STUDY GUIDE

MICROECONOMICS
Explore & Apply

STUDY GUIDE

MICROECONOMICS
Explore & Apply

Ronald M. Ayers
Robert A. Collinge

PEARSON
Prentice
Hall

Upper Saddle River, New Jersey 07458

Executive Editor: Rod Banister
Project Manager: Marie McHale
Manager, Print Production: Christy Mahon
Production Editor & Buyer: Wanda Rockwell
Printer/Binder: Technical Communication Services

Pearson Prentice Hall[TM] is a trademark of Pearson Education, Inc.

10 9 8 7 6 5 4 3 2 1
ISBN 0-13-016425-9

TABLE OF CONTENTS

Preface

Using the *Study Guide* for *Microeconomics: Explore & Apply*

Congratulations on your purchase of the *Study Guide* for *Microeconomics: Explore & Apply*. Each chapter in the *Study Guide* corresponds to a chapter in your textbook. To make the *Study Guide* as easy to use as possible, each chapter is laid out with the following arrangement:

1. **Chapter Review.** Detailed bullet points condense each chapter according to each major heading. Chapter reviews provide convenient summaries, but are not intended to substitute for a careful reading of the text.

2. **Study Checks.** Up to 10 questions and problems per chapter are integrated throughout the Chapter Review. This material helps you get the most out of your reading. Some of the exercises require you to draw a graph or work out a numerical calculation.

3. **Fill in the Blanks.** By completing the sentences, you will be able to test your mastery of the chapter. Once the blanks have been filled in, this section of the study guide also provides a second, brief chapter review.

4. **True/False/Explain.** Twenty-five statements are presented per chapter, including five for the chapter's Explore & Apply section. To get the most out of this feature of the *Study Guide*, you should explain each false statement in the space provided.

5. **Multiple Choice.** Twenty-five multiple choice questions per chapter, including five for each Explore & Apply section, allow you to test and deepen your understanding of the chapter content.

6. **Grasping the Graphs.** Major graphs from the textbook are repeated without some of their descriptive labels. You are to fill in these or other applicable labeling in the space provided.

7.   **Answers.** Answers are provided at the end of each chapter for all items in that chapter. We suggest that you first work through the material on your own, and then refer to the answers to check your work. If you do not understand the reason for an answer, you may wish to reread the relevant section of the chapter.

Do not hesitate to write in answers, make notes, and otherwise personalize *your Study Guide*. Getting actively involved in this way deepens and broadens learning. Although no study guide can guarantee you perfect understanding or a perfect score on an exam, working through these materials will enhance your grasp of economic principles and your ability to apply them.

Part 1

A JOURNEY THROUGH THE ECONOMY

Chapter 1

THE ECONOMIC PERSPECTIVE

CHAPTER REVIEW

- **Economics** studies the allocation of limited resources in response to unlimited wants.

1.1 Scarce Resources, Unlimited Wants

- Economics is about choice. We are forced to choose because of **scarcity**, which means that society does not have enough resources to produce all the goods and services we want to consume. Securing the most value from limited resources is the objective of economic choice.

- We commonly make choices at **the margin,** meaning incrementally—in small steps. Decision making at the margin is about the choice of a little more of this and a little less of that. It's about weighing and balancing the benefits and costs of alternatives.

- It is not a scarcity of money that is at the root of economics. Scarce resources lead to scarce goods, whether or not money is involved.

- Resource allocation refers to the uses to which resources are put. How resources are used depends partly upon *technology*, which refers to the techniques of production. When new technologies are created, among the results can be new ways of doing things, new product choices, and new uses for resources. When society makes choices about what will be produced it is also choosing its allocation of resources.

1.2 Surveying the Economic Landscape

- **Microeconomics** studies the individual parts of the economy. It looks at the choices of individuals in their roles as consumers and as workers. It also includes the choices of businesses—*firms*—which are the companies that produce goods and services as their outputs. Microeconomics also studies the industries within which firms operate, where an *industry* is composed of firms producing similar outputs.

- Microeconomics revolves around the interaction of consumers and producers in markets. Markets can take physical, electronic, or other forms. The common characteristic of all markets is that they make possible the voluntary exchange of resources, goods, and services. Market prices serve as the signals that guide the allocation of resources. Participants in the economy make choices based upon the *incentives* provided by the prices they face, meaning that these prices motivate their actions.

- **Macroeconomics** looks at the big picture. It concentrates on the analysis of economic *aggregates*, total values that describe the economy as a whole.

- The most important aggregate is *gross domestic product (GDP)*, which measures the market value of a country's aggregate output – the market value of the goods and services that a country produces in one year.

- Macroeconomics was first considered a separate field of study following the 1936 publication of *The General Theory of Employment, Interest, and Money* by British economist John Maynard Keynes [1883-1946].

1.3 Three Basic Questions: What, How, and for Whom
- Every economy must answer three basic economic questions:
  1. **What?** What goods and services will be produced and offered for sale and in what quantities?
  2. **How?** How will goods and services be produced? There are numerous production techniques available. Some methods of production use simple hand tools and much labor. Other production methods employ machines or computers in combination with labor.
  3. **For whom?** Who will consume the goods and services that are produced?

- When it comes to deciding what, how, and for whom, society must choose among three kinds of *economic systems*. Government might make the decisions. If so, the economy is termed **command and control.**

- Alternatively, government might stay out of the picture and allow economic choices to be made entirely in the marketplace. In that case, the economy is characterized by laissez-faire free markets, also termed laissez-faire capitalism. Laissez faire means "let it be." **Free markets** are characterized by freedom of choice in both production and consumption. Free markets are associated with capitalism, in which resources are privately owned.

- In practice, all countries have **mixed economies,** meaning that they choose a combination of markets and government. Different countries choose different combinations, with some leaning toward command and control, and others toward laissez faire. The exact mix is influenced by custom, tradition, religion, political ideology, and other factors.

- **There are two primary economic objectives to guide countries in choosing how much government to mix with free markets. The first objective is *equity*, which refers to fairness.**

- **The second economic objective is** *efficiency*, **sometimes called economic efficiency, which means that resources are used in ways that provide the most value**—that maximize the size of the economic pie. Efficiency means that no one can be made better off without someone else becoming worse off. Efficiency has both a technological and allocative component, defined as follows.

- **Technological efficiency** implies getting the greatest quantity of output for the resources that are being used. Conversely, for any given output, technological efficiency requires that a least-cost production technique must be chosen.

- **Allocative efficiency** involves choosing the most valuable mix of outputs to produce.

- **There is frequently a tradeoff between efficiency and equity**, meaning that more equity may result in less efficiency, referred to as more *inefficiency*. Likewise, less equity may result in greater efficiency.

StudyCheck 1

Define the three types of efficiency. Define equity. Why do goals of efficiency and equity often conflict?

- Government *central planning* sets production plans for most goods, which are produced by government-owned state enterprises. The result of command-and-control methods is often inefficiency, in which resources are squandered on the production of the wrong goods and services or wasted through use of the wrong production techniques.

- Centrally planned economies must also match production to consumption. If production fails to match their plans, then the government may be forced to ration goods and services. Government *rationing* occurs when consumers are permitted to buy only limited amounts of the goods they want.

- In the *Wealth of Nations*, published in 1776, Scottish philosopher-economist Adam Smith described how the **invisible hand** of the marketplace leads the economy to produce an efficient variety of goods and services, with efficient production methods as well. Guided by this invisible hand, producers acting in their own self-interests provide consumers with greater value than even the most well-intentioned of governments. An essential ingredient of the invisible hand is *competition*, which pits rival firms against one another in a contest to win the favor of consumers.

- All participants in a market economy, including consumers, businesses, investors, and workers, make choices on the basis of information conveyed by market prices. The collection of prices in product and resource markets is termed the *price system*. **Prices provide information about scarcity. It is the price system that allocates resources in a market economy to their highest-valued uses.**

- Guided by market prices, free-market choices lead the economy toward allocative efficiency. The preferences of consumers dictate answers to the "what" question. Competition provides the incentive for firms to choose least-cost production techniques, thus answering the "how" question. The "for whom" question is answered when people offer their labor and other resources in the marketplace—their incomes reflect the value of these resources to others.

StudyCheck 2

What is the primary advantage of capitalism over central planning? What is a possible disadvantage?

- Sorting out when government intervention is helpful and just how it might best be done is probably the most challenging task facing a nation and one that different countries answer in different ways. The result is that all economies combine government action and the marketplace. Some economies, such as that of Cuba, lie toward the command-and-control end of the spectrum. Others place greater reliance upon the marketplace, but still retain a role for government.

- The following table summarizes the key differences between laissez faire, command and control, and mixed economies

A Brief Comparison of Basic Economic Systems

	Laissez Faire	**Mixed Economy**	**Command and Control**
Key Characteristics	Limited role for government implies a small government with few powers. Low taxes. Private property.	Significant role for government. Taxes take a significant portion of national output. Most production of goods and services occurs in the private sector, but many regulations and some government production.	Government ownership of property and government directives control the production of goods and services.
Organizing Principle	Invisible hand guides free markets.	Mix of free markets and command and control. Emphasis upon markets relative to government varies from country to country.	Central planning of the economy by government.
Daily Life	Large degree of personal freedom. Most goods and services provided by the private sector, including such essentials as food and education. Market prices and market wages.	Moderate limits on personal freedom because of government regulation and taxation. A few essential goods, education for example, provided by government, while others, such as food, provided by the private sector. Market prices, with the possibility of some government price controls. Minimum wage laws and a small degree of other government control of wages.	Severe limits on personal freedom due to government control of the economy. Most goods provided by government. Prices set by government rather than the market. Government-set wages.
Countries Where Applied	None, although the U.S., Australia, and some other countries value laissez faire in principle.	All countries, including China, Russia, and other countries in transition away from command-and-control.	None entirely. Cuba and North Korea come the closest.

1.4 Economic Analysis

•   The practice of economics involves analysis and problem solving. Sometimes these problems force us to think in terms of value judgments; sometimes they are factual. Care must be taken to avoid faulty reasoning that leads to false conclusions. An example is the *fallacy of composition*. This error in reasoning occurs when it is assumed that what is true at the micro level must also be true at the macro level. In other words, the fallacy of composition involves the observation of a truth about some individual component of the economy accompanied by the assumption that this truth will also apply to the economy at large.

- **Normative** statements have to do with behavioral norms, which are judgments as to what is good or bad. Examples of normative statements often include "ought" or "should" in them. They imply that something deserves to happen, such as: "The federal government ought to balance its budget."

- **Positive** statements have to do with fact. They may involve current, historical, or even future fact. Positive statements concern what is, was, or will be. The accuracy of positive statements can be checked against facts, although verifying predictions about the future will have to wait until that future arrives.

- Both positive and normative economics rely upon theory, which is organized thought aimed at answering specific questions. Theories can be tested by logic and, for positive economic theories, by data. Theories are first tested for their internal logic. Does a theory make sense? Sometimes the testing stops there. When feasible, theories are tested by collecting facts to see whether the facts are consistent with the theory. Testing of theories allows us to judge their value, so that the results become more than mere opinion or idle speculation.

- Economics, like other academic fields such as physics, psychology, and political science, makes extensive use of models. A **model** is a simplification of reality that emphasizes features essential to answering the questions we ask of it. A roadmap is a familiar model.

- Economic models remove unneeded detail, keeping only features that are essential. Keep in mind a guiding principle when producing a model. This principle is termed *Occam's razor*, formulated by the 14th century English philosopher William of Occam. Occam argued that reasoning is improved by focusing one's thinking on the most essential elements of an issue. He suggested using a figurative razor to cut away the unnecessary elements from analysis. Occam's razor increases the likelihood that modeling will lead to correct conclusions when the principle is applied correctly.

- To keep models simple, economists make *assumptions*, meaning that they act as though certain things are true without proving them to in fact be true. One common assumption is termed *ceteris paribus*, which is Latin for holding all else constant. The assumption of *ceteris paribus* allows us to look at one thing at a time.

E&A 2.5 From Mao to Now—Market Incentives Take Hold in China

- Like the former Soviet Union and other communist countries, the People's Republic of China was guided by the philosophy of the controversial 19th-century theorist, Karl Marx. Marx had a simple maxim: "From each according to his ability, to each according to his need." This idea was used to justify a strong central government that would allocate resources according to the communist idea of equity. That idea focused on equal outcomes rather than equal opportunities. Equality would be achieved by government ownership of resources and government central planning of the economy.

- Marxist governments expounded a philosophy of *egalitarianism,* in which everyone would get identical access to everything from soap to medical care. Unfortunately for an economy, egalitarianism provides little incentive for people to be productive.

- With central planners attempting to direct the what, how, and for whom of production, bad choices were made and resources were squandered. Everyone had a job, but productivity and purchasing power lagged badly behind the West. China, already the most populous nation on earth, faced a population explosion that promised to lead to mass starvation and unrest unless the economy could be made to perform. Thus, the turn to the market.

- The advantage of a market economy is that the marketplace rewards those producers best able to offer goods and services of value to others. The better a person is at providing things of value to others, the more will be that person's income. A problem arises that, through no fault of their own, people do not all have the same potential.

- Enter government, with its power to tax. Specifically, government redistributes wealth by imposing taxes that take wealth from those who can afford to give and that give to those in need. Taken to an extreme, this redistribution of wealth would eliminate incentives for individuals to behave more productively and lead to stagnation. Therefore, in taxing, government must weigh the trade-off between equity and incentives for efficiency. In the case of China this has meant the willingness to keep taxes relatively low and tolerate inequality in income and wealth.

APPENDIX: Working with Graphs and Data

- Economists draw graphs in order to clarify thoughts and show economic relationships in a way that can be more easily understood than with words alone. Graphs that present factual information are often drawn as line graphs, bar charts, and pie charts, all of which are seen in this book.

- Other graphs represent economic models and contain lines that are referred to as curves. The horizontal line is commonly called the *X* axis and the vertical line the *Y* axis, with the specific labels of the axes varying from graph to graph, depending on what the graph is modeling.

- Each axis of the graph of a model is labeled with the name of a variable, where a variable refers to the name of anything that can change. Within the axes, a relationship between two variables is shown by a curve—a line. Some graphs will have more than one curve in them. Other graphs will only show one curve.

- Curves that slope upward to the right show a *direct relationship,* also termed a *positive relationship,* between the variables. Curves that slope downward to the right show an *inverse relationship,* also termed a *negative relationship.*

• The slope of a curve is measured by the amount of change in the variable on the vertical axis divided by the amount of change in the variable on the horizontal axis. Slope is sometimes referred to as the "rise over the run." Straight lines are linear and always have a constant slope. This means that if you know the slope between any two points on the line, you know the slope everywhere on the line. The slope of a nonlinear curve changes from one point to the next on the curve.

StudyCheck 3

3. Graph the following data points. Show the slope of the resulting line.

Data Point	City	Coat Sales	Average January Temperature
F	Tropical City	100 units	50 degrees
G	North Town	200 units	40 degrees
H	Snowbound	300 units	30 degrees
I	Cold City	400 units	20 degrees
J	Arctica	500 units	10 degrees

StudyCheck 4

4.   If Harry smokes a cigar, 20 people leave the room. If Harry smokes two cigars, 25 people leave the room. Graph this relationship, making sure to label the axes of your graph. Is the relationship positive or negative?

- Merely glancing at a curve is often revealing. When the curve slopes upward to the right, you know that it has a positive slope and thus shows a direct relationship between the variables on the axes. Likewise, when the curve slopes downward to the right, it has a negative slope that portrays an inverse relationship between the variables.

- The slope of a curve provides information at the margin.

- A change in the relationship between two variables is indicated by a shift in a curve. The student should also be aware that **there is a difference between a shift in a curve and a movement along a curve.**

- Some graphs show two different relationships between the variables on the axes. Each relationship will be illustrated by its own curve. An example of this possibility occurs when two curves intersect—cross each other. When two curves intersect, the intersection point will sometimes be of particular interest. **At the intersection point the values of each variable will be identical for both relationships—both curves.**

- *Time-series data* show the values of a variable as time passes. Economists utilize time-series data when changes in the value of a variable over time are the focus of interest. *Cross-sectional data* are fixed at a moment in time, but vary in some other way. In other words, cross-sectional data change because of some cause that is unrelated to the passage of time.

StudyCheck 5

Give an example of time-series data and an example of cross-sectional data.

- Economic research utilizes data in order to identify problems and issues, and to provide evidence about the causes of economic phenomena. Much of the numerical data economists use is collected by various levels of government. Important nongovernmental sources of data include industry trade associations, the United Nations, the Organization for European Community Development (OECD), the International Monetary Fund (IMF), Standard and Poor's, Moody's, and Robert Morris Associates.

FILL IN THE BLANKS

1. _____ studies the allocation of _____ resources in response to unlimited wants. We are forced to choose because of _____, which means that society does not have enough resources to produce all the goods and services we want to consume. We commonly make choices at the _____, meaning incrementally—in small steps.

2. Resource _____ refers to the uses to which resources are put. How resources are used depends partly upon _____, which refers to the techniques of production

3.   _____ studies the individual parts of the economy. It looks at the choices of individuals in their roles as consumers and as workers. It also includes the choices of businesses—_____—which are the companies that produce goods and services as their outputs. It also studies the industries within which firms operate, where an *industry* is composed of firms producing similar outputs.

4.   _____ looks at the big picture. It concentrates on the analysis of economic *aggregates*, total values that describe the economy as a whole. The most important aggregate is _____ _____ _____ (GDP), which measures the market value of a country's aggregate output – the market value of the goods and services that a country produces in one year.

5.   Every economy must answer three basic economic questions: (1) _____? (2) _____? (3) _____ _____?

6.   When it comes to deciding on answers to the three basic questions, society must choose among three kinds of *economic systems*. Government might make the decisions. If so, the economy is termed _____ and _____.

7.   If government stays out of the picture and allow economic choices to be made entirely in the marketplace, the economy is characterized by _____-_____ free markets.

8.   In practice, all countries have _____ economies, meaning that they choose a combination of markets and government.

9.   There are two primary economic objectives to guide countries in choosing how much government to mix with free markets. The first objective is _____, which refers to fairness. The second economic objective is economic _____, which means that resources are used in ways that provide the most value—that maximize the size of the economic pie. This means that no one can be made better off without someone else becoming worse off.

10.   _____ _____ implies getting the greatest quantity of output for the resources that are being used. For any given output, this requires that a least-cost production technique must be chosen.

11.   _____ _____ involves choosing the most valuable mix of outputs to produce.

12.   There is frequently a _____ between efficiency and equity, meaning that more equity may result in less efficiency, referred to as more *inefficiency*. Likewise, less equity may result in greater efficiency.

13.   Government _____ _____ sets production plans for most goods, which are produced by government-owned state enterprises. Government _____ occurs when consumers are permitted to buy only limited amounts of the goods they want.

14.   In the *Wealth of Nations*, published in 1776, Scottish philosopher-economist _____ _____ described how the _____ _____ of the marketplace leads the economy to produce an efficient variety of goods and services, with efficient production methods as well. An essential ingredient is _____, which pits rival firms against one another in a contest to win the favor of consumers.

15.   The use of prices to help answer the three basic questions all economies must answer characterizes the _____ system.

16.   The _____ _____ _____ is error in reasoning that occurs when it is assumed that what is true at the micro level must also be true at the macro level.

17.   _____ statements have to do with behavioral norms, which are judgments as to what is good or bad. Examples often include "ought" or "should" in them.

18.   _____ statements have to do with fact. They may involve current, historical, or even future fact.

19.   _____ is organized thought aimed at answering specific questions. A _____ is a simplification of reality that emphasizes features essential to answering the questions we ask of it.

20.   The 14th century English philosopher William of Occam argued that reasoning is improved by focusing one's thinking on the most essential elements of an issue, a principle termed _____ _____.

21.   To keep models simple, economists make _____, meaning that they act as though certain things are true without proving them to in fact be true.

22.   One common assumption is termed _____ _____, which is Latin for holding all else constant.

E&A   23.   Marxist governments expounded a philosophy of _____, in which everyone would get identical access to everything from soap to medical care.

24.   Government redistributes wealth by imposing _____ that take wealth from those who can afford to give and that give to those in need. Taken to an extreme, this redistribution of wealth would eliminate incentives for individuals to behave more productively and lead to

stagnation. Therefore, in taxing, government must weigh the _____ between equity and incentives for efficiency.

APPENDIX

25.   Some graphs represent economic models and contain lines that are referred to as _____. The horizontal line is commonly called the X axis and the vertical line the Y axis, with the specific labels of the axes varying from graph to graph, depending on what the graph is modeling. Each axis of the graph of a model is labeled with the name of a _____, referring to the name of anything that can change.

26.   Curves that slope upward to the right show a _____ relationship, also termed a positive relationship, between the variables. Curves that slope downward to the right show an _____ relationship, also termed a negative relationship.

27.   The _____ of a curve is measured by the amount of change in the variable on the vertical axis divided by the amount of change in the variable on the horizontal axis, sometimes referred to as the "rise over the run."

28.   A change in the relationship between two variables is indicated by a _____ in a curve.

29.   At the intersection point of two curves the values of each variable will be _____ for both relationships—both curves.

30.   _____-_____ data show the values of a variable as time passes. _____-_____ data are fixed at a moment in time, but vary in some other way.

TRUE/FALSE/EXPLAIN
If false, explain why in the space provided.

1.   Without scarcity, there would be no need for economics.

2.   The essence of scarcity is a lack of money.

3.   Making choices at the margin is about a little more of this and a little less of that.

4.   The right to private property is an essential ingredient of a free market economy.

5.   Allocative efficiency refers to selecting the most valuable combination of goods and services to produce.

6.   The invisible hand of the marketplace refers to the framework of laws and regulations within which firms must operate.

7.   A prediction that the unemployment rate will reach twenty percent in the year 2020 is an example of positive economics.

8.   The best economic models include as much real-world detail as possible.

9.   Goods and services are the same as resources.

10.   Consumer decisions about what to buy will affect the allocation of resources.

11.   Microeconomics is about the big public policy issues.

12.   An industry is a group of firms producing a similar output.

13.   Industry studies are an example of macroeconomic analysis.

14.   Allocative efficiency requires the use of a least-cost production technique.

15.   Economic efficiency encompasses both allocated the efficiency and technological efficiency.

16.   Equity means fairness.

17.   In the last couple of centuries, there has been little relationship between political and economic ideas.

18.   The fallacy of confusion is an error in reasoning which involves assuming that what is true for a part of the economy must also be true for the whole economy.

19.   The following is a normative statement: "Movies today are too violent."

20.   Economic models built on the principle of Occam's razor will include as many details of the real world as possible.

E↔A   21.   China has turned to market incentives to help its economy grow.

22.   Like the former Soviet Union and other communist countries, the People's Republic of China was guided by the philosophy of the controversial 19th-century theorist, Karl Marx.

23.   Lack of incentives for productivity is a major failing of egalitarianism.

24. The ideas of Karl Marx were used by China and the former Soviet Union to justify a strong central government.

25. A philosophy of egalitarianism has guided Western economies to success relative to China and the former Soviet Union.

APPENDIX

26. If two variables have a direct relationship to each other, an increase in one variable is associated with a decrease in the other.

27. A curve with a negative slope shows a direct relationship between variables,

28. When there is a change in the relationship between variables, we can illustrate the change by a shift in a curve.

29. An example of cross-sectional data is the current inflation rates in the countries of Europe.

30. An example of time-series data would be the average unemployment rate in 1995 in the ten largest cities in the United States.

MULTIPLE CHOICE
Circle the letter preceding the one best answer.

1. Most generally, economics is about
   a. money.
   b. profit.
   c. control.
   d. choice.

2.   Making decisions of the margin means to make them
   a.   logically.
   b.   in the marketplace.
   c.   all at once.
   d.   incrementally.

3.   The more redistributional is the tax system,
   a.   the more productive economy is likely to be.
   b.   the less productive the economy is likely to be.
   c.   the more laissez-faire the economy is likely to be.
   d.   the more efficient the economy is likely to be.

4.   Of the following, which is the most likely to involve microeconomics?
   a.   A study of the airline industry.
   b.   A study of inflation.
   c.   A study of economic growth.
   d.   A study of a country's employment.

5.   Keynesian economic theory is most closely associated with
   a.   microeconomics.
   b.   macroeconomics.
   c.   efficiency.
   d.   equity.

6.   The three fundamental economic questions are
   a.   who, what, where?
   b.   how when, why?
   c.   will, won't, whether?
   d.   what, how, for whom?

7.   The two primary economic goals are
   a.   equity and efficiency.
   b.   capitalism and communism.
   c.   efficiency and equality.
   d.   free markets and command and control.

8.   Which of the following is NOT a type of efficiency?
   a.   Allocative efficiency.
   b.   Technological efficiency.
   c.   Economic efficiency.
   d.   Equity efficiency.

9. Which of the following is an example of technological efficiency?
   a. Choosing the best combination of goods and services to produce.
   b. Getting the most toothpicks from the inputs devoted to toothpick making.
   c. Ensuring that everyone has enough money to buy the necessities of life.
   d. Ensuring that everyone has equal opportunities in life.

10. Which of the following is an example of allocative efficiency?
    a. Choosing the best combination of goods and services to produce.
    b. Getting the most toothpicks from the inputs devoted to toothpick making.
    c. Ensuring that everyone has enough money to buy the necessities of life.
    d. Ensuring that everyone has equal opportunities in life.

11. Information about the scarcity of one resource relative to another is most likely to be provided by
    a. government.
    b. prices.
    c. market failures.
    d. normative economic statements.

12. In a capitalist economy, economic activities are coordinated by
    a. tradition.
    b. prices.
    c. government.
    d. business firms.

13. In laissez-faire free markets, the government is responsible for
    a. income redistribution.
    b. policies to improve efficiency.
    c. determining what prices will be charged for goods and services.
    d. nothing.

14. The proper functioning of the invisible hand requires
    a. monopoly.
    b. a fair distribution of income.
    c. competition.
    d. government ownership of large industries.

15. *The Wealth of Nations*, published in 1776, was written by
    a. John Maynard Keynes.
    b. Sir Isaac Arnold.
    c. Karl Marx.
    d. Adam Smith.

16. Which of the following illustrates the fallacy of composition?
   a. If I can sell my product for a higher price, I am better off. Thus, my customers are better off.
   b. If I can sell my product for a higher price, I am better off. Thus, if prices of all products rise, all sellers are better off.
   c. If I can sell my product for a higher price, I am better off. Thus, my customers are worse off.
   d. If customers want my product so much that I can sell it for a higher price, it must be the higher price that attracts the customers.

17. Trying to determine the effect of mad-cow disease upon the sales of beef and poultry would involve
   a. positive macroeconomics.
   b. positive microeconomics.
   c. normative macroeconomics.
   d. normative microeconomics.

18. "I expect that Congress will continue to run a budgetary deficit for the foreseeable future." This statement is an example of
   a. positive macroeconomics.
   b. positive microeconomics.
   c. normative macroeconomics.
   d. normative microeconomics.

19. To the extent that they explain the questions we ask of them, the best models are the
   a. simplest.
   b. most complex.
   c. most descriptive.
   d. most mathematical.

20. The principal of eliminating unnecessary details and models is called
   a. the fallacy of composition.
   b. normative analysis.
   c. positive analysis.
   d. Occam's razor.

E&A 21. If output is divided equally among all citizens, a country is following a policy of
   a. egalitarianism.
   b. equal rights.
   c. equity.
   d. laissez faire.

22.   The primary economic problem of communism has been
        a.   the lack of personal incentive to be productive.
        b.   that people in a communist society are unselfish.
        c.   that following the philosophy of Karl Marx would be inequitable.
        d.   that workers exploit capitalists.

23.   When Mao led the country, the People's Republic of China was guided by the philosophy of Karl Marx, with
        a.   reliance upon free markets to achieve the goal of equality.
        b.   central planning combined with private ownership of resources as the country strived for equality.
        c.   central planning combined with government ownership of resources as the country strived for equality.
        d.   no emphasis upon equality, and no consistent economic system to guide the country.

24.   China's transition to a mixed economy since 1978
        a.   does not allow privately-owned companies.
        b.   imposed price controls on all goods and services.
        c.   resulted in collective farms replacing individual farms.
        d.   included the establishment of a stock market.

25.   In China today, millionaires
        a.   find their wealth taxed away by China's high tax rates.
        b.   do not exist since there is not sufficient wealth to allow anyone to become a millionaire.
        c.   are allowed to exist.
        d.   must hide their wealth since accumulating more than $3,000 is a crime.

APPENDIX
26.   In economics, the concept of a curve would include
        a.   a downward sloping straight line.
        b.   an upward sloping straight line.
        c.   a curving line.
        d.   all of the above.

27.   Direct relationships between variables are illustrated graphically by curves that
        a.   slope upward to the right.
        b.   slope downward to the right.
        c.   are horizontal.
        d.   are vertical.

28.   A decreasingly positive slope is shown in
Multiple Choice Figure 1 as curve
  a.   A.
  b.   B.
  c.   C.
  d.   D.

29.   A increasingly negative slope is shown in
Multiple Choice Figure 1 as curve
  a.   A.
  b.   B.
  c.   C.
  d.   D.

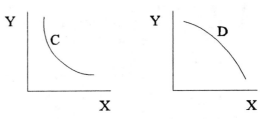

Multiple Choice Figure 1

30.   If you wished to study differences in the
economy between the administrations of
Presidents Carter, Reagan, Bush, Clinton, and GW Bush, you would most likely seek out
  a.   cross-sectional data.
  b.   cross-time data.
  c.   time-series data.
  d.   time-out data.

GRASPING THE GRAPHS
Fill in each box with a concept that applies.

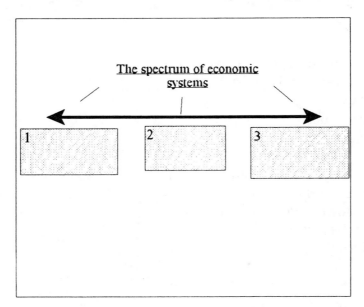

The spectrum of economic
systems

1

2

3

APPENDIX

In the following graph, use the information in the table to identify points.

Hypothetical Data on Yearly Rainfall and Umbrella Sales

Data Point	Community	Yearly Rainfall	Umbrella Sales
A	Center City	30 inches	100 units
B	Moose Haven	40 inches	200 units
C	Blountville	50 inches	300 units
D	Houckton	60 inches	400 units
E	Echo Ridge	70 inches	500 units

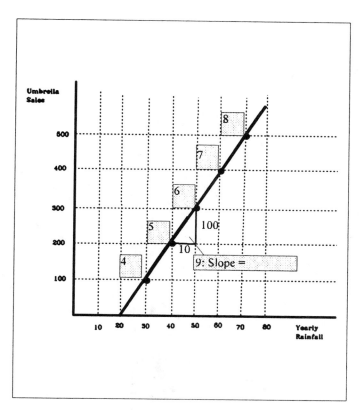

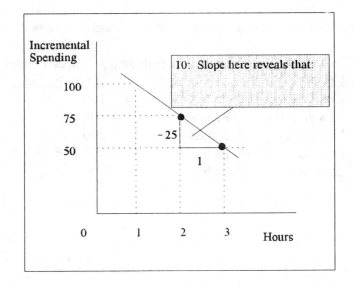

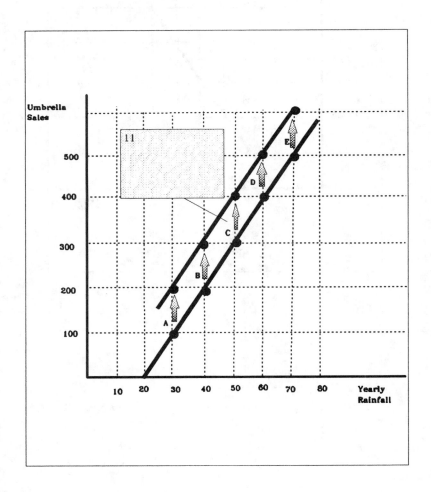

**For additional practice in grasping this chapter's graphs,
visit http://www.prenhall.com/ayers and try *Smart Graph* 1,
along with *Active Graphs* 1, 2, 3, 4, and 5.**

ANSWERS

STUDYCHECKS

1. Economic efficiency is a situation where you cannot make anyone better off without making someone else worse off. It involves getting the most value from available resources. Technological efficiency is to get the most output from given inputs or, conversely, to use the fewest inputs for a given output. Allocative efficiency is to produce the most valuable combination of outputs. Equity is fairness. Equity may call for the redistribution of income, which in turn reduces people's incentives to be productive.

2. Capitalism provides incentives for productivity, and thus "bakes a bigger pie." However, it can slice that pie more unequally than under a Marxist egalitarian philosophy. Capitalism is thus sometimes perceived as inequitable.

3. See StudyCheck 3 Figure.

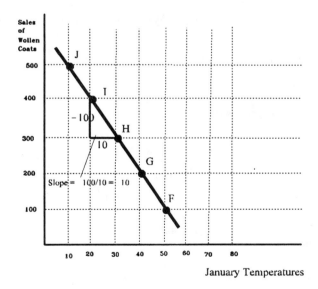

StudyCheck 3 Figure

4.   The relationship is positive. See StudyCheck 4 Figure.

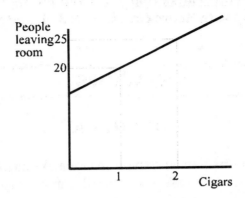

StudyCheck 4 Figure

5.   An example of time-series data is any data that varies over time. Examples are many, including yearly values for GDP, the unemployment rate, and interest rates. Cross-sectional data varies, but in some way other than time. Examples are many, including the value of GDP in a particular year for different countries, and the unemployment rate in a particular year for different countries.

FILL IN THE BLANKS

1.   Economics, limited, scarcity, margin
2.   allocation, technology
3.   Microeconomics, firms
4.   Macroeconomics, gross domestic product
5.   What, How, For whom
6.   command and control
7.   laissez-faire
8.   mixed
9.   equity, efficiency
10. Technological efficiency
11. Allocative efficiency
12. tradeoff
13. central planning, rationing
14. Adam Smith, invisible hand, competition
15. price
16. fallacy of composition
17. Normative
18. Positive

19. Theory, model
20. Occam's razor
21. assumptions
22. ceteris paribus
23. egalitarianism
24. taxes, tradeoff
25. curve, variable
26. direct, inverse
27. slope
28. shift
29. equal
30. Time-series, Cross-sectional

TRUE/FALSE/EXPLAIN

1. True.
2. False, scarcity exists even if there is no money.
3. True.
4. True.
5. True.
6. False, the invisible hand of the marketplace refers to the forces of competition that lead to be efficiency.
7. True.
8. Defaults, the best economic models include only as much detail as necessary to answer the questions that they are to be asked.
9. Defaults, resources are used to produce goods and services.
10. True.
11. False, macroeconomics is about the big public policy issues, wild microeconomics concerns the details of the economy.
12. True.
13. False, industry studies are an example of microeconomic analysis.
14. False, that would be technological efficiency.
15. True.
16. True.
17. False, politics and economics have been so entwined that the field of economics used to be known as political economy.
18. False, that would be the fallacy of composition.
19. True.
20. False, Occam's razor requires models to be a simple as possible.
21. True.
22. True.

23.   True.
24.   True.
25.   False, the attempt to achieve egalitarianism in Communist countries resulted in poor economic incentives and economies that were unsuccessful relative to the market economies of the West.
26.   False, a direct relationship means that an increase in one variable would increase the other variable.
27.   False, a curve with a negative slope shows an inverse relationship between variables.
28.   True.
29.   True.
30.   False, time-series data refers to data across a span of time, such as number of years.

MULTIPLE CHOICE

1.	d	9.	b	17.	b	25.	c
2.	d	10.	a	18.	c	26.	d
3.	b	11.	b	19.	a	27.	a
4.	a	12.	b	20.	d	28.	a
5.	b	13.	d	21.	a	29.	d
6.	d	14.	c	22.	a	30.	c
7.	a	15.	d	23.	c		
8.	d	16.	b	24.	d		

GRASPING THE GRAPHS
Examples of correct answers

1.   laissez-faire free markets
2.   mixed economy
3.   command and control
4.   A
5.   B
6.   C
7.   D
8.   E
9. $-100/10 = -10$
10.   The added revenue from staying open another hour is $25 less than for the previous hour.
11.   The curve has shifted upward, implying more umbrella sales at each level of rainfall.

Visit the Ayers/Collinge companion Website at http://www.prenhall.com/ayers for further activities and exercises for this chapter.

Chapter 2

PRODUCTION AND TRADE

CHAPTER REVIEW

2.1 Scarcity and Choice

- Scarcity means we have to make choices. **Opportunity costs** represent the value of forgone alternatives. The opportunity cost of an action is the value of the single most highly valued alternative choice that has been forgone. The money you pay for an item could have alternatively been spent on something else. The value of the best alternative use of that money is an opportunity cost, but not usually the only opportunity cost. The value of forgone alternative uses of time or other non-monetary resources must also be included.

- *Resources* are combined to produce outputs of goods and services. *Inputs* is another name for resources, which are usually divided into the categories of land, labor, capital, and entrepreneurship. We refer to the ability of a resource to produce output as that resource's *productivity*.

- **Land** refers to all natural resources in their natural states. **Labor** refers to people's capacity to work. It ignores the increased labor productivity from acquired skills and the development of peoples' abilities, which constitute **human capital.** Human capital is a special case of an economy's third resource, capital. **Capital** is anything that is produced in order to increase productivity in the future. Along with human capital, there is also *physical capital*, which includes buildings, machinery, and other equipment. Caution: The definition of capital used in economics differs from that used in finance. Financial capital refers to financial instruments, such as stocks, bonds, and money.

- **Entrepreneurship** is taking personal initiative to combine resources in productive ways. Entrepreneurs take risks, but have the potential to become the economy's movers and shakers. Countries tap the creative potential of entrepreneurship in order to improve the value they get from other resources.

- The possibilities for combining an economy's resources depend upon technology. **Technology** refers to possible techniques of production. Technological advances both improve the selection of goods and services and the manner in which we can produce them.

2.2 Production Possibilities

- The **production possibilities frontier** illustrates scarcity and choice by assuming that only two goods can be produced. It is termed a *frontier* because it represents the limits of output possibilities, given current resources and technology.

- Castaway Island is inhabited exclusively by a castaway named Hank. His options are to catch fish or harvest coconuts. He values both of these foods in his diet and can spend up to eight hours a day to obtain them. The amounts he can obtain are shown in the table below.

Data Point	Fish Caught per Day	Coconuts Collected per Day
A	5	0
B	4	10
C	3	16
D	2	19
E	1	21
F	0	22

- The more fish Hank catches, the fewer coconuts he can collect. The inverse relationship between fish and coconuts illustrates the opportunity cost of Hank using his limited resource, time.

- The opportunity cost of more fish is the number of coconuts forgone. As Hank increases his catch from zero fish (row F in the table) to a maximum of five fish (row A), we see the number of coconuts he collects drop at an increasing rate. In other words, the opportunity cost of the first fish is only one coconut. The opportunity cost of two fish is giving up three coconuts. Then opportunity costs really jump. The opportunity cost of four fish is 12 coconuts, which is quadruple the opportunity cost of two fish. Five fish carry an opportunity cost of 22 coconuts, meaning that Hank must give up all coconuts if he wants to catch five fish. The table below shows these opportunity costs. The final column shows *marginal opportunity cost*, which is the additional opportunity cost from catching one more fish.

Data Point	Fish caught per day	Opportunity Cost (number of coconuts forgone)	Marginal Opportunity Cost (change in number of coconuts forgone)
F	0	0	undefined
E	1	1	1
D	2	3	2
C	3	6	3
B	4	12	6
A	5	22	10

• The numbers for marginal opportunity cost illustrate a principle known as the **law of increasing cost**, which states that as an economy adds to its production of any one good, the marginal opportunity cost of that good will rise. The reason is that resources are often specialized, being more suitable to producing one output than another output. So to increase the output of a good, the most appropriate resources are used first, followed by resources that are increasingly less appropriate for producing that good.

• Because marginal opportunity cost increases as output increases, the production possibilities frontier is bowed outward, meaning that its slope becomes increasingly negative. In contrast, if marginal opportunity cost were constant, the production possibilities frontier would be a straight line with a constant downward slope. In producing any good X, an economy first uses resources that are best suited to producing X. If the economy keeps adding to the production of good X, it uses resources that are increasingly less well suited to X, but increasingly better suited to some other good, Y. The result is that the production of good Y drops at an increasingly rapid rate as X production increases. The production possibilities frontier bows outward because resources are not equally suited to the production of different goods.

• All points within or along the production possibilities frontier are feasible combinations of two goods. For the economy to reach that frontier, it must use all of its resources. It must also use these resources efficiently in the technological sense of getting the most output for given inputs. Otherwise, the economy would be inefficient and at a point inside the frontier. In short, **any point along the production possibilities frontier is a technologically efficient combination of outputs.**

• Points inside the frontier are inefficient and points outside the frontier are currently unattainable.

StudyCheck 1

Draw a production possibilities frontier, labeling the points that are technologically efficient. Also show which combinations of outputs are possible and which ones are currently impossible. Make sure that you label the axes of your graph.

- Allocative efficiency implies a specific point on the production possibilities frontier that is the most valuable combination of outputs. In general, **there will be only one point on the production possibilities frontier that is allocatively efficient**, and we cannot know what it is by sight. However, the invisible hand of the market economy will tend to lead the economy to that point on the production possibilities frontier that is the allocatively efficient combination of outputs.

- Production possibilities will depend on how much of each resource the economy has and on the technology that is available to make use of those resources. As resources increase or technology improves, production possibilities grow and the economy's entire production possibilities frontier shifts outward. **When the production possibilities frontier shifts outward, the economy experiences** *economic growth.* Economic growth occurs when the economy uses expanded production possibilities to produce an output of greater value.

- In the event of natural disasters, the exhaustion of natural resources, or anything else that causes an economy's resource base to shrink, the country's production possibilities will also shrink, which would lead to negative economic growth.

- It takes capital to make use of technological change and increase labor productivity. Since capital represents output that is produced now for the purpose of increasing productivity later, the creation of capital comes at the expense of current consumption.

- When an economy is devoting nearly all of its resources to producing goods for current consumption, the result is that the amount of capital it possesses decreases over time, because of equipment wearing out, buildings falling into disrepair, and other forms of *depreciation*. With its economy producing too little new capital to offset depreciation of existing capital, the production possibilities frontier shifts inward. If the country trades off some current consumption for significantly more production of capital, depreciation can be more than offset. The result is that the production possibilities frontier shifts out over time.

- Technological change can increase productivity across a broad range of industries, as with the better information flows made possible by modern computers and telecommunications. Oftentimes, however, technological change is specific to an industry. In the case of general growth, productivity in both the pretzel and pumpkin industries increases. In the case of specialized growth, productivity increases in only one industry. **Specialized growth thus pivots the production possibilities frontier in the direction of more output in the industry affected by the technological change.**

StudyCheck 2

Using a production possibilities frontier, show how the Internet has expanded economic growth. Briefly note on your graph why this growth occurred.

StudyCheck 3

Draw two production possibilities frontiers, labeling the axes with the goods pretzels and pumpkins. On one of your graphs, show the effects of a general increase in the economy's resources. On the other graph, show the effects of only technological change in the pretzel industry. Label the first graph general growth and the second graph specialized growth.

- To summarize, the production possibilities frontier shows how much of one good can be produced for any feasible amount of another good. If an economy is on its frontier, the opportunity cost of producing more of one good is less of the other good. The production possibilities frontier is bowed outward, consistent with the law of increasing cost. Every point along the production possibilities frontier is technologically efficient. Points inside the frontier imply some unemployed or misallocated resources and are thus inefficient. Points outside the frontier are unattainable with current resources and technology. Economies grow by acquiring resources or better technology, which shifts the frontier outward. If the economy acquires resources that are specialized in the production of a certain good, the production possibilities frontier pivots outward in the direction of more of that good.

2.3 The Circular Flow of Economic Activity

- **Money** is a medium of exchange, meaning that it facilitates the exchange of goods and services. Without money, people would be forced to exchange goods directly, a situation known as **barter.** Barter would be very difficult in a complicated economy.

- Many things have served as money through the years. In prisoner-of-war camps in World War II, cigarettes served as money. Traditionally, gold, silver, and other scarce metals have been considered money, since they are inherently scarce and relatively easy to transport in the form of coins. Paper is even easier to transport, which is why it is the most common form of money in use today. However, for paper or anything else to be used as money, its quantity must be limited, which is why counterfeiting is illegal. Government must also be careful about printing too much currency if it wishes its currency to retain value as money.

- The **circular flow** of economic activity is a model that depicts how markets use the medium of money to determine what goods and services are produced and who gets to buy them. The **output market** is where businesses sell goods and services to consumers.

- The **input market** illustrates that households supply the resources of land, labor, capital, and entrepreneurship. All of these resources are ultimately owned by people, who make up households. The sale of resources to business provides the income that households use to buy products. Since people own businesses, business profits also belong to households. For this reason, the circular flow of inputs and outputs is maintained by a counterflow of dollars. Through taxation, regulation, and production, government influences the mix of goods that is produced and the manner in which resources are used. The circular flow model could be expanded to include foreign commerce, banking, or other economic details, but would become difficult to interpret.

StudyCheck 4

Draw and explain the meaning of the circular flow model of economic activity.

2.4 Expanding Consumption Possibilities through Trade

- For their own self-interest, economies engage in trade with other economies. This is true for national economies, regional economies, local economies, and even personal economies.

- People specialize in their jobs according to their interests and opportunities. They then use the income they earn in order to purchase goods and services. Note that this is a two-part decision. First people decide what to produce; then they decide what to consume. The economies of countries engaged in international trade operate the same way.

- In order to gain from trade, an economy must *specialize* according to its **comparative advantage. An economy has a comparative advantage in producing a good if it can produce that good at a lower opportunity cost than could other economies.** This means the economy chooses to produce those things it does well relative to other things it could be doing.

- Contrary to popular belief, trade is not based on **absolute advantage,** which refers to the ability to produce something with fewer resources than could others. **To gain from trade, specialize according to comparative advantage, whether or not you have any absolute advantage.**

- Countries gain from trade whether or not they have an absolute advantage in anything. The country can start off rich or poor and still gain from trade. While a country is constrained to produce along or inside its production possibilities frontier, it can exchange some of its own output for the output of other countries.

- Goods and services a country sells to other countries are termed **exports.** Exports are traded for **imports,** which are goods and services a country buys from other countries. **Through trade, a country can consume a combination of goods and services that lies outside its production possibilities frontier, meaning that the country's consumption possibilities will exceed its production possibilities.**

- International trade is more important to small countries than to large countries. This is because, the larger is the country, the more opportunities there are to specialize internally.

- If a country has a comparative advantage in producing certain goods, it can produce those goods cheaply relative to the other goods that it could produce. Those goods in which it has a comparative advantage will be the goods it can offer at the best prices in the international marketplace. Thus, without any economic research, economies engaging in international trade naturally tend to export those goods for which they have a comparative advantage and import the rest.

- Consider a model involving two countries, Japan and England, that can each produce only computer memory chips and oil. Assume that all computer memory chips are interchangeable and that oil is also identical. The productivity of workers is shown in the table below. Note that in this example Japan's workers are more productive at both producing oil and manufacturing computer chips, meaning that Japan has an absolute advantage in both computer chips and oil production.

Productivity per Worker in Japan and England

Country	Computer Memory Chips	Barrels of Oil
Japan	10 units per day	4 per day
England	5 units per day	3 per day

- The key to computing comparative advantage is to measure opportunity costs, shown in the table below.

Computing Opportunity Cost and Comparative Advantage

Product Location	Opportunity Cost (C is computer chips and B is barrels of oil)	Opportunity Cost per Unit
Computer chips in Japan	10C for 4B	2/5 barrel of oil (.4B)*
Computer chips in England	5C for 3B	3/5 barrel of oil (.6B)
Oil in Japan	4B for 10C	5/2 computer chips (2.5C)
Oil in England	3B for 5C	5/3 computer chips (1.67C)**

*Lower opportunity cost per unit of computer chips implies comparative advantage in Japan.
**Lower opportunity cost per unit of barrels of oil implies comparative advantage in England.

- In Japan, we see that making a computer chip requires giving up the ability to make 2/5 or .4 barrels of oil, while in England the computer chip costs 3/5 or .6 barrels of oil. Since Japan has a lower opportunity cost of producing the computer chips, it is said to have a comparative advantage in computer chips. Verify for yourself that England has a comparative advantage in oil.

StudyCheck 5

Suppose that there are two countries, Tryhard and Trynot. In Tryhard, each hour of labor can produce either 8 units of good X or 8 units of good Y. In Trynot, each hour of labor can produce either 2 units of good X or 4 units of good Y. Compute the opportunity cost of: a) X in Tryhard; b) Y in Tryhard; c) X in Trynot; d) Y in Trynot. If these countries trade only goods X and Y, which country will produce X? Which will produce Y? Explain.

E&A 2.5 Guns and Butter—Victory from a Strong Economy

- When the United States decided to strengthen its armed forces in the 1980s, the Soviet Union struggled so hard to keep pace that it impoverished its own people and lost its will to exist. The Soviet Union was formally dissolved in 1991 without a shot being fired, breaking up into several different countries, including Russia.

- Now, as we seek to surmount the unfolding terrorist threats of the 21st century, the lessons of America's 20th century success can help guide our way. How has the United States has been able to maintain prosperity during peacetime and yet still have the wherewithal to be victorious in wartime? The secret has been the vibrancy of a strong U.S. economy, meaning that the United States has been able to maintain production possibilities that exceed those of its adversaries.

- Let guns represent military output and butter represent output for civilian consumption. Because of its strong economy, the United States could increase its production of guns to exceed that of the Soviet Union and still have more butter for its civilians. When the Soviets tried to match U.S. spending on guns in the 1980s, their production of butter fell so low that the Soviet people were forced to endure severe hardships.

- To maintain a strong economy, a country must use its existing resources and technology efficiently. Moving from an inefficient economy to an efficient economy allows the production of both more guns and more butter. The economy must use the right people and the right capital to produce the right goods in the right way. By producing more in the present, the economy also has more ability to put aside some current consumption of guns and butter in favor of investing in new capital and better technology that will allow production possibilities to grow over time. In other words, the more efficient an economy is in the present, the more ability it will have to expand its production possibilities for the future.

StudyCheck 6

Labeling the axes as guns and butter, show on a production possibility frontier how an economy can move from being inefficient to being efficient and the changes in output that this could lead to. Show also that the economy can produce more output over time by being efficient.

• The United States has been able to use its production possibilities with relative efficiency and achieve significant economic growth over time by relying in large measure upon the marketplace to allocate resources. The lure of profit in the market economy has motivated people and companies to look for the most valuable products to produce, keep costs as low as possible, and invest in new capital that expands the country's production possibilities frontier. These actions constitute the invisible hand of the marketplace that motivates individuals out for their own self-interest to best serve the needs of others.

- While there are exceptions in which either markets or government policies have failed to achieve efficiency, it is its reliance upon a market economy that has generally allowed the United States to prosper relative to its adversaries with more centralized economies.

- The 20th century has not always brought victory to the U.S. or other prosperous countries. As the U.S. learned in Cuba and Vietnam, citizens of impoverished countries can be stubborn adversaries when their patriotic zeal is aroused. Why not peace, with its promise of prosperity?

- Whether the world in the 21st century sees economic victory or the impoverishment of warfare might hinge in part upon attitudes. Are people of impoverished nations inspired to recreate for themselves the success of the U.S. and other developed countries? Or is that prosperity seen as out of reach and the source of resentment and ongoing conflict?

FILL IN THE BLANKS

1. _____ _____ represent the value of forgone alternatives.

2. _____ are combined to produce outputs of goods and services. They are usually divided into the categories of land, labor, capital, and entrepreneurship. We refer to the ability to produce output as _____.

3. _____ refers to all natural resources in their natural states. _____ refers to people's capacity to work. It ignores the increased labor productivity from acquired skills and the development of peoples' abilities, which constitute _____ _____. _____ is anything that is produced in order to increase productivity in the future. Along with human capital, there is also _____ capital, which includes buildings, machinery, and other equipment. _____ is taking personal initiative to combine resources in productive ways.

4. _____ refers to possible techniques of production. Technological advances both improve the selection of goods and services and the manner in which we can produce them.

5. The_____illustrates scarcity and choice by assuming that only two goods can be produced. It represents the limits of output possibilities, given current resources and technology.

6. Castaway Island is inhabited exclusively by a castaway named Hank. His options are to catch fish or harvest coconuts. He values both of these foods in his diet and can spend up to eight hours a day to obtain them. The amounts he can obtain are shown in the table below.

Data Point	Fish Caught per Day	Coconuts Collected per Day
A	5	0
B	4	10
C	3	16
D	2	19
E	1	21
F	0	22

The opportunity cost of the first fish is _____ coconut. The opportunity cost of two fish is giving up _____ coconuts. The opportunity cost of four fish is _____ coconuts.

7.   Marginal opportunity cost is the additional opportunity cost from catching one more fish. The marginal opportunity cost of the first fish is _____ coconut. The marginal opportunity cost of the second fish is _____ coconuts. The marginal opportunity cost of the fourth fish is _____ coconuts.

8.   The law of _____ _____ states that as an economy adds to its production of any one good, the marginal opportunity cost of that good will rise.

9.   Because marginal opportunity cost increases as output increases, the production possibilities frontier is _____ _____, meaning that its slope becomes increasingly negative. In contrast, if marginal opportunity cost were constant, the production possibilities frontier would be a _____ line with a constant downward slope.

10.   All points within or along the production possibilities frontier are _____ combinations of two goods. For the economy to reach that frontier, it must use all of its resources. It must also use these resources _____ in the technological sense of getting the most output for given inputs. Otherwise, the economy would be inefficient and at a point _____ the frontier. Points _____ the frontier are currently unattainable.

11.   _____ efficiency implies a specific point on the production possibilities frontier that is the most valuable combination of outputs.

12.   As resources increase or technology improves, production possibilities grow and the economy's entire production possibilities frontier shifts _____. When the production possibilities frontier shifts outward, the economy experiences economic _____.

13. When an economy is devoting nearly all of its resources to producing goods for current consumption, the result is that the amount of capital it possesses decreases over time, because of equipment wearing out, buildings falling into disrepair, and other forms of _____. With its economy producing too little new capital, the production possibilities frontier shifts _____.

14. In the case of _____ growth, productivity in a variety of industries increases, and the production possibilities frontier shifts outward along both axes. In the case of _____ growth, productivity increases in only one industry, which pivots the production possibilities frontier in the direction of more output in one industry.

15. _____ is a medium of exchange, meaning that it facilitates the exchange of goods and services. Without money, people would be forced to exchange goods directly, a situation known as _____.

16. The _____ _____ of economic activity is a model that depicts how markets use the medium of money to determine what goods and services are produced and who gets to buy them. The _____ market is where businesses sell goods and services to consumers. The _____ market illustrates that households supply the resources of land, labor, capital, and entrepreneurship.

17. In order to gain from trade, an economy must specialize according to its _____ advantage. An economy has a _____ advantage in producing a good if it can produce that good at a lower opportunity cost than could other economies. This means the economy chooses to produce those things it does well relative to other things it could be doing. Trade is not based on _____ advantage, which refers to the ability to produce something with fewer resources than could others.

18. Goods and services a country sells to other countries are termed _____. _____ are goods and services a country buys from other countries. Through trade, a country can consume a combination of goods and services that lies _____ its production possibilities frontier, meaning that the country's consumption possibilities will exceed its production possibilities.

19. International trade is more important to _____ countries than to _____ countries.

20. Consider a model involving two countries, Japan and England, that can each produce only computer memory chips and oil. Assume that all computer memory chips are interchangeable and that oil is also identical. The productivity of workers is shown in the table below. Note that in this example Japan's workers are more productive at both producing oil and manufacturing computer chips, meaning that Japan has an _____ advantage in both computer chips and oil production. The country with a comparative advantage in computer

memory chip production is _____, while the country with the comparative advantage in oil production is _____.

Productivity per Worker in Japan and England

Country	Computer Memory Chips	Barrels of Oil
Japan	10 units per day	4 per day
England	5 units per day	3 per day

E&A

21. To maintain a strong economy, a country must use its existing _____ and _____ efficiently.

22. Moving from an _____ economy to an _____ economy allows the production of both more guns and more butter.

23. The lure of _____ in the market economy has motivated people and companies to look for the most valuable products to produce, keep costs as low as possible, and invest in new capital that expands the country's production possibilities frontier.

24. These actions constitute the _____ _____ of the marketplace that motivates individuals out for their own self-interest to best serve the needs of others.

25. People of impoverished countries might be _____ to emulate the success of developed countries, or this success might alternatively become a source of _____ and _____.

TRUE/FALSE/EXPLAIN
If false, explain why in the space provided.

1. The opportunity cost of a city park to the city that owns it is best measured by the budget required to police and maintain that park.

2. If you start your own business, you are an entrepreneur.

3. A bowed-out production possibility frontier shows that the incremental opportunity cost of each additional unit of either good will be lower than it was for the preceding unit.

4. Human capital is created when a person acquires knowledge and skills that can increase his or her earnings.

5. Technological change in the widget industry will pivot the production possibility frontier in the direction of more widgets.

6. Other things equal, if a country produces more capital goods, its production possibility frontier will shift out over time.

7. There is only one point on the production possibility frontier that is technologically efficient.

8. The circular flow diagram shows the flow of resources, and the flow of goods and services, while ignoring money.

9. In the circular flow model of economic activity, resources are assumed to be owned by businesses.

10. A country that trades with other countries can consume outside its production possibility frontier.

11. To gain from trade, a country must be able to do something better or with fewer resources than the other country.

12. When we make economic decisions, our goal is always to maximize the opportunity cost of our actions.

13. The countries of Superior and Wannabee produce nothing but fish and movies. The residents of Superior are far better suited to both activities than are the residents of Wannabee. This means that Superior has a comparative advantage in both goods.

14. Relative to most countries, the United States has a comparative advantage in goods that are produced with a high proportion of capital, including human capital.

15. If a country has an unproductive labor force and few other resources, it is better off not trading with other countries.

16. It is impossible for a country to have a comparative advantage in all goods.

17. A country gains by protecting its high-paying jobs.

18. The marketplace identifies the goods for which individuals and countries have comparative advantages.

19. If it takes 12 units of labor to produce gizmos, and 24 units of labor to produce gadgets, the opportunity cost of a gizmo is two gadgets.

20. If workers in country A can produce 10 widgets or 10 gizmos per day, while workers in country B can produce 5 widgets or 1 gizmo per day, the two countries can both gain from trade if country B specializes in the production of widgets.

E&A   21. The Soviet Union was dissolved in 1991 after a violent revolution in which hundreds of thousands of people died.

22.   A vibrant U.S. economy in the 20th century meant the United States could maintain production possibilities in excess of the production possibilities of its adversaries.

23.   The more efficient an economy is in the present, the more ability it will have to expand its production possibilities for the future.

24.   Former Soviet Premier Mikhail Gorbachev has in recent years ridiculed the ways of the Soviet Union.

25.   As the United States learned in Cuba and Vietnam, it is weapons and not patriotic zeal that matters in wartime.

MULTIPLE CHOICE
Circle the letter preceding the one best answer.

1.   Human capital refers to
  a.   money.
  b.   money, but not if it's owned by businesses.
  c.   work effort.
  d.   acquired skills and abilities.

2.   Water flowing down a river represents the resource of
  a.   land.
  b.   technology.
  c.   capital.
  d.   entrepreneurship.

3.   Suppose that the Capitalist Computer Corporation is about to finish a new office building in downtown Richville. When completed, this building will house all Capitalist operations and still have five vacant floors. In order to retain maximum flexibility for future operations, Capitalist Computers has decided to not lease out this extra space. The opportunity cost of this decision is
   a.   the cost of building those five floors.
   b.   the cost of maintaining those five floors while they are vacant.
   c.   the total payments Capitalist Computers could have received by leasing out those five floors.
   d.   zero, because the space remains vacant.

4.   Of the following, the opportunity cost of attending class on any given day is most likely to be
   a.   tuition.
   b.   the cost of books.
   c.   the pleasure of sleeping late.
   d.   a higher grade on the test.

5.   The relationship between marginal opportunity cost and total opportunity cost is:
   a.   Marginal opportunity cost is the sum of all the total opportunity costs.
   b.   Total opportunity cost is the sum of all the marginal opportunity costs.
   c.   Marginal opportunity cost equals total opportunity cost divided by output.
   d.   Total opportunity cost equals marginal opportunity cost divided by output.

6.   Marginal opportunity cost is the _____ of the production possibilities frontier.
   a.   height
   b.   width
   c.   direction
   d.   slope

7.   The outwardly bowed shape of the production possibilities frontier can be explained by
   a.   specialization of resources.
   b.   consumer preferences.
   c.   the circular flow diagram.
   d.   absolute advantage.

8.　In Multiple Choice Figure 2-1,
　　a.　point D is more technologically efficient than point C.
　　b.　point C is more technologically efficient than point D.
　　c.　both points C and point D are equally technologically efficient.
　　d.　neither points C nor D are technologically efficient.

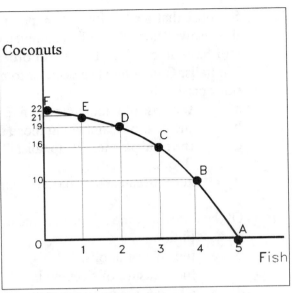

Multiple Choice Figure 2-1

9.　In Multiple Choice Figure 2-1, the marginal opportunity cost of increasing fish production from two to three would be
　　a.　3 coconuts forgone.
　　b.　16 coconuts forgone.
　　c.　6 coconuts forgone.
　　d.　2 fish forgone.

10.　Multiple Choice Figure 2-2 shows ＿＿＿＿＿＿ economic growth.
　　a.　general
　　b.　specialized
　　c.　positive
　　d.　negative

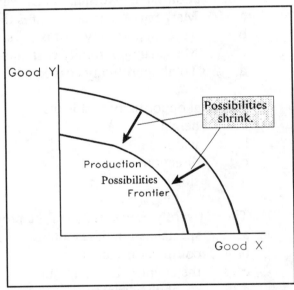

Multiple Choice Figure 2-2

11.　An economy that invests heavily in capital goods in one year will find that, in following years,
　　a.　its production possibility frontier has shifted out.
　　b.　it is consuming a more equitable combination of goods.
　　c.　it is consuming a more efficient combination of goods.
　　d.　it cannot produce as many capital goods.

12.　Exchanging goods for goods is known as
　　a.　stock trading.
　　b.　bond trading.
　　c.　barter.
　　d.　debasement.

13. In a circular-flow graph, spending by business equals
    a.   total profits.
    b.   income to households.
    c.   spending on services, but not on goods.
    d.   the increase in inventories.

14. As a general economic rule, economic well-being in a country is _____ by allowing imports, and _____ by allowing exports.
    a.   increased; increased
    b.   decreased; increased
    c.   increased; decreased
    d.   decreased; decreased

15. When two countries trade with each other,
    a.   both countries' production possibility frontiers shift outward.
    b.   they move from one point to another on their respective production possibility frontiers
    c.   they both move to points outside their respective production possibility frontiers.
    d.   they both move to points inside their respective production possibility frontiers.

16. International trade tends to be most important to
    a.   small, specialized countries.
    b.   large, diversified countries.
    c.   primitive economies.
    d.   communist countries.

17. A country that agrees to trade with another country where workers are paid a considerably lower real wage is likely to see its standard of living
    a.   rise, but exports fall.
    b.   and exports both fall.
    c.   and exports both rise.
    d.   fall, but exports rise.

18. When the United States trades with Mexico and other countries that have an abundance of relatively unskilled labor, the effect on the U.S. labor market is to reduce
    a.   demand for relatively unskilled labor.
    b.   wages for both skilled and unskilled labor.
    c.   employment in all U.S. industries engaged in international trade.
    d.   exports in an amount equal to the increasing imports.

19.   Suppose one acre of land is able to produce 5,000 bushels of rice or 6,000 bushels of wheat in Louisiana. In Arkansas, one acre of land can produce 3,000 bushels of rice or 4,000 bushels of wheat. Arkansas has a comparative advantage over Louisiana in
   a.   only wheat.
   b.   only rice.
   c.   both wheat and rice.
   d.   neither wheat nor rice.

20.   Suppose that M.J. and Rodney are stranded on a tropical island containing streams teeming with delicious fish. There is nothing to do but fish, cook, or relax. It takes Rodney two hours to catch a fish and three hours to cook a fish. M.J. can catch a fish in one hour, and also cook a fish in an hour. Both M.J. and Rodney are indifferent as to whether they'll spend their time fishing or cooking. It is likely that
   a.   Rodney will do most of the fishing and M.J. most of the cooking.
   b.   M.J. will do most of the fishing and Rodney most of the cooking.
   c.   M.J. will do most of both the fishing and cooking.
   d.   Rodney will do most of both the fishing and cooking.

E&A   21.   The 20th century has often been called America's century. Of the following, the most likely explanation is
   a.   the economic and military dominance of the United States and the 20th century.
   b.   the opportunities opened up to the United States in the 20th-century by the Louisiana purchase.
   c.   the opportunities opened up to the United States in the 20th-century by technological change.
   d.   that America claimed ownership of most of the world's resources in that century.

22.   Of the following, the most likely reason for the Soviet Union's demise is that
   a.   it was unable to match the United States militarily in the 1980s.
   b.   it might have been able to match the United States militarily in the 1980s, but its citizens would have been left with a very low standard of living.
   c.   its citizens came to believe that democracy was a better form of government and refused to work until it was established in the Soviet Union.
   d.   access to the Internet caused disenchantment among Soviet youth with the Soviet system.

23.   An economy is better able to grow if it is efficient then if it is inefficient because
   a.   efficiency allows more production from the economies resources.
   b.   efficiency reduces discontent among workers.
   c.   efficiency is equitable.
   d.   greater efficiency is the same thing as economic growth.

24.   The United States economy has been relatively efficient over time in large part due to its reliance upon
   a.   a strong military.
   b.   a market economy.
   c.   a pattern of continuous warfare.
   d.   impoverishment of other nations.

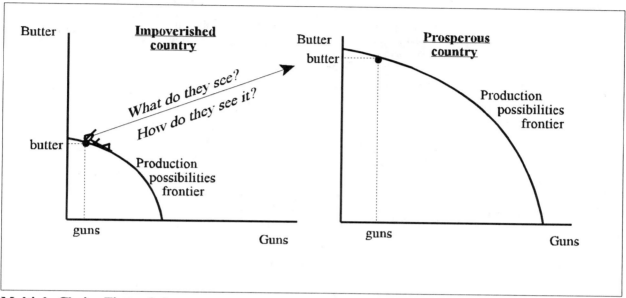

Multiple Choice Figure 2-3

25.   The questions shown in the left side of Multiple Choice Figure 2-3 refer to
   a.   how prosperous countries are viewed by residents of impoverished countries.
   b.   how impoverished countries are viewed by residents of prosperous countries.
   c.   whether residents of impoverished countries believe that prosperous countries have truly achieved technological efficiency.
   d.   whether impoverished countries can achieve the equity that is clearly visible in prosperous countries.

GRASPING THE GRAPHS
Fill in each box with a concept that applies.

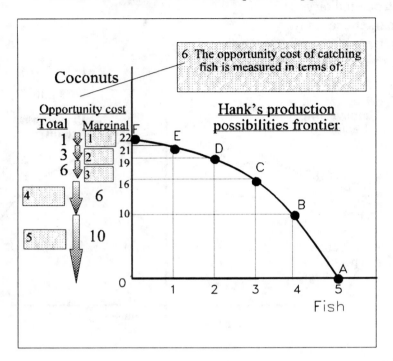

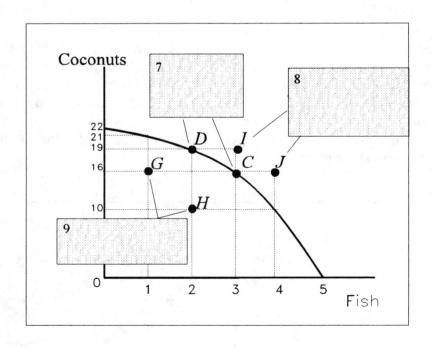

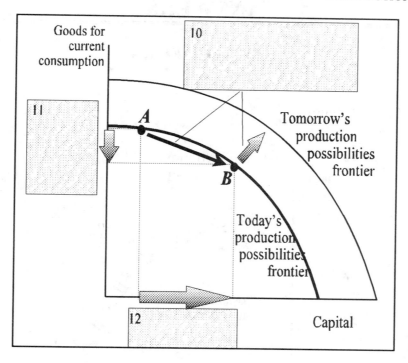

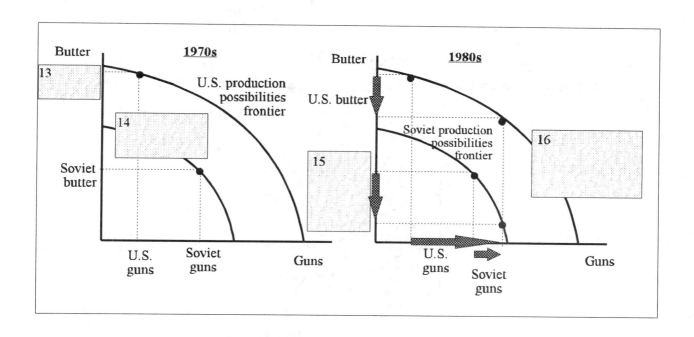

**For additional practice in grasping this chapter's graphs, visit
http://www.prenhall.com/ayers and try *Smart Graphs* 2 and 3,
along with *Active Graphs* 6, 7, and 8.**

ANSWERS

STUDYCHECKS

1.   See StudyCheck 1 figure.

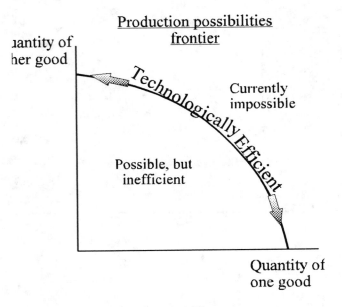

StudyCheck 1 Figure

2.   See StudyCheck 2 Figure.

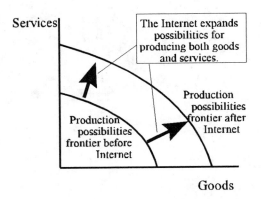

StudyCheck 2 Figure

3.   See StudyCheck 3 Figure.

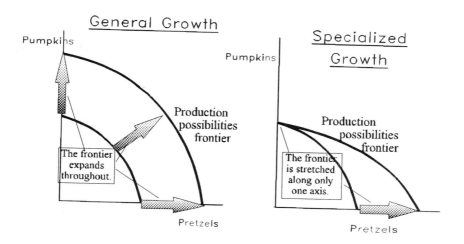

StudyCheck 3 Figure

4.   The circular flow model shows that the sale of resources in the input market provides households with the income to make purchases in the output market. In the aggregate, these flows must be equal in dollar terms. The model is illustrated in StudyCheck 4 Figure.

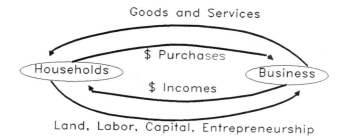

StudyCheck 4 Figure

5.   The opportunity cost of:
            X in Tryhard = 1Y;
            Y in Tryhard = 1X;
            X in Trynot = 2Y;
            Y in Trynot = ½X.
Countries specialize according to which has the lowest opportunity cost of each good. That means that Tryhard will produce X and Trynot will produce Y.

6.   See StudyCheck 6 Figure.

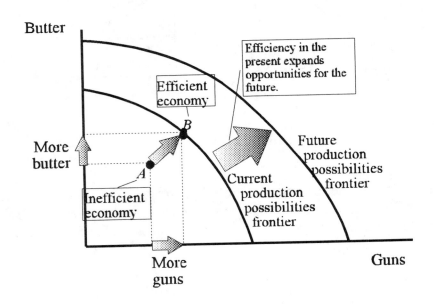

StudyCheck 6 Figure

FILL IN THE BLANKS

1.   Opportunity costs
2.   Resources, productivity
3.   Land, labor, human capital, capital, physical, entrepreneurship
4.   Technology
5.   production possibilities frontier
6.   one, three, ten
7.   one, two, six
8.   increasing costs
9.   bowed outward, straight
10.   efficient, efficiently, inside, outside

11. Allocative
12. outward, growth
13. depreciation, inward
14. general, specialized
15. Money, barter
16. circular flow, output, input
17. comparative, comparative, absolute
18. exports, Imports, outside
19. smaller, larger
20. absolute, Japan, England
21. resources, technology
22. inefficient, efficient
23. profit
24. invisible hand
25. inspired, resentment, conflict

TRUE/FALSE/EXPLAIN

1. False, the opportunity cost is the value that the land, time, and money involved in maintaining the park would have had their next best alternative uses.
2. True.
3. False, the opportunity cost will be higher because the bowed-out shape implies an increasing incremental tradeoff.
4. True.
5. True.
6. True.
7. False, all points are technologically efficient.
8. False, money is an integral part of the circular flow of inputs and outputs.
9. False, resources are assumed to be owned by households.
10. True.
11. False, even though the country might not have an absolute advantage in anything, it can still gain by trading according to its comparative advantage.
12. False, we would seek to minimize opportunity costs.
13. False, although Superior would have an absolute advantage in both goods, it would have a comparative advantage only in one of them.
14. True.
15. False, the country would gain by specializing according to its comparative advantage and trading with other countries.
16. True.
17. False, although workers in those jobs would gain, the country as a whole would lose because its consumption possibilities would diminish.
18. True.

19.   True.
20.   True.
21.   False, although the Soviet Union was dissolved in 1991, it was dissolved peacefully.
22.   True.
23.   True.
24.   True.
25.   False, patriotic zeal has proved very important in warfare in Cuba, Vietnam, and elsewhere.

MULTIPLE CHOICE

1.	d	8.	c	15.	c	22.	b
2.	a	9.	a	16.	a	23.	a
3.	c	10.	d	17.	c	24.	b
4.	c	11.	a	18.	a	25.	a
5.	b	12.	c	19.	a		
6.	d	13.	b	20.	a		
7.	a	14.	a	21.	a		

GRASPING THE GRAPHS
Examples of correct answers

1.   1
2.   2
3.   3
4.   12
5.   22
6.   Coconuts forgone
7.   Either would be possible and efficient.
8.   Neither is possible.
9.   Both are possible, but neither is efficient.
10.   By choosing less current consumption and more capital, the production possibilities frontier grows faster over time.
11.   Current consumption forgone today
12.   Increase in capital produced today
13.   U.S. butter in the 1970s
14.   Soviet production possibilities frontier in the 1970s
15.   Decrease in Soviet butter production from the 1970s to the 1980s
16.   U.S. production possibilities frontier in the 1980s

**Visit the Ayers/Collinge companion Website at http://www.prenhall.com/ayers
for further activities and exercises for this chapter.**

Chapter 3

DEMAND AND SUPPLY

CHAPTER REVIEW

- *Competition* provides consumers with alternatives. The competition by producers to satisfy consumer wants underlies markets, which are characterized by demand and supply. Market economies rely upon competition, and thus upon demand and supply, to answer the three basic economic questions: What? How? For whom?

3.1 Demand

- Demand relates the quantity of a good that consumers would purchase at each of various possible prices, over some period of time, ceteris paribus. Demand is a relationship, not a single quantity. The terms demand, demand schedule, and demand curve all refer to the same thing. For a given price, demand tells us a specific quantity that consumers would actually purchase. This quantity is termed the **quantity demanded**.

- Demand must be defined for a set period of time. Moreover, anything else that might influence the quantity demanded must be held constant. This is termed the *ceteris paribus* condition. It means that we only look at one relationship at a time, where **ceteris paribus** is the Latin for holding all else equal.

- Demand is an inverse relationship between price and quantity demanded. As price rises, quantity demanded falls. As price falls, quantity demanded rises. This relationship is termed the **law of demand**.

- Anything that causes the demand curve to shift is termed a *shift factor*. **An increase in demand occurs when demand shifts to the right. A *decrease in demand* occurs when demand shifts to the left.** Note that a change in the price of the good neither increases nor decreases demand—demand does not shift. Rather, **a price change would change the quantity demanded, which involves *moving along the demand curve*, but would not change the demand curve itself.** A lower price results in a movement down the demand curve, while a higher price causes a movement up the demand curve.

- Some things are more likely to shift demand than are others. As mentioned, consumer income is a likely shift factor. **For *normal goods*, an increase in income shifts demand to the right.** However, there are many goods that people buy less of as their incomes rise. These are termed **inferior goods. An increase in income shifts the demand for inferior goods to the left.**

- Changes in the prices of substitutes and complements also shift demand. A **substitute** is something that takes the place of something else. Different brands of coffee are substitutes. So are coffee and tea. A **complement** is a good that goes with another good, such as ketchup on hot dogs or cream in coffee. **Demand varies directly with a change in the price of a substitute. Demand varies inversely to a change in the price of a complement.**

- **Changes in tastes and preferences will also shift demand.** Over time, as some items become more popular, their demand curves shift out. Other items see their popularity fade and their demand curves shift in. Producers often use advertising in an attempt to influence tastes and preferences toward their particular brand of product.

- Changes in population, in expectations about future prices, or in many other factors can cause demand to shift. **Demand will increase or decrease to the extent that population increases or decreases. A change in consumer expectations about future prices will shift demand in the present.** For example, if you expect prices to fall in the future, you might put off your purchases now, in effect shifting your current demand curve to the left. You would be treating future purchases as a substitute for current purchases. For some products, other factors could be significant, such as conjectures about future technologies that might make products with current technologies obsolete.

StudyCheck 1

List several reasons that demand might decrease, as in part (a) of the following figure. List several reasons that demand might increase, as in part (b) of the following figure.

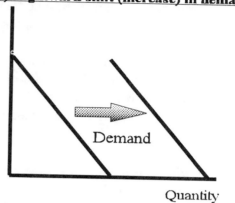

(a) Leftward shift (decrease) in demand

(b) Rightward shift (increase) in demand

3.2 Supply

- **Supply** relates the quantity of a good that will be offered for sale at each of various possible prices, over some period of time, ceteris paribus. This quantity is termed the **quantity supplied.** Note that supply and quantity supplied are not synonyms. Supply refers to the entire set of data that relates price and quantity and is thus also called a *supply schedule* or *supply curve*. Quantity supplied is the quantity associated with a single point on that schedule. As price changes, quantity supplied changes, but supply does not.

- In contrast to the downward-sloping demand curve, the supply curve nearly always slopes upward to the right. This direct relationship between price and quantity supplied is known as the **law of supply.** As price rises, the quantity offered for sale by producers increases. The reason is that a higher price means higher revenue per unit sold, which will in turn cover the cost of producing some additional units.

- An *increase in supply* occurs when the entire supply curve shifts to the right, with more quantity supplied at each particular price. Likewise, a *decrease in supply* occurs when the entire supply curve shifts to the left, showing less quantity supplied at any particular price. A change in price does not shift supply, but rather causes a *movement along supply*.

- Supply's most important shift factors differ from those for demand. When it comes to supply, changes in expectations as to future prices are still important, but it is the expectations by producers, and not by consumers, that matter. The other important supply shift factors are different from the demand shift factors. In addition to producer expectations as to future prices, important shift factors include: 1) the number of firms; 2) prices of inputs; 3) technological change; 4) restrictions in production; 5) prices of substitutes in production; and 6) prices of jointly produced goods.

- **Today's supply curve shifts in the opposite direction from changes in expected future prices.** Supply shifts directly with the change in the number of firms producing a good.

- If the price of labor or other input prices fall, firms see their expenses drop, and are willing to produce more at any given price. Hence, a decline in input prices increases supply, meaning that supply shifts to the right. Were input prices to increase, supply would decrease, meaning that it would shift to the left. In that case, fewer units are offered for sale at any given price. In general, **supply will shift in the opposite direction from changes in input prices.**

StudyCheck 2

List several reasons that supply might decrease, as in part (a) of the following figure. List several reasons that supply might increase, as in part (b) of the following figure.

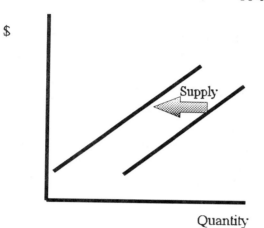

(a) Leftward shift (decrease) in supply

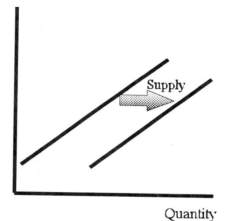

(b) Rightward shift (increase) in supply

- Firms adopt technological change in order to produce more output per unit of input. This has the same effect as a decrease in input prices. **Technological change in the production of any good shifts its supply to the right.**

- Firms sometimes face restrictions in how they are allowed to do business. **Production restrictions decrease supply.**

- **Supply varies inversely to the price of a substitute in production.** Be aware that substitutes in production are not the same as the substitutes in consumption that shift demand.

- Some products are produced jointly, such as beef and leather. An increase in the popularity and price of beef would lead to a movement up the supply curve for beef. The greater quantity supplied of beef means that more cattle are raised for slaughter, which has the effect of shifting the supply of leather to the right. In brief, more leather would be offered for sale at each price of leather, in response to people consuming more steak and hamburger. Thus, **supply varies directly with the prices of products that are jointly produced.**

3.3 Equilibrium—Demand Meets Supply and the Market Clears

- **Demand can be one individual's or the market's as a whole. Likewise, supply can be from one firm or all firms in the market.**

- Market demand is the sum of all the individuals' demands in that market. Summing individuals' demands is straightforward if you remember to add quantities, not prices. For each price, the quantity demanded in the marketplace is the sum of the quantities demanded by all consumers. On the graph of demand, **market demand is the horizontal summation of individuals' demand curves.**

StudyCheck 3

Draw a single graph indicating somebody's demand curve for tacos. Calling this person Larry, label the demand curve "Larry's demand." Be sure to label the axes of your graph, too. On the same graph, draw market demand, given that there are a total of three people willing to buy tacos and that each has a demand curve identical to Larry's.

StudyCheck 4

Graph the supply and demand for MARGARINE. Label price and quantity. Suppose that the price of BUTTER increases. Make appropriate changes in the margarine market.

- Market supply depicts the total quantity offered for sale in the market at each price. To obtain market supply, merely add the quantities offered for sale by all sellers at each price. Graphically, **market supply is the horizontal summation of each seller's supply curve.**

- **There is only one price that *clears the market*, meaning that the quantity supplied equals the quantity demanded.** The market-clearing price and the resulting quantity traded comprise what is known as the **market equilibrium,** meaning that there is no tendency for either price or quantity to change, *ceteris paribus*. Market equilibrium is determined by the intersection of supply and demand.

- At any price above the equilibrium price, there would be a **surplus,** representing the excess of quantity supplied over quantity demanded. In any market in which a surplus occurs, some sellers would cut their prices slightly in order to be the ones that make the sales. Other suppliers would then be without customers, and would consequently lower their own prices enough to capture customers from their competitors. This leapfrogging process would continue until the quantity demanded and supplied are equal, which occurs at the equilibrium price.

- A price that is below the equilibrium price results in a **shortage,** equal to the amount by which quantity demanded exceeds quantity supplied. Whenever there is a shortage in any market, buyers compete against each other for the limited quantities of the goods that are offered for sale at that price. For sellers, shortages provide an opportunity both to raise prices and to increase sales, a doubly appealing prospect. Price would thus rise to its equilibrium value, the point at which the shortage disappears. Thus, without any guidance, the invisible hand of the market eliminates either surpluses or shortages and leads to the market-clearing equilibrium.

- Suppose either supply or demand were to change. For example, suppose an increase in consumer income or a decrease in the price of a complement shifts demand to the right. One of the most common mistakes students make is to think this shift in demand would also shift supply. It would not, because demand is not a shift factor for supply. Rather, the rightward shift in demand leads to a movement up the supply curve and results in a new, higher equilibrium price and quantity. More generally, **a change in supply would cause a movement along demand. Similarly, a change in demand would cause a movement along supply.**

- The market equilibrium will change whenever supply or demand shift. Taken one curve at a time, there are only four shifts possible: 1) An increase in supply, which shifts supply to the right. 2) A decrease in supply, which shifts supply to the left. 3) An increase in demand, which shifts demand to the right. 4) A decrease in demand, which shifts demand to the left.

- The table describes the effects of a shift in demand or a shift in supply:

The Four Basic Cases of Shifting Demand and Supply

Case	Demand	Supply	Equilibrium Price	Equilibrium Quantity
1	No change	Shifts right	Falls	Rises
2	No change	Shifts left	Rises	Falls
3	Shifts right	No change	Rises	Rises
4	Shifts left	No change	Falls	Falls

StudyCheck 5

Using a graph, show the effect on the market equilibrium price and quantity of a decrease in the number of firms supplying a good. Label all curves, the initial price (P1), the final price (P2), the initial quantity (Q1), the final quantity (Q2), and the axes of the graph.

- To understand the effects on price and quantity when there are simultaneous shifts in supply and demand, combine two shifts from the table above. The table shows the outcome of simultaneous shifts:

The Four Cases of Simultaneous Shifts in Demand and Supply

Case	Demand	Supply	Equilibrium price	Equilibrium quantity
5 (cases 1 and 3)	Shift right	Shifts right	Direction uncertain	Rises
6 (cases 2 and 4)	Shifts left	Shifts left	Direction uncertain	Falls
7 (cases 2 and 3)	Shifts right	Shifts left	Rises	Direction uncertain
8 (cases 1 and 4)	Shifts left	Shifts right	Falls	Direction uncertain

•   Notice that in the case of simultaneous shifts, the change in either equilibrium price or quantity is listed as uncertain to indicate that the direction in which the equilibrium price or quantity will move cannot be known without additional information. The direction in which either price or quantity changes will be uncertain when the shifts in demand and supply pull the equilibrium in opposite directions.

StudyCheck 6

Show how a simultaneous increase in both demand and supply can lead to any of the following three outcomes: (a) no change in price; (b) a decrease in price; or (c) an increase in price. Use three separate graphs to show these three cases. In each case, note that the equilibrium quantity increases.

StudyCheck 7

Suppose demand and supply both shift to the left. Using three separate graphs, show how these shifts could lead to a higher price, a lower price, or no change in price, but always lead to a lower quantity.

StudyCheck 8

Using a graph, show the effects on equilibrium price and quantity of a large increase in supply combined with a small increase in demand.

E❖A 3.4 Demanding Better Schools, Supplying Better Schools

- Consistent with the law of demand, the lower the price of a college education, *ceteris paribus*, the greater the number of students who will apply and the more education they will choose. To promote higher education, government offers tax deductions, subsidies, and financial aid that in effect lowers its price.

- High school seniors seriously consider a varied assortment of colleges. In lower grades, however, there is a powerful financial incentive to choose only the government-provided local public school. The reason is that taxpayer financing makes those schools free to the student.

- Inefficient schools are insulated from competitive pressures to reform because even the best private schools find it hard to compete with "free" and it would take moving to a new school district to enroll in a different public school.

- If there were no free public schools, the invisible hand of the market would cause schools to become efficient at responding to the demands of parents. Schools that are most efficient at providing value would gain students, while others would lose them. However, because family incomes differ, the outcome would lead to unequal opportunities for schooling.

- Limited competition is provided by *charter schools*, a form of public school. Much more competition can be achieved through *vouchers,* which provide money that recipients can spend, but restrict that spending to a certain category of goods. *School vouchers* provide parents with money that can only be spent on schooling their children. With vouchers, the money is received by the school of each parent's choosing rather than being spent directly by the government-run public school.

- School vouchers were first proposed in 1955 by Nobel-prize-winning economist Milton Friedman. Today, voucher programs of one sort or another are underway in Ohio, Florida, Texas, and elsewhere.

- Vouchers lower the price of private schooling to parents, thus increasing their quantity demanded. Private schools are willing to offer greater quantities supplied at lower prices because of the supplemental payment they receive from vouchers, a rightward shift in supply when parents are provided vouchers. The result is a lower price and more children enrolled in private schools. In the market for the substitute government-run public schools, which offer unlimited enrollments at a price of "free" to the parents, the result is a decrease in demand and enrollments With vouchers, the location, design, and operation of schools is driven by market demand.

- Opponents of vouchers fear that the competition for voucher money would cause schools to shortchange educational objectives and promote popular, but not very worthwhile, activities. Voucher critics want to see schooling remain in the hands of educational professionals whose motives they perceive as more focused on learning and less on money. Just like inefficient companies in other sectors of the free market, inefficient public schools would whither and die. So, too, would inefficient private schools. The process might be hard on the students.

• Perhaps more experiments with vouchers will clarify the issues. By promoting competition, vouchers offer the promise of improved schools. Will parents demand well for their children or should that choice be left to educational professionals?

StudyCheck 9

Explain the workings of, and motivation for, a system of school vouchers.

FILL IN THE BLANKS

1. _____ by producers to satisfy consumer wants underlies markets. The what, how, and for whom questions are answered in a market economy by _____ and _____.

2. _____ relates the quantity of a good that consumers would purchase at each of various possible prices, over some period of time, ceteris paribus. For a given price, demand tells us a specific quantity that consumers would actually purchase. This quantity is termed the _____ _____.

3. Anything besides price that might influence demand must be held constant, termed the _____ _____ condition, meaning that we only look at one relationship at a time, holding all else equal.

4. The law of demand is an _____ relationship between price and quantity demanded. As price rises, quantity demanded _____. As price falls, quantity demanded _____.

5. Anything that causes the demand curve to shift is termed a shift factor. An increase in demand occurs when demand shifts _____. A decrease in demand occurs when demand shifts _____.

6. The most important shift factors for demand are _____, _____, _____, the prices of _____ or _____, and _____ about future prices.

7. Note that a change in the price of the good neither increases nor decreases demand—demand does not shift. Rather, a price change would change the _____ _____, which involves moving along the demand curve, but would not change the demand curve itself. A lower price results in a movement _____ the demand curve, while a higher price causes a movement _____ the demand curve.

8. For _____ goods, an increase in income shifts demand to the right. However, there are many goods that people buy less of as their incomes rise. These are termed _____ goods, and an increase in income shifts the demand for them to the _____. A _____ is something that takes the place of something else. A _____ is a good that goes with another good. Demand varies directly with a change in the price of a substitute. Demand varies inversely to a change in the price of a complement.

9. Changes in tastes and preferences will also shift demand. Over time, as some items become more popular, their demand curves shift to the _____. Other items see their popularity fade and their demand curves shift to the _____. Demand will increase or decrease to the extent that population increases or decreases. A change in consumer expectations about future prices will shift demand in the present. If you expect prices to fall in the future, you might put off your purchases now, in effect shifting your current demand curve to the _____. You would be treating future purchases as a substitute for current purchases.

10. _____ relates the quantity of a good that will be offered for sale at each of various possible prices, over some period of time, ceteris paribus. This quantity is termed the _____ _____.

11. The direct relationship between price and quantity supplied is known as the _____ ___ _____. As price rises, the quantity offered for sale by producers _____. An

increase in supply occurs when the entire supply curve shifts to the _____, while a decrease in supply occurs when the entire supply curve shifts to the _____. A change in price does not shift supply, but rather causes a _____ _____ _____.

12. In addition to producer expectations as to future prices, important shift factors for supply include the number of _____, the prices of _____ , _____ improvements, restrictions in production, _____ of substitutes in production; and _____ of jointly produced goods.

13. Today's supply curve shifts in the _____ direction from changes in expected future prices. Supply will shift in the _____ direction from changes in input prices. Technological improvements in the production of any good shifts its supply to the _____. Production restrictions _____ supply. Supply varies _____ to the price of a substitute in production. Supply varies _____ with the prices of products that are jointly produced.

14. Market demand is the _____ of all the individuals' demands in that market. Market supply depicts the total quantity offered for sale in the market at each price. To obtain market supply, _____ the quantities offered for sale by all sellers at each price.

15. The market-clearing price and the resulting quantity traded comprise what is known as the market _____, meaning that there is no tendency for either price or quantity to change, *ceteris paribus.*

16. Market equilibrium is determined by the intersection of _____ and _____. At any price above the equilibrium price, there would be a _____, representing the excess of quantity supplied over quantity demanded. price that is below the equilibrium price results in a _____ equal to the amount by which quantity demanded exceeds quantity supplied.

17. Suppose either supply or demand were to change. For example, suppose an increase in consumer income or a decrease in the price of a complement shifts demand to the right. One of the most common mistakes students make is to think this shift in demand would also shift supply. It would not, because demand is not a shift factor for supply. Rather, the rightward shift in demand leads to a movement up the supply curve and results in a new, higher equilibrium price and quantity. More generally, a change in supply would cause a _____ along demand. Similarly, a change in demand would cause a _____ along supply.

18. The market equilibrium will change whenever supply or demand shift. Taken one curve at a time, there are only four shifts possible: 1) An _____ in supply, which shifts supply

to the right. 2) A _____ in supply, which shifts supply to the left. 3) An _____ in demand, which shifts demand to the right. 4) A _____ in demand, which shifts demand to the left.

19. The table describes the effects of a shift in demand or a shift in supply:

The Four Basic Cases of Shifting Demand and Supply

Case	Demand	Supply	Equilibrium Price	Equilibrium Quantity
1	No change	Shifts right	_____	_____
2	No change	Shifts left	_____	_____
3	Shifts right	No change	_____	_____
4	Shifts left	No change	_____	_____

20. To understand the effects on price and quantity when there are simultaneous shifts in supply and demand, combine two shifts from the table above. The table shows the outcome of simultaneous shifts:

The Four Cases of Simultaneous Shifts in Demand and Supply

Case	Demand	Supply	Equilibrium price	Equilibrium quantity
5 (cases 1 and 3)	Shift right	Shifts right	_____	Rises
6 (cases 2 and 4)	Shifts left	Shifts left	_____	Falls
7 (cases 2 and 3)	Shifts right	Shifts left	_____	Direction uncertain
8 (cases 1 and 4)	Shifts left	Shifts right	_____	Direction uncertain

E&A 21. In lower grades, there is a powerful financial incentive to choose only the government-provided local public school. The reason is that taxpayer financing makes those schools _____ to the student. _____ schools are insulated from competitive pressures to reform because even the best private schools find it hard to compete with "free" and it would take moving to a new school district to enroll in a different public school.

22. If there were no free public schools, the invisible hand of the market would cause schools to become _____ at responding to the demands of parents. Schools that are most efficient at providing value would gain students, while others would lose them.

23. Limited competition is provided by _____ schools, a form of public school. Much more competition can be achieved through school _____, which provide parents with money that they must spend on schooling their children.

24. Vouchers lower the _____ of private schooling to parents, thus increasing their quantity demanded. Private schools are willing to offer greater quantities supplied at lower prices because of the supplemental payment they receive from vouchers, a _____ shift in supply when parents are provided vouchers. The result is a lower price and more children enrolled in private schools. In the market for the substitute government-run public schools,

which offer unlimited enrollments at a price of "free" to the parents, the result is a _____ in demand and enrollments.

25. With vouchers, the location, design, and operation of schools is driven by market _____.

TRUE/FALSE/EXPLAIN
If false, explain why in the space provided.

1. A decrease in price shifts demand to the right.

2. A decrease in income decreases demand for a normal good.

3. Technological change has the effect of shifting supply to the left.

4. Market demand is the horizontal summation of all buyers' demands.

5. An increase in supply increases demand.

6. If demand shifts to the right and supply shifts to the left, we know that price will rise.

7. If demand shifts to the right and supply shifts to the left, we know that quantity will not change.

8. An increase in price will result in a decrease in demand.

9.   Demand shifts to the right if the good in question is normal and income increases.

10.   If the wage rate falls, the supply of a good will shift to the left.

11.   If the actual price exceeds the market equilibrium price, there will be a shortage.

12.   If the price of spaghetti increases, demand for meatballs would decrease.

13.   If the price of spaghetti increases, the supply of meatballs would increase.

14.   Both government regulations and restrictive union work rules tend to shift supply to the left.

15.   If the market price is below the equilibrium price, the equilibrium price will fall.

16.   Whenever demand shifts, supply also shifts.

17.   Demand in the present shifts to the left when consumers hear news that the market price is likely to rise in the future.

18.   Supply in the present shifts to the left when producers hear news that the market price is likely to rise in the future.

19.   When additional producers enter the market, the market supply shifts upward.

20.   Generic paper towels would be an example of an inferior good.

E⊕A   21.   Charter schools are public schools that are established by the parents and certified by the state.

22.   School vouchers would reduce competition among schools.

23.   Because you get what you pay for, the quality of education depends only upon how much money is spent, not upon whether schools are run by government or the private sector.

24.   Vouchers are proposed as a way for parents to shop for schools.

25.   Government usually spends about the same amount of your tax money on your children whether or not you send them to a religious school.

MULTIPLE CHOICE
Circle the letter preceding the one best answer.

1.   Which of the following is a statement of the law of demand?
   a.   As the price of a good falls, demand rises, *ceteris paribus*.
   b.   As the price of a good rises, demand rises, *ceteris paribus*.
   c.   As the price of a good falls, the quantity demanded rises, *ceteris paribus*.
   d.   As the price of a good falls, the quantity demanded falls, *ceteris paribus*.

2.   A decrease in the price of french fries would cause
    a.   the demand for hamburgers to shift to the right.
    b.   a movement up the demand curve for hamburgers.
    c.   the demand for hamburgers to shift to the left.
    d.   a movement down the demand curve for hamburgers.

3.   If a good is inferior and income goes up,
    a.   supply of that good will shift to the right.
    b.   supply of that good will shift to the left.
    c.   demand for that good will shift to the right.
    d.   demand for that good will shift to the left.

4.   The market demand curve for a good is the
    a.   horizontal summation of each individual's demand curve.
    b.   horizontal summation of each individual's demand curve minus market supply.
    c.   vertical summation of each individual's demand curve.
    d.   vertical summation of each individual's demand curve minus market supply.

5.   In Multiple Choice Figure1, the quantity demanded by Jill at a price of $2 is given by the length of arrow
    a.   A.
    b.   B.
    c.   C.
    d.   D.

6.   In Multiple Choice Figure 1, the quantity demanded by Jack at a price of $3 is given by the length of arrow
    a.   A.
    b.   B.
    c.   C.
    d.   D.

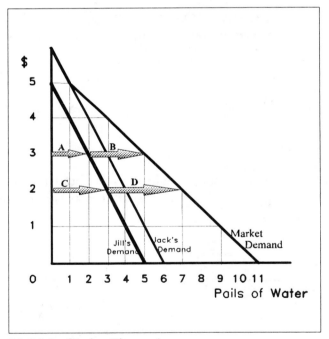

Multiple Choice Figure 1

7.   In Multiple Choice Figure 1, adding together the lengths of arrows C and D tells the market
    a.   supply.
    b.   quantity demanded at a price of $2.
    c.   price.
    d.   quantity supplied at a price of $2.

8.   A decrease in the popularity of blue denim would
     a.   shift the supply of blue denim to the right.
     b.   shift the supply of blue denim to the left.
     c.   cause a movement up the blue denim supply curve.
     d.   cause a movement down the blue denim supply curve.

9.   Ceteris paribus, an increase in the demand for Pepsi would
     a.   increase the supply of Pepsi.
     b.   increase the demand for Coke.
     c.   decrease the supply of Coke.
     d.   increase the quantity of Pepsi supplied.

10. And increase in supply is the same as
     a.   a rightward shift in the supply curve.
     b.   an upward shift in the supply curve.
     c.   a downward shift in the supply curve.
     d.   a leftward shift in the supply curve.

11. If wage rates go down,
     a.   supply shifts to the right.
     b.   supply shifts to the left.
     c.   demand shifts to the right.
     d.   demand shifts to the left.

12. If government regulations increase costs,
     a.   supply shifts to the right.
     b.   supply shifts to the left.
     c.   demand shifts to the right.
     d.   demand shifts to the left.

13. Beef and hides represent
     a.   substitutes in consumption.
     b.   substitutes in production.
     c.   complements in consumption.
     d.   complements in production.

14. In Multiple Choice Figure2, the arrow labeled A is the
    a. surplus if the price is $4.
    b. shortage if the price is $4.
    c. quantity supplied at a price of $4.
    d. quantity demanded at a price of $4.

15. In Multiple Choice Figure 2, the arrow labeled B is the
    a. surplus if the price is $2.
    b. shortage of the price is $2.
    c. quantity supplied at a price of $2.
    d. quantity demanded at a price of $2.

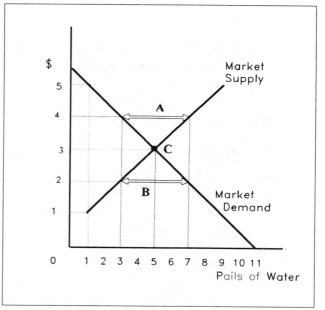

Multiple Choice Figure 2

16. In Multiple Choice Figure 2, point C represents the
    a. surplus at a price of $3.
    b. shortage at a price of $3.
    c. surplus at a price of $2.
    d. market equilibrium.

17. If the market price is above its equilibrium value, the market price will
    a. decrease, because some producers will not sell as much as they would like to at that price and proceed to cut their prices, which causes other producers to do the same.
    b. decrease, because a price that is above the equilibrium price would be illegal according to the law of demand.
    c. remain the same, because the concept of a market equilibrium refers to a tendency for prices to increase, and there is no reason for price to increase if it is already above its equilibrium value.
    d. increase, because a price that is above the market equilibrium tends to rise.

18. If demand shifts to the right, and supply does not shift, the equilibrium
    a. price and quantity will both rise.
    b. price and quantity will both fall.
    c. price will rise and quantity will fall.
    d. price will fall and quantity will rise.

19.   If the demand and supply of a product both increase, then
   a.   both price and quantity must rise.
   b.   price rises, but quantity remains constant.
   c.   quantity rises, but the change in price cannot be predicted without more information.
   d.   price falls, but the change in quantity cannot be predicted without more information.

20.   Which of the following COULD NOT explain an increase in both price and quantity?
   a.   Supply and demand both shift right.
   b.   Supply remains unchanged, and demand shifts right.
   c.   Supply shifts right, and demand shifts left.
   d.   Supply shifts left, and demand shifts right.

E&A 21.   In government-run public schools, a child's school is usually determined by
   a.   where that child lives.
   b.   a lottery system.
   c.   which parents are willing to pay the most.
   d.   competitive testing of skills and abilities.

22.   A charter school is a
   a.   school that would not exist except for school vouchers.
   b.   public school that is established by parents.
   c.   private school with a religious affiliation.
   d.   private school with no religious affiliation.

23.   _____ specify an amount that the holder can spend, but restrict that spending to a certain category of goods.
   a.   Mandates
   b.   Taxes
   c.   Vouchers
   d.   Price supports

24.   The primary purpose of school vouchers is to
   a.   allow parents to express their religious preferences in terms of their children's education.
   b.   standardize educational opportunities for all children.
   c.   get around the Supreme Court ruling that charter schools are unconstitutional.
   d.   promote efficiency through competition among schools.

25.   A major objection to school vouchers is that
    a.   they are inefficient.
    b.   parents are not formally trained in how to best educate their children.
    c.   it would greatly increase the influence of teachers' unions.
    d.   they would cost much more than government-run public schools.

GRASPING THE GRAPHS
Fill in each box with a concept that applies.

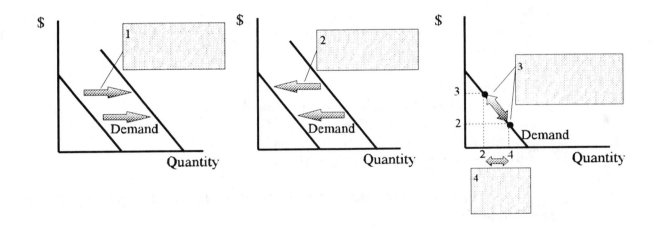

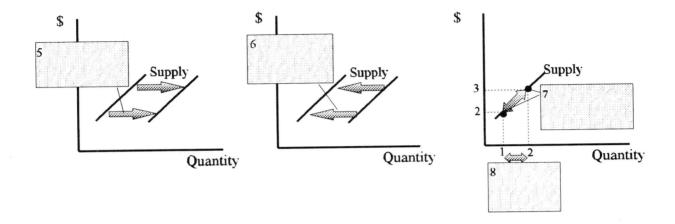

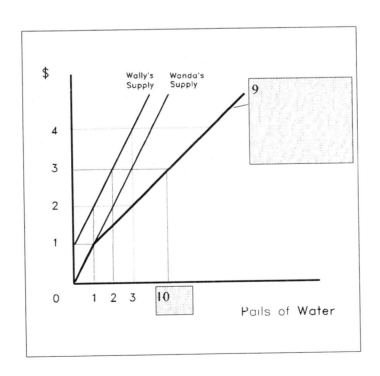

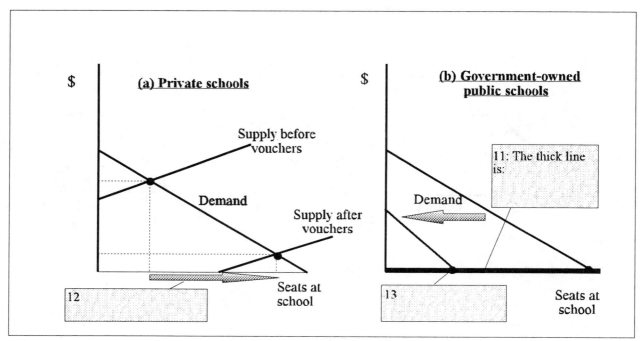

For additional practice in grasping this chapter's graphs, visit
http://www.prenhall.com/ayers and try *Smart Graphs* 4, 5, 6, 7, and 8,
along with *Active Graphs* 10, 11, 12, and 13.

ANSWERS

STUDYCHECKS

1.

Demand decreases (shifts to the left) when:	Demand increases (shifts to the right) when:
The price of a substitute decreases.	The price of a substitute increases.
The price of a complement increases.	The price of a complement decreases.
The good is normal and income decreases.	The good is normal and income increases.
The good is inferior and income increases.	The good is inferior and income decreases.
Population decreases.	Population increases.
Consumers expect price to decrease in the future.	Consumers expect price to increase in the future.
Tastes and preferences turn against the product.	Tastes and preferences turn in favor of the product.

2.

Supply decreases (shifts to the left) when	Supply increases (shifts to the right) when
The number of sellers decreases.	The number of sellers increases.
The price of labor or any other input rises.	The price of labor or any other input falls.
Producers expect prices to rise in the future.	Producers expect prices to decline in the future.
Government, labor union, or other restrictions on production practices increase cost.	Technological change lowers cost.
The price of a substitute in production rises.	The price of a substitute in production falls.
The price of a jointly produced product falls.	The price of a jointly produced product rises.

3.   See StudyCheck 3 Figure.

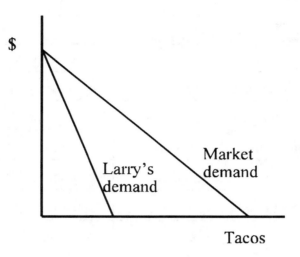

StudyCheck 3 Figure

4.   See StudyCheck 4 Figure.

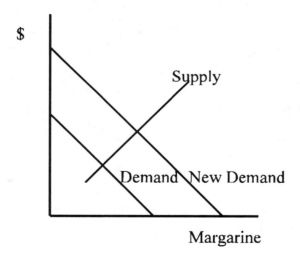

StudyCheck 4 Figure

5.   See StudyCheck 5 Figure.

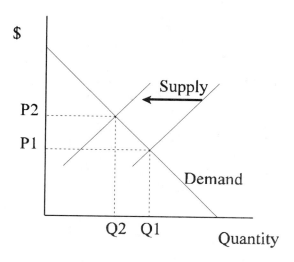

StudyCheck 5 Figure

6.   See StudyCheck 6 Figure.

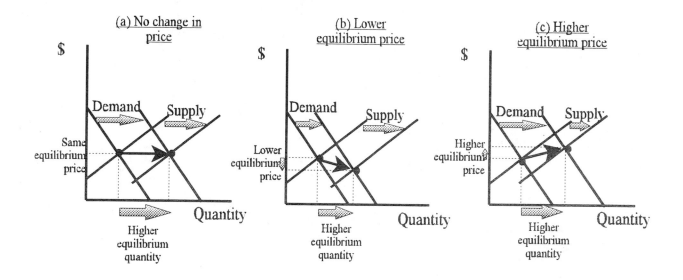

StudyCheck 6 Figure

7.   See StudyCheck 7 Figure.

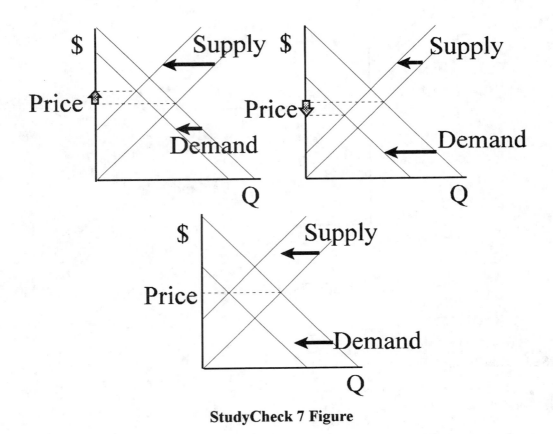

StudyCheck 7 Figure

8.   See StudyCheck 8 Figure.

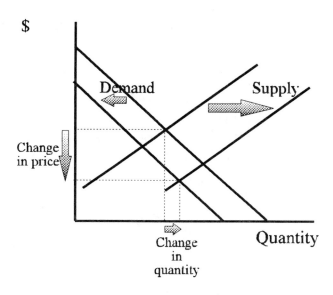

StudyCheck 8 Figure

9.   A school voucher system gives parents vouchers that represent money, but only if spent on schooling for their children. Numerous details would be specified, such as whether the vouchers would apply to parochial schools. The motivation is to introduce competition into the market for children's education. Voucher proponents argue that competition would lead to efficiency, as schools seek to attract parents' voucher spending by offering the most valuable education for the money. Opponents claim that parents will not choose as well as professionally trained educators.

FILL IN THE BLANKS

1.   Competition, demand, supply
2.   Demand, quantity demanded
3.   ceteris paribus
4.   inverse, falls, rises
5.   to the right, to the left
6.   incomes, population, tastes and preferences, substitutes, complements, expectations
7.   quantity demanded, down, up
8.   normal, inferior, left, substitute, complement

9.   right, left, left
10.   supply, quantity supplied
11.   law of supply, rises, right, left, movement along supply
12.   firms, inputs, technological , prices, prices
13.   opposite, opposite, right, decrease, inversely, directly
14.   sum, add
15.   equilibrium
16.   supply, demand, surplus, shortage
17.   movement, movement
18.   increase, decrease, increase, decrease
19.   Case 1: falls, rises; Case 2: rises, falls; Case 3: rises, rises; Case 4: falls, falls
20.   Case 5: direction unknown; Case 6: direction unknown; Case 7: rises; Case 8: falls
21.   free, Inefficient
22.   efficient
23.   charter, vouchers
24.   price, rightward, decrease
25.   demand

TRUE/FALSE/EXPLAIN

1.   False, there is a movement down the demand curve, but the demand curve itself does not shift.
2.   True.
3.   False, supply would shift to the right.
4.   True.
5.   False, an increase in supply would increase the quantity demanded because it would cause the equilibrium price to the lower.
6.   True.
7.   False, without further information, we do not know if the equilibrium quantity will rise, fall, or remain unchanged.
8.   False, it is the quantity demanded that would decrease.
9.   True.
10.   False, supply would shift to the right.
11.   False, there would be a surplus.
12.   True.
13.   False, spaghetti and meatballs are not substitutes in production ,and so the price of one has no effect on the supply of the other.
14.   True.
15.   False, the market price would tend to rise to the market equilibrium but the equilibrium price itself would not change.

16.	False, a shift in demand does not shift supply.
17.	False, consumers would demand more in the present if they expect price to go up in the future.
18.	True.
19.	False, supply shifts to the right.
20.	True.
21.	True.
22.	False, vouchers would increase competition among schools.
23.	False, the efficiency with which money is spent can vary among schools.
24.	True.
25.	False, government usually spends tax money only on schools that are provided by the government and that do not teach religion.

MULTIPLE CHOICE

1.	c	8.	d	15.	b	22.	b
2.	a	9.	d	16.	d	23.	c
3.	d	10.	a	17.	a	24.	d
4.	a	11.	a	18.	a	25.	b
5.	c	12.	b	19.	c		
6.	b	13.	d	20.	c		
7.	b	14.	a	21.	a		

GRASPING THE GRAPHS
Examples of correct answers

1.	Increase in demand
2.	Decrease in demand
3.	Movement along demand
4.	Change in the quantity demanded
5.	Increase in supply
6.	Decrease in supply
7.	Movement along supply
8.	Change in the quantity supplied
9.	Market supply, which is the horizontal summation of Wally's supply and Wanda's supply
10.	5

11.   Supply by the government
12.   Equilibrium quantity after vouchers
13.   Increased private-school enrollment

**Visit the Ayers/Collinge companion Website at http://www.prenhall.com/ayers
for further activities and exercises for this chapter.**

Chapter 4

THE POWER OF PRICES

CHAPTER REVIEW

- The marketplace depends on **price signals**, meaning that the market price sends a message to consumers and producers. The price signals to consumers how much of a good they will wish to buy, and signals to producers how much of a good they will wish to sell.

4.1 Price Signals for Efficient Choice

- Consumers buy something because they expect that they will be better off by doing so. Likewise when producers sell something. So when a consumer buys a good that a producer sells, both parties are better off. The mutual gains from such market exchanges lead the economy to greater efficiency.

- The demand curve depicts the quantity that would be purchased at each of various prices, *ceteris paribus*. Another way of looking at it is that the demand curve shows the maximum price the consumer would pay for each quantity that might be purchased. This maximum price is the consumer's **marginal benefit**—the incremental value of each additional item consumed.

StudyCheck 1

Using a graph, illustrate the concept of marginal benefit.

- Consider Dwight, who is shopping for blue jeans. The table below shows how demand translates into marginal benefit and total benefit. Dwight's *total benefit* from his blue-jean purchases is the sum of his marginal benefit from each pair. So, if he buys 3 pair, the blue jeans would bring Dwight $45 worth of total benefit, where $45 = $20 + $15 + $10.

Dwight's Demand and Benefits from Blue Jeans

(a) Dwight's Demand for Blue Jeans		(b) Dwight's Benefits from Buying Blue Jeans		
Price	Quantity	Quantity	Marginal Benefit	Total Benefit
$20	1	1	$20	$20
$15	2	2	$15	$35
$10	3	3	$10	$45

- Since Dwight must pay for the blue jeans he buys, the value to him of his blue-jean purchases equals the total benefit from the blue jeans minus what he pays. This value is termed **consumer surplus**, which is difference between the total benefit and total cost to the consumer. Graphically, it is the demand curve minus price.

- The table below computes consumer surplus for three different prices of blue jeans. As you can see in that table, **consumer surplus varies inversely with price.** The greater the price the less is consumer surplus and the lower the price the greater is consumer surplus.

Dwight's Consumer Surplus from Blue Jeans

Price	Quantity Bought	Total Benefit	Total Paid	Consumer Surplus
$20	1	$20	$20	$0
$15	2	$35	$30	$5
$10	3	$45	$30	$15

- A supply curve shows the quantity that would be offered for sale at each of various prices, *ceteris paribus*. The supply curve also depicts the minimum price that the producers of a good would be willing to accept for each quantity offered. That minimum price is the producer's *marginal cost*, which is the incremental cost of producing each additional item offered for sale.

StudyCheck 2

Using a graph, illustrate the concept of marginal cost.

- Consider Buddy, who sells blue jeans. The table below shows how supply translates into marginal cost and total cost. Buddy's *total cost* of blue-jeans sold is the sum of his marginal cost from selling each pair. So, if he sells 3 pair of blue jeans, he would incur total costs of $22.50, where $22.50 = $5 +$7.50 + $10.

Buddy's Supply and Costs of Blue Jeans

(a) Buddy's Supply of Blue Jeans		(b) Buddy's Costs of Producing Blue Jeans		
Price	**Quantity**	**Quantity**	**Marginal Cost**	**Total Cost**
$5	1	1	$5	$5
$7.50	2	2	$7.50	$12.50
$10	3	3	$10	$22.50

- The value Buddy receives from the sale of his product equals total revenue minus total cost. This value is termed **producer surplus**, which is the excess of revenue to producers over their costs of production. Graphically, it is the market price minus the supply curve. If the price of blue jeans is $10 in our example, then Buddy would sell three pair for a total revenue of $30, where total revenue is computed by multiplying price by quantity. Subtracting the total cost of $22.50 from the $30 would leave him with a producer surplus of $7.50.

• The table below computes producer surplus for three different prices of blue jeans. As seen in that table, **producer surplus varies directly with price.**

Buddy's Producer Surplus from Blue Jeans

Price	Quantity Sold	Total Cost	Total Revenue	Producer Surplus
$5	1	$5	$5	$0
$7.50	2	$12.50	$15	$2.50
$10	3	$22.50	$30	$7.50

• **Markets are efficient to the extent that they maximize *social surplus*, which is the sum of consumer and producer surplus.** Social surplus is the difference between how much a good is worth and how much it costs to produce. It is the total value the economy gains by having the good produced and consumed. In the blue jeans example, the social surplus at a price of $10 would be $22.50, which equals $15 in consumer surplus for Dwight plus $7.50 in producer surplus for Buddy.

• Any time marginal benefit exceeds marginal cost, social surplus would increase if more of the good were to be produced and sold. That is just what the marketplace does. Producers keep on selling until their marginal cost just equals the market price. Likewise, consumers keep on buying until their marginal benefit equals the market price. This means that marginal benefit equals marginal cost at the market equilibrium price and that social surplus is maximized. Any more output would add more cost than benefit.

• Thus, the *rule of efficiency* states that **the efficient output occurs when society's marginal benefit equals marginal cost.** The marketplace achieves an efficient output through price adjustments. At the market equilibrium price, marginal benefit equals marginal cost and social surplus is maximized. The intersection of demand and supply establishes the efficient quantity. Since demand represents marginal benefit and supply represents marginal cost, the rule of efficiency is satisfied.

• The triangular area of forgone social surplus caused by inefficient pricing is called a **deadweight loss**. The size of the deadweight loss will decrease when the price is closer to the market price, but increase when the price moves farther away from its equilibrium value. Prices that differ from their equilibrium values will not persist because those prices will adjust toward equilibrium. The deadweight loss will in this way eventually disappear.

- Some necessities that have a great deal of intrinsic worth are priced lower than luxuries we could easily do without. For example, people pay much more for a diamond than for a glass of water, which seems paradoxical. The paradox disappears when we realize that price merely tells the value of a good at the margin. The last bit of water is not worth much when water is plentiful. It is the scarcity of diamonds that keeps that price high. To understand the total value of a good, though, we must look beyond price to consumer surplus. The consumer surplus from water purchases is vastly greater than the consumer surplus from diamond purchases.

- Questions of efficiency often arise in the context of international trade. If a country chooses not to engage in international trade, the market prices of its goods and services would reflect only the supply and demand within that country. Those prices are called *domestic* prices. Opening an economy to international trade will change market prices in a country by bringing into its markets a world of new consumers and producers. Countries that trade buy goods and services from other countries—their *imports*. They also sell goods and services to other countries—their *exports*. Whether a country imports a good or exports a good will depend upon whether the good's world equilibrium market price is below or above what the country's price would otherwise have been—its domestic price.

- In other words, **the result of trade is that the price in the domestic market will come to equal the world market price.** If the domestic price rises to meet a higher world price, then the country exports the good. If a lower world price causes the domestic price to drop, then the country imports the good, meaning that it is purchased from producers in other countries. In either case, there are some people within the country who gain and others who lose.

- Allowing imports increases social surplus. Although the lower price will cause producer surplus to shrink, the increase in consumer surplus more than compensates for that loss. Because the gains to consumers more than offset the losses to producers, efficiency calls for allowing imports.

- Allowing exports increases social surplus. Although the higher price will cause consumer surplus to shrink, the increase in producer surplus more than compensates. Because the gains to producers more than offset the losses to consumers, efficiency calls for allowing exports.

- In short, consumers come out winners from imports, but producers lose. Producers come out the winners from exports, but consumers lose. In each case, though, the gains exceed the losses. So, whether it be from imports or from exports, the country as a whole comes out the winner.

StudyCheck 3

Using two graphs, show how a country gains from allowing exports. On your first graph, show the social surplus without trade. On your second graph, show how allowing exports increases this surplus.

4.2 Price Ceilings—Holding Prices Down

• A **price ceiling**, is a law that establishes a maximum price that can be legally charged for a good. With rising populations in competition for scarce land, major cities sometimes choose rent controls as a way to insulate tenants from higher housing costs. **Rent controls** hold the monthly price of rental housing to below its equilibrium level. Price tries to rise, but bumps up against the rent control ceiling. For these rent controls to be meaningful, the ceiling price must be set below the market equilibrium price. The result is a housing shortage, in which less housing is offered for lease, while more housing is demanded.

- One effect of rent controls is to transfer wealth from current landlords to current tenants. Such **transfer payments** in which one party's loss is another's gain are not themselves inefficient since they merely redistribute social surplus. However, when transfer payments are caused by government price controls, there are multiple sources of inefficiency, in which social surplus shrinks. The first inefficiency is the deadweight loss triangle associated with a less-than-efficient overall quantity.

- A second source of inefficiency comes from misallocating apartments that are leased. Since any tenant would be constrained to pay the same rent and there are more potential tenants than available apartments, the landlord would find it easy to discriminate, whether on the basis of income, occupation, or anything else the landlord thinks is important.

- A third inefficiency involves **search costs**, which are the costs of finding an apartment. Since landlords have plenty of prospective tenants for rent-controlled apartments, they do not need to advertise. So some enterprising would-be tenants have taken up such tactics as reading the obituaries or, to get the jump, listening to police radios and checking out emergency rooms. In the absence of rent controls, there would be little or no need for such wasteful behavior.

- **The inefficiencies of rent controls are likely to get worse over time** as demand grows with an increasing population while rent-controlled apartments are allowed to deteriorate.

- While rent controls have problems, there are also problems associated with removing them. The immediate effect of abolishing rent controls is that rents jump to their market equilibrium value.

- There are alternatives to rent controls. One alternative is to identify the needy and assign them housing vouchers. **Housing vouchers** are government grants that the recipient can spend only on housing.

- Local governments have often attempted to protect consumers against **price gouging**, which is the disparaging term for hiking up prices in response to temporary surges in demand. The idea is to promote equity. The cost is in terms of efficiency, though, because high prices in times of emergency prevent shortages and allocate sought-after goods to those who value them the most.

- Profitably high prices also motivate rapid restocking, which means that prices do not stay high for long. Local governments also often have laws against *ticket scalping*—the practice of buying tickets at the price set by concert promoters and then reselling at whatever the market will bear. Scalping is a form of *arbitrage*, which means buying low and selling high. Arbitrage directs goods to their highest-valued uses, thus efficiently allocating seats at concerts, ball games, and other events. As for equity, however, opinions differ.

StudyCheck 4

Using supply and demand analysis, indicate graphically the effects on price, quantity demanded, and quantity supplied resulting from imposition of rent-control legislation which lowers rents below their free-market equilibrium level. Be sure to label: 1) the axes of your graph; 2) supply (S); 3) demand (D); 4) price before rent control (Pb); 5) price after rent control (Pa); 6) quantity demanded after rent control (Qd); 7) quantity supplied after rent control (Qs).

StudyCheck 5

Explain the economic grounds upon which laws against price gouging have been justified. What is the primary economic objection?

4.3 Price Floors—Propping Prices Up

- Although consumers are better off when prices are low, producers prefer them high. Both groups often turn to government for help. If politics dictates propping up prices, government can establish a **price floor**, also termed a **price support**, which sets a minimum price that producers are guaranteed to receive. One way to implement a price floor is for government to agree to buy at that floor price. This approach can cause surpluses to pile up at taxpayer expense. Such is the case of agricultural price supports. Note that the term *surplus* in this context refers to a quantity of output, specifically the excess of what is produced over what is consumed, not to the term social surplus that is also used in this chapter.

- Although only two percent of the United States labor force currently derives a living from agriculture, the political influence of agriculture has been strong enough to maintain agricultural price supports in the U.S. since the 1920s. These price supports have been justified on two counts. One is that they sustain the lifestyle of the family farm, an American tradition. However, the reality is that family farming has continued to decline, and a disproportionate amount of price support payments have gone to large farms and corporations. The second justification is that they ensure a plentiful supply of food for American consumers. This line of reasoning does not withstand the logic of economic analysis.

- The effects of an agricultural price support, holding price above its equilibrium value, are more farm output produced, but less consumed. The result is a surplus. Such agricultural surpluses have averaged many billion dollars' worth of foodstuffs annually in the United States.

- The effect of agricultural price supports is to transfer money from both taxpayers and consumers to those in the agriculture industry. Maintaining a high price redistributes social surplus from consumers to producers. There is a deadweight loss associated with both increased production and decreased consumption.

- Additional deadweight loss can be expected to occur because government must buy and dispose of the surplus quantity, which is nearly impossible to do in an efficient manner. Government cannot merely sell the surplus to the highest bidder, because it must prevent the surplus commodities it buys from being distributed to people who would otherwise purchase that product in the marketplace. To do otherwise would merely mean more of a surplus that government would be forced to buy, because those who received from government would buy less from farmers.

- One option is to give the surplus quantity away in a relatively unpalatable form, such as by turning excess milk into powdered milk. Another option is to export the surplus in a manner that does not compete with other agricultural exports. For example, foreign aid to impoverished countries might work, to the extent that the aid does not supplant other food imports from the donor country.

- The **minimum wage** is a requirement that employers pay no less than a specified wage rate. The higher wage means that more people are willing to work. The higher wage for low-skilled labor also means that fewer jobs are offered. Fast food restaurants, car washes, and other businesses "make do" with fewer people, but train and work them harder. They also may replace some labor with capital, such as automated dishwashers and car-washing equipment. The result is that, along with higher wages comes a surplus of labor—or a shortage of jobs, depending upon how you look at it. Because higher wages are offset by fewer jobs, there is no guarantee that minimum wage laws actually increase the total amount firms spend to employ low-skilled workers.

- As was the case with rent controls, minimum wage requirements facilitate discrimination. With numerous applicants for each job opening, employers can pick and choose as they wish. It would be quite difficult to prove if they choose to discriminate on an illegal basis. While the pay is higher, the jobs and extra pay go to those applicants who need help the least.

- There are alternatives to the minimum wage that target the problem of low wages without controlling price. One alternative is to subsidize the earnings of low-income workers. Such a subsidy is already embedded in the U.S. personal income tax—the earned income tax credit. The drawback is that earnings subsidies come at a high budgetary cost, because they reduce government tax collections or involve actual cash payments.

- Subsidies to education also serve as an alternative to the minimum wage. Such subsidies include free public schooling or government financial assistance to students attending private schools, subsidized student loans for college students, and subsidized tuition at public universities. The more widely available are educational opportunities, the more skills the workforce will acquire. The result is that the supply of low-skilled labor shifts to the left. The leftward shift in supply increases the equilibrium wage for low-skilled labor, which is the purpose of minimum wage laws.

StudyCheck 6

Consider the market for unskilled labor, where a minimum wage prevents the price from reaching an equilibrium. Depict this on a graph, labeling: 1) the axes of the graph; 2) Supply (S); 3) Demand (D); 4) wage (W) in the presence of the minimum wage law; 5) the amount of any surplus or shortage (label either surplus or shortage); 6) the quantity of labor actually employed (LE).

StudyCheck 7

Show the manner in which wage subsidies can increase wages for low-skilled labor.

4.4 Around the World—Black Markets as a Safety Valve

- Price controls are practiced throughout the world. Price support programs have been common in agriculture.

- Any time government tries to hold prices above or below market equilibrium, it provides profit opportunities to those willing to take advantage of them. **Black market** activity is said to occur when goods are bought and sold illegally.

E&A   ### 4.5 The Price of Power

- It was the winter of 2001 when inadequate electricity supplies prompted rolling blackouts in California that cut off electricity to 670,000 households and businesses for two hours at a time.

- In order to increase the efficiency with which electricity was generated and distributed at the wholesale level, California lawmakers deregulated the wholesale electricity market. Deregulation caused the state's wholesale electricity providers to compete for customers. Competition reduces costs through weeding out inefficiencies. *Ceteris paribus*, greater efficiencies in wholesale electricity production and distribution causes the wholesale electricity supply to shift to the right and the price of electricity in the wholesale market to fall. Utilities pay less for the electricity they distribute and these savings are passed along to the utilities' residential and business customers. So California lawmakers felt comfortable promising California voters that their electricity rates would not go up, at least not very much, and might even go down.

- In the real world many things can change at once. In particular, world crude oil prices skyrocketed, more than doubling soon after California's deregulation of wholesale electricity took effect. The prices of natural gas, coal, and other substitutes for crude oil likewise increased. Since oil and other fuels are significant inputs into the production of electricity, rising fuel prices shifted the supply of electricity at the wholesale level significantly to the left. That leftward shift more than offset any rightward shift caused by deregulation. The decrease in the supply of wholesale electricity caused the wholesale price of electricity to rise sharply.

- Left to itself, the marketplace will not allow a shortage for long. The price of electricity at the retail level will rise in response to a shortage. In turn, consumers will consume less electricity, and producers will provide more until an equilibrium is reached. But, because of the lawmaker's promise that consumer electricity prices would be held in check, rates were held down to less than the market equilibrium price. The result in the retail electricity market was a shortage.

- There was no incentive for the utilities to provide additional electricity because the controlled price they were allowed to charge their customers was less than what they were paying for the electricity they bought on the wholesale market. Losses among the California utilities climbed to $13 billion (as reported by SoCal Edison and Pacific Gas & Electric) and they

THE POWER OF PRICES 107

were teetering on the brink of bankruptcy before the state fashioned a plan to keep the power on. Under the terms of that plan, California borrowed $10 billion to tide the utilities through, with California taxpayers responsible for repaying this added debt.

- The restructuring of the electricity industry toward more competition is not just a California event. About half of the states are currently active in this effort, with electricity deregulation moving from the planning stage to reality in state after state. The experience of California, one of the first to deregulate, will be remembered and analyzed for what can be learned. The most vivid memory is sure to be of the electricity shortages caused by the price ceiling.

StudyCheck 8

Using separate graphs, show the effects of deregulation and energy price increases on the equilibrium in California's wholesale electricity market. Explain how this market analysis could have helped California lawmakers avoid the electricity shortages the state experienced in 2001.

FILL IN THE BLANKS

1.   The marketplace depends on price _____, meaning that the market price sends a message to consumers and producers. Consumers buy something because they expect that they will be better off by doing so. Likewise when producers sell something. So when a consumer buys a good that a producer sells, both parties are better off. The mutual gains from such market exchanges lead the economy to greater _____.

2.   The demand curve depicts the _____ that would be purchased at each of various prices, *ceteris paribus*. Another way of looking at it is that the demand curve shows the _____ price the consumer would pay for each quantity that might be purchased, the consumer's _____—the incremental value of each additional item consumed.

3.   Consider Dwight, who is shopping for blue jeans. The table below shows how demand translates into marginal benefit and total benefit. Dwight's total benefit from his blue-jean purchases is the sum of his _____ benefit from each pair. So, if he buys 3 pair, the blue jeans would bring Dwight $_____ worth of total benefit.

Dwight's Demand and Benefits from Blue Jeans

(a) Dwight's Demand for Blue Jeans		(b) Dwight's Benefits from Buying Blue Jeans		
Price	Quantity	Quantity	Marginal Benefit	Total Benefit
$20	1	1	$20	$20
$15	2	2	$15	$35
$10	3	3	$10	$

4.   Since Dwight must pay for the blue jeans he buys, the value to him of his blue-jean purchases equals the total benefit from the blue jeans minus what he pays. This value is termed _____ _____, which is difference between the total benefit and total cost to the consumer. Graphically, it is the demand curve minus _____.

5.   The table below computes consumer surplus for three different prices of blue jeans. As you can see in that table, consumer surplus varies inversely with price. The greater the price the less is consumer surplus and the lower the price the greater is consumer surplus. Dwight's consumer surplus from 3 pairs of blue jeans equals $_____.

Dwight's Consumer Surplus from Blue Jeans

Price	Quantity Bought	Total Benefit	Total Paid	Consumer Surplus
$20	1	$20	$20	$0
$15	2	$35	$30	$5
$10	3	$45	$30	$

6. A supply curve shows the _____ that would be offered for sale at each of various prices, *ceteris paribus*. The supply curve also depicts the _____ price that the producers of a good would be willing to accept for each quantity offered, which is the producer's _____ cost, which is the incremental cost of producing each additional item offered for sale.

7. Consider Buddy, who sells blue jeans. The table below shows how supply translates into marginal cost and total cost. Buddy's total cost of blue-jeans sold is the sum of his _____ cost from selling each pair. So, if he sells 3 pair of blue jeans, he would incur total costs of $_____.

Buddy's Supply and Costs of Blue Jeans

(a) Buddy's Supply of Blue Jeans		(b) Buddy's Costs of Producing Blue Jeans		
Price	Quantity	Quantity	Marginal Cost	Total Cost
$5	1	1	$5	$5
$7.50	2	2	$7.50	$12.50
$10	3	3	$10	$

8. The value Buddy receives from the sale of his product equals total revenue minus total cost. This value is termed _____ _____, which is the excess of revenue to producers over their costs of production. Graphically, it is the market price minus the _____ _____.

9. The table below computes producer surplus for three different prices of blue jeans. As seen in that table, producer surplus varies directly with price. If the price of blue jeans is $10 in our example, then Buddy would sell three pair for a total revenue of $30, where total revenue is computed by multiplying price by quantity. The producer surplus is $_____.

Buddy's Producer Surplus from Blue Jeans

Price	Quantity Sold	Total Cost	Total Revenue	Producer Surplus
$5	1	$5	$5	$0
$7.50	2	$12.50	$15	$2.50
$10	3	$22.50	$30	$

10. Markets are efficient to the extent that they maximize _____ _____, which is the sum of consumer and producer surplus.

11. The rule of efficiency states that the efficient output occurs when society's _____ _____ equals _____ _____. The intersection of _____ and _____ establishes the efficient quantity. The triangular area of forgone social surplus caused by inefficient pricing is called a _____ _____.

12. That people pay much more for a diamond than for a glass of water refers to the _____ of diamonds and water. The explanation for this behavior is that the _____ _____ from water purchases is vastly greater than that from diamond purchases.

13. The market prices of goods and services that reflect only the supply and demand within a country are called _____ prices. Opening an economy to international trade will change market prices in a country by bringing into its markets a world of new consumers and producers. Countries that trade buy goods and services from other countries—their _____. They also sell goods and services to other countries—their _____. Whether a country imports a good or exports a good will depend upon whether the good's world equilibrium market price is _____ or _____ what the country's price would otherwise have been. In other words, the result of trade is that the price in the domestic market will come to _____ the world market price. If the domestic price rises to meet a higher world price, then the country _____ the good. If a lower world price causes the domestic price to drop, then the country _____ the good, meaning that it is purchased from producers in other countries.

14. Allowing imports increases _____ surplus. Although the lower price will cause _____ surplus to shrink, the increase in _____ surplus more than compensates for that loss.

15. Allowing exports increases _____ surplus. Although the higher price will cause _____ surplus to shrink, the increase in _____ surplus more than compensates.

16. A _____ _____ is a law that establishes a maximum price that can be legally charged for a good. _____ _____ hold the monthly price of rental housing to below its equilibrium level.

17. One effect of rent controls is to transfer wealth from current landlords to current tenants. Such _____ _____ in which one party's loss is another's gain are not themselves inefficient since they merely redistribute social surplus. However, when transfer payments are caused by government price controls, there are multiple sources of inefficiency, in which social surplus shrinks. One inefficiency is the _____ _____ triangle associated with a less-than-efficient overall quantity. Another inefficiency involves _____ costs, which are the costs of finding an apartment. There are alternatives to rent controls. One alternative is to identify the needy and assign them _____ _____, government grants that the recipient can spend only on housing.

18. Local governments have often attempted to protect consumers against _____ _____, which is the disparaging term for hiking up prices in response to temporary

surges in demand. Ticket scalping is a form of _____, which means buying low and selling high.

19. If politics dictates propping up prices, government can establish a price _____, also termed a price _____, which sets a minimum price that producers are guaranteed to receive. The effect of holding price above its equilibrium value is a _____.

20. The _____ _____ is a requirement that employers pay no less than a specified wage rate. The result is that, along with higher wages comes a _____ of labor.

21. Any time government tries to hold prices above or below market equilibrium, it provides profit opportunities to those willing to take advantage of them. _____ _____ activity is said to occur when goods are bought and sold illegally.

E↓A 22. In order to increase the efficiency with which electricity was generated and distributed at the wholesale level, California lawmakers _____ the wholesale electricity market.

23. Deregulation caused the state's wholesale electricity providers to compete for customers. Competition reduces costs through weeding out inefficiencies. *Ceteris paribus*, greater efficiencies in wholesale electricity production and distribution causes the wholesale electricity supply to shift to the _____ and the price of electricity in the wholesale market to _____.

24. World crude oil prices subsequently skyrocketed, more than doubling soon after California's deregulation of wholesale electricity took effect. The prices of natural gas, coal, and other substitutes for crude oil likewise increased. Since oil and other fuels are significant inputs into the production of electricity, rising fuel prices shifted the supply of electricity at the wholesale level significantly to the _____, offsetting any rightward shift caused by deregulation, causing the wholesale price of electricity to _____.

25. Because of the lawmaker's promise that consumer electricity prices would be held in check, rates were held down to less than the market equilibrium price. The result in the retail electricity market was a _____.

TRUE/FALSE/EXPLAIN
If false, explain why in the space provided.

1. For an economy to be efficient, it must maximize value, as measured by consumer and producer surplus.

2. Consumer surplus is measured as the difference between demand and market price.

3. If Jack purchases a pail of water for $5 that he was willing to pay $7 for, then Jack's consumer surplus for the pail of water is $7.

4. The paradox of diamonds and water illustrates that it is consumer surplus that truly measures the total value consumers receive from the things they buy.

5. The presence of a price ceiling means that some consumers who value a good quite highly may be unable to buy it.

6. For a price ceiling to be effective, it must be above the market equilibrium price.

7. Rent controls are usually in the short-term interest of renters.

8. Rent controls make discrimination less costly and harder to prove.

9. Under a housing voucher plan, it makes good sense to read the obituaries in order to identify which apartments are likely to come up for rent.

10. Rent controls make it difficult to renovate run-down neighborhoods.

11. While ticket scalping is likely to be efficient, it is commonly considered to be inequitable.

12. So-called price gouging in response to natural disasters can be an efficient way to allocate scarce goods.

13. When a surge in demand causes the price of a good to rise dramatically, economists say that a shortage exists.

14. A price support increases the market equilibrium quantity.

15. Despite being difficult to sell politically, economic analysis suggests that agricultural price supports are an efficient way to provide an income to farmers.

16. Because agricultural price supports promote production, they allow consumers to buy more food.

17. The best way to get rid of surpluses which are accumulated under price support programs is for government to auction off those surpluses in the free market.

18. Minimum wage laws make it easier for employers to discriminate.

19.   Minimum wage laws are likely to prevent those with the poorest work skills from finding a job.

20.   Minimum wage laws reduce employment.

E&A   21.   California experienced electricity blackouts, but never for essential services such as street lights.

22.   Nature was mostly to blame for the electricity blackouts that occurred in California.

23.   The idea of deregulating electricity is to introduce competition that reduces costs by increasing efficiency.

24.   Left to itself, the marketplace will not allow a shortage too last long.

25.   As a result of controlling the price of electricity, the state of California was forced to borrow millions of dollars in order to assist electric companies.

MULTIPLE CHOICE
Circle the letter preceding the one best answer.

1.   Markets are efficient to the extent that they maximize
    a.   social surplus.
    b.   equity.
    c.   marginal benefit.
    d.   producer surplus.

2.   The difference between a consumer's maximum willingness to pay and the price he or she actually pays is termed
a.   equilibrium.
b.   social benefit.
c.   consumer surplus.
d.   opportunity cost.

3.   Suppose Chip's demand for bags of potato chips is:

Price	Quantity demanded
$5	0
$4	1
$3	2
$2	3
$1	4
$0	5

What is Chip's consumer surplus if the price per bag is $1?
a. $16.
b. $12.
c. $6.
d. $4.

4.   Suppose that Jack is willing to pay up to $10 for the first pail of water, $8 for the second, $6 for the third, and $4 for the fourth. If the price of pails of water is $5 each, Jack will buy _____ pails of water and receive a total of _____ worth of consumer surplus.
a.   3; $9
b.   4; $9
c.   4; $13
d.   3; $12

5.   Suppose that the market supply curve offers a quantity of 1 at $1, 2 at $2, 3 at $3, and 4 at $4. If the market price is $4, producer surplus is:
a. $2.
b. $4.
c. $6.
d. $8.

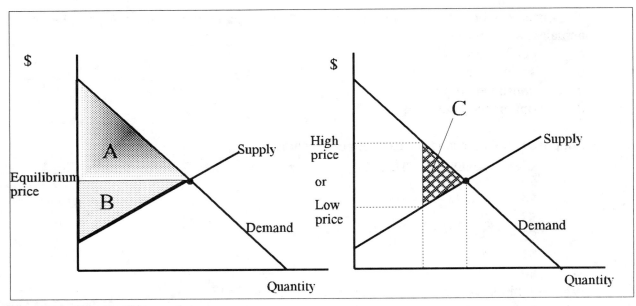

Multiple Choice Figure 1

6. In Multiple Choice Figure 1, consumer surplus is shown by
    a.   area A.
    b.   area B.
    c.   area C.
    d.   area A + B.

7. In Multiple Choice Figure 1, producer surplus is shown by
    a.   area A.
    b.   area B.
    c.   area C.
    d.   area A + B.

8. In Multiple Choice Figure 1, social surplus is shown by
    a.   area A.
    b.   area B.
    c.   area C.
    d.   area A + B.

9. In Multiple Choice Figure 1, deadweight loss is shown by
    a.   area A.
    b.   area B.
    c.   area C.
    d.   area A + B.

10. The rule of efficiency requires that
    a. producer surplus equal consumer surplus.
    b. market prices be fair.
    c. marginal social benefit equal marginal social cost.
    d. people buy low and sell high.

11. The competitive marketplace maximizes
    a. consumer surplus, but not producer surplus.
    b. producer surplus, but not consumer surplus.
    c. the sum of consumer and producer surplus.
    d. the ratio of consumer surplus to producer surplus.

12. An effective price ceiling will result in
    a. an equilibrium quantity.
    b. a shortage.
    c. a surplus.
    d. an efficient allocation of resources.

13. Which of the following is LEAST likely to occur under rent controls?
    a. Landlords will discriminate illegally.
    b. Tenants will find it difficult to move.
    c. The quality of apartments will go down.
    d. The quantity of apartments rented will increase.

14. Once rent controls have been in effect for many years, they are usually difficult to remove. The most likely reason is that
    a. tenants would face huge increases in their rents.
    b. rent controls have had time to prove that they are efficient.
    c. landlords develop a vested interest in keeping the controls in place.
    d. removal of rent controls would violate landlords' property rights.

15. A market-based alternative to rent controls that could ensure affordable housing is
    a. housing price supports.
    b. housing vouchers.
    c. urban renewal.
    d. anti-gouging laws.

16. In Multiple Choice Figure 2, the deadweight loss from reduced consumption is given by
    a. area A.
    b. arrow B.
    c. area C.
    d. arrow D.

17. In Multiple Choice Figure 2, arrow D represents the
    a. deadweight loss from reduced consumption in response to agricultural price supports.
    b. increase in output caused by agricultural price supports.
    c. shortage caused by agricultural price supports.
    d. surplus caused by agricultural price supports.

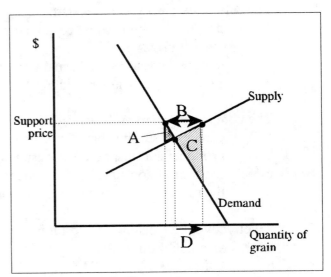

Multiple Choice Figure 2

18. A substantial increase in the minimum wage is likely to be good for
    a. employers, because it would ensure a higher quality workforce.
    b. the most needy - those with the least desirable education and work habits.
    c. new entrants into the labor force seeking to gain experience.
    d. the most employable of the workers currently holding minimum wage jobs.

19. In Multiple Choice Figure 3,
    a. both Dave and Tony are sure to get jobs.
    b. neither Dave nor Tony are likely to get jobs.
    c. although Dave is willing to work for less than Tony, Tony might nonetheless get the job.
    d. although Tony is willing to work for less than Dave, Dave might nonetheless get the job.

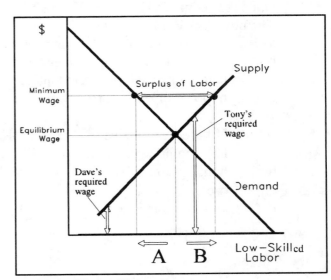

Multiple Choice Figure 3

20.   In Multiple Choice Figure 3, arrow A might be labeled _____ and arrow B labeled
        _____.
        a.   decrease in job applicants; increase in job applicants.
        b.   decrease in jobs; increase in job applicants.
        c.   surplus; shortage.
        d.   shortage; surplus.

E&A 21.   The fundamental reason for electricity shortages in California in 2001 was
        a.   price controls for wholesale electricity, along with deregulation of retail electricity
                prices.
        b.   deregulated wholesale electricity prices along with price controls for retail electricity.
        c.   deregulation of both the wholesale and retail electricity prices.
        d.   price controls in the electricity market at both the wholesale and retail levels.

22.   Multiple Choice Figure 4 shows the effect of controlling the retail price of electricity when
        wholesale prices increase. In this figure,
        the quantity demanded will be given by
        a.   point A.
        b.   point B.
        c.   point C.
        d.   arrow D.

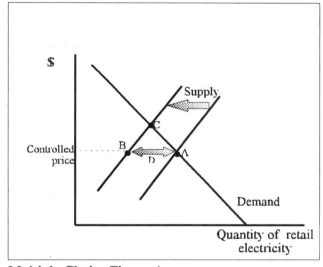

Multiple Choice Figure 4

23.   In Multiple Choice Figure 4, the arrow
        labeled D shows
        a.   a surplus.
        b.   a shortage.
        c.   the quantity demanded.
        d.   the quantity supplied.

24.   The shift in supply shown in Multiple
        Choice Figure 4 was most likely caused
        by
        a.   price controls.
        b.   increased demand.
        c.   increased competition.
        d.   higher oil prices.

25.   Deregulation of wholesale electricity markets has occurred or is in the process of occurring
        a.   nowhere in the world but in California.
        b.   in Russia, Cuba, and California, but nowhere else.
        c.   in numerous states.
        d.   in all fifty states and most countries.

GRASPING THE GRAPHS
Fill in each box with a concept that applies.

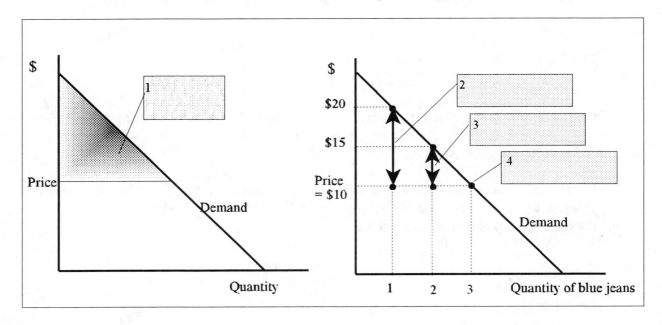

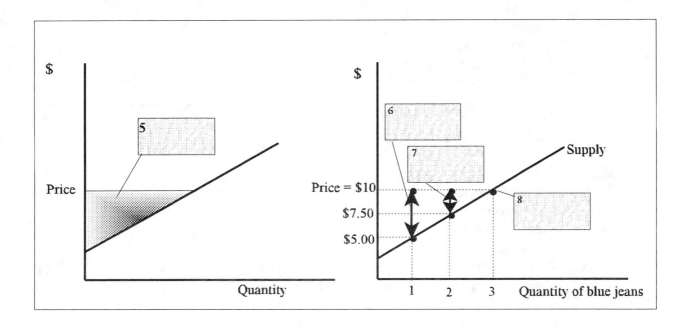

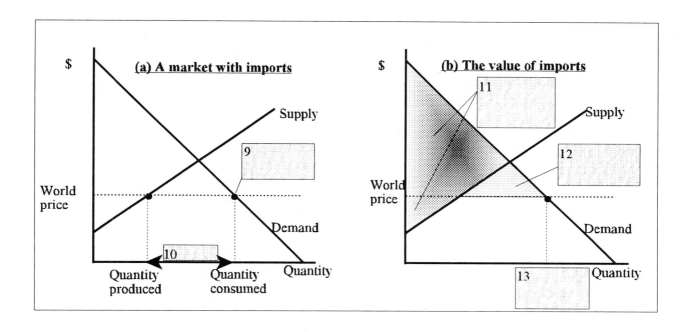

(a) A market with imports

Supply

9

World price

10

Quantity produced   Quantity consumed   Quantity

Demand

(b) The value of imports

11

Supply

World price

12

13

Demand

Quantity

E&A

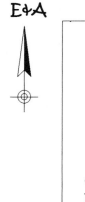

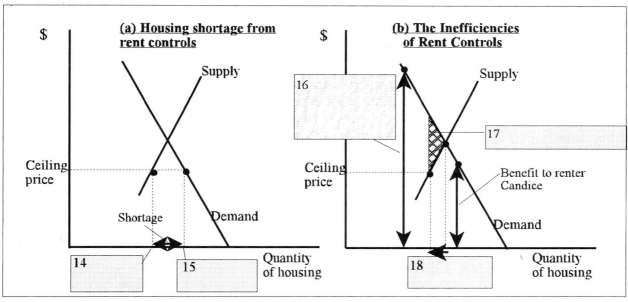

(a) Housing shortage from rent controls

Supply

Ceiling price

Shortage

14   15   Quantity of housing

Demand

(b) The Inefficiencies of Rent Controls

16

Supply

17

Ceiling price

Benefit to renter Candice

Demand

18   Quantity of housing

For additional practice in grasping this chapter's graphs, visit
http://www.prenhall.com/ayers and try *Smart Graph* **9**, along with
Active Graphs **14, 15, 16, 17, 18, 19, and 20.**

ANSWERS

STUDYCHECKS

1.   See StudyCheck 1 Figure.

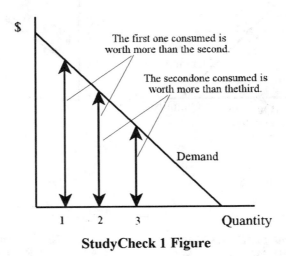

StudyCheck 1 Figure

2.   See StudyCheck 2 Figure.

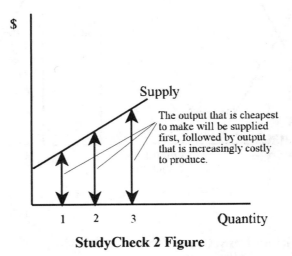

StudyCheck 2 Figure

3. Exports result from a world price that exceeds what the country's equilibrium price would be without trade. In StudyCheck 3 Figure, the higher world price causes the country's consumption to fall and production to rise, with the difference being the amount exported, as shown in (a). The value of social surplus increases by the triangular area shown in (b). However, the gains go disproportionately to producers. Consumer surplus is less because of the higher price.

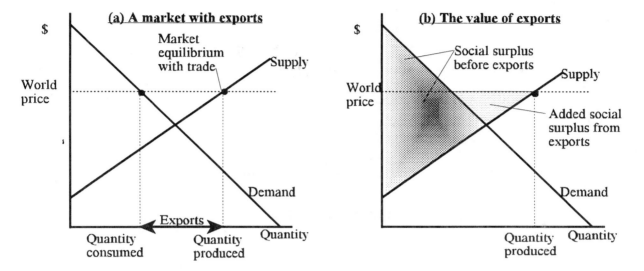

StudyCheck 3 Figure

4. See StudyCheck 4 Figure.

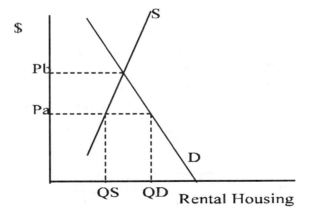

StudyCheck 4 Figure

5. The justification is the perception of equity—windfall profits might seem unfair. The objection is that restricting price is inefficient.

6. See StudyCheck 6 Figure.

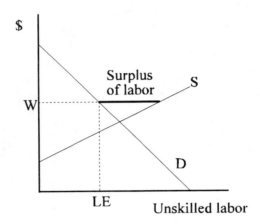

StudyCheck 6 Figure

7. See StudyCheck 7 Figure.

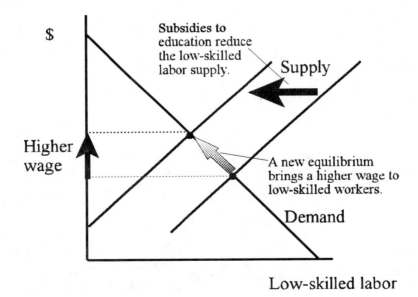

StudyCheck 7 Figure

8. See StudyCheck 8 Figure. Increased ·competition after deregulation was expected to shift supply to the right and lower electricity prices, as shown in (a). However, soaring prices of

crude oil, coal, and natural gas—inputs into the production of electricity—more than offset the effects of deregulation. The result was that electricity supply in fact shifted to the left, causing price to increase as shown in (b). Had California lawmakers recognized this analysis, they might have avoided price ceilings that would not allow electricity retailers to pass along increases in wholesale costs that deregulation could not prevent.

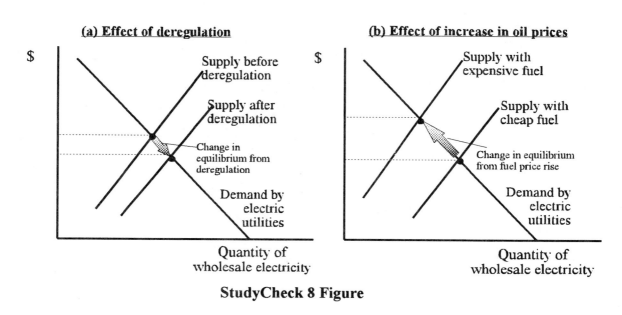

StudyCheck 8 Figure

FILL IN THE BLANKS

1. signals, efficiency
2. quantity, maximum, marginal benefit
3. marginal, $45
4. consumer surplus, price
5. $15
6. quantity, minimum, marginal
7. marginal, $22.50
8. producer surplus, supply curve,
9. $7.50
10. social surplus
11. marginal benefit, marginal cost, demand, supply, deadweight loss
12. paradox, consumer surplus
13. domestic, imports, exports, exports, imports
14. social, producer, consumer
15. social, consumer, producer
16. price ceiling, Rent control

17. transfer payments, deadweight loss, search, housing vouchers
18. price gouging, arbitrage
19. floor, support, surplus
20. minimum wage, surplus
21. black market
22. deregulated
23. right, fall
24. left, rise
25. shortage

TRUE/FALSE/EXPLAIN

1. True.
2. True.
3. False, consumer surplus is $2.
4. True.
5. True.
6. False, a price ceiling will have no effect unless it is below the market equilibrium price.
7. True.
8. True.
9. False, housing vouchers give renters greater purchasing power, but do not cause shortages and so do not require prospective renters to make extraordinary efforts to be the first to see an apartment.
10. True.
11. True.
12. True.
13. False, a surge in demand would cause the price to rise as far as necessary to equate the quantity demanded and the quantity supplied.
14. False, a price support keeps price above the market equilibrium price, but does not change the value of either the market equilibrium price or quantity.
15. False, agricultural price supports are an easy sell politically, but are shown to be inefficient by economic analysis.
16. False, consumers buy as much food as they want to without the existence of price supports, which increase the price such that consumers would want to buy less.
17. False, those surpluses cannot be auctioned off in the free market, as any of the surplus quantity sold would merely displace the sales of farmers who would then line up to sell their output to the government.
18. True.
19. True.
20. True.
21. False, even street lights in San Francisco were disrupted.

THE POWER OF PRICES 127

22. False, the shortages resulted from a combination of deregulated wholesale electricity markets and price controls on retail electricity.
23. True.
24. True.
25. True.

MULTIPLE CHOICE

1.	a	8.	d	15.	b	22.	a
2.	c	9.	c	16.	a	23.	b
3.	c	10.	c	17.	b	24.	d
4.	a	11.	c	18.	d	25.	c
5.	c	12.	b	19.	c		
6.	a	13.	d	20.	b		
7.	b	14.	a	21.	b		

GRASPING THE GRAPHS
Examples of correct answers

1. consumer surplus
2. $10 consumer surplus for first pair
3. $5 consumer surplus for second pair
4. no consumer surplus for third pair
5. producer surplus
6. $5 producer surplus for first pair
7. $2.50 producer surplus for second pair
8. no producer surplus for third pair
9. quantity demanded
10. imports
11. social surplus
12. increase in social surplus from imports
13. quantity consumed
14. quantity supplied
15. quantity demanded
16. This person values housing highly, but may not get any.
17. deadweight loss
18. fewer units rented

Visit the Ayers/Collinge companion Website at http://www.prenhall.com/ayers for further activities and exercises for this chapter.

Part 2

MICROECONOMIC FOUNDATIONS

Chapter 5

ELASTICITY: MEASURING RESPONSIVENESS

CHAPTER REVIEW

- Social and business issues often revolve around the responsiveness of one thing to another—a concept termed **elasticity** in economics.

5.1 Computing Elasticity

- Elasticity measures how one variable changes as a result of another variable changing. Although the names of the variables can be anything, the concept remains the same: Elasticity = Percentage change in one variable (Y)/Percentage change in other variable (X). All elasticities arise from this same underlying formula. Different elasticities merely name the variables differently.

- Elasticity has a broad range of applications. In economics, elasticities are most often used to distinguish the way in which various demand curves differ from one another. There are many other instances in which the concept of elasticity is useful.

- Computing an elasticity is little more than determining a percentage change. In common usage, a percentage change is defined as the change in something divided by what it started out as. For example, if a person's weight rises from 100 pounds to 150 pounds, we say that their weight has risen by 50 percent, that is, by 50/100. Curiously, if the person's weight were to drop from 150 pounds to 100 pounds, the percentage change would be -33 percent, that is, $-50/150 = -1/3$. In other words, weight rose by half but fell by one-third.

- This type of measure will not do for the computation of elasticities. Rather, a measure is needed that is independent of the direction in which the variables are changing. That measure of percentage change is provided by the *midpoint formula*, which computes a percentage change as the change in the variable divided by an amount halfway between the starting and ending amount.

- Consider the variable Y, which changes from a starting value called Y_0 to another value called Y_1. Symbolically, the midpoint formula to compute the percentage change in Y is: Percentage change in Y = change in Y/Y midpoint, where Change in Y = $Y_1 - Y_0$ and Y midpoint =

$(Y_0 + Y_1)/2$. Likewise, the percentage change in variable X is computed as: Percentage change in X = change in X/X midpoint, where Change in X = $X_1 - X_0$ and X midpoint = $(X_0 + X_1)/2$.

- To compute the elasticity of Y with respect to X, divide the percentage change in Y by the percentage change in X: Elasticity of Y with respect to X = Percentage change in Y ÷ Percentage change in X.

5.2 The Elasticity of Demand

- The **elasticity of demand** measures the responsiveness of quantity demanded to changes in price. For this reason it is sometimes called the *price elasticity of demand*. Some price changes are pretty much ignored by consumers, while others elicit a sharp response.

- The formula for the elasticity of demand is given by the percentage change in quantity demanded (Q), divided by the percentage change in price (P). Since price and quantity demanded are inversely related, the computation of the elasticity of demand will always result in a negative value. **For convenience, the elasticity of demand is stated as an absolute value, meaning that the minus sign is dropped.**

- The elasticity of demand using the midpoint formula is: Elasticity of demand = |Percentage change in quantity demanded ÷ Percentage change in price.| Note the vertical bars around the formula, indicating absolute value. Using Q to stand for quantity demanded, we have Percentage change in Q = change in Q/Q midpoint, where Change in Q = $Q_1 - Q_0$, and Q midpoint = $(Q_0 + Q_1)/2$. Similarly, using P to stand for price, Percentage change in P = change in P/P midpoint, where Change in P = $P_1 - P_0$. and P midpoint = $(P_0 + P_1)/2$.

- Note that **the elasticity of demand is not the same as the slope of demand.** The slope of demand divides the change in price by the change in quantity, without reference to percentages.

- Consider Jerry's elasticity of demand for Old Navy t-shirts. At the regular price of $10, he used to furnish his wardrobe with 12 shirts a year. Now that he has discovered that Old Navy lowers the price of the shirts to $8 each when they are on sale, he waits until there is a sale and buys 18 t-shirts a year.   Jerry's elasticity of demand in the price range between $10 and $8 equals 1.8.

Computing Jerry's Elasticity of Demand for t-shirts

---

(1) Set up the problem.

Call the regular price of t-shirts P_0 and the sale price P_1. The quantity purchased by Jerry at the regular price was 12 t-shirts; the quantity purchased at the sale price is 18 t-shirts. The values of the variables are thus:

$P_0 = \$10$ $Q_0 = 12$

$P_1 = \$\ 8$ $Q_1 = 18$

(2) Compute the percentage change in Q

Change in $Q = Q_1 - Q_0 = 18 - 12 = 6$

Q midpoint $= (Q_0 + Q_1)/2 = (12 + 18)/2 = 30/2 = 15$

Percentage change in Q = change in Q/Q midpoint = 6/15

(3) Compute the percentage change in P

Change in $P = P_1 - P_0 = 8 - 10 = -2$

P midpoint $= (P_0 + P_1)/2 = (10 + 8)/2 = 18/2 = 9$

Percentage change in P = change in P/P midpoint = $-2/9$

(4) Substitute into the formula for the elasticity of demand

$|$percentage change in Q/percentage change in P$| = (6/15)/(2/9) = (6/15) \times (9/2) = 54/30 = 1.8$

- The elasticity of demand is classified as inelastic, unit elastic, or elastic, according to its numerical value.

- **Inelastic demand:** Elasticity of demand lies between 0 and 1; in this range, the quantity demanded is relatively unresponsive to changes in price.

- **Unit elastic demand:** Elasticity of demand equal to 1; in this range, the quantity demanded changes proportionally to changes in price.

- **Elastic demand:** Elasticity of demand is greater than 1; in this range, the quantity demanded is relatively responsive to changes in price.

- **Other things equal, the more substitutes there are for a product or the greater the fraction of a person's budget it takes to buy the product, the greater will be its elasticity of demand.** Items that some people will find to be *necessities*—items that it is difficult to do without—tend to have more inelastic demand than *luxuries* that we can easily forego.

- Consumer spending translates into revenue for sellers. The revenue sellers receive equals the quantity sold multiplied by the price, and is called **total revenue**. In other words,

Total revenue = price × quantity

- Total revenue, which is the same as total spending by consumers, can be shown graphically as the rectangular area created when a price and corresponding quantity demanded are multiplied by each other.

StudyCheck 1

Suppose that Sammy buys 1 pair of baseball shoes if the price is $70, 2 pairs at $50, 3 pairs at $30, or 4 pairs at $10. Compute the elasticity of demand between each of these points. Compute the total revenue associated with each quantity (bear in mind that expenditures by Sammy equal total revenues to sellers).

- An increase in price will bring in more revenue only if demand is inelastic, meaning that the fall in quantity demanded is less significant than the rise in price. In contrast, were demand to be elastic, the quantity demanded would be quite responsive to price. Any increase in price would cause a proportionally greater fall in the quantity sold and thus would lower total revenue. The following table summarizes the effects on total revenue of a price change.

The Effect of a Change in Price On Total Revenue

Change in Price	Effect on Total Revenue
Higher Price	If demand is inelastic, total revenue rises. If demand is unit elastic, total revenue remains constant. If demand is elastic, total revenue falls.
Lower Price	If demand is inelastic, total revenue falls. If demand is unit elastic, total revenue remains constant. If demand is elastic, total revenue rises.

- **The longer the time period that quantity demanded adjusts, the greater will be the elasticity of demand.** Time lets people adjust, to substitute toward goods that become relatively less expensive and away from those that become relatively more expensive.

- **The elasticity of demand will vary along most demand curves. Along a downward-sloping, straight-line demand curve, demand is unit elastic at the midpoint, elastic above the midpoint, and inelastic below the midpoint.** The reason is that, when we move down the demand curve, the percentage change in price becomes larger relative to the corresponding percentage change in quantity demanded.

- In the elastic range of demand, total revenue increases as price decreases. Total revenue reaches its maximum when the elasticity of demand is unit elastic, which occurs at the midpoint of demand. In the inelastic range of demand, total revenue decreases as price falls.

- One implication of this analysis is that each firm always seeks to stay out of the inelastic portion of its demand.. When demand is inelastic, firms would find their revenues increasing if they reduce output and increase their price. They will do so until they are out of the inelastic range. The result is this general rule: **Each firm seeks to produce in the elastic range of its demand.** Exactly where in that range firms will produce is unclear because the cost of production must be taken into account when deciding on the specific quantity to produce.

StudyCheck 2

Draw a graph showing the relationship between demand and total revenue. Indicate where demand is unit elastic and where it is inelastic. Why will the firm not produce an output greater than the output associated with unit elasticity?

- There are three cases in which elasticity is constant throughout the demand curve. Demand can be **perfectly inelastic**, meaning that the elasticity of demand is zero. In other words, the quantity demanded will not depend on price. The corresponding demand curve is drawn as a vertical line.

- Demand can be **unit elastic throughout**. The shape of the demand curve is referred to as a rectangular hyperbola, because any total revenue rectangle drawn under that demand curve will have the same area. A demand with this shape slopes downward at a decreasing rate, never touching either axis. Whatever price may be, total revenue remains the same.

- The demand curve can be **perfectly elastic** throughout, meaning that it has an elasticity of infinity and is drawn as a horizontal line. In other words, the slightest increase in price over some threshold price leads to a complete loss of sales. At any price at or below this threshold, unlimited quantities could be sold. This demand is a close approximation to demand facing the firm in the competitive marketplace, in which there is a very large number of other firms. The firm's demand curve in the competitive marketplace is perfectly elastic at the market price.

5.3 Income and Cross Elasticities of Demand: The Sign Matters

- Two additional demand elasticities are also referred to frequently, the income elasticity of demand and the cross elasticity of demand. The **income elasticity of demand** measures how demand responds to income. It is computed by dividing the percentage change in quantity demanded by the percentage change in income. If the income elasticity of demand is positive, an increase in income increases demand. **A positive income elasticity of demand indicates the good is normal.** Conversely, **a negative income elasticity of demand indicates the good is inferior** because demand decreases when income rises.

- Normal goods can be distinguished from inferior goods by the direction of the shift in demand that arises from a change in income. A good is normal when the demand shifts in the same direction as the change in income. When the demand shifts in the opposite direction as income, the good is inferior.

- Finally, the **cross elasticity of demand** measures how the demand for one good responds to changes in the price of another good. Its formula is given by the percentage change in the demand for one good divided by the percentage change in the price of the other. If this value is positive, the demand for the first good changes in the same direction as the price of the other good. **A positive cross elasticity of demand indicates the goods are substitutes,** such as Coke for Pepsi. Thus, if the price of Pepsi increases, so does the demand for Coke.

- If the cross elasticity of demand is negative, the quantity demanded of the good falls as the price of the other good rises, and vice versa. **A negative cross elasticity of demand indicates that the goods are complements,** goods that go together, such as popcorn and movies. If movie tickets become more expensive, fewer people go to the movie theater and less popcorn is sold.

5.4 The Elasticity of Supply

- The **elasticity of supply** measures the responsiveness of quantity supplied to price. Its formula is given by the percentage change in quantity supplied divided by the percentage change in price. The formula used to compute the elasticity of demand can be used to compute the elasticity of supply, except that the variable Q will be quantity supplied rather than quantity demanded. Since price and quantity supplied are directly related to each other, the elasticity of supply will always be positive, thus eliminating the need to take the absolute value, as is done with the elasticity of demand.

- The elasticity of supply can fall within the following three ranges:
  - **Inelastic supply:** Elasticity of supply lies between 0 and 1; in this range, the quantity

supplied is relatively unresponsive to price.

- **Unit elastic supply:** Elasticity of supply = 1; in this range, the quantity supplied changes proportionally to changes in price.
- **Elastic supply:** Elasticity of supply is greater than 1; in this range, the quantity supplied is relatively responsive to changes in price.

- As with demand, supply can be *perfectly inelastic, unit elastic throughout, or perfectly elastic*. A perfectly inelastic supply curve is vertical. Unit elastic supply is any straight line from the origin. This share is implied by unit elastic's definition, in which the percentage change in price must always equal the percentage change in quantity. A perfectly elastic supply curve is horizontal.

5.5 Tax Shifting and the Elasticities of Demand and Supply

- When a product is taxed, how much of that tax will the buyers pay and how much will the sellers pay? Some people mistakenly think that, even if the tax is levied on sellers, all of the tax will just be passed on to buyers in the form of higher prices. In reality, the answer to the question of who ultimately shoulders the burden of the tax depends on the demand and supply elasticities of the product taxed.

- If the addition of the tax causes the tax-inclusive price of the product to change by less than the amount of the tax, then both consumers and producers are sharing in the *burden* of that tax, meaning that they are both worse off. The greater is the elasticity of supply relative to the elasticity of demand, the more of the tax burden will be borne by consumers and the less by producers.

- When the effects of a tax are transferred from one party to another, **tax shifting** is said to occur. *Forward tax shifting* occurs when the seller is taxed but is able to pass along all or part of the tax to buyers in the form of a higher price. Conversely, if the buyer pays a sales tax and the seller feels compelled to charge a lower price in order to make that sale, the result is *backward tax shifting*, in which the buyer has effectively shifted some of the tax backward onto the seller.

- Consider the effect of a tax in which sellers must pay a fixed amount per unit of sales. Because the seller must pay the tax for each unit sold, **the effect of the tax is to shift the supply curve upward by the amount of the tax.** If we have a perfectly inelastic demand curve and an upward-sloping supply curve, the price of the product rises as the market equilibrium changes so that the after-tax price is greater by exactly the amount of the tax. The maximum amount of tax shifting occurs when demand is perfectly inelastic because the entire amount of the tax is passed on to buyers. Notice that in spite of the tax, the perfectly inelastic demand results in no change in the quantity of the product bought and sold.

- When it is supply that is perfectly inelastic, then supply shifts vertically by the amount of the tax, also. However, the shift in supply does not affect the market equilibrium—the equilibrium price and quantity remain unchanged. In this case, no tax shifting can occur.

- Usually, reality lies somewhere in between these extremes, with the **tax burden**—how much the tax costs after taking into account price changes—shared between producers and consumers. **Consumers pay more of the tax if demand is relatively less elastic than supply. Producers pay more of the tax if demand is relatively more elastic than supply**.

- Cigarettes and alcohol are taxed at much higher rates than virtually any other good. The reason is partly because these "goods" are seen as bad. Just as important, it is because the elasticity of demand is low relative to that of other goods. If the elasticity were high, people could more easily switch to other goods with lower tax rates. That would cut into tax revenues.

StudyCheck 3

On two separate graphs, one for each market, show a situation where imposition of a tax on sales of a good would be: (a) shifted totally to the buyer; and (b) borne totally by the seller. In each case, show the amount of the tax and its effect on supply.

5.6 Crime and the Market for Drugs

- The United States has the highest proportion of its citizens behind bars of any developed country. Sixty percent of those prisoners are convicted on drug-related charges. Economic analysis can help to solve the dilemma of why toughening up our enforcement of drug laws seems to make drug-related problems worse.

- Government enforcement of drug laws increases the risk involved in getting illegal drugs to market. The supply curve shifts to the left as costs increase and as risk-averse suppliers leave the industry. Remaining suppliers will be those who shrug off the risk, perhaps because they enjoy it or have become accustomed to the lifestyle. For the most part, however, competition will select those suppliers who are best at circumventing the law.

- Organized crime flourishes under tough drug law enforcement. These organizations offer both connections and firepower to the dealers. In addition, because the drug dealer cannot turn to the police for protection, that dealer becomes easy prey for organized criminals. Here is one source of crime associated with drugs—turf battles in which criminal organizations seek to dominate the sales of drugs in an area.

- On the demand side, tough enforcement of the drug laws makes it much more expensive to support a drug habit. Drug users are often addicted to the drugs they use and would go to great lengths to avoid doing without. In other words, the demand for drugs is inelastic because the quantity purchased does not drop proportionally to increases in price. This means that, the tougher we enforce our drug laws, the more money drug users need. Moreover, the tougher we punish a convicted drug offender for the drug use itself, the less the user cares about adding other crimes to the list.

- Tough enforcement of our drug laws also has the perverse effect of increasing the popularity of the more highly refined drugs, since these drugs are harder to intercept. For instance, "cracking" cocaine to form crack requires only a small amount of cocaine, a drug with very little bulk. Such drugs also tend to be the most addictive.

- There are numerous possible drug control policies between the current war on drugs and a laissez faire hands-off strategy. At the extreme, if all drugs were legalized, that would seem to suggest including prescription pharmaceuticals.

- The addictive nature of drugs leads to an inelastic demand curve. The market price and quantity of drugs in the free market is determined by the intersection of supply and demand. The drug war shifts that supply by increasing the riskiness and cost of supplying drugs. The result is a higher equilibrium price and lower equilibrium quantity.

- Relative to the outcome under the drug war, the free market would appear to offer both good news and bad news. The good news is that the quantity of spending, given by P multiplied by

Q, would be lower without the drug war. This means less crime to raise money to buy drugs. Since drugs would be sold by legitimate businesses in the free market, the violent territorial crime of the drug rings would also largely disappear. The bad news is that drug use would rise, ceteris paribus, because demand always shows an inverse relationship between price and quantity.

- Keep in mind that the demand curve keeps constant everything but price. But moving away from the drug war entails more than just a drop in price. For example, the entire demand curve would shift outward to the extent that users no longer fear being arrested, which would lead to greater usage. Alternatively, the demand curve might shift inward to the extent that drug usage constitutes less of an anti-authority rebellion and is seen more as a matter of responsible personal behavior. Without tough drug laws, there would be no "pushing" because there would be no money in it. There would be no financial incentive to lure schoolchildren to drug use. Free from the pressure of pushers, and without drugs exemplifying rebellion against authority, fewer kids would turn to drugs—demand would shift to the left.

- Some people suggest legalization of many drugs, but only if we impose high sales taxes to discourage purchases and pay for drug-related problems. This policy would be akin to taxing cigarettes in proportion to their external costs—those not captured in the marketplace. While taxes can be reasonable, a prohibitively high tax would reopen the doors to criminal pushers and modern-day bootleggers.

- Moving away from the drug war toward legalization does raise many questions. Some people are concerned about whether quality would diminish in the workplace, especially when that quality involves personal safety.

- Without government prohibitions, the free market would provide its own incentives for a clear-headed workforce. The incredibly high cost of a plane crash in terms of replacing the equipment and settling lawsuits would give airlines strong incentives to screen their personnel for drugs, alcohol, or other judgment-impairing problems. In general, companies that employ workers with impaired judgment would lose out in the competitive marketplace to those firms that are more effective at screening out problem workers.

- Legal or illegal, drugs do cause problems for both users and innocent victims. For example, driving-under-the-influence laws have reduced but not eliminated problems of drunk driving. Would a similar approach provide pedestrians and other drivers adequate protection from drivers hallucinating under the influence of LSD? Questions of law aside, recreational drugs are the source of serious problems. For example seeing cocaine babies and other heart-wrenching consequences of addiction can so enrage people that they want to wipe out drug use at any cost. Does that justify intensifying the drug war. Or is peace the way to victory?

StudyCheck 4

Analyze the effects on crime and drug usage of a reduction in the penalty for the use and sale of recreational drugs.

StudyCheck 5

Consider the market for cocaine. Assume that demand is inelastic, but that the elasticity exceeds zero. Graph: 1) demand (D0); 2) supply (S0); 3) price (P0); 4) quantity (Q0); 5) total revenue (TR0). Suppose the government steps up drug interdiction efforts, which increases the cost of smuggling. On the same graph, repeat the 5 steps above, making any changes that would be appropriate. Assume that demand does not shift. Label supply as S1, price as P1, quantity as Q1, and total revenue as TR1.

FILL IN THE BLANKS

1. Social and business issues often revolve around the responsiveness of one thing to another—a concept termed _____ in economics.

2. Elasticity measures how one variable changes as a result of another variable changing. Although the names of the variables can be anything, the concept remains the same: Elasticity = _____ change in one variable (Y)/ _____ change in other variable (X).

3. The _____ formula computes a percentage change as the change in the variable divided by an amount halfway between the starting and ending amount. To compute the elasticity of Y with respect to X, divide the percentage change in ___ by the percentage change in ___ .

4. The elasticity of demand measures the responsiveness of _____ _____ to changes in _____ . For this reason it is sometimes called the price elasticity of demand.

5. Since price and quantity demanded are inversely related, the computation of the elasticity of demand will always result in a negative value. For convenience, the elasticity of demand is stated as an _____ _____ , meaning that the minus sign is dropped.

6. The elasticity of demand is classified as inelastic, unit elastic, or elastic, according to its numerical value. ___ _____ demand: Elasticity of demand lies between 0 and 1; in this range, the quantity demanded is relatively unresponsive to changes in price. _____ _____ demand: Elasticity of demand equal to 1; _____ demand: Elasticity of demand is greater than 1.

7. Other things equal, the more substitutes there are for a product or the greater the fraction of a person's budget it takes to buy the product, the _____ will be its elasticity of demand.

8. Items that some people will find to be necessities—items that it is difficult to do without—tend to have more _____ demand than luxuries that we can easily forego.

9. Consumer spending translates into revenue for sellers: Total revenue = _____ × _____ .

10.   Total revenue, which is the same as total spending by consumers, can be shown graphically as the _____ area created when a price and corresponding quantity demanded are multiplied by each other.

11.   An increase in price will bring in more revenue only if demand is _____. If demand were to be _____, the quantity demanded would be quite responsive to price. so that any increase in price would cause a proportionally greater fall in the quantity sold and thus would lower total revenue. If demand is unit elastic, total revenue remains _____ no matter the direction of a price change.

12.   The longer the time period that quantity demanded adjusts, the _____will be the elasticity of demand.

13.   The elasticity of demand will vary along most demand curves. Along a downward-sloping, straight-line demand curve, demand is _____ _____ at the midpoint, _____ above the midpoint, and _____ below the midpoint.

14.   In the elastic range of demand, total revenue_____ as price decreases. Total revenue reaches its _____when the elasticity of demand is unit elastic, which occurs at the midpoint of demand. In the inelastic range of demand, total revenue as price falls.

15.   There are three cases in which elasticity is constant throughout the demand curve. Demand can be perfectly inelastic, meaning that the elasticity of demand is _____. In other words, the quantity demanded will not depend on price. The corresponding demand curve is drawn as a _____ line. Demand can be unit elastic throughout. The shape of the demand curve is referred to as a _____ _____ , because any total revenue rectangle drawn under that demand curve will have the same area. A demand with this shape slopes downward at a decreasing rate, never touching either axis. Whatever price may be, total revenue remains the same. The demand curve can be perfectly elastic throughout, meaning that it has an elasticity of _____ and is drawn as a _____line.

16.   The income elasticity of demand, measures how demand responds to income. It is computed by dividing the percentage change in _____ by the percentage change in _____. If the income elasticity of demand is _____ an increase in income increases demand. A positive income elasticity of demand indicates the good is _____ . Conversely, a negative income elasticity of demand indicates the good is _____ because demand decreases when income rises.

17.   The cross elasticity of demand measures how the demand for one good responds to changes in the _____of another good. A positive cross elasticity of demand indicates the goods are _____ . A negative cross elasticity of demand indicates that the goods are _____ .

18. If the addition of a tax causes the tax-inclusive price of the product to change by less than the amount of the tax, then both consumers and producers are sharing in the _____ of that tax, meaning that they are both worse off.

19. When the effects of a tax are transferred from one party to another, tax shifting is said to occur. _____tax shifting occurs when the seller is taxed but is able to pass along all or part of the tax to buyers in the form of a higher price. Conversely, if the buyer pays a sales tax and the seller feels compelled to charge a lower price in order to make that sale, the result is _____ tax shifting, in which the buyer has effectively shifted some of the tax backward onto the seller.

20. Consider the effect of a tax in which sellers must pay a fixed amount per unit of sales. Because the seller must pay the tax for each unit sold, the effect of the tax is to shift the supply curve _____by the amount of the tax. If we have a perfectly inelastic demand curve and an upward-sloping supply curve, the price of the product rises as the market equilibrium changes so that the after-tax price is greater by exactly the amount of the tax. The maximum amount of tax shifting occurs when demand is perfectly _____ because the entire amount of the tax is passed on to buyers. When supply is perfectly inelastic, then supply shifts vertically by the amount of the tax, also. However, the shift in supply does not affect the market equilibrium—the equilibrium price and quantity remain unchanged. In this case, no tax shifting can occur.

E&A 21. Government enforcement of drug laws increases the risk involved in getting illegal drugs to market. The supply curve shifts to the _____ as costs increase and as risk-averse suppliers leave the industry.

22. On the demand side, tough enforcement of the drug laws makes it much more expensive to support a drug habit. Drug users are often addicted to the drugs they use and would go to great lengths to avoid doing without. In other words, the demand for drugs is _____ because the quantity purchased does not drop proportionally to increases in price.

23. The market price and quantity of drugs in the free market is determined by the intersection of _____ and _____.

24. The drug war shifts supply by increasing the riskiness and cost of supplying drugs. The result is a _____equilibrium price and _____equilibrium quantity.

25. The quantity of spending, given by P multiplied by Q, would be _____without the drug war. Drug use would _____, ceteris paribus, because demand always shows an inverse relationship between price and quantity.

TRUE/FALSE/EXPLAIN
If false, explain why in the space provided.

1. All elasticities have the same basic formula, which is the percentage change in one variable divided by the percentage change in another.

2. The elasticity of demand and the price elasticity of demand are the same thing.

3. Computing elasticity of demand involves nothing more than computing the slope of the curve.

4. The elasticity of demand is stated as an absolute value, meaning that the minus sign is dropped.

5. Suppose Molly is willing to buy 10 muffins at 10 cents each, or 30 muffins at 5 cents each. Molly's elasticity of demand in this range is 1.5.

6. Using the midpoint formula, if the price rises from $3 to $4 and the quantity demanded falls from 2 units to 1 unit, then the elasticity of demand equals 7/3.

7. If demand is elastic, its value will be greater than one.

8. The more substitutes there are for a product or the greater the fraction of a person's budget it takes to buy the product, the lower will be the elasticity of demand for the product.

9. Total revenue equals price multiplied by quantity.

10. If demand is inelastic and the price goes up, total revenue rises.

11. If demand is elastic and the price goes down, total revenue falls.

12. The longer the time period over which quantity demanded can adjust, the greater will be the elasticity of demand.

13. Elasticity of demand will be constant along most demand curves.

14. Along a straight-line demand curve, the elasticity of demand is constant at all points.

15. A demand curve that is unit elastic at all points will have the shape of a rectangular hyperbola.

16. The elasticity of supply measures the responsiveness of the quantity supplied to the quantity demanded.

17. Tax burden refers to how much the tax costs after taking into account price changes, and will be affected by the elasticities of demand and supply for the product that is being taxed.

18. The effect of a per-unit tax on sales is to shift the demand curve rightward by the amount of the tax.

19. The more elastic is demand relative to supply, the greater will be the amount of the sales tax burden that is borne by consumers.

20.   So-call sin taxes refer to taxes on the necessities of life, such as taxes on food, shelter, and medical care.

E↔A   21.   On the supply side, the corruption and violence associated with the drug trade occurs because there is much money at stake and because the business is outside the law.

22.   If demand for illegal drugs is inelastic, increasing the enforcement of anti-drug laws is likely to increase spending on those drugs.

23.   Drug pushers would probably lose their businesses if drugs were to be legalized.

24.   An effective way to reduce spending on illegal drugs is to get tough with drug suppliers.

25.   Drug cartels are adamantly opposed to the current drug war, and would prefer to see recreational drugs legalized.

MULTIPLE CHOICE
Circle the letter preceding the one best answer.

1.   Using the midpoint formula, Ally's elasticity of demand for weekday cellular talk time between points A and B in Multiple Choice Figure 1 is
   a.   (1/3)/(1/5) = 1.67.
   b.   (1/5)/(1/3) = .6.
   c. $4.50/ 7 + $5.50/5 = 1.74.
   d.   (1/5)/(1/6) = 1.2

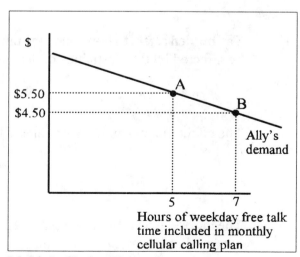

Multiple Choice Figure 1

2.   Ally's elasticity of demand for cellular talk time between points A and B in Multiple Choice
       Figure 1
       a.   is elastic.
       b.   is inelastic.
       c.   is unit elastic.
       d.   cannot be determined without more information.

3.   The shaded area shown in Multiple Choice
       Figure 2 represents
       a.   quantity demanded.
       b.   quantity supplied.
       c.   elasticity.
       d.   total revenue.

4.   If demand is elastic and the price goes
       down, total revenue will
       a.   increase.
       b.   decrease.
       c.   not change.
       d.   first increase and then decrease.

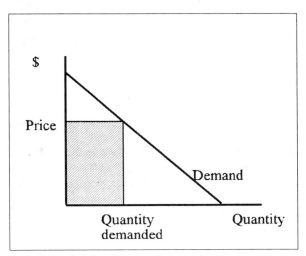

Multiple Choice Figure 2

5.   If demand is unit elastic and the price goes
       down, total revenue will
       a.   increase.
       b.   decrease.
       c.   not change.
       d.   first increase and then decrease.

6.   When the CEO of Amazon.com justified free shipping by saying, "The hope is we'll generate
       enough new business to offset the cost,"he was in effect hoping that demand for his
       company's products would prove to be
       a.   unit elastic.
       b.   elastic.
       c.   inelastic.
       d.   less than his company's elasticity of supply.

7.   The income elasticity of demand is
    a.   the percentage change in quantity supplied divided by the percentage change in quantity demanded.
    b.   the percentage change in income divided by the percentage change in quantity demanded.
    c.   the percentage change in quantity demanded divided by the percentage change in income.
    d.   the change in income divided by the change in price.

8.   A positive income elasticity of demand indicates
    a.   a substitute.
    b.   a complement.
    c.   a normal good.
    d.   an inferior good.

9.   Which of the following is most likely to be an inferior good?
    a.   A book
    b.   A roll of generic paper towels
    c.   Steak
    d.   A genuine wool sweater from the Land's End catalog.

10.   The cross elasticity of demand measures the
    a.   responsiveness of the quantity demanded of one good in response to a change in the price of another good.
    b.   elasticity of supply divided by the elasticity of demand.
    c.   elasticity of demand divided by the elasticity of supply.
    d.   responsiveness of quantity demanded to a change in income.

11.   If the cross elasticity of demand is negative, the goods in question are
    a.   substitutes.
    b.   complements.
    c.   normal.
    d.   inferior.

12.   If thingamajigs are good substitutes for thingamabobs, then
    a.   the cross elasticity of demand between thingamabobs and thingamajigs will be negative.
    b.   the cross elasticity of demand between thingamabobs and thingamajigs will be positive.
    c.   both goods have similar elasticities of demand.
    d.   both goods have similar elasticities of supply.

13. Which graph in Multiple Choice Figure 3 shows perfectly elastic supply?
   a. Graph A
   b. Graph B
   c. Graph C
   d. Unknown without further information

14. Which graph in Multiple Choice Figure 3 shows perfectly inelastic supply?
   a. Graph A
   b. Graph B
   c. Graph C
   d. Unknown without further information

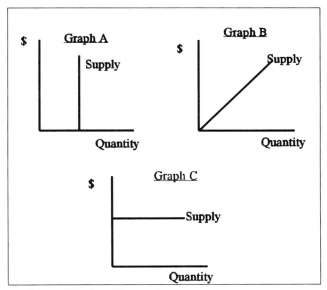

Multiple Choice Figure 3

15. Which graph in Multiple Choice Figure 3 shows unit-elastic supply?
   a. Graph A
   b. Graph B
   c. Graph C
   d. Unknown without further information

16. In Multiple Choice Figure 4, the total amount of taxes is represented by
   a. arrow A.
   b. arrow B.
   c. arrow C.
   d. arrow A + arrow B.

17. In Multiple Choice Figure 4, arrow B represents the
   a. portion of the tax the sellers are able to pass along to buyers.
   b. decrease in the price received by sellers after the tax is paid.
   c. decrease in tax revenue received by government caused by the lower quantity of output.
   d. decrease in the number of sellers.

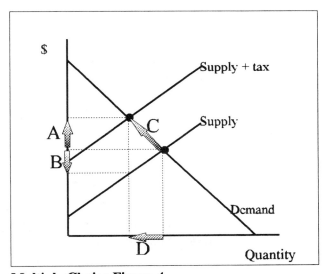

Multiple Choice Figure 4

18.   In Multiple Choice Figure 4, the inefficiencies of taxation are most closely associated with the
        arrow labeled
        a.   A.
        b.   B.
        c.   C.
        d.   D.

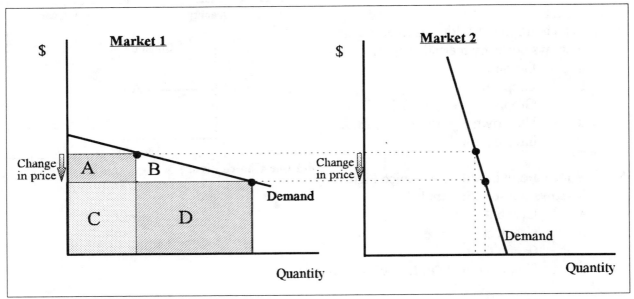

Multiple Choice Figure 5

19.   Consider the price change shown in Multiple Choice Figure 5. In market 1, the total revenue
        after the price change is given by the sum of areas
        a.   A and B.
        b.   A and C.
        c.   C and D.
        d.   A, B, C, and D.

20.   For the price change shown in Multiple Choice Figure 5, the elasticity of demand
        a.   will definitely be higher in market 1.
        b.   will definitely be higher in market 2.
        c.   will definitely be equal in both markets.
        d.   cannot be compared without specific numerical data.

E+A 21. If demand for addictive recreational drugs is inelastic and does not shift, increasing the penalties for the sale and use of those drugs would _____ drug usage and _____ revenues in the drug industry.
   a. increase; increase
   b. increase; decrease
   c. decrease; increase
   d. decrease; decrease

22. If demand for addictive recreational drugs is inelastic and does not shift, increasing the penalties for the sale and use of those drugs would _____ the market price and probably _____ violent crime among drug suppliers.
   a. increase; increase
   b. increase; decrease
   c. decrease; increase
   d. decrease; decrease

23. Suppose that the drug war reduces the supply of a prohibited substance. If spending on this substance increases, then the relevant portion of demand must be
   a. upward-sloping.
   b. elastic.
   c. inelastic.
   d. unitary elastic.

24. Organized crime _____ tough drug law enforcement.
   a. flourishes under
   b. is eliminated by
   c. is not affected by
   d. is greatly diminished (but not eliminated) by

25. If the government were to legalize the use and sale of addictive recreational drugs, it is most likely that there would be
   a. an increase in the number of commercial airline crashes, as pilots and air traffic controllers come to work "strung out" on drugs.
   b. a sharp decline in the income of drug pushers.
   c. an increase in the amount of money people spend on drugs.
   d. an increase in violence among suppliers.

GRASPING THE GRAPHS
Fill in each box with a concept that applies.

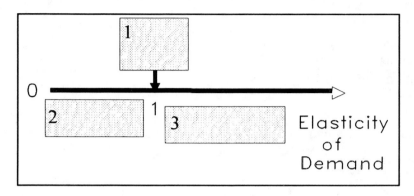

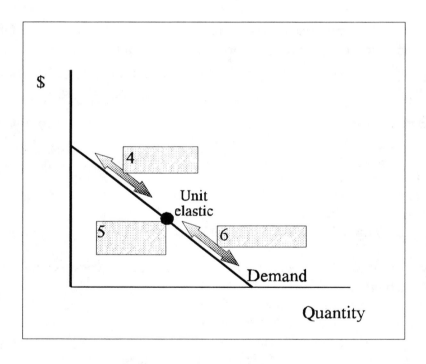

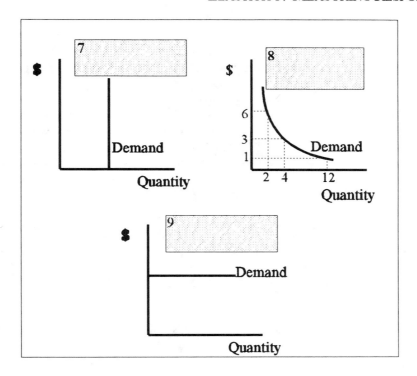

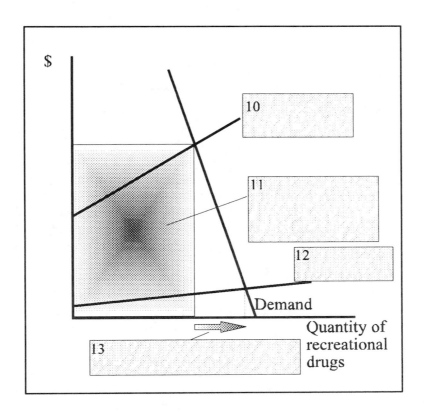

**For additional practice in grasping this chapter's graphs, visit
http://www.prenhall.com/ayers and try *Smart Graphs* 18 and 19,
along with *Active Graphs* 37, 38, 39, 40, 41, and 42.**

ANSWERS

STUDYCHECKS

1.

Point	P	Q	TR	Elasticity (from previous point)
A	$70	1	$70	not applicable
B	$50	2	$100	2
C	$30	3	$90	4/5 (=.8)
D	$10	4	$40	2/7 (=.286)

2.   See StudyCheck 2 Figure.

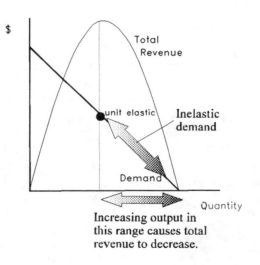

StudyCheck 2 Figure

3.   See StudyCheck 3 Figure.

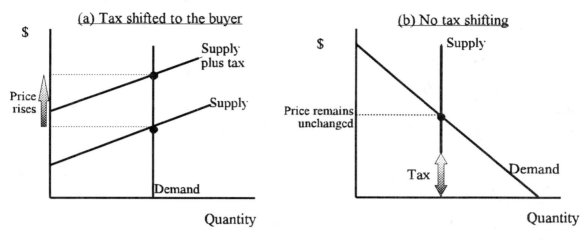

StudyCheck 3 Figure

4.   A reduction in the penalty for the sale of drugs would shift the supply curve down, which would increase drug usage. Because the demand is inelastic, total spending on drugs and its associated crime would be reduced. However, reducing the penalties for drug usage could either offset or accentuate this effect, depending upon whether demand shifts to the right or left. It would shift to the right if the greater tolerance promoted greater usage. However, demand might alternatively shift to the left in response to the decline of drug pushers and their influence as role models, among other factors.

5.   See StudyCheck 5 Figure.

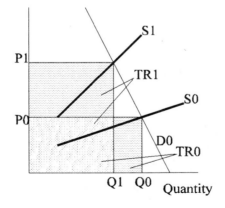

StudyCheck 5 Figure

FILL IN THE BLANKS

1.   elasticity
2.   Percentage, Percentage
3.   midpoint, Y, X
4.   quantity demanded, price
5.   absolute value
6.   inelastic, unit elastic, elastic
7.   greater
8.   inelastic
9.   price, quantity
10.   rectangular
11.   inelastic, elastic, constant
12.   greater
13.   unit elastic, elastic, inelastic
14.   increases, maximum, decreases
15.   zero, vertical, rectangular hyperbola, infinity, horizontal
16.   quantity demanded, income, positive, normal, inferior
17.   price, substitutes, complements
18.   burden
19.   Forward, backward
20.   upward, inelastic
21.   left
22.   inelastic
23.   supply, demand
24.   higher, lower
25.   lower, rise

TRUE/FALSE/EXPLAIN

1.   True.
2.   True.
3.   False, while slope involves computing the change in price and the change in quantity, the elasticity of demand requires that these changes be put in percentage terms and that the percentage change in quantity be divided by the percentage change in price.
4.   True.
5.   True.
6.   True.
7.   True.
8.   False, the more substitutes there are for a product or the greater is the fraction of a person's budget that takes to buy the product, the higher will be the elasticity of demand for the

product.
9.   True.
10. True.
11. False, total revenue would rise.
12. True.
13. False, elasticity of demand will usually vary, and will always vary if the demand curve is a downwardly sloping straight line.
14. False, along a straight-line demand curve, points above the midpoint are elastic, points below the midpoint are inelastic, and the midpoint itself is unit elastic.
15. True.
16. False, the elasticity of supply measures the responsiveness of the quantity supplied to price.
17. True.
18. False, the effect would be to shift the demand curve downward or the supply curve upward, depending on whether the tax is collected from the buyer or seller.
19. False, the more elastic is demand relative to supply, the less will be the amount of the sales tax burden that is borne by consumers.
20. False, sin taxes usually refer to taxes on alcohol and tobacco.
21. True.
22. True.
23. True.
24. False, the amount of spending would increase as authorities get tougher because demand is inelastic for addictive substances.
25. False, drug cartels would lose out in competition with conventional pharmaceutical companies or other companies if drugs were legalized.

MULTIPLE CHOICE

1.	a	8.	c	15.	b	22.	a
2.	a	9.	b	16.	d	23.	c
3.	d	10.	a	17.	b	24.	a
4.	a	11.	b	18.	d	25.	b
5.	c	12.	b	19.	c		
6.	b	13.	c	20.	a		
7.	c	14.	a	21.	c		

GRASPING THE GRAPHS
Examples of correct answers

1.   Unit elastic
2.   Inelastic
3.   Elastic
4.   Elastic
5.   Elasticity = 1
6.   Inelastic
7.   Perfectly inelastic
8.   Unit elastic throughout
9.   Perfectly elastic
10.   Supply with drug war
11.   Total revenue with drug war
12.   Supply in free market
13.   Ceteris paribus, quantity demanded increases when price decreases.

Visit the Ayers/Collinge companion Website at http://www.prenhall.com/ayers for further activities and exercises for this chapter.

CONSUMER BEHAVIOR

CHAPTER REVIEW

6.1 The Law of Demand Revisited

- The law of demand is caused in part by the **substitution effect** of a price change, which occurs when a lower price on a good causes a person to buy more of that good *instead of alternative goods*. Likewise, the substitution effect from increasing the price of a good would drive consumers to buy more of the substitute goods instead of the good with the increased price. The result of the substitution effect is a downward sloping demand curve.

- For a normal good, the **income effect** of a price change will also cause demand to slope down. The income effect occurs when the price change affects consumer purchasing power, termed *real income*, and thus leads to a change in quantity demanded. A higher price reduces real income while a lower price increases real income. In most cases the income effect of a price change will be smaller than the substitution effect because few price changes are very significant in terms of a person's overall purchasing power.

6.2 Utility and Consumer Satisfaction

- Consumers buy in order to obtain **utility**, which is the satisfaction received from the consumption of a good. The utility that people gain from their purchases is subjective, varying from person to person. **Utility is not measurable since satisfaction is not measurable.**

- It would be easy to mistakenly conclude that utility is only provided by the "useful" items we purchase. **Utility does not imply that a good is useful.**

- Although utility is not measurable, it can be modeled as though it were, using the **util** as its unit of measurement.

- We can distinguish between increments to utility and the sum of those increments. For example, suppose you eat two slices of pizza and gain 160 utils from doing so. If the first slice contributed 90 of those utils, then the second slice provided an increment of 70 utils. **Total utility** equals the sum of the utils a person receives from consuming a specific quantity of a good. In this example, your total utility equals 160 utils. **Marginal utility** equals the increments to utility from changes in consumption. Your marginal utility of the second slice of pizza equals 70 utils.

- When you know the amounts of total utility for various amounts of consumption, you can calculate marginal utility by:

  Marginal utility = change in total utility/change in number of units consumed

- Note that the marginal utility curve has a negative slope. Also note that the marginal utility curve crosses the horizontal axis to become negative. When marginal utility is negative we say that a good provides **disutility.**

StudyCheck 1

Suppose Jennie receives 7 utils from her first Dr. Pepper of the day. When she consumes 2, her total utility is 12 utils. Three Dr. Peppers gives her a total utility of 14 utils, and four Dr. Peppers a total utility of 11 utils. Compute Jennie's marginal utility from drinking Dr. Pepper. Why would she turn down a fourth Dr. Pepper?

- Total utility can be computed by summing the marginal utilities. The total utility curve rises so long as marginal utility is a positive number. When marginal utility equals zero, the total utility curve peaks because total utility is at its maximum value. The total utility curve turns downward when marginal utility becomes negative.

StudyCheck 2

Fill in the missing items in the following table:

Packs of Chewing Gum Consumed Weekly	Total Utility	Marginal Utility
0	0	undefined
1	12	_____
2	22	_____
3	28	_____
4	_____	2
5	_____	0
6	27	_____

- **The law of diminishing marginal utility** decrees that the first unit of a good is the most satisfying, after which additional units provide progressively less and less additional utility. There is a **satiation point**, beyond which additional consumption actually reduces total utility. Beyond the satiation point a good has disutility.

- Graphically, total utility rises, reaches a peak, and then falls. Marginal utility decreases, reaches a value of zero, and then turns negative. The relationship between total utility and marginal utility is such that the following are always true:
  - When total utility is increasing, marginal utility will be positive.
  - When total utility is at its maximum, the consumer has reached the satiation point and marginal utility will equal zero.
  - When total utility is decreasing, marginal utility will be negative.

- **The law of diminishing marginal utility applies when consumption occurs over a relatively short time period.**

- The law of diminishing marginal utility suggests that eventually marginal utility becomes 0, as at the satiation point, and then a negative value. Would you buy so much of a good that your next purchase provides you with zero marginal utility? No, because you spend money in order to gain satisfaction. You would be wasting your money if the purchase gave you no increment of satisfaction. For the same reason you would avoid purchasing so much of the good that the marginal utility of the next unit is a negative value. You would refuse to accept a good that has a negative marginal utility value, even if offered free of charge.

- Marginal utility might increase at first. Nonetheless, marginal utility will eventually diminish as you start to get tired of snacking. The law of diminishing marginal utility is generally applicable.

6.3 Maximizing Utility Subject to a Budget Constraint

- The *budget constraint*, a consumer's income, curbs the amount of total utility that can be obtained. **Consumers maximize utility subject to their budget constraint. Utility maximization is achieved when the consumer's choices provide the greatest amount of total utility for a specific amount of income.**

- When a marginal utility is divided by the price, the result is called the **marginal utility per dollar**. The marginal utility per dollar spent upon each good diminishes, which occurs because the marginal utility of each good diminishes.

- When choices provide the same amount of marginal utility per dollar, we say that the consumer is *indifferent* between them.

- The process of maximizing utility leads to **the rule of utility maximization**:

Rule of utility maximization

*To maximize utility, a consumer adjusts spending until the marginal
utility from the last dollar spent on each good is the same.*

- When the rule of utility maximization is followed we say the consumer is in *equilibrium*.

- Fortunately consumers do not need to measure their utility to follow this rule. As noted earlier, there is no way to accurately measure utility, or to convincingly compare utility across different consumers. To follow the rule of utility maximization, we attempt to divide our spending so that the last dollar spent on each good provides the same marginal utility, whatever the good may be. The marginal utility of a dollar we spend on a good equals the marginal utility of the good itself divided by the price we pay for it. For this to be equal for all goods means that:
Marginal utility of X/price of X = marginal utility of Y/price of Y, for all goods X and Y.

- To understand why this equality characterizes consumer equilibrium, consider a consumer who receives greater marginal utility from dollars spent on X than from dollars spent on Y. If X and Y are ice cream and cookies, respectively, the consumer would cut down on purchases of cookies, and use the extra income to buy ice cream. Even though the budget would be the same, total utility would be greater. We would each be quick to seize such opportunities. By doing so, however, we reallocate our spending until the opportunities to increase total utility are no longer there. Increases in the consumption of ice cream will decrease its marginal utility. At the same time, decreases in the consumption of cookies will increase the marginal utility from consuming cookies. This means that the marginal utility per dollar will ultimately be the same for ice cream and cookies.

StudyCheck 3

Explain in your own words the rule that the marginal utility per dollar spent will be equal across the range of goods a consumer buys.

- **When consumers maximize utility their individual demand curves for a good are downward sloping.** In other words, the quantity demanded of a good will change in the opposite direction to a change in its price.

E&A **6.4 Good Choice, Bad Choice: The Choice is Yours**

- Consumers account for some 70 percent of total spending in the U.S. economy. Predicting consumers' choices is difficult since they are determined by numerous considerations.

- Time has utility. People try to allocate time to give them the greatest amount of satisfaction, taking into account time's opportunity cost. The income and other rewards from time spent at work provides satisfaction. Time spent with families and friends provides another form of satisfaction. Time spent on hobbies and interests also offers satisfaction We consider the amounts of satisfaction we receive from each of these and more as we decide how to spend our time.

- Consumers today have more leisure time than previous generations. While time spent doing nothing has utility, there are many goods that are *complements* to leisure time. Examples include sports and entertainment. The utility from an hour of leisure time can sometimes be increased by filling that time with an interesting activity.

- Some goods are time intensive. You might not purchase a chess set because developing the necessary skills and finding the time to play would cut into the utility provided by the alternatives. Many other products require us to spend time with them in order to obtain the satisfaction they provide. Television, computers, and video games are just three examples. The more time you have available to use these products the greater the amount of satisfaction they provide.

- Information has utility. Subscribers to *Consumer Reports* and other magazines receive valuable product information, but at the price of the subscription. Other information has a price too, although not always in terms of money. For example, information cost could include listening to annoying "sales pitches."

- A consumer must decide how much information to purchase. Product information, like other goods, is characterized by diminishing marginal utility. The rule of utility maximization you studied in this chapter may include information as another good. Thus, the last dollar spent on information should have a marginal utility per dollar equal to the marginal utility per dollar of the last dollar spent on the consumer's other purchases.

- *Impulse buyers* make purchases on the spur of the moment without consulting information sources. Impulse buying may appear to be irrational since impulse purchases may provide less utility than well planned purchases. However, impulse buying does not necessarily mean that people are ignoring utility. A consumer's time has utility and impulse buying conserves on time devoted to collecting product information. When the utility of time is taken into account, impulse buying can be viewed as a way to maximize utility.

- Some people visit a public library, an appropriate web site, or watch the news to get information. The federal government often publicizes consumer information in these venues. The government's anti-smoking campaign is an example of such consumer information.

- Other information that influences consumer choices comes from friends and family. Word of mouth is especially important when movie goers select which film to see. The same is true of many other purchases. Some of the choices we make using information supplied by friends end up disappointing us.

- Advertising is intended to affect consumers' choices, generally with the goal of getting us to buy something now. Advertisers will sometimes provide us with useful information in order to loosen our purse strings. The information in the Yellow Pages that relates to opening and closing times, locations, and telephone numbers of businesses is an example of informational advertising. Print advertising for personal computers usually includes numerous technical specifications that promote sales. Other times, advertising seeks to work its effects by influencing our emotions rather than providing us with information. This type of advertising recognizes that utility is subjective.

- You don't need to spend a dollar in order to gain utility. A dollar saved can provide more satisfaction than a dollar spent, at least for some people. Attitudes toward saving and spending may be partially inborn, but are more likely to be the result of the influences of parents, family, and friends. Such attitudes are likely to be formed in childhood. They can be difficult to change.

- Consider the compulsive spender. These people have great difficulty in sticking to a budget, even when financial problems hang over them like a dark cloud. When prudence would dictate paying off their bills, they spend. When they ought to be saving, they spend. When they are sleeping, they are dreaming of spending! Ultimately, the motivations of compulsive spenders fall within the realm of psychology. All an economist can say is that if a dollar is spent it must have provided the individual with more utility than if it had been saved.

- Giving away your wealth can provide you with utility. That explains why Americans contribute many millions of dollars to charity every year. *Altruism*, a concern for others, is consistent with utility maximization. We may obtain satisfaction from charitable contributions because they make us feel good. Altruism may also be motivated by religious or philosophical beliefs.

- Some people make choices that appear to be bad choices to others. The choice to smoke is an example. Overeating is another. Alcohol and drug problems that amount to addictive behavior are a third. Many would like to make different choices, but don't seem to be able to do so.

- Two aspects of utility analysis can help us better understand addictive and other unhealthy behaviors. One aspect of addiction problems is that we are unable to rationally control the things that give us utility. People who aim to keep their weight down for health reasons cannot help it that chocolate cake provides them with significantly more utility than lettuce. In an effort to provide a massive dose of disutility to problem drinkers, doctors will sometimes prescribe Antabuse, a drug that makes them very sick if they drink.

- The other aspect is the time horizon relating to utility. Some things provide immediate gratification, but also produce long-term problems. Thus, the utility comes now, but the disutility later. The farther into the future the disutility the more we are inclined to brush it aside. Some addictions might be cured if only the time horizons of the addicted were longer, so that they took into account future problems caused by their addictions

- To conclude, we have seen that good people often make "good" choices, but sometimes make "bad" choices because those choices furnish utility. But good people are also free to choose. Good choices can replace bad ones. Our families and society can help us to make those good choices.

StudyCheck 4

Economics models people's behavior under the assumption that individuals attempt to maximize utility subject their budget constraints. How can this be justified when we know that individuals do not always act rationally or in their own best interests?

APPENDIX: Indifference Curves, Budget Constraints, and Utility Maximization

- Consumer choice can be illustrated so that we do not require utils. All that is required is that consumers be able to tell which of two choices they prefer or whether they are indifferent between those choices.

- Sometimes people are indifferent to the choices before them. **In economic terms, when people are indifferent to the choices before them, they obtain the same amount of utility from each of those choices.**

- An **indifference curve** shows the combinations of two goods that provide an individual with equal amounts of utility. When we draw an indifference curve we do not need to state the amount of utility. Instead, our thoughts focus on the idea that the combinations shown are equally desirable to the consumer. An indifference curve shows the combinations of two goods that provide the same, constant amount of utility.

- **An indifference curve slopes downward.**   The downward slope occurs because in order for utility to remain constant the consumption of one of the goods must be cut back when more of the other good is consumed.

- The indifference curve is curved rather than a straight line.   A straight-line indifference curve would violate the law of diminishing marginal utility. An indifference curve is drawn as a curved line because that shape is consistent with diminishing marginal utility.

StudyCheck 5

Ray is considering four alternative meals that would leave him equally satisfied, which are:

Combination	Jumbo shrimp	Chicken wings
A	1	8
B	2	5
C	3	3
D	4	2

Plot Ray's indifference curve based on this data. Make sure to label your axes.

- Rather than discuss the curvature of indifference curves in terms of slope, economists prefer to focus on the idea that we can substitute more of one good in place of less of the other good while maintaining a constant level of satisfaction. The **marginal rate of substitution** is the quantity of one good that must be given up as the consumption of the other good increases by one unit and *total utility remains constant*. Holding utility constant, the marginal rate of substitution can be expressed as:

$$\text{marginal rate of substitution} = \frac{\text{change in the consumption of one good}}{\text{change in the consumption of another good}}$$

- This expression applies to changes along an indifference curve because total utility must remain constant when the marginal rate of substitution is computed. The convention is to express the marginal rate of substitution as a positive number. The marginal rate of substitution diminishes as more of a good is consumed, known as the *principle of the diminishing marginal rate of substitution*

- By referring to the formula for the marginal rate of substitution we see that **the marginal rate of substitution is an approximation for the absolute value of the slope of an indifference curve.** Indifference curves are typically convex to the origin. Indifference curves that are convex to the origin will always exhibit a diminishing marginal rate of substitution.

- A consumer has more than one indifference curve between any two goods, reflecting varying levels of satisfaction. An **indifference map** shows a set of indifference curves.

- Consumer choice is limited by the amount of money people can spend and the prices of the goods they buy. The **budget constraint** is a curve that shows a consumer's consumption possibilities for two goods. The budget constraint, also called the budget line, is always a straight line.

- When there are two goods to choose from, the budget constraint is given by the formula: Income = (Price of first good × quantity of first good) + (price of second good × quantity of second good)

- In this formula a consumer knows the prices and income. The quantities of the two goods are the choice variables. The consumer computes various combinations of the two goods that all use up the income.

- Points outside the budget line require more income than is currently available and thus cannot be purchased now. Points inside the budget line are combinations that cost less than the income available.

- When the consumer's income changes, there will be a new budget constraint that shows the new combinations of goods that the consumer is able to purchase.

- The slope of the budget constraint in absolute value terms equals the ratio of the prices of the two goods. Thus, a change in a price will alter the slope of the budget line.

- The consumer's objective is to maximize utility, subject to a budget constraint. **Graphically, utility maximization is achieved when the consumer reaches the highest indifference curve attainable along the budget constraint.** The highest indifference curve will be tangent to the budget line, called the *consumer equilibrium*.

- When two curves are tangent to each other, their slopes are equal at the tangency point. What a consumer is *willing to do* is indicated by the marginal rate of substitution. The ratio of prices tells us what the consumer *must do* since the consumer cannot consume beyond the budget line.

- When there is a change in the price of one of the goods, the utility-maximizing equilibrium point will change. This effect occurs because the slope of the budget line changes with a price change. A lower price will allow the consumer to attain a higher indifference curve; a higher price will push the consumer to a lower indifference curve.

FILL IN THE BLANKS

1. The law of demand is caused in part by the _____ effect of a price change, which occurs when a lower price on a good causes a person to buy more of that good instead of alternative goods. For a normal good, the _____ effect of a price change, which occurs when the price change affects consumer purchasing power and thus leads to a change in quantity demanded, will also cause demand to slope down.

2. Consumers buy in order to obtain _____, which is the satisfaction received from the consumption of a good.   The utility that people gain from their purchases is _____, varying from person to person.

3. Utility is not measurable since _____ is not measurable. Although utility is not measurable, it can be modeled as though it were, using the _____ as its unit of measurement.

4. We can distinguish between increments to utility and the sum of those increments. _____ utility equals the sum of the utils a person receives from consuming a specific quantity of a good. _____ utility equals the increments to utility from changes in consumption.

5.   When you know the amounts of total utility for various amounts of consumption, you can calculate marginal utility by: Marginal utility = _____ in total utility/_____ in number of units consumed.

6.   The marginal utility curve has a _____ slope. Also, the marginal utility curve crosses the horizontal axis to become _____, meaning that a good provides _____ .

7.   Total utility can be computed by summing the _____ utilities. The total utility curve rises so long as marginal utility is a _____ number. When marginal utility equals zero, the total utility curve _____ because total utility is at its maximum value.

8.   The total utility curve turns downward when marginal utility becomes _____. Beyond the satiation point a good has _____. The law of _____ marginal utility suggests that eventually marginal utility becomes zero, as at the satiation point, and then a negative value.

9.   The _____ constraint, a consumer's income, curbs the amount of total utility that can be obtained. Consumers _____ utility subject to this constraint.

10.   When a marginal utility is divided by the _____, the result is called the marginal utility per dollar.

11.   When choices provide the same amount of marginal utility per dollar, we say that the consumer is _____ The process of maximizing utility leads to the rule of utility maximization: To maximize utility, a consumer adjusts spending until the marginal utility from the _____ dollar spent on each good is the _____ .

12.   When the rule of utility maximization is followed we say the consumer is in _____ .

13.   The rule of utility maximization can be stated as: _____ utility of X/price of X = _____ utility of Y/price of Y, for all goods X and Y.

14.   To understand why this equality characterizes consumer equilibrium, consider a consumer who receives greater marginal utility from dollars spent on X than from dollars spent on Y. If X and Y are ice cream and cookies, respectively, the consumer would cut down on purchases of _____, and use the extra income to buy _____. Even though the budget would be the same, total utility would be _____ .

15.   When consumers maximize utility, their individual demand curves for a good are _____ sloping.

E&A   16.   Consumers account for some _____ percent of total spending in the U.S. economy. Predicting consumers' choices is difficult since they are determined by numerous considerations.

17.   Consumers today have more leisure time than previous generations. While time spent doing nothing has utility, there are many goods that are _____ to leisure time. Examples include sports and entertainment.

18.   A consumer must decide how much information to purchase. Product information, like other goods, is characterized by _____ marginal utility. The rule of utility maximization you studied in this chapter may include information as another good. Thus, the last dollar spent on information should have a _____ _____ per dollar equal to the _____ _____ per dollar of the last dollar spent on the consumer's other purchases.

19.   Giving away your wealth can provide you with utility. That explains why Americans contribute many millions of dollars to charity every year. _____, a concern for others, is consistent with utility maximization. We may obtain satisfaction from charitable contributions because they make us feel good.

20.   Some things provide immediate gratification, but also produce long-term problems. Thus, the utility comes now, but the disutility later. The farther into the future the disutility the more we are inclined to brush it aside. Some addictions might be cured if only the time horizons of the addicted were _____, so that they took into account future problems caused by their addictions

Appendix

21.   In economic terms, when people are _____ to the choices before them, they obtain the same amount of utility from each of those choices.

22.   An indifference curve shows the combinations of two goods that provide an individual with _____ amounts of utility. An indifference curve slopes _____.

23.   The _____ _____ ___ _____ is the quantity of one good that must be given up as the consumption of the other good increases by one unit and total utility remains constant.

24.   When there are two goods to choose from, the budget constraint is given by the formula:
Income = _____ +
_____

25.   Graphically, utility maximization is achieved when the consumer reaches the _____ indifference curve attainable along the budget constraint.

TRUE/FALSE/EXPLAIN
If false, explain why in the space provided.

1. The substitution effect of a price change affects consumer purchasing power.

2. The substitution effect of a price change means that when the price of the good goes down, a person buys more of it instead of buying other things.

3. The main difference between the income effect and the substitution effect is that the income effect causes the entire demand curves to shift while the substitution effect causes a movement along the demand curve.

4. Higher prices reduce real income.

5. We cannot accurately measure utility, but can nevertheless use the concept to explain consumer behavior.

6. Utils are hypothetical units of measure of utility.

7. Total utility can be thought of as the sum of all the marginal utilities.

8. As a general rule, an increase in consumption of a good increases the marginal utility from that good.

9. Marginal utility is negative past the satiation point.

10. The law of diminishing marginal utility applies when consumption occurs over an extended period of time, such as a month or a year.

11. To maximize utility, a consumer would buy each good until the marginal utility of the last dollar spent on that good was the same as for any other good.

12. A person maximizes utility by consuming each good to the person's satiation point for that good.

13. When alternative quantities of goods each provide the same amount of total utility, the consumer would be indifferent among them.

14. Suppose the last bag of apples purchased by Johnny had a marginal utility of 10, while the last bag of oranges he purchased had a marginal utility of 8. Apples sell for $1 a bag and oranges sell for $0.50 a bag. To maximize utility, Johnny should have bought more bags of apples and fewer bags of oranges.

15. Suppose the last bag of apples purchased by Johnny had a marginal utility of 10, while the last bag of oranges he purchased had a marginal utility of 8. If apples sell for $1 a bag and oranges also sell for $1, Johnny's purchases of apples and oranges maximized utility.

E&A 16. When the utility of time is taken into account, impulse buying can be viewed as a way to maximize utility.

17.   Acquiring information about a product often provides just as much utility as acquiring the product itself.

18.   If a consumer spends a dollar, that consumer expects it to provide more utility that if the dollar had been saved.

19.   Economics assumes that all behavior maximizes utility, including such behavior and overeating and becoming addicted to drugs or alcohol.

20.   One aspect of the addiction problem is being unable to rationally select the quantity that maximizes utility.

Appendix

21.   Indifference curves slope upward, which indicates greater utility as you move upward along each curve.

22.   The marginal rate of substitution is the absolute value of the slope of an indifference curve.

23.   A budget constraint shows how much of various combinations of two goods a person could purchase, and will shift outward if prices fall.

24.   The consumer maximizes utility by choosing the budget constraint that crosses as many indifference curve as possible.

25.   To derive a demand curve using indifference curves and budget constraints, you would observe consumer choices in response to at least two different prices.

MULTIPLE CHOICE
Circle the letter preceding the one best answer.

1. Total utility can be expressed as
   a. the maximum value of marginal utility.
   b. the marginal utility from the last unit consumed minus the marginal utility from the previous unit consumed.
   c. the sum of the marginal utilities from each unit consumed.
   d. the marginal utility of a good divided by its price.

2. If you are eating at an "all you can eat" restaurant, your best strategy is to continue eating
   a. until your marginal utility starts to diminish.
   b. until your marginal utility becomes zero.
   c. so long as your total utility remains positive.
   d. until your total utility becomes zero.

3. When a consumer buys a good to the point where marginal utility equals zero, then the total utility is
   a. equal to zero.
   b. equal to one.
   c. at its maximum.
   d. at its minimum.

4. When the value of marginal utility is positive but decreasing, total utility must be
   a. equal to zero.
   b. increasing.
   c. decreasing.
   d. at its minimum value.

5. What is the marginal utility of the third candy bar eaten by Kathy, when her total utility behaves as in the following table?

Candy bar #:	1	2	3	4	5
Total utility:	6	11	15	18	20

   a. 4.
   b. 11.
   c. 15.
   d. 32.

Refer to the following table for the next three questions:

Quantity Consumed	Total Utility
0	0
1	10
2	19
3	25
4	28
5	29

6.   The marginal utility of the fourth unit is
    a.   10.
    b.   19.
    c.   28.
    d.   3.

7.   The satiation point
    a.   occurs at a quantity of 1.
    b.   occurs at a quantity of 3.
    c.   occurs at a quantity of 5.
    d.   is not shown to occur at all.

8.   Total utility in the table is measured in
    a.   utils.
    b.   dollars.
    c.   units of output.
    d.   centimeters.

9.   An underlying explanation for the negative slope of demand curves is provided by
    a.   limited incomes of consumers.
    b.   scarcity.
    c.   diminishing marginal utility.
    d.   changes in consumer preferences.

10.   The fact that an ounce of perfume is priced higher than an ounce of gasoline suggests that
    a.   the average utility derived from an ounce of perfume exceeds the average utility derived from an ounce of gasoline.
    b.   the total utility derived from perfume exceeds the total utility derived from gasoline.
    c.   the marginal utility of perfume exceeds the marginal utility of gasoline.
    d.   gasoline is a necessity while perfume is a luxury.

11. In moving from point A to point B in Multiple Choice Figure 1, Denise's total utility from movies would
a.   increase.
b.   decrease.
c.   remain the same.
d.   possibly change, but we cannot say in which direction without data.

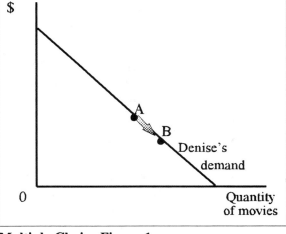

Multiple Choice Figure 1

12. In moving from point A to point B in Multiple Choice Figure 1, Denise's marginal utility from movies would
a.   increase.
b.   decrease.
c.   remain the same.
d.   possibly change, but we cannot say in which direction without data.

13. In moving from point A to point B in Multiple Choice Figure 1, Denise's behavior is obviously consistent with the
a.   satiation point.
b.   law of utility maximization.
c.   law of demand.
d.   law of large numbers.

14. A person who consumes only goods X and Y is in equilibrium when the
a.   ratio of the marginal utility of X to the price of X is equal to the ratio of the marginal utility of Y to the price of Y.
b.   ratio of the marginal utility of X to the marginal utility of Y is equal to the ratio of the price of Y to the price of X.
c.   ratio of the marginal utility of X to the price of Y is equal to the ratio of the marginal utility of Y to the price of X.
d.   marginal utility of X is equal to the marginal utility of Y.

15. In equilibrium, consumers allocate their spending such that the _____ utility of each good _____.
a.   marginal; is the same as for all other goods.
b.   marginal; divided by the price of that good is the same as for all other goods.
c.   total; is the same as for all other goods.
d.   total; divided by total spending on that good is the same as for all other goods.

E+A 16. The relationship between leisure time and sports is that the two are
   a.   inferior goods.
   b.   substitutes.
   c.   complements.
   d.   both common examples of addictive behavior.

17. Someone who makes a purchase on the spur of the moment and without gathering information about the product would be called
   a.   irrational.
   b.   utility neutral.
   c.   an economic man.
   d.   an impulse buyer.

18. In creating commercials intended to cause good feelings among consumers, advertisers are counting on utility being
   a.   objective.
   b.   subjective.
   c.   objectionable.
   d.   subject to the law of demand.

19. Of the following, the situation that is shown in Multiple Choice Figure 2 is most likely to be associated with
   a.   a ride in the country.
   b.   consuming too much alcohol.
   c.   giving a stranger a smile.
   d.   getting a haircut.

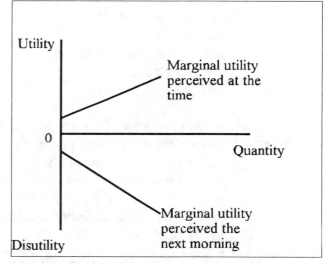

Multiple Choice Figure 2

20. The situation that is shown in Multiple Choice Figure 2 suggest that consumers
   a.   maximize utility.
   b.   face budget constraints that prevent them from maximizing utility.
   c.   maximize utility within the limits allowed by their budgets.
   d.   make some choices that they later realize reduced their total utility.

Appendix

21.   If prices of all goods were to be cut in half, the effect on the budget constraint between any two goods would be to
  a.   pivot the budget constraint to the right.
  b.   pivot the budget constraint to the left.
  c.   shift the budget constraint outward, keeping it parallel to the initial budget constraint.
  d.   shift the budget constraint inward, keeping it parallel to the initial budget constraint.

22.   In Multiple Choice Figure 3, the lines labeled A and B represent
  a.   marginal utility.
  b.   satiation.
  c.   indifference curves.
  d.   budget constraints.

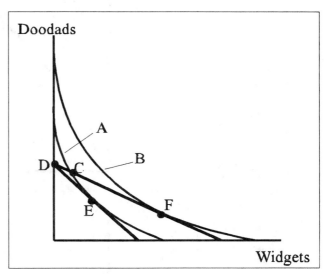

Multiple Choice Figure 3

23.   Multiple Choice Figure 3 shows two alternative prices for
  a.   widgets.
  b.   doodads.
  c.   both widgets and doodads.
  d.   goods other than widgets and doodads.

24.   In Multiple Choice Figure 3, the budget constraint representing the lower of the two prices would cause the consumer to consume at point
  a.   E.
  b.   F.
  c.   C.
  d.   D.

25.   If Multiple Choice Figure 3 were to be used to derive the demand curve, that demand curve would contain information from points
  a.   C and D.
  b.   C and E.
  c.   C and F.
  d.   E and F.

GRASPING THE GRAPHS
Fill in each box with a concept that applies.

Appendix

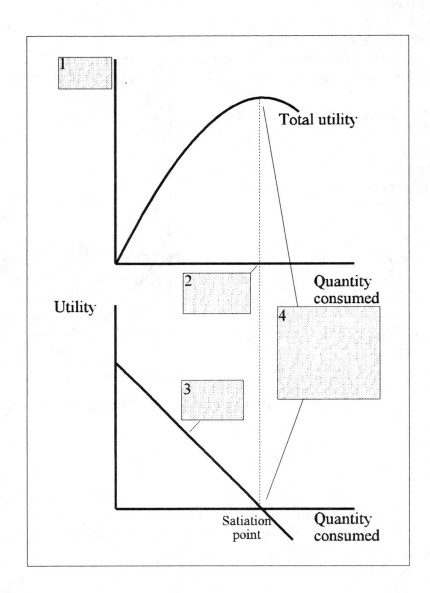

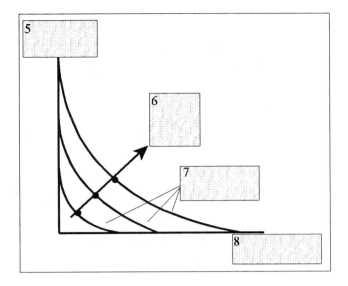

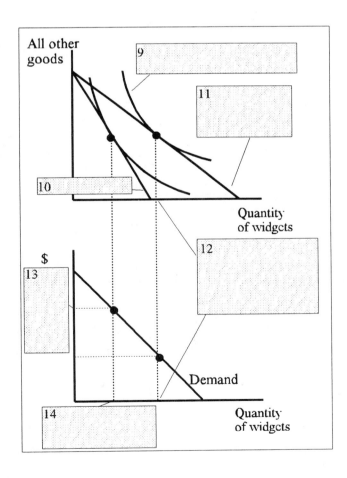

**For additional practice in grasping this chapter's graphs, visit
http://www.prenhall.com/ayers and try *Active Graphs* 43, 44, and 45.**

ANSWERS

STUDYCHECKS

1.   Jennie's marginal utility is:

Dr. Pepper:	#1	#2	#3	#4
Marginal Utility:	7	5	2	-3

Because the marginal utility of the fourth Dr. Pepper is negative, she would not drink it.

2.

Number of packs of Chewing Gum Consumed Weekly	Total Utility	Marginal Utility
0	0	undefined
1	12	12
2	22	10
3	28	6
4	30	2
5	30	0
6	27	-3

3.   If a consumer's utility rises when he or she transfers a dollar from one type of consumption to another, then that consumer is better off doing so. Since people attempt to maximize their utility, they will make all such transfers. Only when the marginal utility per dollar spent is equal across all goods and services do possibilities for such transfers cease.

4.   Models provide simplifications of reality so as to highlight selected significant features of that reality. The assumption that individuals act rationally and in their own self-interests captures the essence of consumer choice, even though there will always be exceptions in which people do not act rationally or act in a manner that is contrary to their own self-interests. The exceptions themselves can be analyzed with reference to the rational model, in which the individual maximizes his or her utility subject to that person's budget constraint.

5.   See StudyCheck 5 Figure.

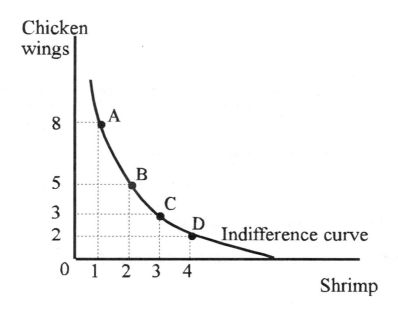

StudyCheck 5 Figure

FILL IN THE BLANKS

1.   substitution, income
2.   utility, subjective
3.   satisfaction, util
4.   Total, Marginal
5.   change, change
6.   negative, negative, disutility
7.   marginal, positive, peaks
8.   negative, disutility, diminishing
9.   budget, maximize

10.   price
11.   indifferent, last, same
12.   equilibrium
13.   Marginal, marginal
14.   cookies, ice cream, greater
15.   downward
16.   70
17.   complements
18.   diminishing, marginal utility, marginal utility
19.   Altruism
20.   longer
21.   indifferent
22.   equal, downward
23.   marginal rate of substitution
24.   Price of first good × quantity of first good, price of second good × quantity of second good
25.   highest

TRUE/FALSE/EXPLAIN

1.   False, the income effect changes consumer purchasing power.
2.   True.
3.   False, the two effects together are responsible for the slope of the demand curve.
4.   True.
5.   True.
6.   True.
7.   True.
8.   False, marginal utility ordinarily decreases as the quantity consumed increases.
9.   True.
10.   False, the law of diminishing marginal utility applies when consumption occurs over a short period of time.
11.   True.
12.   False, the existence of a budget constraints means the person cannot consume all goods to their satiation points.
13.   True.
14.   False, since the marginal utility of another dollar spent on oranges exceeds the marginal utility of another dollar spent on apples, Johnny should reallocate his spending towards more oranges and fewer apples.
15.   False, the rule is to consume each good up to the point where the marginal utility of another dollar spent on that good as the same as for any other good.
16.   True.

17. False, information is used as a way of screening products, but it is ordinarily the products themselves that provide consumers with utility.
18. True.
19. False, while the model with utility maximization does assume that individuals maximize utility, it is merely a model and is not intended to represent every facet of reality.
20. True.
21. False, indifference curve slope downward and represent alternative combinations of two goods that provide the same utility.
22. True.
23. True.
24. False, the maximize utility, the consumer would choose the point on the budget constraint that is tangent to an indifference curve.
25. True.

MULTIPLE CHOICE

1.	c	8.	a	15.	b	22.	c
2.	b	9.	c	16.	c	23.	a
3.	c	10.	c	17.	d	24.	b
4.	b	11.	a	18.	b	25.	d
5.	a	12.	b	19.	b		
6.	d	13.	c	20.	d		
7.	d	14.	a	21.	c		

GRASPING THE GRAPHS
Examples of correct answers

1. Total utility
2. Satiation point
3. Marginal utility
4. Marginal utility is zero when total utility is at a maximum.
5. Quantity of one good
6. More is better.
7. Indifference curves
8. Quantity of other good
9. Highest obtainable indifference curve
10. Budget constraint
11. The budget constraint pivots outward when the price of widgets falls.
12. The chosen quantity is repeated on the demand curve.

13.   At a higher price . . .
14.   . . . the quantity demanded is lower.

**Visit the Ayers/Collinge companion Website at http://www.prenhall.com/ayers
for further activities and exercises for this chapter.**

Chapter 7

THE FIRM AND PRODUCTION

CHAPTER REVIEW

- **Firms** take inputs of resources and produce outputs of goods and services to be sold in the marketplace.

7.1 Business Basics

- Certain elements of business economics are common to all firms. Choosing a legal form, obtaining financing, computing profit or loss, making the best use of personnel, and producing a good or service are universal experiences for firms.

- A firm can choose to operate in one of the following three legal forms: sole proprietorship, partnership, or corporation.

- If you commence in a less than formal fashion, you'll become a *sole proprietorship*—a business with a single owner. The owner is legally liable for injuries caused to or by the employees acting in the course of their duties. The owner is also personally liable for all debts and taxes of the business. If your firm doesn't earn enough income from sales, the owner will have to tap into personal resources to pay off creditors and the tax collector. You'll report the business's profits or losses on your personal tax return.

- If you can find one or more people with whom to start your business, you can form a *partnership*. Partnerships are similar to proprietorships. Each partner can hire employees. Each partner is also liable for business debts that the business is unable to pay.

- To avoid the disadvantages of proprietorships and partnerships, many firms are formed as corporations. A **corporation** is a firm that is a legal entity, a thing separate from the people who own, manage, and otherwise direct its affairs. Corporations tend to be big business. While they account for only about 21 percent of businesses in the United States, they earn over 91 percent of the revenues.

(a) Percentage of Firms by Legal Form

Proprietorships 73%
Partnerships 6%
Corporations 21%

(b) Percentage of Revenues by Legal Form

Proprietorships 6%
Partnerships 3%
Corporations 91%

- Unlike other forms of business, corporations can issue shares of **stock**, which are shares of ownership in the corporation that can be traded on a stock exchange. In addition to being able to issue stock, two major advantages of the corporate form of business are *limited liability* and *perpetual existence*. Limited liability means that the owners are not personally liable for the debts of the business. Perpetual existence means the corporation can outlive its owners, providing that it avoids dissolution through bankruptcy.

- The major disadvantage to the corporate form of business is the need to pay a corporation income tax, which takes up to 39 percent of profits. There are also reporting and procedural requirements that other forms of business do not face. These disadvantages explain why few small businesses choose to incorporate. The following table summarizes the key advantages and disadvantages of the legal forms of business.

Comparing the Legal Forms of Business

Type of Business	Advantages	Disadvantages
Sole Proprietorship	Easy to start	Unlimited liability
Partnership	Access to partner's funds	Unlimited liability
Corporation	Access to funds through issuance of shares of stock; limited liability; perpetual existence	Corporate income tax; corporate reporting and procedural requirements

- In order to operate, firms must have *financial capital*, the money needed to start or grow a business. Firms can choose one or more of the following four options:
  - Use personal funds
  - Use retained earnings
  - Borrow
  - Issue shares of stock.

- In the case of many small businesses, startup financial capital comes from the owners' personal savings. New small businesses often are unable to obtain funds from other sources.

- *Retained earnings* are a firm's savings. Just as the name suggests, retained earnings are monies kept from a business's earnings for the purpose of financing its operations. A business that has never had any earnings, such as a new business, will have no retained earnings. Retained earnings are also called *internal funds*. **Internal funds make up the majority of funds used to finance the operations of U.S. firms.**

- Corporations and other firms with established track records and valuable assets are likely to be able to borrow financial capital from banks or other lenders. Only corporations are able to borrow funds by issuing bonds, where a **bond** is a promise to repay borrowed funds at some future date. Businesses that borrow funds must not only repay them, but also pay interest to the lenders, where *interest* is a periodic payment as a percentage of the face value of a bond or loan. While small startups cannot easily borrow from banks, or issue bonds, the owners of these businesses will often borrow funds from friends and relatives. Most firms use a combination of retained earnings and borrowed funds to finance their expansion.

- Only corporations have the option of issuing shares of stock. The corporation receives revenue from the initial sale of its stock, but not later when the stock "trades" from one owner to another. Stock exchanges, such as the New York Stock Exchange, the so-called "Big Board," are *secondary markets*, meaning that already existing shares of stock are traded there.

- A corporation's market value is given by: market value of corporation = number of shares of stock × market price per share. The market price of a share of stock is determined by demand and supply in the *stock market*, in which shares of stock are bought and sold, often on a stock exchange.

- **Only new issues of stock provide funds to a corporation.** When new shares are issued, they are sold through so-called public offerings.

- When firms look to sources outside themselves for financing, they are said to be seeking *external funds*. Stocks, bonds, and loans provide external funds. Historically, loans have provided about 60 percent of external funds for U.S. business, with bonds providing about 30 percent and stocks about 2 percent. (Other sources of external funds, such as government, provided the remainder.)

- External funds are not, however, the primary source of funds for firms. All the external sources of funds—including stocks, bonds, and loans—provide only about 25 percent of the funds that firms use. Thus, as stated earlier, retained earnings provide most financing for firms.

- U.S. firms, especially corporations, are not restricted to this country in their search for external funds. Financial markets today are global in scope as financial capital flows relatively freely across international borders.

7.2 The Goal of Maximum Profit

- **Profit**, also called **economic profit**, is the difference between total revenue and total cost:
$$\text{Profit} = \text{total revenue} - \text{total cost.}$$

- **Total revenue** is the sum of income received by a firm. For a firm selling a single product at a single price, total revenue equals the quantity sold multiplied by its price:
$$\text{Total revenue} = \text{price} \times \text{quantity.}$$

- **Total cost**, which must be subtracted from total revenue to compute profit, is the sum of the firm's expenses.

- To say that a firm maximizes profit means that it earns the greatest amount of total profit that it is capable of earning. **The economic analysis of firms usually assumes the goal of profit maximization.**

- To explain the behaviors of firms, we must distinguish between two components of total cost. All of the costs accountants aim to measure are termed **explicit costs**, no matter what the accountants call them. Explicit costs are all internal to the firm, in the sense that they depend upon decisions that the firm makes.

- There are other costs that accountants do not measure. These are **implicit opportunity costs**, **implicit costs** for short, that are associated with non-purchased inputs. These costs are the value that the firm's capital and entrepreneur's time would have in their best alternative uses.

- Implicit costs vary with forces external to the firm, in the sense that the firm has no control over them. Examples include interest rates from alternative investments and the opportunity cost of the entrepreneur's time. Accountants do not try to measure these costs, because they vary in unforeseeable ways over time and among entrepreneurs. Because the value of alternatives cannot be known, accountants ignore implicit opportunity costs when calculating profit:
$$\textit{Accounting profit} = \text{total revenue} - \text{explicit costs}$$
$$\text{Economic profit} = \text{Accounting profit} - \text{implicit opportunity costs}$$

- **Normal profit** represents the portion of accounting profit that just covers implicit opportunity costs. From an economic perspective, **normal profit is a cost. It is the accounting profit needed to keep the firm in business.** For this reason, normal profit is the same as a firm's implicit costs. A firm must earn at least a normal profit for its resources to continue to be employed in their current use.

- If a normal profit is not present or expected in the future, the owners of the firm would make plans to eventually go out of business and *liquidate*—sell off—the firm's assets. Substituting for implicit cost in the equation for economic profit:

    Economic profit = accounting profit − normal profit.

- Successful companies are well aware of their implicit costs and the notion of normal profit, even if they cannot know its exact amount. The owners invest their time and money expecting to do at least as well with them as they could elsewhere.

- **Because implicit costs are subtracted from accounting profit to obtain economic profit, economic profit will always be less than accounting profit.**

StudyCheck 1
Describe the relationship between economic profit, accounting profit, and normal profit.

- There are three possible outcomes when economic profit is computed:
    - The firm can earn a positive profit, meaning that total revenue exceeds total cost.
    - The firm can earn a negative profit, meaning that total revenue is less than total cost. A negative profit is called a **loss.** When a firm incurs a loss, it may be able to continue in business for awhile. However, if it continues to incur losses, its resources will eventually be put to different uses and the firm will be out of business.
    - The firm can earn zero profit, meaning that total revenue equals total cost. Zero profit is also called **breakeven**, meaning that the firm earns just enough revenue to provide it with a normal profit, but no more. While a firm would prefer to earn a positive profit, breakeven alone is enough to keep it in business.

- While the owners of a firm may seek to maximize profit, not all of the firm's employees are likely to share that goal. Managers and staff often have their own, personal agendas. This brings about a **principal-agent problem,** which refers to the difficulties of making employees, who are called agents, act in accordance with the will of the owners, who are called principals. Also, employees are often guilty of *shirking,* which is usually known on the job as "goofing off." The bigger the company, the more distance there is between the owners and the employees and the more pronounced the principal-agent problem is likely to be.

- One way of facing up to the principle-agent problem is to provide employees with economic incentives to maximize the firm's profits. These incentives are sometimes highly personal, as in the case of sales commissions. More often, they depend on the performance of the company as a whole and also of the division of the company in which the employee works. These incentives can take a variety of forms, including: *1) stock-option plans* in which employees are provided the option to buy stock at a fixed price, irrespective of what the market price of the stock might become. Employees thus have the collective incentive to increase the profitability of the company so that its stock price will go up. *2)incentive pay* systems that let employees share in the profitability of the firm. An example of incentive pay is the traditional holiday bonus, the value of which depends upon how well the company has done.

StudyCheck 2

Should corporations donate a portion of their profits to charity? Whether your answer is yes or no, provide a justification.

7.3 Producing the Product

- In order to earn a profit, a firm must have something to sell. It must produce a good or service using labor, capital, and perhaps other inputs. The relationship between the amounts of inputs and the quantities of output a firm produces is called its **production function.**

- Production decisions are made by firms in either a long-run or a short-run context. The **long run** is a time period in which all inputs are *variable,* meaning that their quantities can be changed. For this reason, the long run is sometimes called the *planning horizon.*

- Actual production occurs in the **short run,** a time period where at least one input is fixed. The quantity of a *fixed* input cannot be changed.

- While firms employ numerous inputs, our model of the firm simplifies matters by assuming only two inputs. Specifically, assume that labor is a variable input and that capital is a fixed input in the short run. It may be helpful to think of a unit of labor as an hour of work, and a unit of capital as an hour's use of machinery.

- Modeling production with only two inputs highlights the distinction between variable and fixed inputs. The implications pertaining to labor apply in the real world to any variable input, including variable capital inputs such as pencils and light bulbs. Likewise, the connotations for capital apply to any fixed input, including long-term employment contracts.

- In the short run, when capital is fixed, the amount of output depends on the amount of labor. The output produced is said to be the *product* of labor, since nothing is produced without workers.

- **Total product** refers to the total quantity of output produced. We will thus use the terms total product and total output interchangeably.

- The additional total product from additional units of labor is termed the *marginal product of labor,* or **marginal product** for short: Marginal product = change in total product/change in labor.

- In contrast, **average product** is the quantity of output per worker: Average product = total product/total labor.

- Consider a firm that increases its employment of labor from 100 units of labor to 101 units of labor, and experiences an increase in total product from 50,000 units to 51,000 units. The marginal product of the 101st unit of labor is 1,000 units of output. Average product for 100 units of labor is 50,000/100, which equals 500 units, and for 101 units of labor is 51,000/101, which equals approximately 505 units of output.

- Notice that average product increased in the preceding example. **Average product will increase when marginal product is greater than the initial average product, decrease when marginal product is less than average product, and remain constant when marginal product is equal to average product.**

- The relationship between averages and marginals is more general than just average and marginal product. In general, a marginal above average pulls average up; a marginal below average pulls average down; and a marginal equal to average will not change the average. That rule applies no matter what the marginals and averages are in reference to.

- Marginal product is subject to the **law of diminishing returns,** which states that, **when additional units of labor or any other variable input are added to a fixed input, the marginal product of the variable input must eventually decrease.**

- Once a firm reaches the point of diminishing returns, each successive unit of labor will add less and less to total product. This is shown in the shape of total product.

- Marginal product equals the slope of total product. To understand why, recall the definition of marginal product, which is: the change in total product divided by the change in labor. Also recall that the slope of a curve is found by "rise over run." The "rise" is the change in the variable on the vertical axis—the change in total product. The "run" is the change in the variable on the horizontal axis—the change in labor. "Rise over run," the slope of total product, is thus equivalent to marginal product. The slope of total product decreases after the point of diminishing returns. When the slope of total product is decreasing, marginal product must be decreasing as well.

- The law of diminishing returns assumes that all labor is of equal quality, which signifies that diminishing returns occur for reasons other than those relating to differences in labor quality. For example, although the 101st unit of labor in the earlier example had a marginal product equal to 1,000 units of output, the law of diminishing returns suggests that a 102nd unit of labor will exhibit a marginal product of less than 1,000 units.

- The explanation for the law of diminishing returns is found in the commonsense proposition that adding more and more labor to a fixed amount of capital reduces the amount of capital each unit of labor has to work with. Eventually, the effect of less capital per worker reveals itself in the form of diminishing returns. **Because there is a fixed input, the law of diminishing returns applies only in the short run.**

- **Marginal product intersects average product at the maximum point on average product but in the declining portion of marginal product.** This is because average product is pulled up when marginal product lies above it, and pulled down when marginal product lies below it. **Diminishing returns are associated with the downward-sloping part of** marginal product; negative returns are illustrated by the portion of marginal product that lies below the horizontal axis.

StudyCheck 3

Describe the total product curve and its relationship to marginal product.

StudyCheck 4

Graph the total product of labor curve, labeling the axes and giving the curve an appropriate shape. Label the point on the curve at which marginal product is at a maximum.

7.4 BUSINESS—ETHICAL IN PRINCIPLE, NOT ALWAYS IN PRACTICE

- The invisible hand described by Adam Smith is a fundamental concept in economics. It explains how self interest can be in the public interest. Yet Adam Smith was no advocate of unbridled greed, and had even authored an earlier work, entitled *The Theory of Moral Sentiments* (1759), about morality and virtue.

- In his renowned *The Wealth of Nations* (1776), Adam Smith made clear that competition is the key to reining in business self interest and making sure that the public gets the most for their money. Without it, firms would conspire together in a "conspiracy against the public interest."

- News of insider trading, misreported profits, bogus stock "buy" recommendations from stockbrokers who were busy selling the stocks they were recommending, excessive salaries, overabundant stock options, and much more has highlighted questions of *business ethics*, the fairness and honesty of business. Unfortunately, the invisible hand is often not present to keep unfairness and dishonesty in check.

- In a particularly glaring case, the misrepresentation of the financial condition of the Houston-based Enron Corporation by its auditors, the accounting firm of Arthur Anderson, camouflaged Enron's deteriorating financial condition and impending bankruptcy on December 2, 2001. The indictment and conviction of Arthur Anderson for obstruction of justice followed within months, and the firm itself was absorbed by another accounting firm soon after.

- For consumers, when businesses see a clear profit motive, lawsuits might not be necessary to achieve the desired result. For example, a few years ago, the owners of some vehicles produced by Ford began to see the paint on their vehicles peeling. On a case-by-case basis, Ford paid the costs. On the face of it, Ford cut its profit by the amount of the expenses it incurred on behalf of the car owners. However, by having a defect fixed at its own expense, Ford was perhaps also ensuring itself greater future profit.

- A good *reputation* can be critical for the long-term profitability of a firm. Johnson & Johnson, the maker of Tylenol, ensured its good reputation by its actions after several people died when someone poisoned bottles of Tylenol that had been sitting on store shelves in 1982 and 1986. The company, at a huge cost, immediately recalled all bottles of Tylenol. The company was praised for its quick action, and Tylenol is as popular today as ever.

- In contrast, Ford's reputation suffered badly when Ford Explorers were discovered in 2001 to be equipped with blow-out prone tires that caused deadly accidents. A June 2001 CNN/USA Today/Gallop Poll reported that 51 percent of those polled had an unfavorable opinion of the Ford Explorer. Although Ford responded to the problem by offering to replace the tires, public opinion had turned against Ford, and the maker of the tires, Bridgestone-Firestone.

- Since monitoring within the firm is imperfect, it is often up to employees to be ethical enough to not take credit for other people's work. Other ethical challenges encompass laws and regulations that can sometimes be eluded. Examples include the illicit dumping of toxic wastes, industrial espionage in which firms steal ideas from one another, and sexual harassment in the workplace. How well firms face up to these challenges is a matter of ethics, which are often a part of company policies. Detailed codes of ethics are found in many large businesses, and in professional societies, such as the American Accounting Association. Business schools also preach ethics to their students. That business ethics is front and center in the business world makes the ethical lapses that surface all the more disturbing.

- Despite all the ethical challenges within business, **the basic nature of business is highly ethical. Rather than being a *zero-sum game* in which the winner wins only what the loser loses, business is a *positive-sum game* that can bring benefits to all involved.** The reward of profit goes to firms that are best at responding to consumer wishes.

StudyCheck 5

Why is business ethical in principle?

FILL IN THE BLANKS

1. Firms take inputs of _____ and produce outputs of goods and services to be sold in the marketplace.   A firm can choose to operate in one of the following three legal forms: _____ _____, _____, or _____.

2. A _____ _____ is a business with a single owner. If you can find one or more people with whom to start your business, you can form a _____.

3. A _____ is a firm that is a legal entity, a thing separate from the people who own, manage, and otherwise direct its affairs. While they account for only about 21 percent of businesses in the United States, they earn over 91 percent of the revenues.

4. Unlike other forms of business, corporations can issue shares of _____, which are shares of ownership in the corporation . Two major advantages of the corporate form of business are _____ _____, which means that the owners are not personally liable for the debts of the business, and _____ _____, which means the corporation can outlive its owners, providing that it avoids dissolution through bankruptcy.

5. In order to operate, firms must have financial capital, the money needed to start or grow a business. Firms can choose one or more of the following four options: 1) _____ _____, 2) _____ _____, 3) _____, and 4) _____.

6. _____ _____ are a firm's savings. Just as the name suggests, these are monies kept from a business's earnings for the purpose of financing its operations.

7. Only _____ have the option of issuing shares of stock. The corporation receives revenue from the initial sale of its stock, but not later when the stock "trades" from one owner to another. Stock exchanges, such as the New York Stock Exchange, the so-called "Big Board," are _____ markets, meaning that already existing shares of stock are traded there. A corporation's market value is given by: market value of corporation = number of shares of stock × _____ _____ per share. Only new issues of stock provide funds to a corporation.

8. When firms look to sources outside themselves for financing, they are said to be seeking _____ _____, which are provided by stocks, bonds, and loans.

9. External funds are not the primary source of funds for firms. All the external sources of funds—including stocks, bonds, and loans—provide only about _____ percent of the funds that firms use. _____ _____ provide most financing for firms.

10. Profit, also called economic profit, is equal to:

    _____ _____ – _____ _____.

11. Total revenue is the sum of income received by a firm. For a firm selling a single product at a single price,

    Total revenue = _____ × _____.

12. The economic analysis of firms usually assumes the goal of _____ _____.

13. To explain the behaviors of firms, we must distinguish between two components of total cost. All of the costs accountants aim to measure are termed _____ costs, no matter what the accountants call them.

14. There are other costs that accountants do not measure. These are _____ opportunity costs that are associated with non-purchased inputs. These costs are the value that the firm's capital and entrepreneur's time would have in their best alternative uses.

15. Accounting profit = total revenue – _____ costs; Economic profit = Accounting profit – _____ opportunity costs. _____ profit represents the portion of accounting profit that just covers implicit opportunity costs.

16. Because implicit costs are subtracted from accounting profit to obtain economic profit, economic profit will always be _____ than accounting profit.   There are three possible outcomes when economic profit is computed: The firm can earn a positive profit, meaning that total revenue _____ total cost. The firm can earn a negative profit, meaning that total revenue is _____ than total cost. A negative profit is called a loss. When a firm incurs a loss, it may be able to continue in business for awhile. However, if it continues to incur losses, its resources will eventually be put to different uses and the firm will be out of business.. The firm can earn zero profit, meaning that total revenue _____ total cost. Zero profit is also called _____, meaning that the firm earns just enough revenue to provide it with a normal profit, but no more.

17. While the owners of a firm may seek to maximize profit, not all of the firm's employees are likely to share that goal. Managers and staff often have their own, personal agendas. This brings about a _____-_____ problem, which refers to the difficulties of making employees act in accordance with the will of the owners.

18. The relationship between the amounts of inputs and the quantities of output a firm produces is called its production function. Production decisions are made by firms in either a long-run or a short-run context. The long run is a time period in which all inputs are _____, meaning that their quantities can be changed. For this reason, the long run is sometimes called the planning horizon. Actual production occurs in the short run, a time period where at least one input is _____.

19. _____ _____ refers to the total quantity of output produced. The additional total product from additional units of labor is termed the _____ product of labor. _____ product is the quantity of output per worker. Average product will _____ when marginal product is greater than the initial average product, _____ when marginal product is less than average product, and _____ _____ when marginal product is equal to average product.

20. Marginal product is subject to the law of _____ _____, which states that, when additional units of labor or any other variable input are added to a fixed input, the marginal product of the variable input must eventually decrease. Marginal product equals the _____ of total product. Marginal product intersects average product at the _____ point on average product but in the declining portion of marginal product. This is because average product is pulled up when marginal product lies above it, and pulled down when marginal product lies below it. Diminishing returns are associated with the downward-sloping part of _____ product; negative returns are illustrated by the portion of _____ product that lies below the horizontal axis.

E&A 21. The _____ _____ described by Adam Smith is a fundamental concept in economics. It explains how self interest can be in the public interest.

22. In his renowned *The Wealth of Nations* (1776), Adam Smith made clear that _____ is the key to reining in business self interest and making sure that the public gets the most for their money. Without it, firms would conspire together in a "conspiracy against the public interest."

23. News of insider trading, misreported profits, bogus stock "buy" recommendations from stockbrokers who were busy selling the stocks they were recommending, excessive salaries, overabundant stock options, and much more has highlighted questions of _____ _____, the fairness and honesty of business.

24. Despite all the ethical challenges within business, the basic nature of business is highly ethical. Rather than being a _____-_____ game in which the winner wins only what the loser loses, business is a _____-_____ game that can bring benefits to all involved.

25. The reward of _____ goes to firms that are best at responding to consumer wishes.

TRUE/FALSE/EXPLAIN
If false, explain why in the space provided.

1. Sole proprietorships are the most numerous type of business.

2. Limited liability is a characteristic of corporations.

3. External funds, such as through borrowing and stock issuance, make up the majority of funds used to finance the operations of U.S. businesses.

4. The number of shares of a stock multiplied by its market price represents the market value of a corporation.

5. When shares of stock are sold on the secondary market, the firm that issued those shares receives the money paid for the shares.

6. Economic profit is computed by subtracting both explicit costs and implicit opportunity costs from total revenue.

7. Normal profit is that part of accounting profit that just covers implicit opportunity costs.

8. When total revenue is more than required to pay all explicit and implicit costs, the firm is said to earn an economic profit.

9.   Breakeven occurs when total revenue is sufficient to provide the firm with just a normal profit, and no more.

10.   In the long run all inputs are variable.

11.   In the short run all inputs are fixed.

12.   The change in total product divided by the change in labor defines average product.

13.   When marginal product is greater than average product, average product increases.

14.   The law of diminishing returns applies in the short run.

15.   In the region of diminishing, but positive, returns, total product will decrease.

16.   The law of diminishing returns occurs because additional labor is always inferior in quality to the labor that was hired before it.

17.   Diminishing returns applies to the average product curve.

18.   An average product curve rises, reaches a maximum, and then falls.

19. At the maximum point of marginal product, marginal product and average product intersect.

20. Marginal product can never be a negative value.

E+A 21. According to Adam Smith, self interest can be in the public interest.

22. The ethical conduct of business outside the boundaries of the law.

23. After poisoned Tylenol was discovered on store shelves, the maker of Tylenol incurred huge costs in order to preserve the company's reputation and long-term profitability.

24. The scandals at Enron and elsewhere in the business world reveal that businesses do not have codes of ethics.

25. Business is a zero-sum game.

MULTIPLE CHOICE
Circle the letter preceding the one best answer.

1. Which is NOT one of the three legal forms of business?
   a. corporation
   b. cooperative
   c. partnership
   d. sole proprietorship

2.   Approximately what percentage of revenues are received by corporations?
      a.   10 percent
      b.   50 percent
      c.   75 percent
      d.   90 percent

3.   When a firm raises financial capital through a bond, that firm is
      a.   using personal funds of the owner.
      b.   using retained earnings.
      c.   borrowing.
      d.   issuing stock.

4.   The major source of funds for U.S. firms is
      a.   stock.
      b.   bonds.
      c.   bank loans.
      d.   retained earnings.

5.   In everyday trading of AT&T stock on the New York Stock Exchange, the stock is usually
      a.   sold by AT&T.
      b.   bought by AT&T.
      c.   neither bought nor sold by AT&T.
      d.   both bought and sold by AT&T.

6.   Economics usually assumes that firms
      a.   maximize revenue.
      b.   minimize costs.
      c.   maximize unit sales of the product they produce.
      d.   maximize profit.

7.   Which of the following definitions of profit is correct?
      a.   Profit = Total revenue
      b.   Accounting profit = Total revenue − implicit costs
      c.   Accounting profit = Total revenue − explicit costs − implicit costs
      d.   Economic profit = Total revenue − explicit costs − implicit costs

8.   The type of profit needed to keep a firm in business is called
      a.   economic profit
      b.   accounting profit
      c.   excess profit.
      d.   normal profit.

9.   A loss is indicated when
      a.   total revenue equals total cost.
      b.   total revenue is greater than total cost.
      c.   total revenue is less than total cost.
      d.   the firm is subject to diminishing returns.

10.   If total revenue equals $100 a week, explicit costs equal $50 a week, and implicit costs equal $30 a week, then economic profit for the week is
      a.   identical to accounting profit at $50.
      b.   identical to accounting profit at $20.
      c. $20, which is less than the accounting profit of $50.
      d.   zero, since normal profit equals $20.

11.   Shirking illustrates
      a.   profit maximization.
      b.   the law of diminishing returns.
      c.   the principal-agent problem.
      d.   the definition of break even.

12.   Which best describes the principal-agent problem?
      a.   "Don't put all your eggs in one basket."
      b.   "Put all your eggs in one basket and watch that basket."
      c.   "If you want something done right, do it yourself."
      d.   "The attorney who represents himself has a fool for a client."

13.   Which of the following actions would be most likely to reduce the effects of the principal-agent problem?
      a.   Offering workers a higher salary.
      b.   Offering workers a lower salary.
      c.   Sharing ownership of the company with employees.
      d.   Tight security precautions against industrial espionage.

14.   If one worker can produce one unit of output, and a second worker would allow output to rise to four units,
      a.   negative returns exist.
      b.   the marginal product of labor is rising.
      c.   the marginal product of the second worker is less than that of the first.
      d.   marginal cost is rising.

15. When the marginal product of labor is zero,
    a. the total product of labor is negative.
    b. the total product of labor is at a maximum.
    c. the firm is maximizing profits.
    d. the marginal product of capital must also be zero.

16. Average product and marginal product are
    a. never equal.
    b. always equal.
    c. equal only at the point where their curves intersect.
    d. equal at all points in the region of diminishing returns.

17. The average product curve will always slope downward when the marginal product curve is
    a. rising.
    b. falling.
    c. above it.
    d. below it.

18. When diminishing returns are present, and additional variable input is added to production, total product will
    a. remain constant.
    b. decrease.
    c. increase.
    d. become a negative value.

19. Marginal product equals the slope of
    a. total product.
    b. average product.
    c. both total product and average product
    d. neither total product nor average product

20. If you see a marginal product curve, and a portion of it is below the horizontal axis, the best explanation is
    a. a slip of the artist's pen since marginal product should not ever be below the horizontal axis.
    b. increasing returns.
    c. the law of diminishing returns.
    d. negative returns.

E&A   21.   The Enron case involved
    a.   an unsafe consumer product.
    b.   drug dealing.
    c.   worker exposure to toxic waste.
    d.   misrepresentation of the company's financial position.

22.   The government agency that watches over the stock market is the
    a.   Securities and Exchange Commission.
    b.   New York Stock Exchange.
    c.   Federal Reserve.
    d.   U.S. Treasury.

23.   Regarding codes of ethics in the business world,
    a.   many business have them.
    b.   few businesses have them.
    c.   business schools and professional associations have neglected them.
    d.   Enron's code of ethics stated that "all's fair in love, war, and business."

24.   In a zero-sum game,
    a.   everyone wins.
    b.   everyone loses.
    c.   the winner wins what the loser loses.
    d.   there are no winners nor losers.

25.   In a positive sum game
    a.   everyone wins.
    b.   everyone loses.
    c.   the winner wins what the loser loses.
    d.   there are no winners nor losers.

GRASPING THE GRAPHS
Fill in each box with a concept that applies.

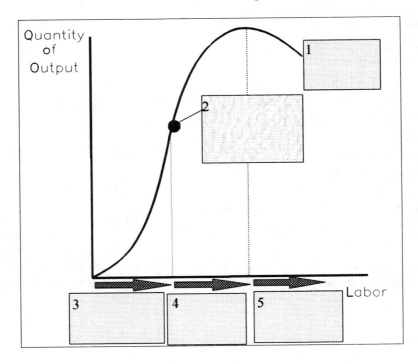

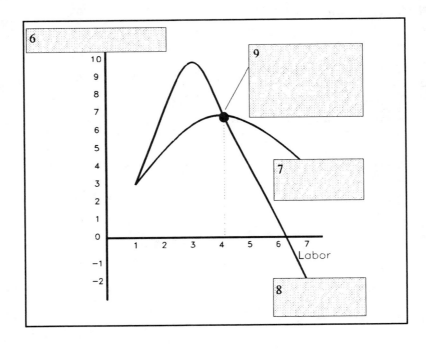

For additional practice in grasping this chapter's graphs,
visit <u>http://www.prenhall.com/ayers</u> and try *Smart Graph* 20,
along with *Active Graphs* 46, and 7.

ANSWERS

STUDYCHECKS

1.   Economic profit is computed by subtracting all explicit and implicit costs from total revenues. Possibilities for economic profit attract the entry of new firms. The accounting profit necessary to keep existing firms in business in the long run is termed normal profit. From an economic standpoint, normal profit is a cost, the opportunity cost of keeping resources in their current uses. Thus, the accounting profits reported by firms will be more than their economic profits.

2.   The response should note that corporations are owned by many shareholders. This raises the issue of whether the individual shareholders are better positioned to make charitable decisions on their own, or of whether there is a corporate responsibility to do so. The response might also note that firms that compete with other firms must keep expenses low and must provide a product of value to others in order to remain in business.

3.   The firm's total product curve tells how much output will be produced by different quantities of labor in the short run, holding all other inputs constant. Total product rises increasingly rapidly at first, as firms experience increasing marginal product. When the point is reached at which marginal product starts to diminish, the total product curve starts to rise less rapidly because marginal product is the slope of total product. Total product decreases when marginal product is negative.

4.   See StudyCheck 4 Figure.

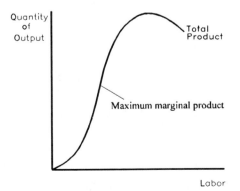

StudyCheck 4 Figure

5.   A successful business must provide a product of greater value than production cost, which is intrinsically ethical in that no one is forced to consume the product.

FILL IN THE BLANKS

1.   resources, sole proprietorship, partnership, corporation
2.   sole proprietorship, partnership
3.   corporation
4.   stock, limited liability, perpetual existence
5.   personal funds, retained earnings, borrow, issue shares of stock
6.   Retained earnings
7.   corporations, secondary, market price
8.   external funds
9.   25, Retained earnings
10. total revenue, total cost
11. price, quantity
12. profit maximization
13. explicit
14. implicit
15. explicit, implicit, Normal
16. less, exceeds, less, equals, breakeven
17. principal-agent
18. variable, fixed
19. Total product, marginal, Average, increase, decrease, remain constant
20. diminishing returns, slope, maximum, marginal, marginal
21. invisible hand
22. competition
23. business ethics
24. zero-sum, positive-sum
25. profit

TRUE/FALSE/EXPLAIN

1.   True.
2.   True.
3.   False, internal funds (retained earnings) represent the majority of financing for U.S. businesses.

4.   True.
5.   False, the seller receives the money.
6.   True.
7.   True.
8.   True.
9.   True.
10. True.
11. False, at least one input is fixed, but the others are variable.
12. False, average product equals total product divided by labor.
13. True.
14. True.
15. False, total product will decrease when there are negative returns.
16. False, diminishing returns occurs because additional variable input is added to a fixed input.
17. False, diminishing returns applies to marginal product.
18. True.
19. False, marginal product and average product will be equal at the maximum point of average product.
20. False, marginal product is negative in the region of negative returns.
21. True.
22. False, there are laws against fraud, consumer protection laws, safety laws, truth-in-lending laws, and many more.
23. True.
24. False, many firms have codes of ethics, but employees sometimes violate the codes.
25. False, business is a positive-sum game.

MULTIPLE CHOICE

1. b	8. d	15. b	22. a
2. d	9. c	16. c	23. a
3. c	10. c	17. d	24. c
4. d	11. c	18. c	25. a
5. c	12. c	19. a	
6. d	13. c	20. d	
7. d	14. b	21. d	

GRASPING THE GRAPHS
Examples of correct answers

1. Total product
2. Point of diminishing returns
3. Increasing marginal product
4. Decreasing marginal product
5. Negative marginal product
6. Output
7. Average product
8. Marginal product
9. Marginal product intersects average product at its maximum.

Visit the Ayers/Collinge companion Website at http://www.prenhall.com/ayers for further activities and exercises for this chapter.

Chapter 8

COSTS
AND PROFIT-MAXIMIZING OUTPUT

CHAPTER REVIEW

• Firms must know their cost of production in order to produce the profit-maximizing quantity of output. As you have learned, economic costs include both the explicit costs and implicit opportunity costs.

8.1 Short-Run Costs

• In the previous chapter you learned that we assume a firm's goal is profit maximization. To achieve that goal, a firm must select the quantity of output that maximizes profit. That decision involves both costs and revenues.

• *Fixed inputs* are those resources used by a firm that remain constant in amount in the short run. In contrast, the amount of *variable inputs* can change. Firms that produce output incur both fixed and variable costs in the short run, with a **fixed cost** being the expense associated with the use of the firm's fixed inputs.

• **Total fixed cost, the sum of all fixed expenses, remains constant in the short run regardless of the quantity of production.** Neither increases nor decreases in the firm's quantity of output will change the amount of total fixed cost since this expense is unrelated to the firm's quantity of production.

• **Variable cost** increases as the quantity of output rises and declines as output falls, because a firm's use of variable inputs varies directly with production.

• *Total cost* includes *total fixed cost* and *total variable cost*, as follows:
    Total cost = total fixed cost + total variable cost.

• **Total cost, like total variable cost, will vary directly with output in the short run.** To simplify, we will assume that labor is the only variable input and capital the only fixed input. Thus, variable costs are exclusively related to the use of labor (workers) and fixed costs are exclusively related to the use of capital (machines).

- Some costs that a firm incurs are called **sunk costs**, meaning that they are irreversible—they cannot be recovered. **Sunk costs are irrelevant to decision making.**

- In the short run with capital fixed in quantity and labor variable, the firm must ask itself how much output to produce and thus how much labor to employ. The answer will depend in part on costs, with costs in turn depending on both the quantity of labor and the *wage rate*, which is the price per unit of that labor.

- To make the decision as to how much labor to employ, the first step is to construct a *labor requirements curve*, which shows the amount of labor needed to produce any given quantity of output. The labor requirements curve is nothing more than the total product curve you studied in the previous chapter with the axes interchanged minus the portion for which marginal product would be negative.

- A firm's total variable cost of output will equal the labor requirement for that output multiplied by the wage rate:

  Total variable cost = wage rate × labor.

- This equation shows that total variable cost equals the cost of labor employed because we assume that labor is the only variable input. Likewise, with capital as the only fixed input, we have:

  Total fixed cost = per unit cost of capital × amount of capital employed.

- Total fixed cost is constant at all outputs. Thus, the total fixed cost curve is flat, with a slope equal to zero. When total fixed cost and total variable cost are added to obtain total cost, the total cost curve appears with the same shape as the total variable cost curve. This means that the slopes of both total cost and total variable cost are identical. The total variable cost curve starts at the origin, while the total cost curve starts at the point where the total fixed cost curve intersects the vertical axis.

- **Marginal cost** is the additional cost of an additional unit of output, computed by taking the change in total cost and dividing it by the change in the quantity of output. Marginal cost is also called *incremental cost* because it measures the additions to total cost of one-unit increments in output.

- Marginal cost is also equal to the slope of the total cost curve. This interpretation of marginal cost requires you to recall that a slope is the "rise over the run." In other words, the slope of a curve is the change in the variable on the vertical axis divided by the change in the variable on the horizontal axis. Since a graph of total cost measures total cost on the vertical axis and the quantity of output on the horizontal axis, the change in total cost divided by the change in quantity is the slope of the total cost curve.

- Each of the following is a different way to express marginal cost:
  - change in total cost ÷ change in quantity;
  - change in total variable cost ÷ change in quantity;
  - slope of total cost;
  - slope of total variable cost.

- The change in total cost is identical to the change in total variable cost because the only other component of total cost is total fixed cost, and that does not vary with output. For the same reason, the slope of total cost and the slope of total variable cost are equal.

- In addition to presenting costs in total or at the margin, costs are often stated per unit, meaning on average. Specifically, **average cost** equals total cost divided by the quantity of output:

- Average cost = total cost ÷ quantity of output.

- Average cost is also called *average total cost* because it is the total of both the fixed and variable components of average costs:
  Average cost = average fixed cost + average variable cost,
  where
  Average fixed cost = total fixed cost ÷ quantity of output
  and
  Average variable cost = total variable cost ÷ quantity of output.

- **Marginal cost intersects both average cost and average variable cost at their respective minimum points.** The difference between the average variable cost and the average cost curves is average fixed cost.

- Average cost, like average variable cost, decreases before reaching a minimum and then increasing. Notice that average variable cost begins to increase before average cost. Average cost includes the effect of average fixed cost, which is constantly declining as output increases. Ultimately, the downward pull of average fixed cost is offset enough by the upward pull of average variable cost. When that happens, average cost begins to increase.

- Cost curves shift—change position— when an input price associated with that cost curve changes. For example, an increase in the wage rate paid to labor will result in a new total variable cost curve that lies above the old one. Correspondingly, a decrease in wage rates would decrease costs and shift the curves down.

- When labor productivity rises, costs fall. When productivity falls, costs rise. This common sense applies to marginal cost and average variable cost in relation to marginal product and average product, respectively. For example, the smaller the marginal product of an additional worker, the greater the marginal cost of additional output. By the same token, the lower is the average product of employees, the greater will be the average cost of the output that is produced. Thus the general appearance of the marginal and average cost curves is opposite to the corresponding marginal and average product curves shown in the previous chapter. The result is that marginal cost is shaped like the letter J, while average cost is shaped more like the letter U. Average cost is at a minimum where it is intersected by marginal cost.

- The wage rate for the marginal unit of labor divided by the output of that labor reveals the marginal cost per unit of output. Thus, the lower is marginal productivity, the higher is marginal cost, as follows:

    Marginal cost = change in total cost ÷ change in quantity

- **Marginal cost varies inversely with marginal product.** Since the change in total cost for the extra hour of work is simply the wage rate and the change in quantity is the worker's marginal product, marginal cost can be expressed as follows:

    Marginal cost = wage rate ÷ marginal product

- Similar reasoning shows that **average variable cost varies inversely with average product.** This statement can be demonstrated by working through the following steps. First, recall the definition of average variable cost:

    Average variable cost = total variable cost ÷ quantity.

    Since total variable cost is the wage rate × labor,

- Average variable cost = wage rate × labor ÷ quantity

    which can be restated as:

    Average variable cost = wage rate ÷ average product,

    because labor/quantity is nothing more than the inverse of quantity/labor, which is the definition of average product. Dividing the wage rate by average product reveals the average variable cost of output.

StudyCheck 1

Draw on a single graph some hypothetical firm's average cost, average variable cost, and marginal cost curves, making sure that the curves are consistent with one another. Be sure to label each curve and the axes of your graph.

StudyCheck 2

Fill in the missing cost data below, given that labor costs $100 per unit and that total fixed cost equals $40.

Labor	Output	Total Variable Cost	Total Cost	Marginal Cost	Average Cost
0	0	$0		undefined	undefined
1	10	$100		$10	
2	22				
3	30				
4	36				
5	40				
6	42	$600		$50	

8.2 Maximum Profit in the Short Run

- Firms produce to earn profit, which is equal to total revenue minus total cost. What quantity of production will maximize profit? The answer lies in comparing costs and revenues.

- Many firms have no choice but to sell their output for the going market price. For example, if you were to plant a field of soybeans, you would know that the marketplace determines the price. You could charge more than the market price, but you would not sell any soybeans. You could charge less than the market price, but there would be no reason to forgo the extra revenue. In other words, the price you receive would be at the mercy of the marketplace and you would be called a **price taker**.

- **For price takers, every additional unit of output adds an amount of revenue equal to the market price of the output.** This additional income is termed **marginal revenue.**
  Marginal revenue = change in total revenue/change in quantity
  and for price taking firms:
  Marginal revenue = market price

- The reasoning we have followed allows the firm to identify the profit-maximizing quantity of flour to produce by following the **rule of profit maximization**:
  ### Rule of profit maximization
  Produce to the point at which marginal revenue equals marginal cost.

- The rule of profit maximization is followed any time firms adjust their outputs. Most generally, it means that the firm should take an action whenever that action adds more to revenue than to cost. Specifically, **if an increase in output comes with higher marginal revenue than marginal cost, the firm should produce more. If marginal cost exceeds marginal revenue, the firm should produce less. The only time it should be satisfied is when the two are equal.** If no equality is possible, the rule is to keep producing more as long as marginal cost does not exceed marginal revenue.

StudyCheck 3

Using a graph, illustrate how a profitable price-taking firm chooses how much to produce. Show price, marginal revenue, marginal cost, average cost, and the quantity produced (Q*).

- Marginal revenue to a price-taking firm equals the market price. Because price and marginal revenue are equal for a price taker we can restate the rule of profit maximization accordingly:

Rule of profit maximization for a price taker
Produce to the point where price equals marginal cost

- The general case of profit maximization by a price taker can be illustrated graphically. Marginal revenue is illustrated by a horizontal line that also portrays the market price. Equating the market price to marginal cost leads to a profit-maximizing quantity. If average cost at this quantity is less than average revenue, given by the market price, the firm will be earning a profit. If average cost at the profit-maximizing output exceeds price, the firm will incur a loss.

• When a firm sells all of its output at a single price, that price is the firm's *revenue per unit* of that output, otherwise known as *average revenue*.

Average revenue = total revenue/quantity = price.

• Multiplying average revenue by quantity thus equals total revenue. By the same token, multiplying average cost by quantity would yield total cost. Thus, a firm's total profit can be expressed as:

Profit = quantity × (average revenue − average cost),

or, equivalently,

Profit = quantity × (price − average cost).

This computation applies the length times width formula for the area of a rectangle.

• The vertical difference between price and average cost at the quantity of output the firm produces is the average profit per unit of output. When average profit is multiplied by the quantity produced, the result equals total profit.

StudyCheck 4

Graph a price-taking firm that produces widgets at a profit. Label: 1) the axes of the graph; 2) Price; 3) Marginal Cost; 4) Average Cost; 5) the profit-maximizing output; 8) Profit (diagonally shade the area). Be sure to label the axes.

- If the market price falls sufficiently, there comes a point where price is just equal to average cost, which would imply that total revenue and total cost would be equal. Such a situation is called *break even* and results in zero economic profits, but because total revenue is enough to pay implicit costs, the firm earns a *normal profit*. Breakeven is illustrated graphically when the price is at the minimum point of the average cost curve.

- If price were to fall below the breakeven level, the firm would incur losses. **A firm will experience a loss when the price falls below the minimum value of average cost. When a firm operates at a loss, it will seek to minimize the loss.** The *rule of loss minimization* is the same as the rule of profit maximization:

  ### Rule of loss minimization
  Produce to the point where marginal revenue equals marginal cost.

- The amount of loss can be computed as:
  Loss = quantity × (price − average cost)
  When there is a loss the computation of profit results in a negative value.

StudyCheck 5

Show a price-taking firm that loses money by producing widgets, but would lose more money if it stopped. Label: 1) the axes of the graph; 2) price; 3) marginal cost; 4) average cost; 5) average variable cost; 6) the loss-minimizing output; 9) losses (diagonally shade area).

- **A profit maximizing firm will never lose more than the amount of its total fixed cost.** Whether the firm is profitable or operates at a loss, it will determine its quantity of output by equating marginal revenue to marginal cost. However, when price drops so low that revenues are insufficient to pay variable costs, the firm can avoid those costs by ceasing production altogether. If the firm ceases producing output but retains the capital that would allow it to resume production later, the firm is said to be **shut down**.

- Since fixed costs must be paid even if the firm produces nothing, **shutdown results in a loss that is equal to the firm's fixed cost.** The *shutdown rule* is as follows:

  <u>**Shutdown rule**</u>
  Shut down if total revenue is less than total variable cost.

- By dividing both total revenue and total variable cost by the quantity of output, the shutdown rule can equivalently be stated in terms of average revenue and average variable cost. For a firm that charges a single price, this shutdown rule thus becomes:

  <u>**Shutdown rule in terms of price**</u>
  Shut down if price is less than average variable cost

- When price falls below average variable cost, shutting down minimizes the loss, which is limited to fixed cost. The fixed cost must be paid even when the firm shuts down. The only way that fixed cost can be avoided is for the firm to go out of business.

- The shutdown rule identifies the only exception to the rule of equating marginal cost to marginal revenue. **Shutdown occurs in the short run.** If a firm incurs continuing losses over the long run, it will **exit** the industry, meaning that it will go out of business. This action is the opposite to the **entry** of new firms, which would occur if the industry appears profitable. **Entry and exit occur in the long run.**

- The following table summarizes the revenue and cost conditions that lead a profit-maximizing firm to make the output decisions it does. The revenue and cost comparisons in the table are first stated in terms of price and the relevant average cost. By multiplying both the price and the cost by the quantity of output, each comparison is restated in terms of total revenue and the relevant total cost.

Four Outcomes of Short-Run Profit Maximization

Comparison of Revenue and Cost	Set Marginal Revenue = Marginal Cost and produce?	Outcome
Price > average cost or Total revenue > total cost	Yes	Profit, maximized
Price < average cost, and Price > average variable cost or Total revenue < total cost, and Total revenue > total variable cost	Yes	Loss, minimized
Price = average cost or Total revenue = total cost	Yes	Breakeven (normal profit)
Price < average variable cost or Total revenue < total variable cost	No, shut down	Loss, minimized (equal to total fixed cost)

StudyCheck 6

Fill in the following table and answer the accompanying questions. The abbreviations used in the table stand for labor, quantity, total variable cost, total fixed cost, total cost, marginal cost, average cost, price total revenue, and profit, respectively.

L	Q	TVC	TFC	TC	MC	AC	P	TR	Profit
0	0			$10			$2.45		
1	11	$20					$2.45		
2	21						$2.45		
3	30						$2.45		
4	38						$2.45		
5	45						$2.45		

a.   What is the profit-maximizing quantity?

b.   What is total profit at the profit-maximizing quantity?

c.   What is the value of marginal revenue? Is marginal revenue the same at each quantity produced?

d.   What is the value of marginal cost at the profit-maximizing quantity?

e.   State the rule of profit maximization that involves marginal cost. How does it apply in this case?

8.3 Long-Run Choices

- The long run is the period of time it takes for all inputs to become variable. Since no production can occur without at least some inputs fixed in the short run, such as equipment and a place to use it in, the long run is also termed the *planning horizon*. The firm will choose from different technologies, requiring different proportions of various sorts of capital and labor.

- The production characteristics of a firm in the short run are determined by decisions made in the long run, before the *scale*—size—of the firm is selected. Changing the firm's scale can change its **long-run average cost**—cost per unit of output when all inputs are variable. When the long-run average cost drops as the firm proportionally expands its use of all its inputs, then **economies of scale**, also called *increasing returns to scale*, are present. For example, doubling the size of a firm might allow it to more than double the amount of output. That benefit would occur if the greater scale allowed more efficient use of inputs.

- Conversely, **diseconomies of scale,** also called *decreasing returns to scale*, which result in increasing per unit cost of output as firm size increases, might occur if the organization grows beyond a size that can easily be managed.

- Competitive pressures motivate firms to achieve economies of scale and avoid diseconomies of scale. When all economies of scale have been achieved and diseconomies averted, the firm is said to experience **constant returns to scale.** There is usually a range of possible firm sizes that exhibit constant returns to scale. Within this range, a proportional change in all inputs leads to the same proportional change in output. For example, if this region of constant returns to scale is sufficiently large, doubling the amount of inputs will double the amount of output. The following table summarizes the response of output according to the type of returns to scale assuming that all inputs in production double.

Returns to Scale and Response of Output

Type of Returns to Scale	When All Inputs Double, Output:
Economies of scale (increasing returns to scale)	More than doubles
Diseconomies of scale (decreasing returns to scale)	Less than doubles
Constant returns to scale	Doubles

- Price takers seek to reach constant returns to scale, because such firms have the lowest possible per-unit costs, which gives them a competitive advantage over other firms that have not achieved constant returns to scale.

- Economies of scale are associated with decreasing long-run average cost, diseconomies of scale with increasing long-run average cost, and constant returns to scale with constant long-run average cost.

- Businesses can often identify any possible economies of scale by asking some commonsense questions as the firm grows in size. Economies of scale would be associated with affirmative answers to any of these questions:
    - Would a larger factory allow a more productive layout of machines?
    - Can larger-scale machines be found that produce the output more cheaply than current machines?
    - Can jobs be broken down into a narrower range of tasks so that greater specialization of labor can be achieved?
    - Will suppliers give discounts for the larger orders that will be placed in the future?

- Technological change can shift the long-run average cost curve downward by leading to cost-saving innovations in production techniques. In choosing whether to adopt new technologies, the same principle applies as in any business decision. The goal is to maximize profit. If a firm expects the marginal revenue from an action to exceed its marginal cost, the rule says, "Do it!" If not, don't.

E&A **8.4 Adjusting to Technology—Fewer Farmers, More Food**
- The financial hardships of farming the land have caused the farm population to dwindle from 30 percent of the U.S. population in 1920 to less than 2 percent today.

- The problem facing farmers is one of abundance and changing technology. Technology has increased the productivity of farm labor and capital, making much of both obsolete in the process. Today, there are tractors and many different kinds of specialized mechanical planting and harvesting equipment. In the long run in economic terms, farming has moved through a series of short runs characterized by different ways of farming. The technological change over time has also included the development of new crop varieties, fertilizers, and techniques of production.

- In farming, all firms must sell at the same market price, despite some of them having cost advantages over others. For example, some farms spread across wide, flat expanses, while others are nestled in river valleys. The result of differences in the physical characteristics of farms is that technological change increases the profit of some farmers while harming others—farmers who cannot adapt to these changes but nevertheless experience the consequent declines in farm output prices. Farmers who are unable to sell their crops at the market price without suffering economic losses will be forced to leave their farms in the long run.

- The average number of acres per farm has been increasing, while the number of farms has been shrinking. Fluctuations in farm income make it difficult for small farms to keep going. There has also been a surge in prices paid by farmers for seed, equipment, fertilizer, and so forth, relative to the prices they receive when they sell their crops. The numbers tell us that farmers are caught in a price squeeze. Thus, there are shrinking employment opportunities in farming.

- Even though farms disappear, farmland is usually not abandoned. Rather, it becomes part of someone else's farm. When one farmer loses money working a particular piece of acreage, why should another farmer be able to take it over and earn a profit?

- An important reason is economies of scale in farming, such as those associated with the use of large-scale equipment, which causes the average cost of farm output to decrease as farms grow larger. For example, farmers waste less time maneuvering their combines when their fields are large. This means that a bushel of corn, wheat, or other commodity can be produced at a lower per unit cost on large farms. Economies of scale are identified with the downward sloping part of the U-shaped long-run average cost curve. Economies of scale do have limits, though. Since bringing in the crop and equipment uses time and fuel, fields that extend too far can lead to diseconomies of scale, in which average costs rise.

- Government programs to help farmers have attempted to drive up prices through supply restrictions and price supports. The price supports are maintained through *deficiency payments* that compensate farmers for the difference between the support price and any lower market price. The result has been that some farmers have become wealthy while others cannot scrape out a living.

- To use agricultural price supports to keep every farmer in business would require a price of output that would provide even the highest cost producer with at least a normal profit.

- There are several objections to crop prices that keep all farmers farming. For one thing, consumers have to pay the higher prices. Since food is a necessity, high food prices hit the poor the hardest. Another problem concerns where to draw the line at government efforts to help people whose incomes are not enough to keep them in their present line of work.

- Over six decades of price supports failed to stop the exodus from the farm. For this, we should be grateful. If 30 percent of Americans were still to live on farms, as was true in 1920, many goods and services that we enjoy consuming would simply not be available. People would be growing food instead of, for example, assembling cars, building houses, and making movies.

- In farm policy, Washington has tough choices to make. Farming has changed, but how much aid should government provide to farmers in trying to ease the pain experienced by those who are adversely affected by that change? That question will be answered by consideration of both economics and politics.

StudyCheck 7

Explain why agricultural price supports were ineffective in preventing the exodus from the family farm.

FILL IN THE BLANKS

1. Economic costs include both _____ costs and _____ _____ costs. We assume a firm's goal is _____ _____.

2.   _____inputs are those resources used by a firm that remain constant in amount in the short run. In contrast, the amount of _____ inputs can change.

3.   _____ _____ _____, the sum of all fixed expenses, remains constant in the short run regardless of the quantity of production. _____cost increases as the quantity of output rises and declines as output falls.

4.   Some costs that a firm incurs are called _____costs, meaning that they are irreversible—they cannot be recovered. These costs are irrelevant to decision making.

5.   A _____ _____curve shows the amount of labor needed to produce any given quantity of output. This curve is nothing more than the total product curve with the axes interchanged minus the portion for which marginal product would be negative.

6.   A firm's total variable cost of output will equal the labor requirement for that output multiplied by the wage rate:
Total variable cost = _____ _____ × _____.

7.   Total fixed cost is _____at all outputs. Thus, the total fixed cost curve has a slope equal to _____. When total fixed cost and total variable cost are added to obtain total cost, the total cost curve appears with the same shape as the total variable cost curve. This means that the slopes of both total cost and total variable cost are _____. The total variable cost curve starts at the _____, while the total cost curve starts at the point where the _____ _____ _____curve intersects the vertical axis.

8.   _____ cost is the additional cost of an additional unit of output, computed by taking the change in total cost and dividing it by the change in the quantity of output. Marginal cost is also called _____ cost because it measures the additions to total cost of one-unit increments in output. Marginal cost is equal to the _____ of the total cost curve.

9.   The change in total cost is identical to the change in _____ _____ cost because the only other component of total cost is total fixed cost, and that does not vary with output. For the same reason, the slope of total cost and the slope of total variable cost are equal.

10.   In addition to presenting costs in total or at the margin, costs are often stated per unit, meaning on average. Specifically, average cost equals total cost divided by the quantity of output:
Average cost = _____ _____ ÷ quantity of output.

11. Marginal cost intersects both average cost and average variable cost at their respective _____ points. The difference between the average variable cost and the average cost curves is _____ _____ cost. Marginal cost is shaped like the letter _____, while average cost is shaped more like the letter _____. Average cost is at a _____ where it is intersected by marginal cost.

12. Marginal cost varies inversely with marginal product. Since the change in total cost for the extra hour of work is simply the wage rate and the change in quantity is the worker's marginal product, marginal cost can be expressed as follows:

Marginal cost = wage rate ÷ _____ product

Similar reasoning shows that average variable cost can be expressed as:

Average variable cost = wage rate ÷ _____ product.

13. Many firms have no choice but to sell their output for the going market price. In other words, the price they receive is at the mercy of the marketplace and they are called _____ _____.

14. For price takers, every additional unit of output adds an amount of revenue equal to the market price of the output. This additional income is termed _____ _____, and is equal to: change in total revenue/change in quantity. For price taking firms: Marginal revenue = market price.

15. The reasoning we have followed allows the firm to identify the profit-maximizing quantity of flour to produce by following the rule of profit maximization:

Rule of profit maximization

Produce to the point at which _____ _____ equals _____ _____.

16. If an increase in output comes with higher marginal revenue than marginal cost, the firm should produce _____. If marginal cost exceeds marginal revenue, the firm should produce _____.

17. For a price taker we can restate the rule of profit maximization accordingly:

Rule of profit maximization for a price taker

Produce to the point where _____ equals marginal cost

When a firm sells all of its output at a single price, the price is the firm's revenue per unit of that output, _____ _____ = total revenue/quantity = price.

18. If the market price falls sufficiently, there comes a point where price is just equal to average cost, which would imply that total revenue and total cost would be equal. Such a situation is called _____ _____ and results in _____ economic profits, but because total revenue is enough to pay implicit costs, the firm earns a _____ profit. A firm will experience a loss when the price falls below the _____ value of _____

cost. When a firm operates at a loss, it will seek to minimize the loss. The rule of loss minimization is the same as the rule of profit maximization.

19.   If the firm ceases producing output but retains the capital that would allow it to resume production later, the firm is said to be shut down. Since fixed costs must be paid even if the firm produces nothing, _____ results in a loss that is equal to the firm's fixed cost. The shutdown rule is as follows:

<u>Shutdown rule</u>
Shut down if _____ _____ is less than total variable cost.
or, equivalently,

Shutdown rule in terms of price
Shut down if _____ is less than average variable cost

20.   The production characteristics of a firm in the short run are determined by decisions made in the long run, before the scale—size—of the firm is selected. Changing the firm's scale can change its long-run average cost—cost per unit of output when all inputs are variable. When the long-run average cost drops as the firm proportionally expands its use of all its inputs, then _____ of scale, also called _____ returns to scale, are present. Conversely, _____ of scale, also called _____ returns to scale, which result in increasing per unit cost of output as firm size increases, might occur if the organization grows beyond a size that can easily be managed.

E↓A 21.   The financial hardships of farming the land have caused the farm population to dwindle from 30 percent of the U.S. population in 1920 to less than _____ percent today.

22.   In farming, all firms must sell at the market _____, despite some of them having cost advantages over others.

23.   The average number of acres per farm has been _____ _____, while the number of farms has been _____.

24.   There are _____ of scale in farming, such as those associated with the use of large-scale equipment, which causes the average cost of farm output to decrease as farms grow larger.

25.   Government programs to help farmers have attempted to drive up prices through supply restrictions and price supports. The price supports are maintained through _____ payments that compensate farmers for the difference between the support price and any lower market price.

TRUE/FALSE/EXPLAIN
If false, explain why in the space provided.

1. Total cost equals total fixed cost plus total sunk cost.

2. Sunk costs are irreversible and irrelevant to decision making.

3. The value of a firm's capital is equal to the cost of producing it.

4. To maximize profit, a firm will always seek to produce where total revenue equals total cost.

5. For a price-taking firm, the rule of profit maximization is to produce the point where price equals marginal cost.

6. A firm should always shut down if total revenue is less than total cost.

7. Marginal cost measures the increase in costs that results from an increase in output.

8. Average cost is calculated by taking the change in total cost, and dividing it by the change in output.

9. The slope of total cost equals average cost.

10. The slope of total cost is always equal to the slope of total variable cost.

11.   Marginal cost equals the wage rate divided by marginal product.

12.   A graphical representation of loss would be a rectangle with a vertical height equal to the difference between price and average variable cost.

13.   A firm should shut down in the short run if price is less than average variable cost.

14.   The marginal cost curve intersects the average cost curve at the latter's minimum point.

15.   Average variable cost equals average cost divided by average product.

16.   The rule of profit maximization is to produce until marginal revenue equals marginal cost.

17.   Marginal revenue equals price for a price taker.

18.   If total revenue is below total variable cost, a firm loses the least money if it shuts down.

19.   In the long run there are no fixed costs.

20.   The planning horizon is somewhere between the short run and long run.

E&A 21. Government deficiency payments compensate farmers for any difference between their agricultural incomes and the incomes that they would need in order to avoid poverty.

22. Long-run average cost in agriculture shifts down in response to technological advances.

23. Historically, government farm policy has included efforts to restrict the supply of farm output.

24. As a result of farm aid, some farmers are wealthy and others cannot even scrape out of living.

25. Economic analysis suggests that aid to farmers results in lower food prices for consumers.

MULTIPLE CHOICE
Circle the letter preceding the one best answer.

1. The result of multiplying the wage rate by the quantity of labor employed by the firm is
    a. total fixed cost.
    b. total variable cost.
    c. total sunk cost.
    d. total cost.

2. Marginal cost of output equals the
    a. wage rate.
    b. marginal product of labor divided by the wage rate.
    c. wage rate divided by the marginal product of labor.
    d. wage rate minus marginal revenue.

3.   Calculate the average variable cost of 4 units of output from the information given:

Output	Total Cost
0	$100
1	150
2	190
3	250
4	350
5	500

   a. $100.
   b. $350.
   c. $250
   d. $62.50

4.   In Multiple Choice Figure 1, the arrow labeled A represents
   a.   average cost.
   b.   average variable cost.
   c.   average fixed cost.
   d.   marginal cost.

5.   In Multiple Choice Figure 1, the curve labeled B represents
   a.   average cost.
   b.   average variable cost.
   c.   average fixed cost.
   d.   marginal cost.

6.   In Multiple Choice Figure 1, the curve labeled C represents
   a.   average cost.
   b.   average variable cost.
   c.   average fixed cost.
   d.   marginal cost.

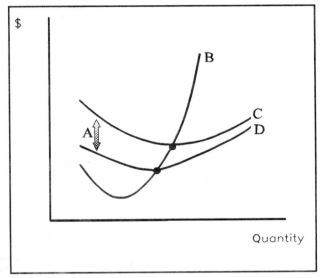

Multiple Choice Figure 1

7.   In Multiple Choice Figure 1, the curve labeled D represents
   a.   average cost.
   b.   average variable cost.
   c.   average fixed cost.
   d.   marginal cost.

8.   The law of diminishing returns explains why
      a.   fixed costs do not change as output changes.
      b.   only marginal costs matter in decision making.
      c.   marginal costs begin to increase at some point.
      d.   both marginal cost and marginal revenue fall as output rises.

9.   The shifts shown in Multiple Choice Figure 2 are most likely caused by
      a.   a higher price.
      b.   a lower price.
      c.   higher wage rates.
      d.   lower wage rates.

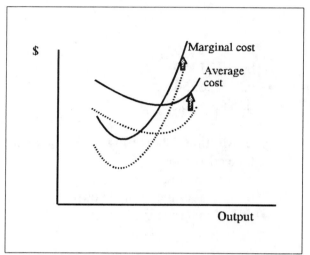

Multiple Choice Figure 2

10.   What kind of firm is a price taker?
      a.   A firm that sets and controls the market price.
      b.   A firm with no choice but to sell its output for the going market price.
      c.   A firm owned by a religious organization.
      d.   All sole proprietorships and partnerships, but never corporations.

11.   A price-taking firm is currently producing 1000 units of output. The market price of the output equals $5 per unit. Its total fixed costs equal $200, while its total variable costs are currently $150. Which statement is correct?
      a.   This firm is losing so much money that it should shut down.
      b.   This firm is maximizing profit.
      c.   This firm is earning a profit, but it is impossible to say from the information given, whether the firm is maximizing profit.
      d.   This firm is at break even, but it could earn a profit if it increased its selling price.

12.   If, at an output of 100 pounds of flour, a flour mill has total fixed costs of $50 and total variable costs of $300, then the average cost is
      a. $300.
      b. $350.
      c. $3.00.
      d. $3.50.

13. The double-headed arrow in Multiple Choice Figure 3 shows
    a. average cost.
    b. marginal cost.
    c. average revenue.
    d. average profit per unit.

14. To maximize profit, the firm shown in Multiple Choice Figure 3 would
    a. continue producing the quantity indicated.
    b. shut down in the short run and exit the industry and the long run.
    c. decrease its output until it produces at the minimum point on its marginal cost curve.
    d. decrease its output until it produces at the minimum point on its average cost curve.

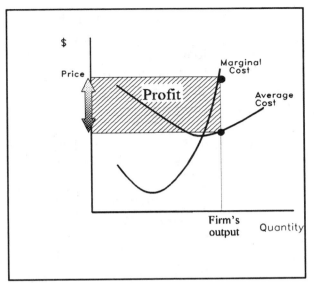

Multiple Choice Figure 3

15. The break-even quantity
    a. is what the firm will always seek to produce.
    b. occurs at the point where the price line is tangent to the average cost curve.
    c. provides a firm with profit.
    d. results in losses.

16. The loss-minimizing firm shown in Multiple Choice Figure 4 faces a market price of
    a. A.
    b. B.
    c. C.
    d. D.

17. The firm in Multiple Choice Figure 4 would
    a. continue producing in the short run and exit the industry in the long run.
    b. shut down in the short run and exit the industry and the long run.
    c. increase the market price until it earns a profit.
    d. increase its output until it produces at the minimum point on its average cost curve.

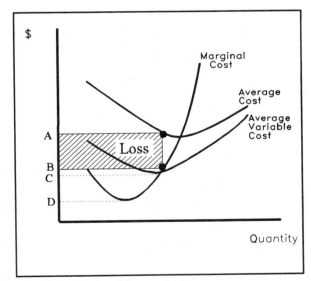

Multiple Choice Figure 4

18.   Economies of scale occur in the _____. If economies of scale are present, average cost ____ with increases in output.
    a.   long run; falls
    b.   long run; increases
    c.   short run; falls
    d.   short run; increases

19.   To maximize profit in the long run and to be able to meet the competition from other companies, a firm seeks a size for which it has
    a.   economies of scale.
    b.   constant returns to scale.
    c.   diseconomies of scale.
    d.   maximized its average cost of production.

20.   The effect of a technological advance would be to shift long-run average cost
    a.   to the right.
    b.   to the left.
    c.   up.
    d.   down.

E&A 21.   Approximately __ percent of the U.S. population lives on farms.
    a.   2
    b.   5
    c.   10
    d.   15

22.   Which economic concept provides the most likely explanation for the decline in the number of farms in the United States?
    a.   Limited liability.
    b.   Perpetual existence.
    c.   Diminishing returns.
    d.   Technological change.

23.   If the farmers of Multiple Choice Figure 5 are all growing the same homogeneous output, which would be the first to exit the industry in response to a lower price?
    a.   Farmer A
    b.   Farmer B
    c.   Farmer C
    d.   All are equally likely to exit.

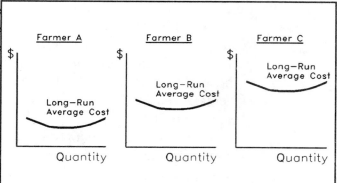

Multiple Choice Figure 5

24. If the farmers of Multiple Choice Figure 5 are each growing the same homogeneous output and are each profitable, which would be the most profitable?
    a. Farmer A
    b. Farmer B
    c. Farmer C
    d. Each farmer's profit would be identical to the profit of each other farmer.

25. The cost curves facing the farmers of Multiple Choice Figure 5 are most likely to differ from one another in response to differences in
    a. price.
    b. the quantity produced.
    c. the characteristics of the land being farmed.
    d. consumer demand for the product.

GRASPING THE GRAPHS
Fill in each box with a concept that applies.

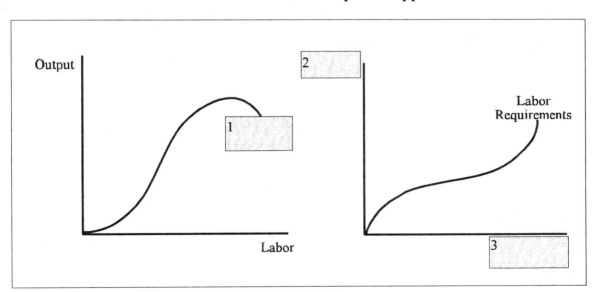

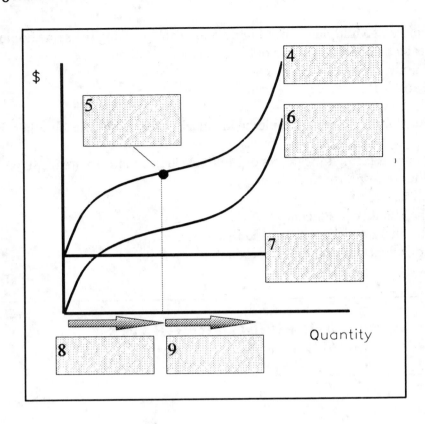

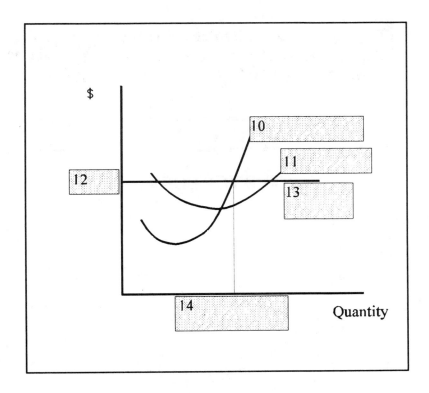

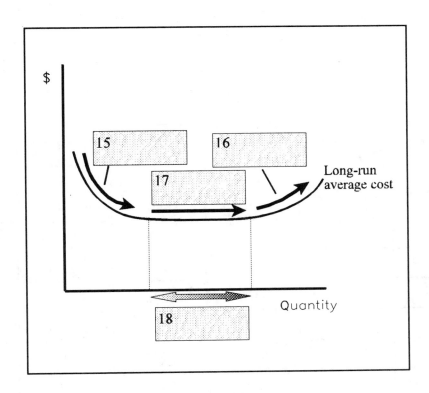

For additional practice in grasping this chapter's graphs, visit http://www.prenhall.com/ayers and try *Smart Graphs* 21 and 22, along with *Active Graphs* 48, 49, 50, 51, and 52.

ANSWERS

STUDYCHECKS

1.   See StudyCheck 1 Figure.

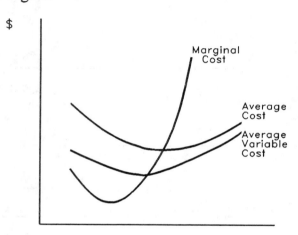

StudyCheck 1 Figure

2.

Labor	Output	Total Variable Cost	Total Cost	Marginal Cost	Average Cost
0	0	$0	$40	undefined	undefined
1	10	$100	$140	$10	$14
2	22	$200	$240	$8.33	$10.91
3	30	$300	$340	$12.50	$11.33
4	36	$400	$440	$16.67	$12.22
5	40	$500	$540	$25	$13.5
6	42	$600	$640	$50	$15.24

3.   See StudyCheck 3 Figure.

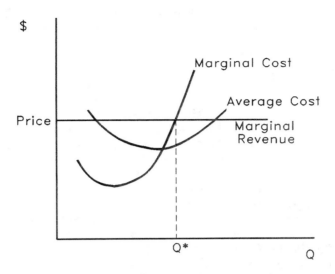

StudyCheck 3 Figure

4.   See StudyCheck 4 Figure.

5.   See StudyCheck 5 Figure.

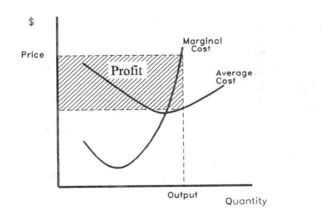

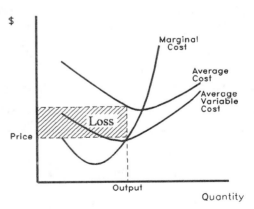

StudyCheck 4 Figure   **StudyCheck 5 Figure**

6.   See the following table.

L	Q	TVC ($)	TFC ($)	TC ($)	MC ($)	AC ($)	P ($)	TR ($)	Profit ($)
0	0	0	10	10	--	--	2.45	0.00	-10.00
1	10	20	10	30	2	3	2.45	24.50	-5.50
2	21	40	10	50	1.82	2.38	2.45	51.45	1.45
3	30	60	10	70	2.22	2.33	2.45	73.50	3.50
4	38	80	10	90	2.5	2.37	2.45	91.20	1.20
5	45	100	10	110	2.86	2.44	2.45	110.25	0.25

Note that total variable cost equals the wage rate multiplied by the number of units of labor employed. Also note that all costs that occur at an output of zero must be fixed costs.

a.   30.
b. $3.50.
c. $2.45, yes.
d. $2.22.
e.   Set marginal revenue equal to marginal cost. In this case, the firm should keep producing until marginal cost is closest to marginal revenue without exceeding marginal revenue. That occurs at a marginal cost of $2.22.

7.   Technological change in farming meant that average costs of production dropped for large farms relative to small farms. If the price supports had been so high that they would have kept all of the high-cost small farms in business, the owners of larger farms would have gotten rich at the public's expense. Thus, price supports were not kept that high, and served mainly to ease the transition out of small-scale farming.

___

FILL IN THE BLANKS

1.   explicit, implicit opportunity, profit maximization
2.   Fixed, variable
3.   Total fixed cost, Variable
4.   sunk
5.   labor requirements
6.   wage rate, labor
7.   constant, zero, identical, origin, total fixed cost
8.   Marginal, incremental, slope

9. total variable
10. total cost
11. minimum, average fixed, J, U, minimum
12. marginal, average
13. price takers
14. marginal revenue
15. marginal revenue, marginal cost
16. more, less
17. price, average revenue
18. break even, zero, normal, minimum, average
19. shutdown, total revenue, price
20. economies, increasing, diseconomies, decreasing
21. 2
22. price
23. increasing, decreasing
24. economies
25. deficiency

TRUE/FALSE/EXPLAIN

1. False, total cost equals total fixed cost plus total variable cost.
2. True.
3. False, the value of a firm's capital comes from the value of the future productivity of that capital, not on what was paid for it in the past.
4. False, producing to the point for which total revenue equals total cost would cause profit to be zero, not maximized, which would require producing to the point were marginal revenue equals marginal cost.
5. True.
6. False, a firm should only shut down if total revenue is less than total variable cost.
7. True.
8. False, average cost is total cost divided by total output.
9. False, the slope of total cost equals marginal cost.
10. True.
11. True.
12. False, the rectangle showing loss would have a vertical height equal to average cost minus price.
13. True.
14. True.
15. False, average variable cost equals total variable cost divided by the quantity of output.
16. True.
17. True.

18. True.
19. True.
20. False, the planning horizon is the long run.
21. False, government deficiency payments make up the difference between the support price and the market price.
22. True.
23. True.
24. True.
25. False, farm aid is intended to increase food prices so as to increase the income to farmers.

MULTIPLE CHOICE

1.	b	8.	c	15.	b	22.	d
2.	c	9.	c	16.	b	23.	c
3.	d	10.	b	17.	a	24.	a
4.	c	11.	c	18.	a	25.	c
5.	d	12.	d	19.	b		
6.	a	13.	d	20.	d		
7.	b	14.	a	21.	a		

GRASPING THE GRAPHS
Examples of correct answers

1. Total product
2. Labor
3. Output (total product)
4. Total cost
5. Point of minimum marginal cost
6. Total variable cost
7. Total fixed cost
8. Decreasing marginal cost
9. Increasing marginal cost
10. Marginal cost
11. Average cost
12. Price
13. Marginal revenue
14. Profit-maximizing output
15. Economies of scale

16. Diseconomies of scale
17. Constant returns to scale
18. Optimal plant size

**Visit the Ayers/Collinge companion Website at <u>http://www.prenhall.com/ayers</u>
for further activities and exercises for this chapter.**

Part 3

OUTPUT MARKETS

Chapter 9

PURE COMPETITION

CHAPTER REVIEW

9.1 Types of Markets

- Different markets are commonly called *industries*. When we buy water we typically face just one seller. When we shop for groceries there might be several supermarkets in our neighborhood to pick from. Once inside the supermarket, there may be dozens of shampoos that we might purchase. Thus, each of these markets is different from the others in terms of the number of sellers.

- Markets also differ according to whether the product is homogeneous or differentiated. **Homogeneous products** are identical, whichever firm produces them, and are often called *commodities*. For example, the #2 grade yellow corn produced by Farmer Brown, Farmer Jones, and other farmers is homogeneous because there are no differences among their crops. Additional examples include cattle, gold and silver bullion, copper, steel, aluminum, and lumber.

- In contrast, **differentiated products** will vary from one producer to the next. These differences lead to four basic **market structures**, which are models of the way markets work. They are:
    - **Monopoly**—a market with only one seller of a good without close substitutes. For example, a municipal sewage service or water supply is a monopoly. A monopoly firm maintains a significant amount of control over the price of its product.
    - **Oligopoly**—a market with more than one seller, where at least one of those sellers can significantly influence price. Oligopoly is usually characterized by just a few significant sellers of a product that can be either homogeneous or differentiated. Passenger airlines and crude oil are both provided in oligopoly markets.
    - **Monopolistic competition**—a market with numerous firms selling a differentiated product and with only a slight ability to control price. Retailers such as dry cleaners and music stores are examples.
    - **Pure competition**—a market in which there are many buyers and sellers of a homogeneous product. The model of pure competition underlies the supply and demand analysis in chapters 3 and 4.

- The table below shows a grid of market structures according to the number of firms and differentiation of the product among them. The four market structures can be arranged according to the amount of **market power**—influence over price by the individual firm. Purely competitive firms have no market power. Monopolistically competitive firms have slight market power. Oligopolistic firms may exhibit a significant degree of market power, while monopoly firms usually have more market power than any other type of firm.

Market structure by product and number of firms

	Homogeneous product	Differentiated product
One firm	Monopoly [example: city drinking water]	Not applicable
Few firms	Oligopoly [example: gasoline refineries]	Oligopoly [example: automobiles]
Many firms	Pure competition [example: farmers]	Monopolistic competition [example: restaurants]

StudyCheck 1

Describe the spectrum of market structures.

- Pure competition is characterized by the following:
  - **Numerous buyers and sellers.** As a result, **each firm and consumer is a price taker,** with firms selling their output at the market price and consumers paying that same market price.

- **A homogeneous product.** The market prices of these items are widely available in newspaper and other media reports. Because products are identical, individual firms reap no benefits from advertising: **firms do not advertise in pure competition.**
- **Costless entry and exit of firms.** In the long run, it is easy for firms to start up, called entering an industry, or leave an industry, which is called exit. Firms might leave an industry by going out of business or by shifting the use of their resources to another industry. For example, Farmer Brown might plant barley instead of corn.

9.2 The Firm's Demand and Supply Curves

- **The central implication of pure competition is that firms are price takers.** Each firm must decide how much to produce based upon the market price, over which it has no control. That price is set by the intersection of supply and demand in the marketplace.

- The equilibrium market price becomes the firm's demand curve. **Although market demand slopes downward to the right, the demand facing each firm is horizontal (perfectly elastic) at the market price.** The horizontal demand means that the firm is able to sell as much as it wishes at the market price. It has no reason to sell for less than the market price because its horizontal demand curve means that it can sell as much as it wishes at that price. Also, it cannot sell anything if it charges more than the market price. Thus, **a price taker always sells at the market price.**

StudyCheck 2

Using two separate graphs, show how the firm in pure competition gets its demand curve from the market.

- The individual firm chooses the quantity of output it produces based upon its demand and its supply. The firm's goal is to maximize profit, a goal that is accomplished by producing at the point where marginal revenue equals marginal cost. The market price equals the price taking firm's marginal revenue. The market price equals the firm's demand curve, too. That makes the firm's demand curve its marginal revenue curve. In the next section we show you that the firm's marginal cost curve is also its short-run supply curve. Thus, the rule of profit maximization, produce at the point where marginal revenue equals marginal cost, is equivalent to producing at the point where the firm's demand and supply curves intersect.

- At any price above the shutdown price, the profit-maximizing price-taking firm equates marginal revenue and marginal cost. Because the price-taking firm's marginal revenue equals the market price, the firm produces the quantity associated with its marginal cost curve at that price. For this reason, the *firm's short-run supply curve* **is that part of its marginal cost curve that lies above average variable cost.** This supply curve shows the quantity that the firm will offer for sale at each of various possible prices. Market supply sums the quantities offered by each firm at each price.

9.3 The Long Run: Entry, Exit, and Efficiency

- In the short run, the market price could be sufficiently high that the firm earns profits, or it could be so low that the firm loses money. However, the **long-run equilibrium market price results in the expectation of zero profit for a firm that is considering entry into the industry.** Recall that zero profit as economists use the term means that the firm is earning a *normal profit* measured in accounting terms—normal profit is the accounting profit necessary to keep the firm in business.

- The adjustment to long-run equilibrium occurs in the following way: The market supply curve will shift until the market price is just sufficient to cover average cost. When price equals average cost, firms will earn a normal profit and no more shifting will occur. This outcome is indicated graphically by the firm's demand curve being tangent to its average cost curve at the minimum point of average cost.

- The free entry and exit that characterize pure competition explains why long-run equilibrium occurs. Entry and exit affect market supply. The expectation of short-run profit attracts new entrants. Their output shifts the market supply to the right. Entry would continue to occur, increasing market supply and driving market price down, until expected profit falls to zero.

- Likewise, the occurrence of long-run losses would prompt the exit of firms. Exit shifts the market supply curve to the left. The decrease in market supply would continue until price rises to the level of zero expected profit for firms contemplating entry or exit. Even so, some existing firms will remain profitable in the long run, such as farms with exceptionally fertile and tillable soil.

StudyCheck 3

Describe how the competitive market moves from a short-run equilibrium to a long-run equilibrium.

- Chapter 4 examined the efficiency of the marketplace. Recall, **the competitive market equilibrium produces an allocatively efficient amount of output. Competition also forces firms to keep costs in check, thus inducing technological efficiency as well.** For these reasons, the model of pure competition is often used as the standard of efficiency by which other market structures are judged.

- Consider the efficiency of the purely competitive market output. Recall that social surplus from the production of any one good equals the difference between the total value consumers place on all units of that good and the extra cost of producing all those units. Supply represents the marginal cost of production and demand the marginal benefit. At the market equilibrium, these two are equal, an outcome that maximizes social surplus and is thus allocatively efficient. In other words, pure competition produces goods up to the point where the value of the last unit of a good is just equal to what that last unit is worth.

- Consider the effect of moving away from the competitive output. Were producers forced to produce more than the competitive output, the value of those extra units would be less than they cost to make, thereby reducing social surplus. Likewise, were producers forced to produce fewer units, the cost savings would be less than the loss of value from those units. Hence, for any particular good, the competitive market price induces consumers and firms to maximize surplus value from that good, which is efficient.

9.4 Long-Run Supply

- When there is entry of new firms into a purely competitive industry it is possible that industry costs will be affected. In the following sections we explain how entry affects costs.

- The expansion or contraction of industries over time sometimes affects the costs of production in that industry. In response to entry, input prices might remain unchanged, rise, or fall, which gives rise to the following three industry types:
    1. **constant-cost industry**—An increase in the industry's output does not affect input prices.
    2. **increasing-cost industry**—An increase in the industry's output causes input prices to rise.
    3. **decreasing-cost industry**—An increase in the industry's output causes input prices to fall.

- Constant-cost industries are the most common. These industries use few highly specialized resources.

- Increasing-cost industries are characterized by the use of scarce resources for which an increase in output increases the price of those resources.

- There are a number of examples of decreasing-cost industries in which increases in industry output result in lower prices. Oftentimes, it is small industries that see decreasing costs as they get large. For example, as the electronics industry expanded in the area of California that became known as Silicon Valley, the movement of skilled labor to the area, the development of specialty suppliers, and increased transportation facilities contributed to lower production costs. Similarly, the rise of the automobile in the early 1900s generated a huge infrastructure of suppliers that drove down costs as the industry expanded.

- These three types of industry are best analyzed with the model of perfect competition, which is a variant upon the model of pure competition. Specifically, the model of **perfect competition** adds to the assumptions of pure competition the assumption that all firms are identical, with identical access to resources and technology, with all information fully and freely available. The uncomplicated nature of perfect competition makes it very useful for illustrative purposes, such as for long-run industry costs.

- In a constant-cost industry, the entry of new firms would have no effect upon the production costs of other firms in the industry. Thus, under perfect competition's assumption that all firms are identical, expansion of the industry would lead to the same equilibrium output price. Any higher price would be profitable and thus attract new entrants that would bring price down. Any lower price would be unprofitable and thus lead to exit that would bring price up.

- In an increasing-cost industry, the entry of new firms would not only increase industry output, but would also shift up the cost curves of each firm in that industry. Thus, expansion of the industry would lead to a higher equilibrium price of output. Conversely, in a decreasing-cost industry, the entry of new firms would lower production costs for all firms and thus lead to a lower equilibrium price of output.

- These effects are seen by looking at **long-run supply**, which tells how much will be produced at each of various possible short-run market-equilibrium prices. Consider the effect of an increase in demand for the product of a perfectly competitive industry, the model that assumes all firms have identical cost curves. The increased demand generates profits which attract new entrants into the industry. Newly entering firms shift supply to the right. How far it shifts depends upon which of the three types of industries it is. The long-run supply curve connects the initial market equilibrium and the new market equilibrium. Long-run supply is seen to be flat for a constant-cost industry, to slope upward for an increasing-cost industry, and to slope downward for a decreasing-cost industry.

StudyCheck 4

Describe long-run aggregate supply and its characteristics in perfect competition. In your answer, distinguish increasing-cost industries, constant-cost industries, and decreasing-cost industries. Also note how perfect competition differs from pure competition.

E&A   9.5 Discrimination: What a Difference Market Structure Makes

- Because price and quality are more significant to buyers than who makes a good, the marketplace, theoretically at least, should offer opportunities to everyone. How well the promise of opportunity is actually realized in an industry, however, tends to depend at least partly upon its market structure.

- Discrimination occurs in the private marketplace, but seldom in markets characterized by pure competition. For example, it was the racially segregated lunch counters at the monopolistically competitive Woolworth five and dime stores that attracted the attention of civil rights organizations in the south of the early1960s. Likewise, large oligopolistic corporations are often accused of having glass ceilings that prevent the rise of qualified women and minorities. But in agriculture, mining, and other industries characterized by pure competition, accusations of discrimination are rarely heard.

- Two features of the purely competitive model work to prevent discrimination. One feature is the homogeneous product which means that the firm has no opportunity to vary the product in discriminatory ways. For example, whites-only restaurants, country clubs, and other facilities are examples of product differentiation, one that provides customers with a slightly different environment in which to take advantage of the firm's services. Depending upon biases among prospective customers, such product differentiation might allow the discriminating firm to increase profits. The firm would be tailoring its product to a market niche, the niche of people with similar biases.

- Firms in market structures that allow product differentiation might choose to discriminate because, by turning away some customers, they might attract other customers who do not wish to associate with the customers who are turned away. For example, looked at in the this way, in the deep south of half a century ago the decision of Woolworth's to not serve blacks at its lunch counters was necessary in order to keep its white customers. Discrimination against African Americans increased the profit of Woolworth's relative to a color blind store policy since whites had more purchasing power than blacks.

- There might be an additional element to this story, though. The denial of service to blacks by Woolworth's was not necessarily voluntary. Racial segregation was a matter of state law and a deeply ingrained custom in the south. Segregation was legally mandated in many southern states. Maybe that was because it was recognized that the profit motive in the free marketplace mostly worked against the perpetuation of discrimination.

- In a purely competitive market, in contrast, the product must remain homogeneous. There is no opportunity to tailor the output to biases, whether the be mandated by law or merely by customer preferences. There is no such thing as Whites-only coal or women-only wheat. No one asks about the race or ethnicity of the roustabout on the offshore drilling platform. Customers do not care which workers produced the lead for the number 2 pencils they use.

For this reason, and unlike and in other market structures, pure competition prevents discrimination in terms of the product itself.

• Pure competition also gives firms a strong profit incentive to avoid discrimination. Profit can be viewed as a source of funds to "pay" for discrimination. Pure competition make profits hard to come by. A firm that is considering entering or exiting the purely competitive market can expect a normal profit, meaning zero economic profit. Using normal profit to pay for discrimination is a luxury such firms can ill afford. In short, to the extent that discrimination occurs on the basis of anything other than a person's abilities, the firm finds itself facing higher production costs. It is quite possible that a firm can turn itself from being profitable to one with a loss as a result of such discrimination.

• For example, discriminating against qualified low-wage minority or female workers by denying them employment would force the firm to hire others, perhaps higher-wage white and/or male labor. The practice of not hiring minority or female workers thus shifts the cost of production upward for discriminating firms. In pure competition, a firm that inflicts higher input costs on itself can find itself going from profit to loss. Such self-inflicted losses will lead the discriminating firms to ultimately go out of business.

• Consider a firm that starts out profitable, but that sees its average cost curve shift upward because it chooses to hire only high-cost white labor. The market price of its output is not sufficient to pay those costs. The firm will have to choose. It will either have to change its hiring practices or, in the long run, go out of business.

• Society does not rely upon the economic incentives discussed here to rein in discrimination. Instead, civil rights laws have made much discrimination illegal. These laws have undoubtedly reduced blatant instances of discrimination. However, discrimination has taken new, more subtle forms, but ones not immune to the economic incentives of competition and profit.

StudyCheck 5

Of the four market structures, which is likely generate to the least racial discrimination? Explain.

FILL IN THE BLANKS

1.   Different markets are commonly called _____. Markets often differ from the others in terms of the number of _____.

2.   _____ products are identical, whichever firm produces them, and are often called commodities.

3.   _____ products will vary from one producer to the next.

4.   There are four basic market structures, which are models of the way markets work. They are:
   *   _____—a market with only one seller of a good without close substitutes.
   *   _____—a market with more than one seller, where at least one of those sellers can significantly influence price. This market is usually characterized by just a few significant sellers of a product that can be either homogeneous or differentiated.
   *   _____ _____—a market with numerous firms selling a differentiated product and with only a slight ability to control price. Retailers such as dry cleaners and music stores are examples.
   *   _____ _____—a market in which there are many buyers and sellers of a homogeneous product.

5.   The four market structures can be arranged according to the amount of _____ _____—influence over price by the individual firm.

6.   _____ _____ firms have no market power. _____ _____ firms have slight market power. _____ firms may exhibit a significant degree of market power, while _____ firms usually have more market power than any other type of firm.

7.   Pure competition is characterized by the following:
   *   _____. As a result, each firm and consumer is a _____ _____, with firms selling their output at the market price and consumers paying that same market price.
   *   A _____product: identical products
   *   _____ entry and exit of firms. In the long run, it is easy for firms to start up, called entering an industry, or leave an industry, which is called exit. Firms might leave an industry by going out of business or by shifting the use of their resources to another industry.

8. The central implication of pure competition is that firms are price takers. Each firm must decide how much to produce based upon the market price, over which it has no control. That price is set by the intersection of _____ and _____ in the marketplace.

9. The equilibrium market price becomes the firm's _____ curve. Although market demand slopes downward to the right, the demand facing each firm is _____ (perfectly elastic) at the market price. A price taker always sells at the _____ price.

10. The individual firm chooses the quantity of output it produces based upon its demand and its supply. The firm's goal is to maximize profit, a goal that is accomplished by producing at the point where marginal revenue equals marginal cost. The market price equals the price taking firm's marginal revenue. The market price equals the firm's demand curve, too. That makes the firm's demand curve its _____ _____ curve.

11. At any price above the shutdown price, the profit-maximizing price-taking firm equates marginal revenue and marginal cost. Because the price-taking firm's marginal revenue equals the market price, the firm produces the quantity associated with its marginal cost curve at that price. For this reason, the firm's short-run supply curve is that part of its _____ _____ curve that lies above average variable cost. This supply curve shows the quantity that the firm will offer for sale at each of various possible prices. Market supply _____ the quantities offered by each firm at each price.

12. In the short run, the market price could be sufficiently high that the firm earns profits, or it could be so low that the firm loses money. However, the long-run equilibrium market price results in the expectation of _____ profit for a firm that is considering entry into the industry. As economists use the term, this means that the firm is earning a _____ profit.

13. The adjustment to long-run equilibrium occurs in the following way: The market supply curve will shift until the market price is just sufficient to cover average cost. When price _____ average cost, firms will earn a normal profit and no more shifting will occur. This outcome is indicated graphically by the firm's demand curve being _____ to its average cost curve at the minimum point of average cost.

14. The free entry and exit that characterize pure competition explains why long-run equilibrium occurs. Entry and exit affect market supply. The expectation of short-run profit attracts new entrants. Their output shifts the market supply to the _____. Entry would continue to occur, _____ market supply and _____ _____ price, until expected profit falls to _____.

15.   Chapter 4 examined the efficiency of the marketplace. Recall, the competitive market equilibrium produces an _____efficient amount of output. Competition also forces firms to keep costs in check, thus inducing _____efficiency as well. For these reasons, the model of pure competition is often used as the standard of efficiency by which other market structures are judged.

16.   The expansion or contraction of industries over time sometimes affects the costs of production in that industry. In response to entry, input prices might remain unchanged, rise, or fall, which gives rise to the following three industry types:
•   _____ industry—An increase in the industry's output does not affect input prices.
•   _____ industry—An increase in the industry's output causes input prices to rise.
•   _____ industry—An increase in the industry's output causes input prices to fall.

17.   _____ industries are the most common. These industries use few highly specialized resources. _____ industries are characterized by the use of scarce resources for which an increase in output increases the price of those resources.

18.   These three types of industry are best analyzed with the model of perfect competition, which is a variant upon the model of pure competition. Specifically, the model of perfect competition adds to the assumptions of pure competition the assumption that all firms are _____, with identical access to resources and technology, with all information fully and freely available.

19.   These effects are seen by looking at _____ _____ _____, which tells how much will be produced at each of various possible short-run market-equilibrium prices.

20.   Long-run supply is _____ for a constant-cost industry, slopes _____ for an increasing-cost industry, and slopes _____ for a decreasing-cost industry.

E&A   21.   Discrimination occurs in the private marketplace, but seldom in markets characterized by _____ _____. For example, it was the racially segregated lunch counters at the _____ _____Woolworth five and dime stores that attracted the attention of civil rights organizations in the south of the early1960s. Likewise, large _____ corporations are often accused of having glass ceilings that prevent the rise of qualified women and minorities.

22.   Two features of the purely competitive model work to prevent discrimination. One feature is the _____ product which means that the firm has no opportunity to vary the product in discriminatory ways.

23. There might be an additional element to this story, though. The denial of service to blacks by Woolworth's was not necessarily voluntary. Racial segregation was a matter of _____ _____ and a deeply ingrained _____ in the south.

24. Pure competition also gives firms a strong _____ incentive to avoid discrimination. Profit can be viewed as a source of funds to "pay" for discrimination. Pure competition makes profits hard to come by. A firm that is considering entering or exiting the purely competitive market can expect a _____ profit, meaning _____ economic profit.

25. Consider a firm that starts out profitable, but that sees its average cost curve shift _____ because it chooses to hire only high-cost white labor. The market price of its output is not sufficient to pay those costs. The firm will have to choose. It will either have to change its hiring practices or, in the long run, ___ ____ ___ _____.

TRUE/FALSE/EXPLAIN
If false, explain why in the space provided.

1. Commodities are products that are differentiated.

2. Increasing market power goes hand-in-hand with increasing barriers to entry.

3. A monopoly is an industry in which there is only one supplier that produces an output for which there are no good substitutes.

4. Firms in monopolistic competition have more market power than firms in oligopoly.

5. A firm has market power when it is able to force consumers to buy products that they really do not want.

6. Purely competitive markets are characterized by high barriers to entry.

7.   Barriers to entry are present in all types of markets.

8.   The restaurant industry is a good example of oligopoly.

9.   In pure competition, there are many firms, each of which is a price taker and sells a homogeneous output.

10.   The Internet has increased the market power of sellers of rare books.

11.   A firm's short-run supply curve is that part of its marginal cost curve that lies above its average fixed cost curve.

12.   Entry or exit is motivated by profit or loss.

13.   Economic efficiency is achieved in purely competitive markets.

14.   Competition forces firms to minimize long-run average costs.

15.   Long-run equilibrium in pure competition is characterized by economic profit for potential new entrants.

16.   An increase in an increasing-cost industry's output causes input prices to rise.

17. An increase in a decreasing-cost industry's output causes input prices to rise.

18. A long-run supply curve can slope upward or be flat, but cannot slope downward.

19. If an increase in the demand for fish led to an expansion of the fishing industry and, as a consequence, the cost of fishing boats increased, the industry fits the increasing-cost model.

20. A long-run supply curve is drawn by connecting an initial point of market equilibrium to a new point of market equilibrium that results from an increase in demand and the subsequent shift in short-run supply.

E&A 21. Government has helped fight discrimination, but it also at times has helped maintain it.

22. Homogeneous products are more likely to be associated with discrimination than are differentiated products.

23. Economic analysis shows that discrimination is most likely when markets are characterized by pure competition.

24. One problem with pure competition is that there is nothing to prevent firms from discriminating on the basis of race, color or creed, unless government intervenes.

25. Firms that discriminate in their hiring on the basis of anything other than the ability to get the job done are likely to face higher costs than do their competitors who do not discriminate.

MULTIPLE CHOICE
Circle the letter preceding the one best answer.

1. Which market structure is characterized by no barriers to entry?
   a. Pure competition.
   b. Monopoly.
   c. Monopolistic competition.
   d. Oligopoly.

2. If placed in the order of increasing barriers to entry, market structures would read as follows:
   a. Oligopoly, monopoly, monopolistic competition, pure competition.
   b. Monopoly, oligopoly, monopolistic competition, pure competition.
   c. Monopolistic competition, pure competition, oligopoly, monopoly.
   d. Pure competition, monopolistic competition, oligopoly, monopoly.

3. Of the following, the best example of a product likely to be produced in pure competition would be
   a. soybeans.
   b. Zippy's Spicy Soy Sauce.
   c. Enjoy Your Soy brand cookies.
   d. socks.

4. The supply of drinking water to residents of a city is likely to the be characterized by
   a. pure competition.
   b. monopoly.
   c. oligopoly.
   d. monopolistic competition.

5. In which of the following market structures will firms NOT advertise?
   a. Pure competition.
   b. Monopoly.
   c. Oligopoly.
   d. Monopolistic competition.

6. For a firm in pure competition, demand will be
   a. upward-sloping.
   b. downward-sloping.
   c. hump-shaped.
   d. horizontal.

7. The market supply curve equals the horizontal summation of each firm's
    a. average total cost of production.
    b. marginal cost of production above average cost.
    c. marginal cost of production above average variable cost.
    d. price.

8. In Multiple Choice Figure 1, Graph 1 represents _____ and Graph 2 represents _____ .
    a. market demand; market supply
    b. market supply; market demand
    c. the market; the firm
    d. the firm; the market

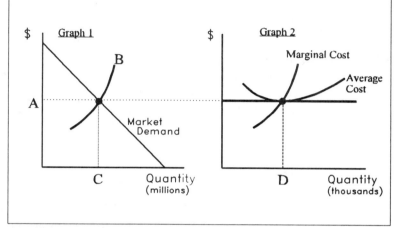

Multiple Choice Figure 1

9. In Multiple Choice Figure 1, the line at point A represents both
    a. price and the firm's demand.
    b. price and the firm's supply.
    c. price and market supply.
    d. the firm's demand and the firm's supply.

10. In Multiple Choice Figure 1, market supply is labeled as
    a. A.
    b. B.
    c. C.
    d. D.

11. For the firm in pure competition,
    a. supply is perfectly elastic.
    b. supply is perfectly inelastic.
    c. demand is perfectly elastic.
    d. demand is perfectly inelastic.

12. If a purely competitive firm is faced with a loss, it is most likely to
    a. increase the price that it charges for its output.
    b. increase its advertising budget.
    c. expanded its production facilities.
    d. plan to eventually exit the industry.

13. In Multiple Choice Figure 2, exit occurs when supply shifts in the direction shown by the arrow labeled
    a. A.
    b. B.
    c. C.
    d. D.

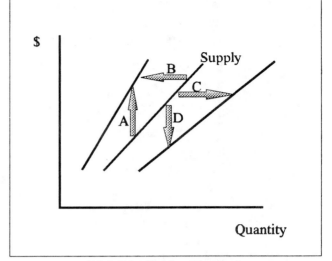

14. In Multiple Choice Figure 2, entry occurs when supply shifts in the direction shown by the arrow labeled
    a. A.
    b. B.
    c. C.
    d. D.

Multiple Choice Figure 2

15. The difference between pure competition and perfect competition is that, in perfect competition, firms
    a. are not price takers.
    b. have identical access to resources and information.
    c. produce differentiated products.
    d. have market power.

16. The long-run supply curve in a constant-cost perfectly competitive industry is
    a. horizontal.
    b. upward sloping.
    c. downward sloping.
    d. steeper than the short-run supply curve.

17. In a decreasing-cost industry, an increase in the industry's output causes input prices to
    a. remain constant and the long-run supply curve to slope upward.
    b. rise and the long-run supply curve to slope downward.
    c. decrease and the long-run supply curve to be horizontal.
    d. decrease and the long-run supply curve to slope downward.

18. An increasing-cost industry is characterized by
    a. a flat long-run supply curve.
    b. an upward-sloping long-run supply curve.
    c. a downward-sloping long-run supply curve.
    d. a vertical long-run supply curve.

19. The analysis of long-run supply starts with
    a. an increase in supply.
    b. a decrease in supply.
    c. an increase in the number of firms.
    d. a change in demand.

20. In the long run, a perfectly competitive decreasing-cost industry that experiences an initial increase in demand will respond with
    a. an increase in supply of equal proportion to the increase in demand.
    b. an increase in supply of a lesser proportion than the increase in demand.
    c. an increase in supply of a greater proportion than the increase in demand.
    d. a decrease in supply of equal proportion to the increase in demand.

E♦A 21. A chief advantage that firms that do not discriminate have over firms that practice racial and gender discrimination is
    a. a larger demand for their product.
    b. better locations.
    c. exemption from the law of diminishing returns.
    d. a larger pool of available labor from which to hire.

22. In markets that are not purely competitive, discrimination could prove profitable if
    a. customers are unaware of the discrimination.
    b. customers are aware of the discrimination, but do not care.
    c. customers are aware of the discrimination and do not like it.
    d. the discrimination allows the firm to differentiate its product from the products of its competitors, and in a way that some customers are willing to pay extra for.

23. In purely competitive markets and without government regulation, widespread discrimination against minorities is
    a. likely, because competitive markets do not have government regulators to ensure that firms do not respond to the biases of their owners.
    b. likely, because the large number of competitive firms means that consumers cannot keep track of which ones discriminate and which ones do not.
    c. unlikely, because widespread discrimination means that nondiscriminating firms would be able to hire the minority workers more cheaply, and thereby be able to profitably undercut the prices charged by discriminating firms.
    d. unlikely, because competitive firms must be sensitive to the needs of their customers, including minority customers.

24.   Suppose that Multiple Choice Figure 3 represents the effect of discrimination on a firm's costs.   After practicing discrimination, this firm finds that it is
a.   profitable, more so than before.
b.   profitable, but less so than before.
c.   unprofitable, whereas before it had been profitable.
d.   unprofitable, whereas before it had been breaking even.

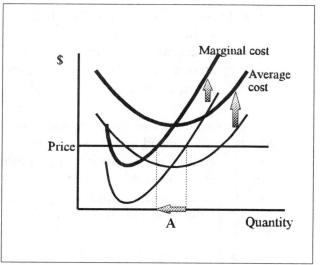

Multiple Choice Figure 3

25.   In Multiple Choice Figure 3, the arrow labeled A represents the decrease in
a.   output after the firm starts to discriminate in hiring.
b.   hiring after the firm starts to discriminate in hiring.
c.   output after the firm starts to discriminate in terms of which customers it will serve.
d.   customer count after the firm starts to discriminate in terms of which customers it will serve.

GRASPING THE GRAPHS
Fill in each box with a concept that applies.

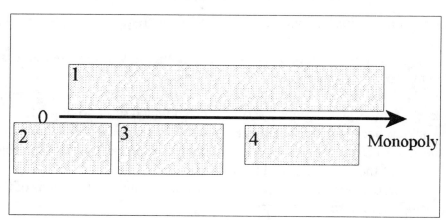

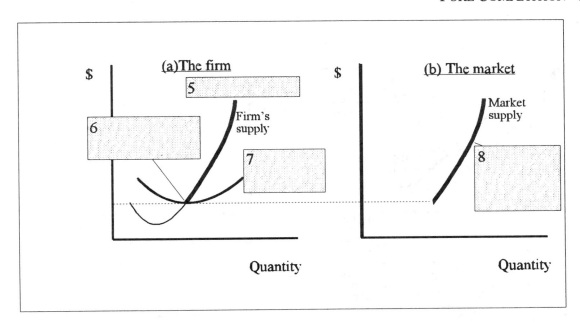

(a)The firm

$

5

6

Firm's
supply

7

(b) The market

$

Market
supply

8

Quantity

Quantity

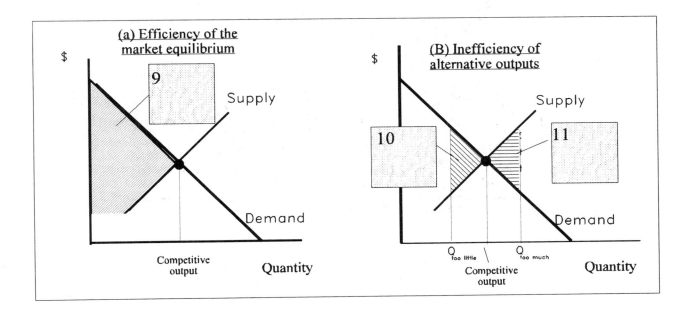

(a) Efficiency of the
market equilibrium

$

9

Supply

Demand

Competitive
output

Quantity

(B) Inefficiency of
alternative outputs

$

10

11

Supply

Demand

$Q_{too\ little}$ $Q_{too\ much}$

Competitive
output

Quantity

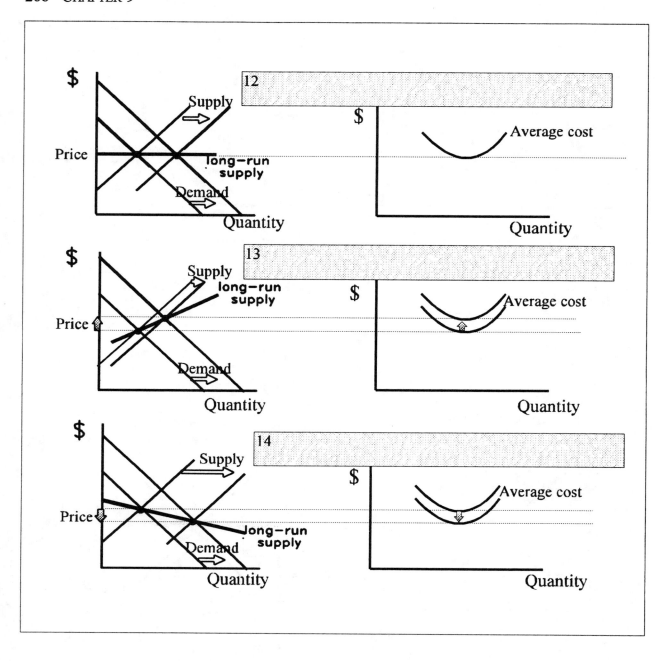

For additional practice in grasping this chapter's graphs,
visit **http://www.prenhall.com/ayers** and try *Smart Graphs* **23** and **24,**
along with *Active Graphs* **53** and **54.**

ANSWERS

STUDYCHECKS

1. Market structures can be arranged according to barriers to entry. Barriers to entry confer market power, which is the ability to set prices. At one extreme is the model of pure competition. Because purely competitive firms have no market power, they are price takers. Purely competitive firms produce a homogeneous product. At the other extreme of market structure is monopoly, which has only one producer because of high barriers to entry. When barriers to entry are less pronounced than under monopoly, multiple firms may coexist. If one or more of these firms has a significant ability to influence price, the market structure is termed oligopoly. Products of oligopolists may be homogeneous or differentiated. Monopolistic competition occurs when there are many firms, each with a differentiated product that confers a slight ability to influence price.

2. See StudyCheck 2 Figure.

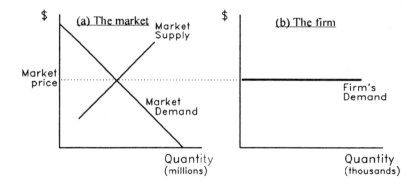

StudyCheck 2 Figure

3. Long-run supply is the quantity that will be supplied in a long-run market equilibrium at each price. To reach long-run equilibrium, short-run market supply adjusts to the right if there is profit, or to the left if there is loss. When a potential entrant expects neither a profit nor a loss, the purely competitive market is in equilibrium.

4. In perfect competition in which all firms are identical, long-run equilibrium occurs when firms' economic profits are zero. If the industry is constant-cost, input prices remain constant no matter how much the industry produces. This means that the zero-profit price does not change and that the long-run supply·curve is horizontal. In an increasing-cost industry, expansion of industry output drives up input prices. The result is that the zero-profit price

is higher when industry output is higher. For this reason, long-run supply slopes upward. Conversely, in a decreasing-cost industry, long-run supply slopes downward.

5.   Pure competition, in which all firms have homogeneous outputs, gives firms powerful profit incentives to avoid racial discrimination. Any firm that discriminates would raise its costs of production. Since all firms are price takers, firms with higher costs would find themselves at a competitive disadvantage to other firms that do not discriminate. Those losses would tend to drive firms that discriminate out of the industry. In other market structures, the possibilities for excess profit in the long run or for product differentiation can allow discriminating firms to continue to exist and perhaps flourish if there is a market for that discrimination. For example, a whites-only restaurant would appeal to a different market segment than an integrated restaurant or a blacks-only restaurant. In pure competition, in contrast, the product is homogeneous.

FILL IN THE BLANKS

1.   industries, sellers
2.   Homogeneous
3.   Differentiated
4.   Monopoly, Oligopoly, Monopolistic competition, Pure competition
5.   market power
6.   Purely competitive, Monopolistically competitive, Oligopolistic, monopoly
7.   Numerous buyers and sellers, price taker, homogeneous, Costless
8.   supply, demand
9.   demand, horizontal (flat), market
10.   marginal revenue
11.   marginal cost, sums
12.   zero, normal
13.   equals, tangent
14.   right, increasing, decreasing market, zero
15.   allocatively, technological
16.   constant-cost, increasing-cost, decreasing-cost
17.   Constant-cost, Increasing-cost
18.   identical
19.   long-run supply
20.   horizontal (flat), upward, downward
21.   pure competition, monopolistically competitive, oligopolistic
22.   homogeneous
23.   state law, custom
24.   profit, normal, zero
25.   upward, go out of business

TRUE/FALSE/EXPLAIN

1. False, commodities are homogeneous products.
2. True.
3. True.
4. False, firms in oligopoly have more market power than firms in monopolistic competition.
5. False, a firm has market power to the extent that is able to set the price at which it sells its product.
6. False, pure competition involves no barriers to entry.
7. False, while barriers to entry are present in monopoly, oligopoly, and monopolistic competition, they are not present in pure competition.
8. False, given the large number of potential eating spots, the restaurant industry is a good example of monopolistic competition.
9. True.
10. False, by improving information flow and the competition that it brings, the Internet has reduced the market power of sellers of rare books.
11. False, a firm's short run supply curve is that part of its marginal cost curve that lies above its average variable cost curve.
12. True.
13. True.
14. True.
15. False, the long-run equilibrium will not occur until no more potential entrants expect profit.
16. True.
17. False, increasing the output in a decreasing-cost industry would cause input prices to fall.
18. False, in a decreasing-cost industry, the long-run supply curve would have a downward slope.
19. True.
20. True
21. True.
22. False, homogeneous products are less likely to be associated with discrimination than are differentiated products.
23. False, discrimination is most likely when markets are **not** characterized by pure competition.
24. False, since firms are priced takers in pure competition, they are motivated to keep costs as low as possible in order to maximize profit. To the extent that discrimination increases costs, it punishes a firm's owners by reducing their profit or causing them to face losses.
25. True.

MULTIPLE CHOICE

1.	a	8.	c	15.	b	22.	d
2.	d	9.	a	16.	a	23.	c
3.	a	10.	b	17.	d	24.	c
4.	b	11.	c	18.	b	25.	a
5.	a	12.	d	19.	d		
6.	d	13.	b	20.	c		
7.	c	14.	c	21.	d		

GRASPING THE GRAPHS
Examples of correct answers

1. Higher barriers to entry are associated with more market power.
2. Pure competition
3. Monopolistic competition
4. Oligopoly
5. Marginal cost
6. The firm's supply starts here (it is the marginal cost curve above the average variable cost curve).
7. Average variable cost
8. Market supply is the horizontal summation of all firms' supply curves.
9. The competitive output maximizes social surplus.
10. Surplus forgone from producing too little.
11. Reduction in social surplus caused by producing too much.
12. A constant-cost industry: changes in industry output do not change the firm's average cost; long-run supply is horizontal.
13. An increasing-cost industry: increases in industry output increase the firm's average cost; long-run supply slopes upward.
14. A decreasing-cost industry: increases in industry output decrease the firm's average cost; long-run supply slopes downward.

**Visit the Ayers/Collinge companion Website at <u>http://www.prenhall.com/ayers</u>
for further activities and exercises for this chapter.**

Chapter 10

MONOPOLY AND ANTITRUST

CHAPTER REVIEW

- This chapter examines the market structure of **monopoly,** in which one firm supplies the entire market. As the only seller in a market, a monopoly firm holds more market power than any other kind of firm.

10.1 Sources of Monopoly

- **A monopoly is characterized by a single firm selling an output for which there are no close substitutes.** Goods substitute for one another when they fill the same need. Whether there are close substitutes for a good or service is often not obvious.

- Monopoly is caused by very high **barriers to entry**, which exist when investors or entrepreneurs find obstacles to joining a profitable industry. Barriers to entry include anything that makes producing and selling output more difficult for a new firm than for an existing firm. Monopoly represents the ultimate barrier to entry—one so high that only one firm makes up the entire industry. The cause could be any of the following:
    - **Monopoly by law**—also called **legal monopoly**—when one firm is protected by law from competition, and there are no close substitutes for the good.
    - **Monopoly by possession**—when one firm is the only owner of a resource needed to produce a good, and there are no close substitutes for the resource or for the good.
    - **Natural monopoly**—when it is cheaper for one firm to produce the entire industry's output than it would be for two or more firms to produce the same output. Again, there must be no close substitutes for the good. Natural monopoly might be called monopoly by technology, as technological advances can sometimes replace it with competition.

- Barriers to entry bring about market power. This market power reveals itself in the slope of the firm's demand curve. If the demand curve slopes down only slightly, it is probably because there are many close substitutes for the firm's product, which leaves the firm with only a little ability to control price. Holding units of measurement constant, **the steeper the demand curve, the more is the firm's market power and the greater is its ability to determine price.**

- If the firm's demand is horizontal, it is a price taker with no market power. The firm would have market power if its demand curve slopes down. **Monopoly represents the most market power, in which case the firm's demand is identical to market demand.** The monopolist's demand would slope down relatively steeply.

- No firm's market power is absolute, because no firm can raise prices without reducing the quantity demanded. Even a monopoly will find that if it raises price enough, it will reach the point where the demand curve intersects the price axis. At that point, the quantity demanded equals zero. The firm would never want to raise price nearly that high. Rather, it seeks the price that will sell its profit maximizing quantity. For this reason, a firm with market power is called a **price maker**, in contrast to the price taker found in pure competition.

- Natural monopoly occurs when one firm can supply the entire market at a lower per unit cost than could two or more separate firms. This means that natural monopoly will occur any time that the minimum point on long-run average cost occurs near or to the right of market demand.

- **Natural monopoly occurs when there are substantial economies of scale.** A potential entrant will think twice about challenging a natural monopolist. To realize economies of scale, the entrant would need to start large, so large that the entrant and the established firm could not both survive. Water companies and local gas and electric companies are examples of *public utilities*, which have distribution lines of pipes, wires, and cables that have traditionally made them natural monopolies. Recent years has seen advances in technology that have eliminated or scaled back what were once thought to be natural monopolies.

StudyCheck 1

Using two separate graphs, show one natural monopoly that has declining costs throughout, and another that does not.

StudyCheck 2

Should government restrict entry into a natural monopoly market? Explain.

10.2 The Profit-Maximizing Monopoly

- In competition, firms are price takers and have only to find the intersection between the market price and their marginal cost in order to maximize profit. In the long run, competitive firms will have no expectation of profit by entering or exiting an industry. In contrast, monopoly firms must set the price and could potentially earn large and lasting profit.

- Recall from the elasticity chapter that total revenue is maximized when the elasticity of demand equals one, which occurs at the midpoint of a straight-line demand curve. Since the market demand is the demand facing the monopoly firm, it, too, would maximize its revenue when elasticity equals one. Even if production cost were zero, the monopoly would not produce any more than the revenue-maximizing output, since to do so would lower its total revenue, and thus its profit. With a positive marginal cost of production, the monopoly firm will produce less than the revenue-maximizing output. This means that **the monopoly firm always chooses to produce in the elastic range of demand.**

- **The rule of profit maximization for a monopoly is the same as for all other firms: produce at the point where marginal revenue equals marginal cost.**

- Marginal revenue is the slope of total revenue. Marginal revenue equals zero when total revenue is at a maximum since the slope of total revenue equals zero at its maximum. Maximum total revenue occurs at the same quantity associated with the midpoint of a straight-line demand curve. The midpoint is also the point of unit elasticity. Observe that marginal revenue slopes down twice as fast as demand, intersecting the horizontal axis under the midpoint of demand.

- For monopoly and other firms with downward-sloping demand curves and that charge a single price, marginal revenue is less than that price. The intuition is that, if such a firm wants another sale, it will have to offer potential buyers a lower price. The lower price would then apply to every unit of output that it offers for sale. The result is that the marginal revenue from an extra unit of output would equal the price of that unit minus the price reduction on every other unit sold. For this reason, **a downward-sloping demand curve is associated with a marginal revenue curve that slopes down even more steeply.**

StudyCheck 3

Using a graph, show why marginal revenue for a monopoly is less than price.

- To find its profit-maximizing price and quantity, the monopoly firm will calculate its marginal revenue at various quantities. It will then compare marginal revenue to marginal cost at each quantity. At some point the two must be equal, because marginal revenue declines as more output is produced and sold, while marginal cost rises because of the law of diminishing returns. Once the profit-maximizing quantity is determined, the firm will charge the highest price possible that allows it to sell that amount of output. This price is given by the point on the demand curve that corresponds to the output that the firm has chosen.

- Under monopoly, the quantity that will be supplied at any particular price depends on demand. Other things equal, the more elastic is demand, the lower will be the price it charges. The result is different prices associated with the same quantity, depending on demand. Since there is no unique relationship between price and quantity supplied, and unlike a firm in pure competition, **the monopolist has no supply curve.**

StudyCheck 4

Show how, for any given output, the monopolist's price will be lower when the elasticity of demand is higher.

- Monopolies can sometimes be quite profitable, since there are no other competitors to undercut their prices. However, merely because a firm is a monopoly does not mean it has a profit. A monopoly firm might find that the best it can do is to break even or even to lose money.

StudyCheck 5

Using a graph, show how a profit-maximizing monopolist can to do no better than break even. Show the quantity that the monopolist will produce and the price it will charge.

- Allocative efficiency requires that each good be produced up to the point at which its marginal cost of production just equals the marginal benefit from its consumption. Yet firms produce to the point where marginal cost equals marginal revenue. It is only because the market price is identical to marginal revenue for price-taking firms that pure competition is efficient.

- In contrast, at any given point in time, monopoly is allocatively inefficient because the quantity that equates marginal cost and marginal revenue falls short of the quantity that equates marginal cost and demand. The result is that the profit-maximizing quantity is less than the efficient quantity. The inefficiency, called **deadweight loss**, shows the benefits that consumers would have received from the additional output minus the cost the firm would have incurred to produce it. It is shown graphically as a triangular area.

- While the monopolist does not face competition directly, it does face the threat of *potential competition* from new producers or new products. If a monopolist prices its product too high, new substitutes may be developed that draw away the monopolist's customers. Alternatively, a new firm may take the risk of challenging the monopolist's turf. To avoid these possibilities, a monopolist might practice **limit pricing,** which is charging the highest price customers will pay, subject to the limit that the price not be so high that it attracts potential competitors. **The limit price will be lower than the short-run profit-maximizing price.**

- Although an unregulated monopoly will not normally produce an efficient quantity at each point in time, it does have the potential to generate profits that it could invest in research and development to enhance its monopoly status. Competitive firms have neither the incentive nor financial ability to pursue research and development. In addition, the lure of monopoly profit is a powerful motivating force for investment. For these reasons, the overall efficiency of monopoly is a matter of debate. While producing too little and charging too much in the short run, monopoly profits might bring about new and better products in the long run.

- The short-run inefficiency of monopoly could be eliminated if the monopolist were able to practice price discrimination in such as way as to perfectly match prices to the demand curve, where **price discrimination** occurs when a firm charges different prices for different units of output and the differences are not based on the cost of providing the product.

- Matching prices exactly to the demand curve is the extreme of **perfect price discrimination**, in which the firm charges a different price to each customer equal to the most that the customer would be willing to pay for the good to avoid doing without it entirely. In other words, the monopolist would capture all consumer surplus by charging the set of prices given by the demand curve. By choosing the quantity for which marginal cost and marginal revenue are equal, the monopolist would also be equating marginal cost and marginal benefit. The result would be an efficient output. Perfect price discrimination would require that the monopolist not only know how much that amount would be, but also be able to prevent customers that are charged low prices from reselling the product to other customers charged higher prices.

- Another example of price discrimination is **multi-part pricing**, in which the price depends on the quantity consumed. For example, the monopolist might set the price very high for the first units consumed, since those are the hardest to do without. Price for additional units could be lower. Since there is no competition, the monopolist would not need to worry about other firms undercutting its prices. If used in this manner, multi-part pricing causes marginal revenue to fall somewhere between the extremes of the monopolist with a single price and one able to practice perfect price discrimination. As a result, multi-part pricing can lead to greater efficiency. Multi-part pricing is often used by municipal electricity or water companies.

10.3 Antitrust and Regulation

- There are various ways in which public policy can address the inefficiencies of monopoly and protect consumers from unfairly high prices. The remedies include breaking up the monopoly, regulating the monopoly, and government ownership. This section discusses these policies and their drawbacks.

- By 1890, public outrage over various alleged abuses of the marketplace by the trusts led to calls for action. Congress responded by passing the *Sherman Act* by the overwhelming vote of 52 to 1 in the Senate and 242 to 0 in the House. This act is the foundation of **antitrust** law—public policies designed to limit the abuse of market power—and is enforced by the Justice Department. The focus of the act is on the conduct of a business, although specific illegal actions are not spelled out. In general, it prohibits contracts, combinations, and conspiracies in restraint of trade. It also forbids attempts to monopolize markets, but does not make monopoly itself illegal.

- The *Federal Trade Commission Act* and the *Clayton Act* were signed into law in 1914, thus completing the job of laying the foundation for today's antitrust enforcement. The Clayton Act supplements the Sherman Act by listing specific illegal actions, such as acquiring stock in a competing firm when that action would lessen competition. The Federal Trade Commission (FTC) was created to oversee markets, with the goal of eliminating unfair trade practices. Other antitrust legislation has augmented these laws by preventing firms from taking anti-competitive actions that would give them excessive market power.

- Be aware that both government and competing firms can file antitrust complaints. A violator of the antitrust laws can be forced to pay up to three times the damages it inflicts on other firms. It can also be fined, broken into competing parts, and its employees imprisoned. Sometimes accused firms will sign a consent decree, in which they agree to change their behavior without admitting guilt.

- **The antitrust laws neither make monopoly illegal nor apply only to monopoly. Rather, they are intended to curb abuses of market power**, of which monopolists have the most. They limit the manner in which firms can compete to what is efficient for society and fair to consumers and potential competitors. In considering what constitutes a violation of the law, the Federal Trade Commission will consider the practices listed in the following table. These practices, including the price discrimination we discussed in the previous section, are not intrinsically illegal. Rather, the behavior becomes illegal when competition is lessened in a significant way, without having overriding business justifications. This judgment is made in court and is known as *the rule of reason*.

Potentially Punishable Practices: A Glossary of Antitrust Terms

Exclusive dealing	A firm prohibits its distributors from selling competitors' products.
Exclusive territories	A firm assigns a geographic area to a distributor and prohibits other distributors from operating in that territory.
Predatory pricing	A firm prices a product below the marginal cost of producing it to drive rivals out of business.
Price discrimination	A firm charges different customers different prices for the same product.

Refusals to deal	A firm prohibits rivals from purchasing/using scarce resources (called essential facilities) that are needed to stay in business.
Resale price maintenance	A manufacturer sets a minimum retail price for its product.
Tie-In sales	A firm conditions the purchase of one product upon the purchase of another.

• If a monopoly is a natural monopoly, government will typically either own it or regulate it with **rate-of-return regulation** that restricts the monopolist from charging more than average cost. For this reason, rate-of-return regulation is also known as **average-cost pricing.** While it is marginal cost that is used to determine efficiency, average cost is often a close approximation and does at least guarantee that the firm will neither earn excessive profit nor go out of business.

StudyCheck 6

Using a graph, show how rate-of-return regulation can reduce the price charged by the monopolist to the point where the monopoly just breaks even. Show the profit-maximizing quantity and the actual quantity under regulation. Show also how this quantity might still be less than the efficient quantity.

- The regulation of industry by the federal government, undertaken to ensure "fair prices," has a long history. The Interstate Commerce Commission (ICC), disbanded in the 1970s, was created by Congress in 1887 to regulate the railroads, the primary means of transporting many kinds of goods at the time. In the 1920s and 1930s, as trucking took a larger share of the transportation market, it seemed natural to extend regulation to that industry as well. Airline regulation was also established as regularly scheduled passenger service took hold in the 1930s. Note that regulation was instituted even though these industries were not characterized by monopoly.

- A problem with rate-of-return regulation is that the regulated monopolist has little incentive to control costs or to provide innovative services. Thus, over time, regulation can impede change in production techniques and in the development of new products For this reason, rate-of-return regulation can cause technological inefficiencies even as it corrects allocative inefficiencies. Regulation can also have the effect of stifling new competition, favoring existing firms at the expense of potential competitors. For example, during the more than 30-year period that the airlines were regulated, start-ups of new airlines were few.

- To avoid the inefficiencies of regulation, economists recommend discarding the market process as little as possible. For example, it might be possible to award a **franchise monopoly**—a right to be the exclusive provider of a service—to the firm that offers to provide the service at the lowest price. In theory, that process should achieve technological efficiency as firms compete for the monopoly franchise. It would also lead to average-cost pricing without regulators needing to know anything about what average costs actually are.

- Instead of awarding a monopoly franchise to the lowest bidder in terms of price, franchises can instead be auctioned by local governments as a way of generating revenue. The result would be pricing above average cost, with the profit going to the locality. For example, some cities restrict taxicab service to one or a few companies willing to bid the highest for service rights. By restricting the number of rights granted, cities can generate monopoly profits for the industry that will be passed along to the city in the form of high bids for those rights.

- The concern that regulation breeds inefficiencies over time and sets up barriers to entry has led to the **deregulation** of some industries, in which government allows market forces to determine price and output. For example, the efficiency of air transportation was significantly increased by deregulation in the late 1970s.

- Deregulation of electricity has also become reality in some states, as technology has advanced to the point where the natural monopoly inherent in power transmission lines can be separated from the production of that power. Deregulation allows power providers the freedom to compete to feed electricity into the power grid, thereby keeping electricity prices as low as possible.

- As an alternative to regulation, the federal government has also engaged in government ownership of industry. The giant electric utility, the Tennessee Valley Authority (TVA), is a familiar example to those living in the southeastern states of the United States. The U.S. Postal Service is familiar to even more people.

- Many countries with a history of widespread government ownership have reduced that ownership over the last two decades. These countries, such as Great Britain, Russia, and Brazil, have turned to **privatization**, in which government turns over some of its production to privately owned companies. This can involve an outright sale of government facilities or merely the *contracting out* of services.

- In some instances, privatization may not be feasible because the industry is unprofitable, when there is no price that would avoid a loss, since the average cost curve is everywhere above demand. It might be in the public interest to *subsidize*—help pay for—production of additional output. Direct government ownership is not the only way to accomplish this task, but is often the one that is chosen.

E&A 10.4 **The United States Postal Service—A Monopoly in the Public Interest?**
- What is probably the oldest monopoly in America is rich in tradition. For instance, the first postmaster general was Benjamin Franklin, given the title by the Continental Congress in 1775, even before the creation of the Post Office itself. For more than two centuries the Post Office has grown along with the country.

- The Postal Reorganization Act of July 1, 1971 established the U.S. Postal Service from what had formerly been the Department of the Post Office. The Postal Service is overseen by a Board of Governors appointed by the President and approved by the Senate. It is intended to be self-supporting.

- In 2001, the Postal Service earned $65.9 billion in total revenue. If it were a private sector company, that revenue would have placed it as the 12th largest on the *Fortune 500* list of the largest U.S. companies. Unfortunately, that revenue was not enough to offset expenses of $67.6 billion, which meant that the Postal Service lost $1.68 billion. To try to make up that loss, in June 2002 the basic rate for mailing a letter increased from 34 cents to 37 cents. That increase of nearly 9 percent outstripped the expected inflation rate of about 4 percent. In addition to rate increases to enhance revenue, the Postal Service seeks ways to cut costs.

- Why has the Postal Service gotten into financial difficulty? On the revenue side, growth has been restrained because the volume of mail was decreased by the growing popularity of electronic mail and the 2001 economic slowdown. On the cost side, wage and benefit costs for the nearly 776,000 Postal Service employees have grown rapidly. At the same time, the number of new addresses that must be served grows by about 1.7 million each year. The cost of transporting the mail, attributable to increased energy costs, rose significantly in both 2000 and 2001. Following the discovery that anthrax-laced letters had been sent through the mail in late 2001, the costs of cleaning up anthrax-contaminated postal facilities also were significant, as are the continuing costs of irradiating selected mail to kill any of the deadly spores that might be mailed in the future.

* The result has been debate in the Senate as to whether first-class mail delivery should remain exclusively in the hands of the U.S. Postal Service. New Zealand (since 1998) and Sweden (since 1994) have abolished their postal monopolies, with Germany scheduled to soon follow suit. Even though the trend is toward greater competition in postal services, entrusting delivery of the mail to a governmental postal monopoly is still the norm in countries around the globe.

* The U.S. Postal Service is such a monopoly, guaranteed by the postal monopoly statutes and, according to some interpretations, even by the U.S. Constitution. Rivals such as UPS and FedEx are allowed to deliver packages and urgent correspondence, but must charge at least $3 per item or twice the Postal Service rate. Thus, the law is a barrier to entry that prohibits the rise of competition in postal services.

* The postal monopoly includes at least two elements of law that act as barriers: 1) control over household mailboxes, and 2) a monopoly on the delivery of first-class mail, which includes personal correspondence, post cards, and many business transactions. These restrictions explain why private companies do not deliver to household mailboxes, nor do they deliver your bills, or letters from friends and family.

* Even if the postal monopoly laws did not provide a measure of protection to the Postal Service through barriers to entry, it would still have a leg up on its competitors. Specifically, the Postal Service pays no federal income taxes, no state income taxes, and no property taxes. It can also violate certain government regulations with impunity. For example, the Postal Service is exempt from traffic and parking fines.

* *Privatization* of the Postal Service would be one option that might increase efficiency in mail delivery. Firms could then compete on an equal footing against one another to capture their share of the first-class mail business, just as they do for parcel delivery. Competition would force firms to seek to understand and follow the wishes of postal customers, and provide that service at a low cost.

* Privatization of first class mail delivery would have many hurdles to overcome. One of the first effects of privatization might be confusion, as a jumble of companies vied against each other for customers. Companies would find themselves on overlapping routes, and realize that combining operations would be more efficient by eliminating that overlap. If the postal services are a natural monopoly, only the one most efficient company would survive. However, we see more than one survivor in the package delivery business, so perhaps two or even more companies might be able to profitably coexist.

- Another hurdle is that the Postal Service is committed to *universal access,* in which mail service is offered at equal rates to everyone, despite some addresses being more expensive to serve than others. In this way, local urban delivery of first-class mail subsidizes delivery of first-class mail across greater distances and to rural areas. A more competitive marketplace would price on the basis of cost and eliminate this *cross subsidization,* in which the revenue from some services helps to pay for other services. Competitors would lower prices of the more profitable services and raise prices of the others.

- Dozens of government-provided goods and services have been turned over to the private sector in one place or another. Private sector provision of services such as garbage collection are testimony to the acceptance of privatization. Yet there is often resistance when services are privatized. The reasons are many.

- Privatization of the Postal Service might involve layoffs, which the postal workers' unions would oppose. Competition might lead to nonunion workers being hired, which would also be opposed by the unions. For these reasons and because of the public's high regard for letter carriers, Congress might find itself embroiled in controversy if it were to pass legislation to privatize postal services.

- With unrestricted privatization, prices of each type of service would tend toward the marginal cost of that service. Prices would be efficient, but whether they would seem fair might depend on the personal impact of the price changes. Politicians often worry about equity as well as efficiency, with equity commonly carrying the most weight in the political process. That process of choice is called democracy!

StudyCheck 7

Describe the most likely effects of rescinding the Postal Statues and allowing private companies to compete against the USPS in the delivery of first-class mail.

FILL IN THE BLANKS

1. A monopoly is characterized by a single firm selling an output for which there are no close _____, goods that fill the same need.

2. Monopoly is caused by very high _____ ____ _____, which exist when investors or entrepreneurs find obstacles to joining a profitable industry.

3. Barriers to entry include anything that makes producing and selling output more difficult for a new firm than for an existing firm. Monopoly represents the ultimate barrier to entry—one so high that only one firm makes up the entire industry. The cause could be any of the following: monopoly by _____ —also called legal monopoly—when one firm is protected by law from competition, and there are no close substitutes for the good; monopoly by _____—when one firm is the only owner of a resource needed to produce a good, and there are no close substitutes for the resource or for the good; _____ monopoly—when it is cheaper for one firm to produce the entire industry's output than it would be for two or more firms to produce the same output.

4. Barriers to entry bring about _____ power. This power reveals itself in the slope of the firm's demand curve. If the demand curve slopes down only slightly, it is probably because there are many close _____ for the firm's product, which leaves the firm with only a little ability to control price. Holding units of measurement constant, the _____ the demand curve, the more is the firm's market power and the greater is its ability to determine price. If the firm's demand is horizontal, it is a _____ _____ with no market power.

5. No firm's market power is absolute, because no firm can raise prices without reducing the quantity demanded. Even a monopoly will find that if it raises price enough, it will reach the point where the demand curve intersects the price axis. At that point, the quantity demanded equals _____.

6. _____monopoly occurs when one firm can supply the entire market at a lower per unit cost than could two or more separate firms. This will occur any time that the minimum point on long-run average cost occurs near or to the right of market demand.

7. Natural monopoly occurs when there are substantial _____ of scale.

8. In competition, firms are price takers and have only to find the intersection between the market price and their _____ cost in order to maximize profit. In the long run, competitive firms will have no expectation of profit by entering or exiting an industry. In contrast, monopoly firms must set the price and could potentially earn large and lasting profit.

9.   The rule of profit maximization for a monopoly is the same as for all other firms: produce at the point where _____ _____ equals _____ _____.

10.   Marginal revenue is the slope of total revenue. Marginal revenue equals zero when total revenue is at a _____ since the slope of total revenue equals zero at its maximum. Maximum total revenue occurs at the same quantity associated with the midpoint of a straight-line demand curve. The midpoint is also the point of unit elasticity. Observe that marginal revenue slopes down twice as fast as demand, intersecting the horizontal axis under the _____ of demand.

11.   For monopoly and other firms with downward-sloping demand curves and that charge a single price, marginal revenue is _____ than that price. The intuition is that, if such a firm wants another sale, it will have to offer potential buyers a lower price.

12.   Under monopoly, the quantity that will be supplied at any particular price depends on demand. Other things equal, the more elastic is demand, the lower will be the price it charges. The result is different prices associated with the same quantity, depending on demand. Since there is no unique relationship between price and quantity supplied, and unlike a firm in pure competition, the monopolist has no _____ curve.

13.   Allocative efficiency requires that each good be produced up to the point at which its _____ _____ of production just equals the _____ _____ from its consumption. Yet firms produce to the point where marginal cost equals marginal revenue. It is only because the market price is identical to marginal revenue for price-taking firms that pure competition is efficient.

14.   In contrast, at any given point in time, monopoly is allocatively inefficient because the quantity that equates marginal cost and marginal revenue falls short of the quantity that equates marginal cost and demand. The result is that the profit-maximizing quantity is _____ than the efficient quantity. The inefficiency, called deadweight loss, shows the benefits that consumers would have received from the additional output minus the cost the firm would have incurred to produce it. It is shown graphically as a triangular area.

15.   If a monopolist prices its product too high, new substitutes may be developed that draw away the monopolist's customers. Alternatively, a new firm may take the risk of challenging the monopolist's turf. To avoid these possibilities, a monopolist might practice _____ pricing, which is charging the highest price customers will pay, subject to the limit that the price not be so high that it attracts potential competitors.

16.   Matching prices exactly to the demand curve is the extreme of _____ _____ _____, in which the firm charges a different price to each customer equal to the most that the customer would be willing to pay for the good to avoid doing

without it entirely. The result would be an _____output. Another example of price discrimination is _____ pricing, in which the price depends on the quantity consumed.

17. By 1890, public outrage over various alleged abuses of the marketplace by the trusts led to calls for action. Congress responded by passing the _____ _____. In general, it prohibits contracts, combinations, and conspiracies in restraint of trade. It also forbids attempts to monopolize markets, but does not make monopoly itself illegal. The _____ _____ _____ Act and the Clayton Act were signed into law in 1914, thus completing the job of laying the foundation for today's antitrust enforcement.

18. The antitrust laws neither make monopoly illegal nor apply only to monopoly. Rather, they are intended to curb abuses of _____ _____, of which monopolists have the most. They limit the manner in which firms can compete to what is efficient for society and fair to consumers and potential competitors. Behavior becomes illegal when competition is lessened in a significant way, without having overriding business justifications. This judgment is made in court and is known as the _____ _____ _____.

19. If a monopoly is a natural monopoly, government will typically either own it or regulate it with _____ regulation that restricts the monopolist from charging more than average cost.

20. The concern that regulation breeds inefficiencies over time and sets up barriers to entry has led to the _____ of some industries, in which government allows market forces to determine price and output. Many countries with a history of widespread government ownership have reduced that ownership over the last two decades. These countries, such as Great Britain, Russia, and Brazil, have turned to _____, in which government turns over some of its production to privately owned companies. This can involve an outright sale of government facilities or merely the *contracting out* of services.

E✛A 21. The _____ _____Act of July 1, 1971 established the U.S. Postal Service from what had formerly been the Department of the Post Office. The Postal Service is overseen by a Board of Governors appointed by the _____ and approved by the Senate. It is intended to be self-supporting.

22. The U.S. Postal Service is such a monopoly, guaranteed by the postal monopoly statutes and, according to some interpretations, even by the U.S. Constitution. Rivals such as UPS and FedEx are allowed to deliver packages and urgent correspondence, but must charge at least $3 per item or twice the Postal Service rate. Thus, the law is a _____ ____ _____ that prohibits the rise of competition in postal services.

23. The postal monopoly includes at least two elements of law that act as barriers: 1) control over household _____, and 2) a monopoly on the delivery of _____-_____ mail, which includes personal correspondence, post cards, and many business transactions.

24. Another hurdle is that the Postal Service is committed to _____ access, in which mail service is offered at equal rates to everyone, despite some addresses being more expensive to serve than others. In this way, local urban delivery of first-class mail subsidizes delivery of first-class mail across greater distances and to rural areas. A more competitive marketplace would price on the basis of cost and eliminate this _____ _____, in which the revenue from some services helps to pay for other services. Competitors would lower prices of the more profitable services and raise prices of the others.

25. With unrestricted privatization, prices of each type of service would tend toward the _____ _____ of that service, meaning that prices would be efficient.

TRUE/FALSE/EXPLAIN
If false, explain why in the space provided.

1. Exclusive ownership of a unique resource with no close substitutes could be the basis for monopoly.

2. The best example of natural monopoly is a taxicab company.

3. A negative value for marginal revenue indicates that total revenue decreases.

4. The demand curve faced by a monopolist is vertical.

5. If a firm is able to sell any number of units of output that it wishes at a price of $5 per unit, the firm is a monopoly.

6.   The rule of profit maximization for monopoly is the same as for any other firm, which is to produce the output for which marginal cost equals marginal revenue.

7.   The price charged by a monopolist will equal the monopolist's marginal cost.

8.   For a monopoly, profit equals the difference between price and marginal cost, multiplied by the quantity produced.

9.   For any given quantity of output, the higher is the elasticity of demand, the lower will be the price charged by the monopolist.

10.   One unique feature of monopoly is that the monopoly can always generate a profit.

11.   A monopoly that breaks even produces at the minimum point on its average cost curve.

12.   Unless it is able to practice perfect price discrimination, a monopoly is likely to produce less than an efficient quantity of output at any given point in time.

13.   Price discrimination occurs when a firm charges different customers different prices because there is a difference in the cost of serving those customers.

14.   If the monopolist can practice perfect price discrimination, then its marginal revenue is the same as its demand.

15. Antitrust laws are public policies that are designed to limit the abusive market power by monopolies.

16. According to the antitrust laws, monopolies are by their nature illegal.

17. Federal courts have ruled that Microsoft Corporation is a monopoly.

18. Deregulation involves increasing the extent to which government owns the means of production so there will be less need to regulate private industry.

19. One form of privatization involves the contracting out of public services to private firms.

20. Rate-of-return regulation of monopoly is designed to provide a monopolist with a normal profit.

E⊕A 21. The postal monopoly laws are a barrier to entry.

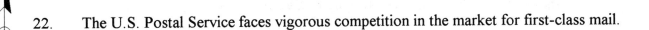

22. The U.S. Postal Service faces vigorous competition in the market for first-class mail.

23. There has been a public outcry in favor of allowing private companies the right to deliver first-class mail.

24. The argument in favor of privatization is that operating efficiencies could be captured and passed on to the public as improvements in both price and service.

25. With a competitive, privatized postal service, the price of each type of service would tend toward the marginal cost of providing that service.

MULTIPLE CHOICE
Circle the letter preceding the one best answer.

1. A natural monopoly occurs when
   a. government grants a patent to a firm.
   b. government prohibits the entry of new competitor firms.
   c. one firm can produce at lower average cost than can any combination of two or more firms.
   d. the product that is monopolized pertains to natural resources.

2. In deciding how much output to produce, the profit-maximizing firm with market power will choose the output for which
   a. average cost is minimized.
   b. marginal revenue equals marginal cost.
   c. total revenue is maximized.
   d. price equals average variable cost.

3. On a graph showing a firm's average costs and price, profit per unit equals _____, while total profit equals _____.
   a. the area of a rectangle; the area of a rectangle
   b. the area of a rectangle; the length of a line segment
   c. the length of a line segment; the area of a rectangle
   d. the length of a line segment; the length of a line segment

4. A firm with market power can be distinguished from a purely competitive firm in that the firm in pure competition
   a. sells all units at the same price, but the firm with market power must reduce price in order to sell another unit.
   b. has a constant average cost, but the firm with market power has a J-shaped average cost curve.
   c. will not maximize profit at the output where marginal revenue equals marginal cost.
   d. advertises, but the firm with market power does not.

5.   Profit for a firm with market power is calculated as
      a.   marginal revenue minus marginal cost.
      b.   marginal revenue plus marginal cost.
      c.   total revenue minus total cost.
      d.   price minus total cost.

Use data from the following table to answer the next four questions.

PRICE	QUANTITY	MARGINAL COST
$22	4	$5
$20	5	$2
$18	6	$3
$16	7	$7
$14	8	$13
$12	9	$20

6.   The marginal revenue from the ninth unit of output is
      a. $6.
      b. $4.
      c. $3.
      d.   -$4.

7.   The profit-maximizing quantity is
      a.   5.
      b.   6.
      c.   7.
      d.   8.

8.   If the total cost of producing 3 units of output is $90, the total cost of producing 5 units of
      output is
      a. $97.
      b. $150.
      c. $180.
      d. $187.

9.   If the total cost of producing 3 units of output is $90, the maximum profit for this firm is
      a. $80.
      b. $8.
      c.   -$8.
      d.   -$80.

10. Referring to Multiple Choice Figure 1, the monopolist will always choose a quantity of output that lies in range
    a. A, where demand is elastic.
    b. B, where demand is elastic.
    c. A, where demand is inelastic.
    d. B, where demand is inelastic.

11. At the quantity of output associated with point C in Multiple Choice Figure 1,
    a. the elasticity of demand is 0.
    b. marginal revenue is maximized.
    c. total revenue is maximized.
    d. profit is always maximized.

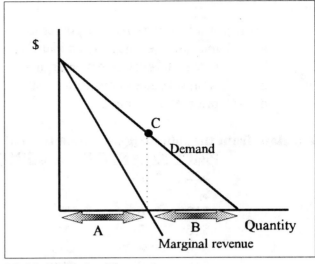

Multiple Choice Figure 1

12. The firm in Multiple Choice Figure 2 is most likely to be
    a. perfectly competitive.
    b. monopolistically competitive.
    c. an oligopolist.
    d. a monopolist.

13. To maximize profit, the firm in Multiple Choice Figure 2 will produce the quantity associated with point
    a. A.
    b. B.
    c. C.
    d. D.

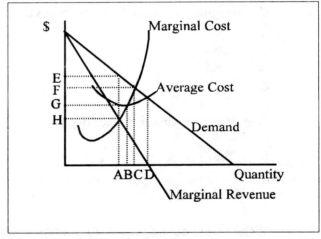

Multiple Choice Figure 2

14. To maximize profit, the firm in Multiple Choice Figure 2 will charge a price of
    a. E.
    b. F.
    c. G.
    d. H.

15. If the firm in Multiple Choice Figure 2 is maximizing profit, its profit will be equal to the quantity of output multiplied by the difference between points
    a. E and F.
    b. G and H.
    c. E and G.
    d. F and H.

16. In Multiple Choice Figure 3, the profit-maximizing firm would charge the price given by
a.   A.
b.   B.
c.   C.
d.   D.

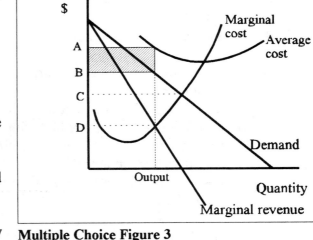

17. In Multiple Choice Figure 3, the rectangular shaded area corresponds to
a.   profit, which is maximized.
b.   profit, which could be increased by increasing output.
c.   loss, which is minimized.
d.   loss, which could be reduced by increasing output.

Multiple Choice Figure 3

18. A regulated firm that does not price discriminate and that produces the quantity of output shown in Multiple Choice Figure 4 would
a.   have a profit that is maximized.
b.   have a loss that is minimized.
c.   just break even.
d.   be producing an efficient quantity.

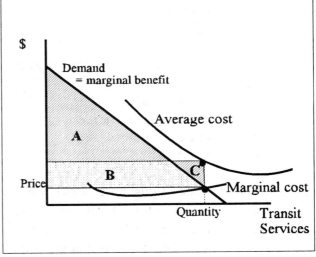

19. In Multiple Choice Figure 4, consumer surplus is given by
a.   area A.
b.   area B.
c.   areas A plus C.
d.   areas A plus B.

Multiple Choice Figure 4

20. Price discrimination
a.   results when an increase in costs forces a firm to raise its price.
b.   results when an increase in demand causes a price increase.
c.   is illegal in the United States.
d.   occurs when one consumer pays a higher price than another, and there is no difference in cost to justify the price difference.

E+A 21. Of the following, the best example of a monopoly by law is
    a. a local electric company.
    b. the U.S. Postal Service.
    c. AT&T.
    d. a local telephone company.

22. If a company offers to deliver non-urgent mail in competition with the United States Postal Service, that company would
    a. also find itself in competition with many other companies.
    b. also find itself in competition with just a few other companies.
    c. find itself in competition with no other company, because competition with the USPS would be unprofitable.
    d. find itself in competition with no other company, because competition with the USPS would be illegal.

23. Most of the budget for the United States Postal Service is spent on
    a. fuel.
    b. wages.
    c. equipment.
    d. advertising.

24. When one group of customers helps to pay for the provision of a good to another group of customers, the result is
    a. universal access.
    b. cross-subsidization.
    c. price discrimination.
    d. privatization.

25. Privatization of postal services is advocated by those worried about
    a. privacy in the handling of mail.
    b. inequities in the delivery of mail.
    c. inefficiencies in postal service practices.
    d. whether the free market could make a profit delivering mail.

GRASPING THE GRAPHS
Fill in each box with a concept that applies.

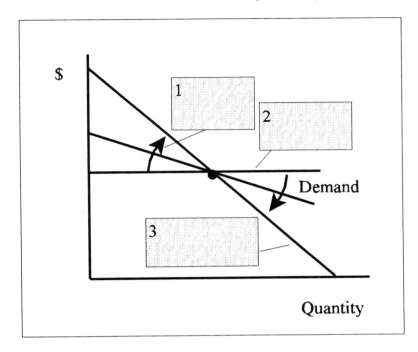

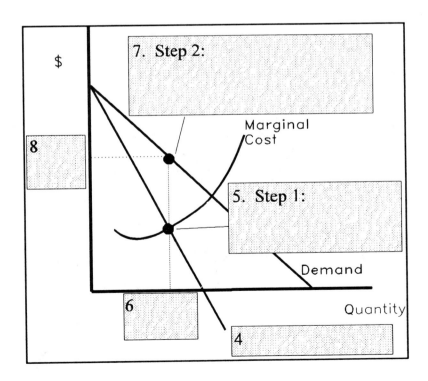

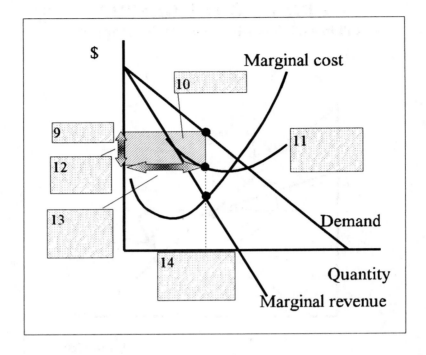

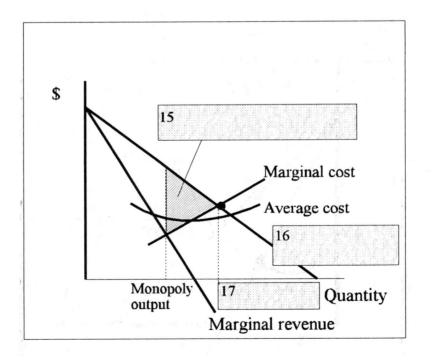

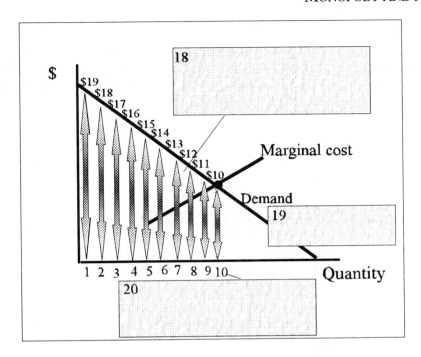

For additional practice in grasping this chapter's graphs,
visit http://www.prenhall.com/ayers and try *Smart Graphs* 25, 26, and 27,
along with *Active Graphs* 55 and 56.

ANSWERS

STUDYCHECKS

1.   See StudyCheck 1 Figure.

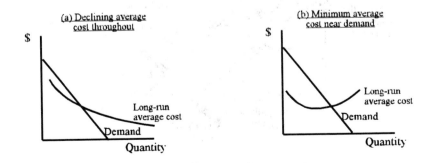

StudyCheck 1 Figure

2.   If a monopoly is a natural monopoly, there is no need to restrict entry in order to obtain a monopoly—it happens in the free marketplace. Because a single firm will have lower production costs than any combination of firms, competition to be that single firm will promote efficiency. Restrictions on entry remove the threat of potential competition and thus lead to technological inefficiency.

3.   See StudyCheck 3 Figure.

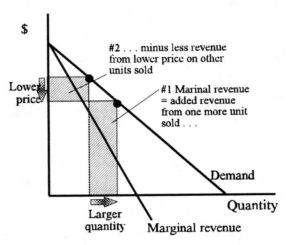

StudyCheck 3 Figure

4.   See StudyCheck 4 Figure.

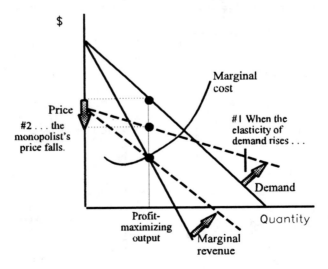

StudyCheck 4 Figure

5.   See StudyCheck 5 Figure.

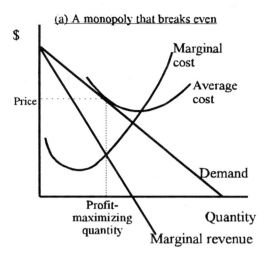

StudyCheck 5 Figure

6.   See StudyCheck6 Figure.

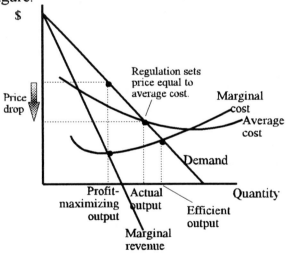

StudyCheck 6 Figure

7.   If competition were allowed, it is possible that only one provider would survive. This result would occur if first-class mail delivery is a natural monopoly. Whether a natural monopoly or not, first-class mail delivery would be different if government were to allow competition. One difference is that firms would compete to provide services at lowest cost. Another difference is that firms would compete to adapt their services to consumers' demands, such as by providing longer weekend service hours. Unrestricted competition would also eliminate cross-subsidization, such as the subsidization of high-cost rural services by urban customers.

However, competition could bring a confusion of choice and leave rural communities worse off, arguments in favor of retaining the status quo.

FILL IN THE BLANKS

1. substitutes
2. barriers to entry
3. law, possession, Natural
4. market, substitutes, steeper, price taker
5. zero
6. Natural
7. economies
8. marginal
9. marginal revenue, marginal cost
10. maximum, midpoint
11. less
12. supply
13. marginal cost, marginal benefit
14. less
15. limit
16. perfect price discrimination, efficient, multi-part
17. Sherman Act, Federal Trade Commission, Clayton
18. market power, rule of reason
19. rate-of-return
20. deregulation, privatization
21. Postal Reorganization, President
22. barrier to entry
23. mailboxes, first-class
24. universal, cross subsidization
25. marginal cost

TRUE/FALSE/EXPLAIN

1. True.
2. False, although a city might create a legal monopoly by awarding an exclusive franchise to one taxicab company, there are numerous competing taxicab companies in cities that do not create legal monopolies.
3. True.
4. False, the demand curve faced by a monopolist is the same as market demand, which is downwardly sloping.

5. False, a monopoly is not a price taker.
6. True.
7. False, the price will be given by the point on the demand curve that lies above the intersection of marginal cost and marginal revenue.
8. False, profit equals the difference between price and average cost, multiplied by the quantity produced.
9. True.
10. False, some monopolies are unprofitable at best.
11. False, if the best that a monopoly can do is to break even, it will find itself producing at the point on demand that is tangent to average cost. Since demand slopes downward, this point does not correspond to the minimum point on average cost, which would have a slope of 0.
12. True.
13. The false, price discrimination involves the firm charging different customers different prices when there is no difference in the cost of serving those customers.
14. True.
15. True.
16. False, antitrust laws do not outlaw monopoly.
17. True.
18. False, deregulation involves reducing the amount of regulation on private industry, not increasing government ownership of the means of production.
19. True.
20. True.
21. True.
22. False, the U.S. Postal Service is protected by a legal monopoly that prohibits competition in the delivery of first-class mail.
23. False, there is little popular outcry in favor of eliminating the monopoly status of the U.S. Postal Service.
24. True.
25. True.

MULTIPLE CHOICE

1.	c	8.	a	15.	c	22.	d
2.	b	9.	b	16.	b	23.	b
3.	c	10.	a	17.	c	24.	b
4.	a	11.	c	18.	d	25.	c
5.	c	12.	d	19.	d		
6.	d	13.	a	20.	d		
7.	b	14.	a	21.	b		

GRASPING THE GRAPHS
Examples of correct answers

1. Increasing market power
2. No market power, price taker
3. Monopoly has the most market power.
4. Marginal revenue
5. Produced the quantity of output for which marginal cost equals marginal revenue.
6. Profit-maximizing output
7. Charge the price given by demand at the profit-maximizing output.
8. Profit-maximizing price
9. Price
10. Profit
11. Average cost
12. Average profit per unit
13. Quantity produced
14. Profit-maximizing output
15. Short-run deadweight loss from monopoly
16. Demand = marginal benefit
17. Efficient quantity
18. The set of prices charged by the monopolist practicing perfect price discrimination
19. Demand equals marginal benefit.
20. With perfect price discrimination, the efficient quantity equals the profit-maximizing quantity.

**Visit the Ayers/Collinge companion Website at <u>http://www.prenhall.com/ayers</u>
for further activities and exercises for this chapter.**

Chapter 11

OLIGOPOLY
AND MONOPOLISTIC COMPETITION

CHAPTER REVIEW

11.1 Oligopoly—Domination by a Few Large Firms

- Oligopoly is characterized by multiple firms, one or more of which will produce a significant portion of industry output. Many oligopoly markets consist of just a few firms. Oligopoly firms are **mutually interdependent,** with the actions taken by one firm inducing other firms to take counteractions. Thus strategy and counter strategy is the norm in oligopolistic markets.

- Mutual interdependence frequently revolves around the pricing decisions of oligopoly firms. Mutual interdependence can also involve product design.

- **Oligopoly products may be differentiated or homogeneous.** Automobile production is an oligopoly industry that produces **differentiated products**—products that vary from one producer to the next. Output of oligopolies is not always differentiated, however. Steel, aluminum, and copper are homogeneous commodities produced by oligopolistic firms.

- Market power is the ability of a firm to control the price it charges for its output. Purely competitive firms have no market power because they must sell their outputs for the market price. Monopoly firms have the most market power because they have no competitors. In many markets, there is neither pure competition nor monopoly. For this reason we need a method to assess how much market power firms possess.

- One widely used measure of market power is the **four-firm concentration ratio.** To compute a four-firm concentration ratio, add the sales of the four largest firms in a market and divide by total sales:
  > Four-firm concentration ratio = (sales by four largest firms in an industry/sales by all firms in an industry) × 100

- A four-firm concentration ratio equals the percentage of sales accounted for by the four largest firms in a market. A four-firm concentration ratio cannot be greater than 100 since

100 percent of industry sales accounts for all the sales in a market. Since a monopoly market consists of only one firm, the four-firm concentration ratio must equal 100 in that case. An oligopoly with just two, three, or four firms will also have a four-firm concentration ratio equal to 100. At the lower end of the scale, a concentration ratio will approach a value of zero when there are many small firms in an industry. For example, when there are 100 firms of equal size in a market, the four-firm concentration ratio would equal 4.

StudyCheck 1

Suppose there are two industries, each consisting of 4 firms. In the first industry the largest of the four firms has a 70 percent market share. In the second industry the largest of the four firms has a 25 percent market share. What will the four-firm concentration ratio be in each industry? Is the concentration ratio misleading in this example? Explain.

- A **merger** occurs when one firm combines with another to form a single firm.

- In contrast, a *spinoff* has a firm splitting off a portion of its operations into a new company, or selling that unit to an existing firm.

- There are three types of mergers:
    - **Horizontal merger** occurs when a firm merges with another in the same line of business.
    - **Vertical merger** occurs when a firm acquires another firm that supplies it with an input, or acquires another firm that buys the product of the acquiring firm.
    - **Conglomerate merger** occurs when firms in unrelated businesses merge.

- The objective of a vertical merger that sees a firm acquiring one of its suppliers of inputs is to secure reliable delivery of the input. When the vertical merger instead involves a firm acquiring another firm that sells its product, the objective is to ensure a ready market for the firm's output.

- A conglomerate merger brings together firms whose lines of business have no obvious relationship to each other. Many large corporations produce a wide variety of goods and services, and so can be viewed as conglomerates.

- Mergers have antitrust implications. Horizontal mergers result in the elimination of a competitor. Proposed mergers must be approved by the U.S. Department of Justice before they are allowed to take place. The Justice Department examines merger proposals, especially those involving horizontal mergers, for their potential effects on competition in the marketplace. One question the Justice Department asks is whether prices will rise because of a merger. While policy in this area is somewhat muddy, it is safe to say that mergers that are deemed by the Justice Department to significantly weaken competition and raise prices are not allowed to be consummated.

StudyCheck 2

If a chain of cafeterias sought out a partner for a horizontal merger, what type of firm would it seek to merge with? If it sought out a partner for a vertical merger, what type of firm would it wish to merge with?

11.2 Oligopoly Models

- Oligopoly is the only market structure for which there are a variety of models. The appropriate model depends upon the specific circumstances of the industry.

- **Contestable markets** occur when new rivals can enter or exit the market quickly and cheaply. Contestability can characterize either oligopoly or monopoly. The "quick in and quick out" characteristic of contestable markets limits the ability of the firm or firms already in the market to raise prices. If prices become too high in a contestable market, entry of new firms will occur since such entry is easy. Congressional deregulation of the airline industry in the 1970s brought contestable markets to life in the airports of our major cities, as large carriers can enter or exit a city's market with relative ease. In contrast, the automobile industry is costly and difficult to enter and thus does not meet the criteria of a contestable market.

- The **price leadership** model is based on observable oligopoly behavior. In some oligopolistic industries, when one firm changes its selling price, the remaining firms in the industry copy that change. The firm initiating the price change is called the price leader; the copycats are termed followers. At one time or another the cigarette, automobile, and steel industries have exhibited the pattern of price leadership. In effect, the followers in a price-leadership oligopoly have voluntarily placed themselves in the role of price takers. They count on the price leader to set a price that will allow them to stay in business. In the remainder of this section, we examine in greater detail additional models of oligopoly.

- In analyzing oligopoly markets, we must go beyond the models of pure competition and monopoly. For example, OPEC (The Organization of Petroleum Exporting Countries) has played a major role in causing the price of petroleum and its products to fluctuate wildly over the past decades.

- OPEC is neither a price taker nor the only supplier of the world's oil, so neither the purely competitive model nor the monopoly model apply. However, used in conjunction with one another, the monopoly and pure competition models can actually reveal what motivates OPEC decisions.

- OPEC is made up of 11 developing countries that produce crude oil: Algeria, Indonesia, Iran, Iraq, Kuwait, Libya, Nigeria, Qatar, Saudi Arabia, the United Arab Emirates, and Venezuela. OPEC is an example of a **cartel,** a form of oligopoly in which firms in an industry collude (or in this case countries). *Collusion* means that firms jointly plan price and output. The objective of a cartel is to behave like a monopoly, increasing price to the profit-maximizing monopoly price. To achieve the higher price, the cartel reduces its output and assigns output quotas to its members. While cartels are illegal within the U.S., they exist internationally for such items as coffee, tin, and diamonds, in addition to crude petroleum.

- Cartels are difficult to keep together for three reasons:
    - While firms have a collective incentive to keep output low and price high, they have an individual incentive to take advantage of the high price and produce extra output. In other words, each cartel member has the incentive to cheat by selling more than its production quota under the cartel agreement. Alternatively, the member could simply leave the cartel.
    - If barriers to entry are not absolute, high cartel profits could induce competition from new entrants or existing firms who are not members of the cartel.
    - Over time, higher prices can lead to the development of substitutes for the cartel's product.

StudyCheck 3

List three reasons that cartels are commonly ineffective over time.

- The real price of oil today is much lower than the nominal price because much of the rise in the nominal price over time has been due to inflation. OPEC's market power became apparent during late 1973 when it allegedly withheld supplies from the world crude-oil market. The nominal price of oil tripled by 1974. Since then, OPEC's market power has fluctuated, depending upon demand and supplies of oil from other non-OPEC producing countries. OPEC's share of world crude oil production since 1980 is also shown. OPEC's share dipped during the 1980s before rising. Today, that share is only slightly lower than it was in 1980. Other things equal, a rising share for OPEC increases its market power.

- While OPEC tries to behave like a monopolist, it faces competition from many small price-taking oil producers who are not OPEC members. These include the U.S., Russia, Norway, Britain, and many other countries. To understand this aspect of OPEC behavior, we turn to the model of a **dominant firm with a competitive fringe**, an oligopoly model that combines the competitive and monopoly models. In this model, the dominant firm, typically the largest in the industry, has a cost advantage over many smaller fringe firms. The dominant firm has no control over other producers, and thus allows them to produce as much as they want at the market price. However, the production decisions of the dominant firm force that price to below what it would be if the competitive fringe firms were the only suppliers. This lower price allows the dominant firm a significant share of the market.

StudyCheck 4

In the model of the dominant firm with the competitive fringe, why are the fringe producers deemed to be price takers? Does this mean the market is purely competitive? Explain.

• In application to the world oil market, the competitive fringe consists of all oil producers that are not members of OPEC. OPEC behaves like the dominant firm. Its demand curve is called a *residual demand*, because at any given price, the dominant firm could sell the residual difference between the market quantity demanded and the quantity supplied by the competitive firms. For example, suppose the price of crude is $15 a barrel, and market demand is 6 million barrels per day at that price.   If the competitive fringe offers for sale a quantity of 1 million barrels of crude per day, then the dominant firm's demand would equal the difference of 5 million barrels. In other words, if the price were $15, OPEC would see its demand as 5 million barrels per day, the shortage in the market at that price. The price of $15 and quantity demanded of 5 million barrels would be one point on the OPEC demand curve. OPEC would compute its residual demand for all other prices in order to arrive at the other points on its demand curve.

• The residual quantity demanded is zero if price equals the equilibrium price under pure competition, where market demand and the competitive supply intersect. Below that price, the residual quantity demanded is positive. The dominant firm determines the actual price in the marketplace. It maximizes its own profit, by producing the output for which its marginal cost equals its marginal revenue. The dominant firm then charges the highest price on its demand curve that would allow it to produce that quantity. That price becomes the market price that faces the price-taking firms in the competitive fringe. The total quantity produced in this market is the sum of the quantities produced by the fringe and by the dominant firm.

• The mathematics of **game theory** can be employed to deepen the understanding of oligopoly markets. The method analyzes the behavior of parties whose interests conflict. The tool of analysis is the *payoff matrix*.

• In game theory, as in life, the outcome of one player's decision will also depend on a decision made by another. For example, a firm cannot predict the effect of a price cut on its profits unless it considers what competitors will do. If competitors leave their price unchanged, the effects on the price-cutting firm will be very different than if competitors cut their price to match or outdo the price cut of the first price cutter. As in poker, chess, and other games, many additional strategies also provide insights into oligopoly behavior. Some strategies are quite complex and involve the use of advanced mathematics.

• An example of a game is illustrated by the *prisoner's dilemma*. Two persons, Al and Happy, are suspected by police of being partners in crime. They are arrested, and an interrogation takes place in separate rooms, where each prisoner is told the following:

> *If your partner confesses, while you keep your mouth shut, we'll throw the book at you. Your partner will get off with 1 year in jail, but you'll do 20 years of hard time. On the other hand, if you confess while your partner keeps quiet, you will get 1 year of jail time, while your partner gets 20. If you both confess, you'll both get 5 years. If you both clam up, we've still got the evidence to send you away for 3 years in the slammer.*

• The following figure summarizes the situation in terms of a *payoff matrix* that shows the gains or losses from making a decision when mutual interdependence is present. The payoff matrix in the prisoner's dilemma reveals that whatever Al does, Happy is better off confessing. Whatever Happy does, Al is better off confessing. Guilt or innocence makes no difference. In the parlance of game theory, confessing is the *dominant strategy* for both Al and Happy. Collusion between Al and Happy, in the form an oath by both to keep quiet, offers a lighter sentence than the 5 years they both receive by confessing. However, the police have separated them for the very purpose of preventing collusion. The police have in effect stacked the deck, preventing the pursuit by Al and Happy of their joint interests.

Payoff Matrix—Prisoner's Dilemma

	Al confesses	Al keeps quiet
Happy confesses	Al get 5 years Happy gets 5 years	Al gets 20 years Happy gets 1 year
Happy keeps quiet	Al gets 1 year Happy gets 20 years	Al gets 3 years Happy gets 3 years

• To see how the prisoner's dilemma applies to oligopoly, consider an oligopoly with only two firms, X-co and Y-co, in which each firm must choose between a high price and a low price for its product. The payoff matrix might look as follows:

Payoff Matrix—Prisoner's Dilemma in 2-firm Oligopoly

	X-co chooses high price	X-co chooses low price
Y-co chooses high price	X-co gets $10 million profit Y-co gets $10 million profit	X-co gets $15 million profit Y-co faces $5 million loss
Y-co chooses low price	X-co faces $5 million loss Y-co gets $15 million profit	X-co gets $1 million profit Y-co gets $1 million profit

- The dilemma facing each firm is that it knows that the best collective solution for the two of them is for both to charge a high price. That solution would bring $20 million in profits to their industry. However, if X-co charges a high price, Y-co's best strategy is to charge a low price and earn a larger profit by pulling customers away from X-co. Y-co's profit would be $15 million and X-co would lose $5 million. Alternatively, if X-co were to charge a low price, Y-co's best strategy is to also charge a low price so as to avoid losing customers to X-co. Y-co would only earn $1 million in profit, but that would be better than a $5 million loss. Thus, charging a low price is the dominant strategy for Y-co.

- Charging a low price is also the dominant strategy for X-co, by the same reasoning. Whether Y-co charges a high price or a low price, X-co's best strategy is to charge a low price. Thus, the firms are led to each charge a low price and share equally in a $2 million profit rather than in a $20 million profit. So, even though each firm knows that their collective best interest involves charging high prices, they are led to each charge low prices!

- Because the firms in this example know that they are better off with high prices, they have an incentive to agree to each keep prices high. Such a bargain would involve collusion and lead to a cartel. The antitrust laws in the U.S. are intended to prevent collusion and thus keep prices low.

- Even if firms do form a cartel to keep prices high, the prisoner's dilemma game still comes into play. Each cartel member knows that by cooperating among themselves and raising price while cutting quantity, the member firms making up the cartel can achieve the greatest profit. But reasoned self-interest says that it pays to cheat on the arrangement by increasing sales through secret price cuts. If a member cheats while other members do not, the cheater is better off. If a member does not cheat while other members do, the honest member suffers. No matter what the other members do, a particular member of the cartel is better off by cheating. Cheating is a major reason that OPEC's power has dwindled over time.

- At any given point in time, it is always in each firm's interest to charge a low price, even if that means cheating on a cartel agreement. This drives the industry price down. Yet firms know that their long term interests are served by a high industry price.

- Fare wars routinely break out in the airline industry because it is in each carrier's self interest to undercut the price of its rivals and take away the rivals' customers. Yet the airlines know that the result is that the rivals do likewise and industry profits plummet. Although airlines are prohibited by U.S. law from colluding on airfares, they have various ways of signaling each other for their collective good. For example, airlines often raise prices, wait a few days to see if rivals match the fare increases, and then lower them again if they do not. In effect, such airlines are signaling their willingness to call off mutually destructive fare wars. Such signaling is not illegal and is widely practiced. The signals become illegal, however, when a firm sends direct messages to specific competitors.

StudyCheck 5

Describe the prisoner's dilemma as it pertains to oligopoly.

- Prices in oligopoly sometimes seem sticky, meaning resistant to change. The **kinked demand curve** model offers an explanation. In this model, any firm that raises its price loses a significant fraction of its customers to other firms that are assumed to keep their prices constant. However, if a firm lowers its price, it does not gain customers from other firms because the other firms in the industry would feel the competitive need to lower their prices, too. The result is that the firm would face a relatively flat demand curve for price increases, losing many customers to competitors that keep their prices constant. However, were the firm to lower its price, it would face a steep demand because its competitors would retain their own customers by matching the price drops. The result is a kink in demand at the current price.

- The mathematics of marginal revenue cause the marginal revenue curve to be discontinuous directly below that kink. Following the rule of profit maximization, namely to produce to the point were marginal revenue equals marginal cost, firms would ordinarily produce the quantity of output associated with the kink in demand. Even if marginal cost changes, it is likely to still intersect marginal revenue in the discontinuous portion and thus change neither are output nor price. For example, marginal cost could rise or fall within the range of the discontinuity without changing either price or quantity produced. For this reason, the kinked demand curve leads to so-called sticky prices, namely prices that tend to remain unchanged over time.

- The kinked demand curve model represents a particular kind of behavioral game. As with other models, the kinked demand curve model only applies when firms behave according to the assumptions of the model. One reason that there are so many models within oligopoly is that firms do not all play the same game or use the same strategies.

11.3 Monopolistic Competition—All Around Us

- Much of our time is spent dealing with firms operating in markets characterized by **monopolistic competition**, a market structure with many firms, product differentiation, and relatively easy entry of new firms. Many retailers operate in monopolistically competitive markets. In addition, many of the products they sell are also produced by firms in monopolistic competition.

- Monopolistically competitive firms face demand curves that slope downward slightly, because although they are the only providers of their version of the product, other firms offer close substitutes. The result is that firms have only a limited ability to affect prices.

- For this reason, the model of price and output determination under monopolistic competition is akin to that of pure monopoly, but with two exceptions. Each firm faces a demand curve that is:
    - highly elastic, which gives it a relatively flat appearance;
    - influenced by the firm's own actions and the actions of competitors.

- For example, the firm has the incentive to advertise and vary its product as a way of increasing its demand at the expense of its competitors.

- Like all profit-maximizing firms, the monopolistically competitive firm produces where marginal cost equals marginal revenue. The firm chooses the price on its demand curve that corresponds to the profit-maximizing quantity. Because demand is highly elastic, marginal revenue slopes down only slightly, too. One consequence is that, like monopoly, the firm does not produce the efficient output (given by the intersection of marginal cost and demand). Unlike monopoly, however, the monopolistically competitive firm chooses a quantity that is very nearly efficient in the short run. What's more, competition among firms also leads them to develop valuable variations on the product over time.

- Facing losses, monopolistically competitive firms look for ways to change their advertising or vary their product in order to get to profitability. These changes can potentially affect both the firm's demand and its costs of production.

- If the monopolistically competitive firm cannot cover its variable costs of production, it will shut down, just like firms in any other market structure. If the firm cannot find a way to eventual profitability, it will exit the industry in the long run. **Firms will continue to exit or enter until a long-run equilibrium is reached in which additional entrants would expect zero profits.**

- Monopolistically competitive firms do not minimize their average costs of production. Nor do they produce the efficient quantity. These deviations from pure competition are the price we pay for the diversity of choices that monopolistically competitive firms offer us.

StudyCheck 6

In long-run equilibrium, a firm contemplating entering a monopolistically competitive industry would expect to earn how much economic profit? Explain.

11.4 Ways to Compete

- It's a big market out there, or so it might seem to a firm in monopolistic competition or oligopoly. A firm in either type of market will be always on the lookout for ways to grab a bigger market share. The firm will also seek was of getting additional revenue from its customers. This section looks at some of the ways it achieve these goals.

- The firm's demand is always defined under the condition of *ceteris paribus*, meaning that everything except the firm's price is held constant. Since oligopoly firms are interdependent, each firm's demand will shift when its competitors change their prices and products. Likewise, the demand facing a firm in monopolistic competition will be affected by the availability of many substitute products of other firms in the industry. Unlike the firm in pure competition, however, the oligopolistic or monopolistically competitive firm is not a helpless victim of market circumstances. Rather, in these market structures, the firm can actively seek to change its own demand curve through the use of product differentiation and advertizing.

- The key to riches in monopolistic competition is successful product differentiation in such things as style, taste, shape, size, color, texture, quality, location, packaging, advertising, and service.

- The differentiated nature of products in monopolistic competition and much oligopoly makes it likely that firms will advertise. Some ads focus on facts, such as Yellow Pages ads with addresses, phone numbers, and hours of operation. On the other hand, much advertising is designed to work on consumers' imaginations and stick in their memories. Advertising slogans permeate our language. Successful advertising, slogans, and sales promotions increase the demand for a firm's version of the industry's output. In addition, advertising that creates customer loyalty for existing firms and their well-known brands forms a barrier to the entry of new firms. Successful advertising shifts demand (and marginal revenue) to the right.

- When advertising or otherwise differentiating its product, the profit-maximizing firm is still guided by the same principle that guides its choice of quantity of output: marginal cost equals marginal revenue. **If the marginal revenue generated by advertising exceeds the marginal cost of that advertising, advertising raises profits. Otherwise it does not. Similarly, the profit-maximizing firm will adjust its hours of operation, selection of merchandise, and every other aspect of product differentiation with this same principle in mind.** For example, if a store's marginal revenue from staying open an extra hour in the evening exceeds the marginal cost of staying open the extra hour, the store will choose to stay open that extra hour.

- You and your roommate are both flying home on the same airline and to the same city, but your roommate paid $200 more than you did . . . is there something wrong with your ticket? More likely, you bought your ticket further in advance and are the beneficiary of *price discrimination*, which is the selling of a good or service at different prices when such differences are not caused by differences in production costs. Price discrimination under monopoly was discussed in the previous chapter. Examples under monopolistic competition and oligopoly include discounts for senior citizens and students, and coupons that give those who redeem them lower prices.

- Price discrimination is feasible when different prices can be charged to different market segments. For example, it costs no less to screen a movie in a theater filled with children than to show it to adults. Yet adult ticket prices are usually twice those of children's, because adults are less deterred by higher prices—demand for adult tickets is less elastic than demand for children's tickets.

- A firm cannot practice price discrimination if buyers who are offered goods at a low price can resell those goods to other buyers at a higher price, called *arbitrage*. Everyone would then buy at or near the same low price. For example, pricing adult movie tickets higher than children's would accomplish nothing if adults could see a movie with a child's ticket. The only tickets that a theater could sell would be child's tickets, purchased by children and then profitably resold to adults at a price less than the regular adult price.

- There are various ways to implement price discrimination. For example, when airlines require Saturday night stays and advance purchases for flyers to get the lowest rates, much of the reason has to do with price discriminating between the leisure traveler with a relatively elastic demand and the business traveler who's demand is relatively inelastic. Airlines know that business travelers often must make plans at the last minute and rarely want to spend the weekend away from home. So requiring advance purchases and Saturday night stays is a good way of identifying that traveler. Merely asking at the counter if a person is a business traveler would not work, not when the penalty for a correct answer is to pay more—typically a lot more!

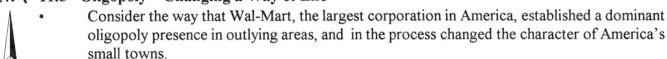

E&A   11.5   Oligopoly—Changing a Way of Life

- Consider the way that Wal-Mart, the largest corporation in America, established a dominant oligopoly presence in outlying areas, and in the process changed the character of America's small towns.

- Consider the four-firm concentration ratios for several categories of retailing. Depending on how broadly retail trade is defined, retailing is either very competitive or very concentrated. Retail trade itself is highly competitive with countless stores of all types vying for the consumer's dollar. When we look at discount stores, however, the four largest firms have an 87 percent market share. Of those four firms, Wal-Mart is by far the largest. Furthermore, Wal-Mart competes with other kinds of retailers, including electronics stores, nurseries, drug stores, and clothing stores.

- Drive through the heart of many small towns. Where there once were hardware stores, drug stores, and groceries, there are now vacant store fronts. To understand why, keep driving until you see the Wal-Mart at the edge of town. The homogeneous Wal-Mart "big box," each one virtually identical to any other anywhere in America, has superseded the differentiation offered by traditional local retailers.

- How did this happen? It was the collective choices of consumers in the free market. Wal-Mart offers reliable one-stop shopping, eliminating the need to crank up the car to make several trips to scattered stores. Just as the "milkman" of yesteryear was largely done in by the convenience of shopping in supermarkets, and the lower price of milk sold in supermarkets, many small-town merchants have found themselves done in by Wal-Mart.

- In spite of the benefits Wal-Mart offers shoppers, many communities have witnessed organized protests when Wal-Mart announces that it is coming to town. Protesters aim to keep Wal-Mart out of their towns. Growing bigger is, however, integral to the Wal-Mart philosophy of business. All other retailers are dwarfed by Wal-Mart.

- The Wal-Mart strategy for growth was simple and effective—find many small markets that it could dominate because there was no other large retailer in town, and then use that base to grow into the more competitive urban areas. In short, Wal-Mart became the dominant oligopolist of the small town, even as it was one of many monopolistic competitors in the big city.

•   Wal-Mart quashes both local flavor, and the personal ties between businesses and their customers that existed in the days when a merchant knew most customers by their first names. It does offer benefits in exchange: convenience, variety, and low prices. How are those low prices achieved? Wal-Mart's business plan emphasizes efficiency in production and distribution. Wal-Mart works with its suppliers to try to reduce their cost of production. Wal-Mart also strategically locates distribution facilities to keep down the cost of restocking its stores.

•   Some small-town competitors of Wal-Mart also claim a third factor is at work in those low prices: an illegal act called *predatory pricing*, pricing below cost to drive the competition out of business, and then raising prices later to recoup those losses. Whether charges of predatory pricing are true or not (they have not been yet proven in court), Wal-Mart's small competitors often have a difficult time staying in business. Wal-Mart has not achieved monopoly status in most small towns, though. The reason is that some competing stores manage to stay in business by offering product differentiation, taking less profit, and becoming more efficient. Likewise, there is competition to Wal-Mart from online or catalog shopping, but not without shipping fees and hassles of returning or exchanging items.

•   The transformation brought about by Wal-Mart in rural America is but a recent example of oligopoly as an agent of change. As observed by Joseph Schumpeter in his 1942 book entitled *Capitalism, Socialism, and Democracy* (1942), new technology provides the impetus for economic growth and higher living standards. "The perennial gale of creative destruction," as Schumpeter termed it, has supplanted one way of doing things with another for as long as mankind has lived.

•   Schumpeter hypothesized that a prerequisite to innovation is the market power conferred upon firms by oligopolistic market structures. Monopoly and pure competition are not well suited to initiate innovation, in his view. He perceived monopoly firms as possessing the wherewithal, but not the motivation, to conduct research, because monopolists lack the competitive pressures felt by firms in oligopoly markets. Schumpeter also thought that firms in pure competition and monopolistic competition lack the pool of economic profits required to finance research and development.

•   Viewed in light of Schumpeter's thoughts, Wal-Mart is at the forefront of the "gale of destruction" that is taking place in small towns today. Like earthquakes, tornadoes, floods, and hurricanes, the case of Wal-Mart is just the latest gale of destruction. Schumpeter would say to keep an eye out for more, because oligopoly and a changing way of life go hand in hand.

StudyCheck 7
What would explain whether Wal-Mart could be viewed as an oligopolist or a monopolistic competitor in your community?

FILL IN THE BLANKS

1. Oligopoly is characterized by multiple firms, one or more of which will produce a significant portion of industry output. Many oligopoly markets consist of just a few firms. Oligopoly firms are _____ _____with the actions taken by one firm inducing other firms to take counteractions. Thus strategy and counter strategy is the norm in oligopolistic markets.

2. Mutual interdependence frequently revolves around the _____decisions of oligopoly firms. Mutual interdependence can also involve product design.

3. Oligopoly products may be _____ or _____.
   Automobile production is an oligopoly industry that represents the former. Steel, aluminum, and copper industries that represent the latter.

4. Market power is the ability of a firm to control the price it charges for its output. Purely competitive firms have _____ market power because they must sell their outputs for the market price. Monopoly firms have the _____ market power because they have no competitors.

5. One widely used measure of _____ _____ is the four-firm concentration ratio. To compute a four-firm concentration ratio, add the sales of the four largest firms in a market and divide by total sales:
   Four-firm concentration ratio = (sales by four largest firms in an industry/sales by all firms in an industry) × 100

6.   A four-firm concentration ratio equals the percentage of sales accounted for by the four largest firms in a market. A four-firm concentration ratio cannot be greater than _____. Since a monopoly market consists of only one firm, the four-firm concentration ratio must equal _____ in that case. An oligopoly with just two, three, or four firms will also have a four-firm concentration ratio equal to _____. At the lower end of the scale, a concentration ratio will approach a value of _____ when there are many small firms in an industry.

7.   A _____ occurs when one firm combines with another to form a single firm. In contrast, a _____ has a firm splitting off a portion of its operations into a new company, or selling that unit to an existing firm.

8.   There are three types of mergers:
   •   _____ merger occurs when a firm merges with another in the same line of business.
   •   _____ merger occurs when a firm acquires another firm that supplies it with an input, or acquires another firm that buys the product of the acquiring firm.
   •   _____ merger occurs when firms in unrelated businesses merge.

9.   Mergers have antitrust implications. Horizontal mergers result in the elimination of a competitor. Proposed mergers must be approved by the U.S. _____ ____ _____ before they are allowed to take place. This government agency examines merger proposals, especially those involving horizontal mergers, for their potential effects on competition in the marketplace. One question asked is whether prices will rise because of a merger.

10.   _____ _____ occur when new rivals can enter or exit the market quickly and cheaply.

11.   The _____ _____ model is based on the case that when one firm changes its selling price, the remaining firms in the industry copy that change.

12.   OPEC is made up of 11 developing countries that produce crude oil: Algeria, Indonesia, Iran, Iraq, Kuwait, Libya, Nigeria, Qatar, Saudi Arabia, the United Arab Emirates, and Venezuela. OPEC is an example of a _____, a form of oligopoly in which firms in an industry collude (or in this case countries). Collusion means that firms jointly plan _____ and _____. The objective of a cartel is to behave like a _____, increasing price to the profit-maximizing monopoly price. To achieve the higher price, the cartel _____ its output and assigns output _____ to its members. Cartels are _____ within the U.S. Cartels are _____ to keep together.

13. The model of a _____ _____ _____ ___ _____
_____ is an oligopoly model that combines the competitive and monopoly models. In this model, the dominant firm, typically the largest in the industry, has a cost advantage over many smaller fringe firms. The dominant firm has no control over other producers, and thus allows them to produce as much as they want at the market price. However, the production decisions of the dominant firm means that the market price is _____ what it would be if the competitive fringe firms were the only suppliers.

14. In application to the world oil market, the competitive fringe consists of all oil producers that are not members of OPEC. OPEC behaves like the dominant firm. Its demand curve is called a _____ demand, because at any given price, the dominant firm could sell the difference between the market quantity demanded and the quantity supplied by the competitive firms. For example, suppose the price of crude is $15 a barrel, and market demand is 6 million barrels per day at that price. If the competitive fringe offers for sale a quantity of 1 million barrels of crude per day, then the dominant firm's demand would equal the difference of ____ million barrels.

15. The mathematics of game theory can be employed to deepen the understanding of oligopoly markets. The method analyzes the behavior of parties whose interests conflict. The tool of analysis is the _____ _____. An example of a game is illustrated by the _____ _____. Two persons, Al and Happy, are suspected by police of being partners in crime. They are arrested, and an interrogation takes place in separate rooms, where each prisoner is told the following: *If your partner confesses, while you keep your mouth shut, we'll throw the book at you. Your partner will get off with 1 year in jail, but you'll do 20 years of hard time. On the other hand, if you confess while your partner keeps quiet, you will get 1 year of jail time, while your partner gets 20. If you both confess, you'll both get 5 years. If you both clam up, we've still got the evidence to send you away for 3 years in the slammer.* In this game, no matter what the other person does, each person is better off _____.

16. Prices in oligopoly sometimes seem _____, meaning resistant to change. The _____ demand curve model offers an explanation. In this model, any firm that raises its price loses a significant fraction of its customers to other firms that are assumed to keep their prices constant. However, if a firm lowers its price, it does not gain customers from other firms because the other firms in the industry would feel the competitive need to lower their prices, too. The result is a _____ in demand at the current price. The mathematics of marginal revenue cause the marginal revenue curve to be _____ directly below that kink.

17. Much of our time is spent dealing with firms operating in markets characterized by _____ _____, a market structure with many firms, product differentiation, and relatively easy entry of new firms. Monopolistically competitive firms face demand curves that slope downward _____, because although they are the only

providers of their version of the product, other firms offer close substitutes. The result is that firms have only a limited ability to affect prices.

18. Under monopolistic competition each firm faces a demand curve that is _____ _____, which gives it a relatively flat appearance. Like in monopoly, the monopolistically competitive firm does not produce the _____ output (given by the intersection of marginal cost and demand), although it is very nearly so.

19. If the monopolistically competitive firm cannot cover its variable costs of production, it will _____ _____, just like firms in any other market structure. If the firm cannot find a way to eventual profitability, it will _____ the industry in the long run. Monopolistically competitive firms do not minimize their average costs of production. Nor do they produce the efficient quantity. These deviations from pure competition are the price we pay for the diversity of choices that monopolistically competitive firms offer us.

20. _____ _____ is the selling of a good or service at different prices when such differences are not caused by differences in production costs.

E&A 21. When we look at discount stores, the four largest firms have an _____ percent market share. Of those four firms, Wal-Mart is by far the largest.

22. The Wal-Mart strategy for growth was simple and effective—find many small markets that it could dominate because there was no other large retailer in town, and then use that base to grow into the more competitive urban areas. In short, Wal-Mart became the dominant _____ of the small town, even as it was one of many _____ _____ in the big city.

23. Some small-town competitors of Wal-Mart also claim a third factor is at work in those low prices: an illegal act called _____ pricing, pricing below cost to drive the competition out of business, and then raising prices later to recoup those losses.

24. The transformation brought about by Wal-Mart in rural America is but a recent example of oligopoly as an agent of change. As observed by Joseph Schumpeter in his 1942 book entitled *Capitalism, Socialism, and Democracy* (1942), new _____ provides the impetus for economic growth and higher living standards. "The perennial gale of creative destruction," as Schumpeter termed it, has supplanted one way of doing things with another for as long as mankind has lived.

25. Schumpeter hypothesized that a prerequisite to innovation is the market power conferred upon firms by _____ market structures.

TRUE/FALSE/EXPLAIN
If false, explain why in the space provided.

1. Mutual interdependence can occur in the realm of both pricing decisions and product design.

2. If there are 20 firms of equal size that make up an industry, the four-firm concentration ratio must equal 500.

3. A four-firm concentration ratio equal to 100 always indicates a monopoly market.

4. A four-firm concentration ratio that approaches zero indicates that the industry consists of numerous small firms.

5. If the Internet browser market once contained two firms but now contains only one, the industry concentration would have increased according to the four-firm concentration ratio.

6. Every merger also creates an equivalent spinoff.

7. Horizontal mergers reduce the number of competitors in a market.

8. If one computer manufacturer merges with another computer manufacturer, the merger is termed a vertical merger.

9. A contestable market is characterized by quick and easy entry and exit.

10. In the price leadership model, the followers of the price leader are in effect price takers.

11. Cartels are found in monopolistically competitive markets.

12. Cartels are illegal in the United States.

13. Members of a cartel have a collective interest in keeping price high, but have individual interests in charging a lower price than other cartel members.

14. The OPEC cartel's market power has remained constant over time.

15. The method of game theory is most fruitfully applied to the study of monopolistically competitive firms, rather than monopoly, oligopoly, or purely competitive firms.

16. Entry is difficult in monopolistically competitive markets.

17. Advertising provides a way to differentiate products.

18. Advertising may create a barrier to entry.

19. Firms can sometimes segment their markets, and price discriminate on the basis of demand elasticity.

20.   For price discrimination to be feasible, arbitrage must be possible.

21.   Wal-Mart's growth strategy involved creating small town monopolies.

22.   Wal-Mart has been accused of predatory pricing, which means that the retailer enters markets with high prices and slowly lowers them to increase its market share.

23.   Schumpeter's idea of the "perennial gale of creative destruction" is that no good can come from technological change.

24.   The "perennial gale of creative destruction" refers to the effects of misguided government policies.

25.   According to Shumpeter, the more competitive are markets, the more technological advancement is likely.

MULTIPLE CHOICE
Circle the letter preceding the one best answer.

1.   Mutual interdependence is a characteristic of
    a.   pure competition.
    b.   monopoly.
    c.   oligopoly.
    d.   monopolistic competition.

2.   If ten firms of equal size make up an industry, the four-firm concentration ratio equals
    a.   25.
    b.   40.
    c.   100.
    d.   250.

3.   A cartel is a type of
    a.   monopoly.
    b.   oligopoly.
    c.   monopolistic competition.
    d.   cellular phone.

4.   In terms of their long-term effectiveness, cartels are
    a.   able to consistently increase their market power over time.
    b.   pretty effective, since they were legalized in the U.S. during the Bush administration.
    c.   usually able to bring all producers into the cartel in the way that the OPEC cartel has all oil-producing nations as members.
    d.   hard to keep together.

5.   Contestable markets are characterized by
    a.   numerous firms, each holding a very small fraction of the market.
    b.   high brand-name recognition that prevents new firms from competing.
    c.   a need for expensive advertising before potential new firms attempt to enter the market.
    d.   potential new rivals that can enter or exit the market quickly and cheaply.

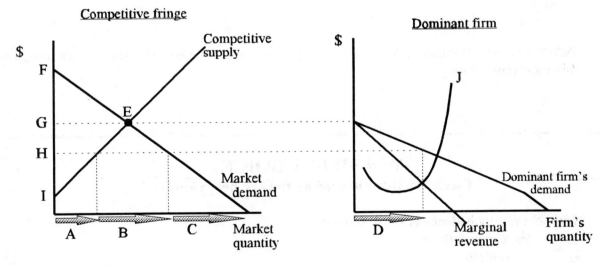

Multiple Choice Figure 1

6.   In the model of a dominant firm with a competitive fringe that is shown in Multiple Choice Figure 1, which two arrows should have identical lengths?
    a.   A and D.
    b.   B and C.
    c.   C and D.
    d.   B and D.

7.   In the model of a dominant firm with a competitive fringe that is shown in multiple Choice
       Figure 1, the quantity that will be supplied by the competitive fringe and equals the length of
       a.   arrow A.
       b.   arrow B.
       c.   arrow C.
       d.   arrows A + B + C.

8.   In the model of a dominant firm with a competitive fringe that is shown in Multiple Choice
       Figure 1, the starting point from which the model proceeds is given by point
       a.   E.
       b.   F.
       c.   G.
       d.   H.

9.   In the model of a dominant firm with a competitive fringe that is shown in Multiple Choice
       Figure 1, the price that will actually be charged by firms in the competitive fringe is
       a.   F.
       b.   G.
       c.   H.
       d.   I.

10.   In Multiple Choice Figure 1, the curve labeled with the letter J represents
       a.   the dominant firm's average cost.
       b.   supply by a single firm in the competitive fringe.
       c.   the dominant firm's marginal cost.
       d.   residual supply.

11.   Game theory focuses on
       a.   how the market structure of monopolistic competition allows firms to trick one
              another.
       b.   how the market structure of pure competition allows firms to trick one another.
       c.   the strategic interaction of firms in an oligopoly market.
       d.   the strategic interaction of firms in an purely competitive market.

12. In Multiple Choice Figure 2, the price charged by a profit-maximizing firm would be
    a.   A.
    b.   B.
    c.   C.
    d.   D.

13. In order to obtain the efficient quantity of output in Multiple Choice Figure 2, the price would need to be
    a.   A.
    b.   B.
    c.   C.
    d.   D.

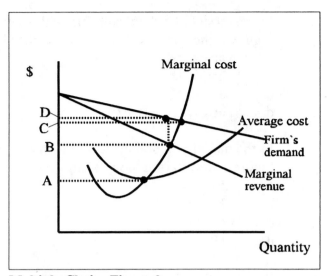

Multiple Choice Figure 2

14. We can tell that the firm in Multiple Choice Figure 2 is in monopolistic competition by observing that
    a.   marginal revenue is less than demand.
    b.   marginal cost intersects the minimum point of average cost.
    c.   the firm's demand curve slopes downward only slightly.
    d.   marginal cost is shaped like the letter J.

15. The vertical height of the profit rectangle for the firm shown in Multiple Choice Figure 3 would equal the distance between
    a.   A and B.
    b.   A and C.
    c.   B and C.
    d.   C and D.

16. The quantity given by point F in Multiple Choice Figure 3 is
    a.   greater than the quantity that would be efficient in the short run.
    b.   less than the quantity that would be efficient in the short run.
    c.   equal to the quantity that would be efficient in the short run.

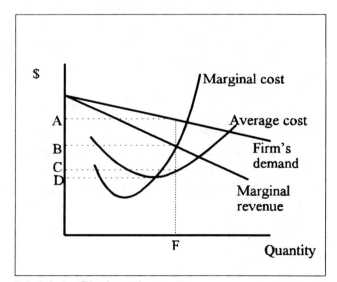

Multiple Choice Figure 3

d.   possibly greater than, equal to, or less than the quantity that would be efficient in the short run—we cannot know without further information.

17.   The shifts shown in Multiple Choice Figure 4 are most likely to be caused by
     a.   advertising.
     b.   higher wages for the firm's workers.
     c.   lower wages for the firm's workers.
     d.   the prisoners dilemma.

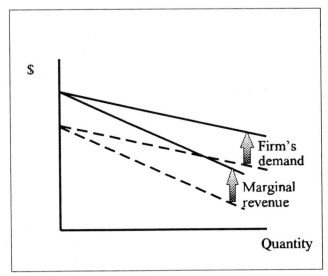

Multiple Choice Figure 4

18.   A conglomerate merger occurs when firms
     a.   producing the same product collude.
     b.   producing the same product combine.
     c.   in unrelated businesses collude.
     d.   in unrelated businesses combine.

19.   Price discrimination
     a.   results when an increase in costs forces a firm to raise its price.
     b.   results when an increase in demand causes a price increase.
     c.   is illegal in the United States.
     d.   occurs when one consumer pays a higher price than another, and there is no difference in cost to justify the price difference.

20.   If you ran a major U.S. airline and sought to maximize its profit, the fares you would charge a business traveler and a vacationer would most likely be
     a.   the same.
     b.   different, with the vacationer charged the higher fare.
     c.   different, with the business traveler charged the higher fare.
     d.   sometimes the same and sometimes different in order to keep em guessing.

E&A   21.   Which statement is correct about retailing?
     a.   Concentration in retailing in general is very high.
     b.   Concentration in discount stores is very high.
     c.   Wal-Mart competes only with other discount stores.
     d.   Wal-Mart is a retail monopoly wherever its stores are located.

22.   Wal-Mart has been accused by its critics of predatory pricing, which is
       a.   legal.
       b.   illegal.
       c.   legal in some towns, but illegal in others.
       d.   legal in some states, but illegal in others.

23.   Which market structure is most conducive to the development of new technologies according
       to Schumpeter?
       a.   Pure competition.
       b.   Monopoly.
       c.   Oligopoly.
       d.   Monopolistic Competition.

24.   Wal-Mart is
       a.   a monopoly in most small towns, but not big cities.
       b.   not a monopoly in most small towns because of competition.
       c.   a monopoly in most small towns and most big cities.
       d.   a monopolistic competitor in most small towns, but an oligopolist in most big cities.

25.   According to Schumpeter, to start the "perennial gale of creative destruction" requires that
       firms have
       a.   a weather forecast handy.
       b.   government assistance.
       c.   a pool of economic profits.
       d.   a detailed knowledge of world history.

GRASPING THE GRAPHS
Fill in each box with a concept that applies.

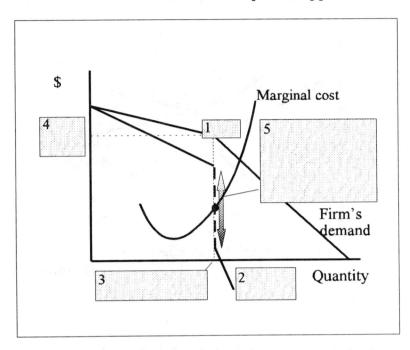

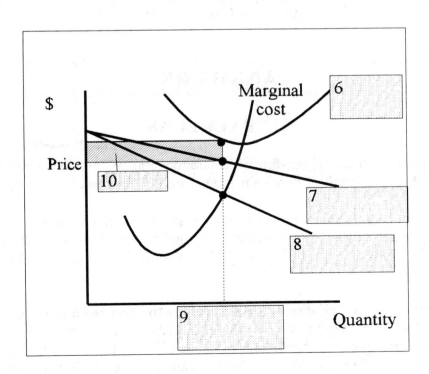

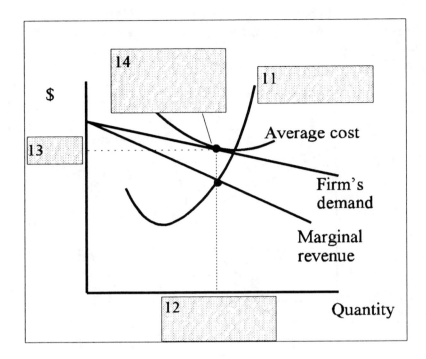

For additional practice in grasping this chapter's graphs, visit
http://www.prenhall.com/ayers and try *Smart Graphs* 28, 29, and 30,
along with *Active Graphs* 57, 58, and 59.

ANSWERS

STUDYCHECKS

1.   Both industries will have a four-firm concentration ratio of 100. This is misleading since the industry where the largest firm has a market share of 70 percent is more concentrated.

2.   Seeking a horizontal merger, it would look for another cafeteria chain to merger with. If it seeks a vertical merger, then it would look toward one of its suppliers to merge with. Perhaps the produce company that supplies it with fresh vegetables would be targeted to merge with.

3.   One reason is that member firms have an incentive to cheat and increase output in order to take advantage of the higher price caused by the cartel. Another reason is that higher prices attract new sources of supply of that are outside of the cartel. A third reason is that higher prices cause consumers to seek out substitutes and firms to develop substitutes over time.

4.   The fringe firms are price takers because they have no market power, and so they follow the price set by the dominant firm. The market is an oligopoly because the dominant firm does have significant market power

5.   The prisoner's dilemma is an example of game theory, in which each player operates independently but knows what is in the collective interest. In application to oligopoly, each firm knows that joint profits are maximized by setting the monopoly price. Each firm also knows that, individually, it could do better to set its price a little lower and gain market share. However, if each firm acts in this manner, the net effect is that both firms are worse off.

6.   Expected economic profit equals zero because of the relatively easy entry in monopolistic competition. Lack of expected economic profit means that entry ceases when the market is in long-run equilibrium.

7.   The number of other significant sellers in the market place and the degree of mutual interdependence would help you to determine the market in your community. The more retailers that compete with Wal-Mart, the closer the market will be to monopolistic competition. For example, the presence of Lowe's, Home Depot, K-Mart, Target, Old Navy, and other large retail chains in your community makes Wal-Mart one of a number of monopolistic competitors.

FILL IN THE BLANKS

1.   mutually interdependent
2.   pricing
3.   differentiated, homogeneous
4.   zero, most
5.   market power
6.   100, 100, 100, zero
7.   merger, spinoff
8.   Horizontal, Vertical, Conglomerate
9.   Department of Justice
10.   Contestable markets
11.   price leadership
12.   cartel, price, output, monopoly, reduces, quotas, illegal, difficult
13.   dominant firm with a competitive fringe, below
14.   residual, 5
15.   payoff matrix, prisoner's dilemma, confessing
16.   sticky, kinked, kink, discontinuous
17.   monopolistic competition, slightly
18.   highly elastic, efficient

19. shut down, exit
20. Price discrimination
21. 87
22. oligopolist, monopolistic competitors
23. predatory
24. technology
25. oligopolistic

TRUE/FALSE/EXPLAIN

1. True.
2. False, the four-firm concentration ratio would equal 20. Each firm would have a 5 percent market share since there are 20 firms of equal size. Any four firms would thus have a 20 percent market share.
3. False, although a monopoly market would have a four-firm concentration ratio of 100, so would an oligopoly market of two, three, or four firms.
4. True.
5. False, in either case the four-firm concentration ratio would be zero.
6. False, mergers combine firms while spinoffs separate them.
7. True.
8. False, the merger is horizontal.
9. True.
10. True.
11. False, cartels are found in oligopoly markets.
12. True.
13. True.
14. False, the OPEC cartel's market power has fluctuated over time.
15. False, game theory is most applicable in oligopoly.
16. False, entry is relatively easy in monopolistic competition, as evidenced by the large number of firms.
17. True.
18. True.
19. True.
20. False, arbitrage (buying low and selling high) must be difficult or impossible for price discrimination to work.
21. False, Wal-Mart was a small town oligopolist.
22. False, predatory pricing involves pricing low to drive competitors out of business.
23. False, technological changes improves living standards.
24. False, the "perennial gale of creative destruction" refers to changes in ways of doing things.
25. False, Schumpeter believed that oligopoly markets would be the most likely to initiate technological change.

MULTIPLE CHOICE

1.	c	8.	a	15.	b	22.	b
2.	b	9.	c	16.	b	23.	c
3.	b	10.	c	17.	a	24.	b
4.	d	11.	c	18.	d	25.	c
5.	d	12.	d	19.	d		
6.	d	13.	c	20.	c		
7.	a	14.	c	21.	b		

GRASPING THE GRAPHS
Examples of correct answers

1. Kink
2. Marginal revenue
3. Profit-maximizing quantity
4. Sticky price
5. Marginal cost can vary within this range without affecting quantity or price.
6. Average cost
7. The firm's demand
8. Marginal revenue
9. Loss-minimizing quantity
10. Loss
11. Marginal cost
12. Profit-maximizing quantity
13. Price
14. Breakeven is the best this firm can do.

**Visit the Ayers/Collinge companion Website at http://www.prenhall.com/ayers
for further activities and exercises for this chapter.**

Part 4

INPUT MARKETS

Chapter 12

MARKETS FOR LABOR
AND OTHER INPUTS

CHAPTER REVIEW

- The *labor market* involves the exchange of labor services. **Unlike the product market, in which firms are sellers and individuals are buyers, in the labor market firms purchase labor services and individuals supply their labor services to firms.**

- The market price of labor services is the *wage rate*—the amount an employee is paid per hour. The quantity of labor services is usually measured by the number of hours of labor services exchanged in the marketplace.

12.1 The Market Demand for Labor—A Derived Demand

- A market demand curve for labor shows the quantity of labor that employers in a labor market wish to employ at various wage rates. The lower is the wage rate, other things equal, the greater will be the quantity of labor demanded.

- **Labor demand slopes downward, meaning that higher wage rates decrease the quantity of labor demanded, whereas lower wage rates increase the quantity of labor demanded.**

- Economists often study the labor demands in three distinct labor market segments:
  - *By occupation:* Occupational labor demands are distinct for dissimilar occupations because labor is associated with human capital that is specific to the occupation—*specific human capital.*
  - *By geography:* The demand for labor varies geographically because of differences in the economies of towns and regions.
  - *By industry:* An industry demand curve for labor shows the quantity of labor employed by all firms in an industry at various wage rates. Various industries may compete for the same pool of workers.

- Labor demand is a **derived demand,** which means the demand for labor exists only because there is a demand for an employer's output. Other things equal, an increase in the demand for a good will increase the demand for labor in that industry.

StudyCheck 1

Explain why labor demand is termed "derived demand."

12.2 The Equilibrium Wage Rate

- Workers supply their labor to the labor market in exchange for the wages and salaries that they can earn. The positive slope of the market supply of labor tells us that higher wage rates attract a greater quantity of labor supplied. Just as labor demand can vary by occupation, area, and industry, so too can labor supply.

- The market demand for labor together with the market supply determine the market wage rate. The market wage rate is also called the *equilibrium wage rate,* since this wage rate results in the quantity demanded of labor being equal to the quantity supplied of labor. A market wage rate higher than the equilibrium wage rate causes a surplus of labor. Likewise, a market wage rate below the equilibrium wage rate causes a shortage of labor.

- The equilibrium wage rate will change when there is a change in labor demand or supply. The market wage rate will increase when there is an increase in labor demand or a decrease in labor supply. A lower market wage rate is brought about by a decrease in labor demand or an increase in labor supply.

- A **purely competitive labor market** exists when the demand for labor and the supply of labor establish an equilibrium wage rate and quantity of labor. Characteristics include the following:
  - There are many buyers and sellers of labor services in the market.
  - The services of labor are homogeneous.
  - The labor market is free of barriers to entry and exit.

- In a purely competitive labor market, employers are *wage takers,* which means that each will be able to hire as much or as little labor as it wishes at the going market wage rate. **Since one employer by itself cannot influence this market wage rate, employers that are wage takers are said to have zero market power over wages.**

- **For a wage-taking firm, the wage rate is the supply curve of labor to the firm.** In other words, the firm can purchase as many units of labor as it wishes at the market wage rate.

- The value to the firm of any given worker's labor is the revenue resulting from the sale of that worker's marginal product. This added revenue is termed the **marginal revenue product of labor**, defined as the increase in the firm's total revenue arising from the employment of an additional unit of labor. Marginal revenue product can be computed in two ways:
  (a) Marginal revenue product = change in total revenue ÷ change in labor
  or
  (b) Marginal revenue product = marginal revenue × marginal product.
  Which ever way it is computed, **marginal revenue product measures the value of an additional unit of labor to the firm.** The marginal revenue product curve slopes downward as more labor is employed.

- If the firm is not a price taker in the output market then it is a *price maker*. Price making occurs in monopoly, oligopoly, and monopolistically competitive markets. The computation of marginal revenue product for a price maker is slightly more complicated than when the firm is a price taker. Rather than multiplying marginal product by price to compute marginal revenue product, instead marginal product is multiplied by marginal revenue. The reason is that, for a price maker, marginal revenue is less than price.

- The result is that the marginal revenue product curves for price making firms slope downward more steeply than for their purely competitive counterparts. There are two reasons for the downward slope when the firm is a price maker. First, as in the case of the price taker, the marginal product of labor decreases as the quantity of labor is increased. Second, for a price maker, price must be decreased in order to sell the additional output that is produced when more labor is employed. The decrease in price also contributes to the decrease in marginal revenue product.

- To understand how much labor the firm will employ, we must introduce one more concept. The **marginal cost of labor** equals the addition to total cost when there is a one unit increase in the quantity of labor. *Wage taking* firms purchase each unit of labor services at the market wage rate. **The market wage rate equals the marginal cost of labor for a wage taker**. For example, if the market wage rate is $16 per unit of labor, adding any additional unit of labor will always increase the firm's total cost by $16. Thus, the marginal cost of labor is $16 in this instance. When the market wage rate changes because of shifts in the market demand and supply of labor, the marginal cost of labor to the firm will change to match the new market wage rate.

- A firm will employ the quantity of labor that maximizes its profit. This quantity of labor can be determined by comparing the marginal revenue product of each unit of labor to its marginal cost: Profit maximization requires a firm to hire additional units of labor so long as labor's marginal revenue product equals or exceeds its marginal cost. Thus, the firm follows the following hiring rule:

Hiring Rule

Hire up to and including but not beyond the point for which marginal revenue product equals the marginal cost of labor.

- In other words, a firm continues adding labor as long as the revenue it receives from the output produced by one more unit of labor is at least sufficient to cover the added cost resulting from employing that unit of labor. The firm aims to employ labor at the point where the marginal revenue product is equal to the marginal cost of labor.

- If there is no quantity of labor that exactly satisfies the equality stated in the hiring rule, the firm will stop hiring when the next hire's marginal revenue product would be less than the marginal cost of labor. After all, firms do not want to pay someone more than the market value of that person's output.

- When the firm is a wage taker in the labor market, the marginal cost of labor curve is horizontal (perfectly elastic). **The marginal revenue product curve is also the firm's demand curve for labor because it shows how much labor the firm will employ at various wage rates.** The firm's labor demand curve is downward sloping.

- The firm's labor demand curve may shift. For example, *ceteris paribus*, a price-taking firm will increase its demand for labor if the market price of the firm's output increases or if the marginal product of the firm's labor increases. Labor demand would decrease if the price of output fell or if the marginal product of labor decreased.

StudyCheck 2					
Fill in the table and answer the questions that follow.					
Number of Workers	**Output**	**Marginal Product**	**Output Price ($)**	**Total Revenue ($)**	**Marginal Revenue Product ($)**
0	0		3		
1	8		3		
2	15		3		
3	21		3		
4	26		3		
5	30		3		

a. Suppose the wage rate is constant at $17 per hour. How many workers would this firm employ? _____

b. Suppose the wage rate is constant at $15.01. How many workers would be hired? _____

c. What is the maximum wage consistent with all five workers being hired? _____

d. Does your work suggest that the firm's derived demand curve for labor is its marginal revenue product schedule? Explain.

StudyCheck 3

Using a graph for reference, show the level of employment for a wage taking firm. Be sure to label the axes.

12.3 Market Power Over the Wage Rate

- Just as there are four types of output markets, so there are four types of labor markets. The type of market in which a firm sells its output does not determine the type of market in which it buys its labor inputs.

- The model of pure competition in the labor market assumes that both employers and employees are wage takers, meaning that they have no market power over the wage rate. However, market power is often present in the labor market and can drive wage rates either up or down from the competitive level. To the extent that workers gain control of the labor market, the wage rate will increase to more than the competitive level. The wage rate will decrease to less than the competitive level to the extent that employers dominate. These effects are captured in the following labor market models:
  - **monopsony**—only one employer of labor services;
  - **monopoly**—only one seller of labor services, a labor union;
  - **bilateral monopoly**—only one employer and only one seller of labor services.

- In the labor market, a firm can have market power over the wage rate. Fewness of employers creates *monopsony power* for firms. **Monopsony employers are able to pay workers less than the competitive wage rate.** The extreme case of monopsony is *pure monopsony*—one buyer of labor's services. The best example of monopsony occurs in geographically isolated mill towns. The mill provides a reason for the town to exist because most of its citizens work there. As the major employer, the mill can offer less than the competitive wage rate to prospective workers. Highly specialized types of labor, such as astronauts or fighter pilots, may also face monopsony in their country's labor market.

- Consider a pure monopsony firm—the only employer of labor in a labor market. The marginal cost of labor curve is upward sloping rather than horizontal as in the case of pure competition in the labor market. Note that, **unlike in the purely competitive labor market, the marginal cost of labor exceeds the wage rate in monopsony.** The reason is that employing additional workers increases the wage rate paid to all workers, not just to the additional workers.

- The monopsonist will follow the profit-maximizing rule, which says to employ labor to the point where the marginal revenue product equals the marginal cost of labor. The monopsonist makes its hiring decision in the following two steps:
  - Step 1: It employs the amount of labor for which the marginal cost of labor equals marginal revenue product.
  - Step 2: It pays as little as possible for that labor. The wage rate is given by the supply curve of labor at the quantity of labor chosen in step 1.

- Note that if a monopsonized labor market could be transformed into a purely competitive one, the employment of labor would increase to the point where the supply and demand curves for labor intersect. This demonstrates that **monopsony labor markets are characterized by less**

employment and a lower wage rate than are purely competitive labor markets. These aspects of monopsony have sometimes led economists to refer to the "exploitation" of labor by monopsony employers.

StudyCheck 4
Using a graph for reference, explain why a monopsonist hires fewer workers than would a competitive firm. Be sure to label the axes.

- Monopolies in the output market possess market power because of they can raise prices above the level indicated by the intersection of supply and demand. Monopolies are able to command a higher price for their output by reducing the supply of output. *Labor unions,* which we discuss more fully in the next chapter, are analogous to monopolies. They are like monopolies in that unions eliminate competition for jobs among workers in order to raise the price of their members' labor services.

- Just as a monopoly in the output market is the sole seller of a good or service, a labor union could be the sole provider of labor to an employer. If a union is successful in monopolizing the supply of labor's services, it can drive wages higher than would occur in competition. Because labor demand curves slope downward, the employment of union labor will be reduced below the competitive level. If the union behaves as a profit-maximizing monopoly, it will restrict the quantity of labor supplied to the point where marginal revenue equals marginal cost. Union members will be paid more for their work, but that there will be fewer people working. While unions often have other objectives than simple profit maximization, this reasoning illustrates the tradeoff between higher wages and fewer job opportunities in unionized industries.

- In order to cut the supply of labor to an employer, the union must be able to restrict the size of its membership. One way to restrict membership is to place excessive and hard-to-meet skill or experience requirements on those seeking to join the union. Many workers who might be employed in a competitive labor market will not be able to surmount such an artificial barrier to entry in the union labor market.

- Bilateral monopoly occurs when a monopsony buyer of labor's services must obtain those services from a monopoly seller, such as a labor union. Professional sports leagues are often a bilateral monopoly. The National Football League, Major League Baseball, and the National Basketball Association are each organized so that the owners' association presents a united front when negotiating with the players' union. Both sides need each other, but disagreements arise over wages and working conditions. **Under a bilateral monopoly, the wage depends on bargaining power—whether the employer or representative of the employees bargains more effectively.** The wage bargain that is struck could result in a wage at the competitive level, below it, or above it.

12.4 The Employment of Other Inputs

- Economists categorize resource inputs into four types: land, labor, capital, and entrepreneurship. So far, we have seen how employers decide how much labor to employ. But labor needs capital, such as tools, machines, and their own skills. Labor may also need natural resources from the land in the form of raw materials. The marginal revenue product can be calculated for any input, as can its marginal cost. **The rule for the profit maximizing amount of labor applies to other inputs: Employ an input up to the point where its marginal revenue product equals its marginal cost.** The marginal revenue product of capital is computed in the same way as the marginal revenue product of labor was computed. The firm will employ capital up to the point where its marginal revenue product equals the marginal cost of capital.

- Computing the cost of capital is not always easy or simple, but is often not as difficult as it might at first appear. In the simplest case, the firm will lease capital at a fixed price per unit. However, even if it owns the capital it uses, the firm pays a price in terms of revenues forgone from leasing that capital to another firm. For this reason, the marginal cost of capital is usually called the *rental price of capital*. The purchase price of capital is irrelevant to its rental price.

- Whatever the purchase price might be or might have been, a firm will employ additional capital so long as the marginal revenue product of capital exceeds the rental price of capital. When the two are equal, the firm stops expanding its employment of capital. If the capital is *lumpy*, meaning that it cannot be varied in minute amounts, the firm will not see an exact equality between marginal revenue product and rental price, but will definitely plan to add no capital that it thinks will have a marginal revenue product of less that the rental price.

E&A   12.5   Internationalizing the Workforce

- A portion of U.S. imports are made by foreign firms employing foreign workers, but some of these imports are made by foreign workers who work in factories owned by U.S.-based firms called *multinational firms*.

- Not all U.S. multinational firms export their overseas production to the U.S. For example, both Ford Motor Company and General Motors are multinational firms that operate automobile assembly plants and other manufacturing facilities in many countries around the globe. Most of the goods produced in those plants stay in the countries where they are made.

- The home base of their employers is of no consequence to the workers who produce the cars. Since multinationals must abide by the labor laws where they operate, and typically follow local employment practices and customs, it matters not to the workers where their employers live.

- While the U.S. is known as the home base for many multinationals, numerous multinationals are also based elsewhere. Whatever its home base, a multinational will have facilities and employ workers in multiple countries. For this reason, multinational firms face an international workforce, being forced to deal with workers who are protected by different labor laws, speak different languages, have different work ethics, and possess varying educations. Sometimes the firm will require that its workforce learn a common language to use in internal communications. Sometimes that language is not even native to the country the company calls its home. In the case of the French telecommunications giant Alcatel, for example, employees were told to learn English because that language dominates the telecommunications world.

- Workplace diversity is the norm in many countries. Employers are comfortable hiring the foreign born. To some extent this is because the foreign born help plug skill gaps in the workforce. Foreign-born workers are allowed to work in the U.S. when an employer can demonstrate that no American-born worker is available to fill the job. The following table shows the latest data on the number of immigrants admitted to the U.S. for employment reasons. For the years shown, the total number is over a million immigrants, about 10 percent of all immigrants allowed into the U.S. These immigrants were allowed into the U.S. because their employers certified that American workers to fill those jobs could not be found.

U.S. Employment-based Immigration

Year	Number of Immigrants
1990	58,192
1991	59,525
1992	116,198
1993	147,012
1994	123,291
1995	85,336
1996	117,499
1997	90,607
1998	77,517
1999	56,817
2000	107,024

- There can be a downside to employing these workers. Language barriers are an obvious example. So is the paperwork required by the Immigration and Naturalization Service that is required to legally employ them.

- Some employers claim they hire the foreign born because they will do the jobs that American workers will not do. These jobs include low-prestige jobs like janitorial work, the physically demanding jobs like picking crops, and other low-paying jobs. This claim is controversial. Some of these jobs are filled by workers who are in the U.S. working illegally. Since their employers are violating the law and subject to criminal penalties if caught, and subject to seeing their workers deported, some of those employers pay less than the minimum wage. Many times such employers justify their illegal behavior by claiming that they cannot find Americans who will do these jobs.

- Some countries, such as Japan, make it virtually impossible for foreigners to work. However, the internationalization of the workforce that characterizes the U.S. today also applies in many other countries. In England, for instance, workers from the countries that were part of the old British empire are commonly employed because the laws make it easy for that to happen.

- Self-employed entrepreneurs who are foreign-born are another dimension to the internationalizing of the workforce. Thousands of foreign-born entrepreneurs have similarly changed consumer preferences in the U.S. From foreign cuisine to kung fu lessons, exotic new products have been successfully introduced into this country by foreigners.

- The Internet and new communications technologies that are arising around the Internet are internationalizing the workforce in a different way from what has previously been discussed. Many employers are exploiting the potential of the world-wide web to internationalize their operations. Thus, jobs that in the past would have required American firms to fill them with American workers can now be filled with foreign workers who *stay in their home country*. For example, work on computer applications coordinated from the U.S. can be accomplished with programers who live in India or most anyplace else in the world.

- The Internet is fundamentally changing the way that labor is employed. For this reason, a worker faces competition for jobs not only from fellow citizens, but from labor in other countries. By the same token, a worker in the U.S. might draw a paycheck from a foreign firm.

- Change in the labor market is nothing new, but rather as ancient as civilization. Throughout world history, the employment of labor and other inputs has adjusted to change. The internationalization of the workforce is just the latest in a long list of changes brought about by globalization. The U.S. economy, and America's workers, have proven resilient enough to accommodate these changes, as more workers found employment in the last decade than at any time in U.S. history.

StudyCheck 5

Explain the role of the Internet in internationalizing the workforce.

FILL IN THE BLANKS

1. The _____ _____ involves the exchange of labor services. Unlike the product market, in which firms are sellers and individuals are buyers, in this market firms purchase labor services and individuals supply their labor services to firms.

2. The market price of labor services is the _____ _____—the amount an employee is paid per hour. The quantity of labor services is usually measured by the number of hours of labor services exchanged in the marketplace.

3. A _____ demand curve for labor shows the quantity of labor that employers in a labor market wish to employ at various wage rates. The _____ is the wage rate, other things equal, the greater will be the quantity of labor demanded.

4. Labor demand slopes _____, meaning that higher wage rates decrease the quantity of labor demanded, whereas lower wage rates increase the quantity of labor demanded.

5. Labor demand is a _____ demand, which means the demand for labor exists only because there is a demand for an employer's output. Other things equal, an increase in the demand for a good will increase the demand for labor in that industry.

6. Workers supply their labor to the labor market in exchange for the wages and salaries that they can earn. The _____ slope of the market supply of labor tells us that higher wage rates attract a greater quantity of labor supplied.

7. The market demand for labor together with the market supply determine the market wage rate. The market wage rate is also called the _____ wage rate, since this wage rate results in the quantity demanded of labor being equal to the quantity supplied of labor.

8. A market wage rate higher than the equilibrium wage rate causes a _____ of labor. Likewise, a market wage rate below the equilibrium wage rate causes a _____ of labor.

9. The equilibrium wage rate will change when there is a change in labor demand or supply. The market wage rate will increase when there is an increase in labor demand or a decrease in labor supply. A lower market wage rate is brought about by a _____ in labor demand or an _____ in labor supply.

10. A purely competitive labor market exists when the demand for labor and the supply of labor establish an equilibrium wage rate and quantity of labor. Characteristics include the following:
    - There are _____ buyers and sellers of labor services in the market.

- The services of labor are _____.
- The labor market is free of _____ to entry and exit.

11. In a purely competitive labor market, employers are _____ _____, which means that each will be able to hire as much or as little labor as it wishes at the going market wage rate. Since one employer by itself cannot influence this market wage rate, employers that are wage takers are said to have _____ market power over wages.

12. For a wage-taking firm, the wage rate is the _____ curve of labor to the firm. In other words, the firm can purchase as many units of labor as it wishes at the market wage rate.

13. The value to the firm of any given worker's labor is the revenue resulting from the sale of that worker's marginal product.   This added revenue is termed the _____ _____ _____ of labor, defined as the increase in the firm's total revenue arising from the employment of an additional unit of labor.

14. The _____ _____ of labor equals the addition to total cost when there is a one unit increase in the quantity of labor. *Wage taking* firms purchase each unit of labor services at the _____ _____ _____.

15. The profit maximizing firm follows the following hiring rule: Hire up to and including but not beyond the point for which _____ _____ _____ equals the marginal cost of labor.

16. When the firm is a wage taker in the labor market, the marginal cost of labor curve is _____ (perfectly elastic). The marginal revenue product curve is also the firm's demand curve for labor because it shows how much labor the firm will employ at various wage rates. The firm's labor demand curve is _____ sloping.

17. In addition to pure competition, we have the following labor market models:
   - _____—only one employer of labor services;
   - _____—only one seller of labor services, a labor union;
   - _____ _____—only one employer and only one seller of labor services.

18. Fewness of employers creates monopsony power for firms. Monopsony employers are able to pay workers _____ than the competitive wage rate.

19. Consider a pure monopsony firm—the only employer of labor in a labor market. The marginal cost of labor curve is _____ sloping rather than horizontal as in the case of pure competition in the labor market. If a monopsonized labor market could be transformed into

a purely competitive one, the employment of labor would _____ to the point where the supply and demand curves for labor intersect.

20.   If a union is successful in monopolizing the supply of labor's services, wages will be _____ than would occur in competition. Because labor demand curves slope downward, the employment of union labor will be _____ than the competitive level. _____ _____ occurs when a monopsony buyer of labor's services must obtain those services from a monopoly seller, such as a labor union.

E&A   21.   A portion of U.S. imports are made by foreign firms employing foreign workers, but some of these imports are made by foreign workers who work in factories owned by U.S.-based firms called _____ firms.

22.   Foreign-born workers are allowed to work in the U.S. when an employer _____ _____.

23.   For the years 1990 through 2000, the total number of employment-based immigrants is over a _____ people, about _____ percent of all immigrants allowed into the U.S.

24.   Self-employed _____ who are foreign-born are another dimension to the internationalizing of the workforce. From foreign cuisine to kung fu lessons, exotic new products have been successfully introduced into this country by foreigners.

25.   Jobs that in the past would have required American firms to fill them with American workers can now be filled with foreign workers who stay in their home country. The _____ is fundamentally changing the way that labor is employed. For this reason, a worker faces competition for jobs not only from fellow citizens, but from labor in other countries.

TRUE/FALSE/EXPLAIN
If false, explain why in the space provided.

1.   Labor demand curves slope downward, just like product demand curves.

2.   The demand for labor is a derived demand.

3.   Marginal revenue product is calculated as the change in total revenue divided by the change in the quantity of output.

4.   Labor is assumed to be homogeneous in a purely competitive labor market.

5.   The marginal revenue product of labor is the revenue from the sale of a worker's marginal product.

6.   In a purely competitive labor market, each firm is a wage maker.

7.   For a wage taker, the marginal cost of labor equals the wage rate.

8.   A firm's demand curve for labor is its marginal cost of labor curve.

9.   A union that represents all potential workers would be an example of a monopsony.

10.   If a particular labor market is characterized by monopsony, it will pay workers less and thus employ more of them than if that labor market were characterized by pure competition.

11.   A wage-taking firm maximizes profit by hiring up to the point where the wage rate equals marginal revenue.

12.   If a firm sells its output at a constant price of $2 per unit, and if one more worker would add seven more units, then the worker's marginal revenue product equals $14.

13. A decrease in labor demand would result from a decrease in the marginal product of labor.

14. In determining the wage rate to pay, a monopsony first sets the marginal cost of labor equal to the marginal revenue product of labor and then sets the wage rate according to the corresponding point on the supply curve of labor.

15. Pure monopsony occurs when there is one seller of a product.

16. A monopsony labor market occurs when there are many employers in the market.

17. Monopsony firms pay competitive wages.

18. A labor union would be a monopoly in a labor market, if it is the sole seller of labor services.

19. Under a bilateral monopoly, the wage rate will definitely be higher than under monopoly.

20. The profit maximizing employment of capital occurs at the point where capital's marginal revenue product equals its marginal cost.

E&A 21. U.S. imports come only from foreign-owned factories.

22. Multinational firms are based in many countries of the world, including the U.S.

23.   One reason to hire a foreign-born immigrant is that sometimes native born workers with the right skills cannot be easily found.

24.   All immigrants to the U.S. are allowed into the country for employment reasons.

25.   . In Japan it is very easy for the foreign-born to get jobs.

MULTIPLE CHOICE
Circle the letter preceding the one best answer.

1.   The vertical axis of a graph of labor demand will be labeled
   a.   price.
   b.   good X.
   c.   wage rate.
   d.   quantity of labor.

2.   Occupational labor demand is associated with
   a.   industries.
   b.   particular geographic areas.
   c.   specific products.
   d.   specific human capital.

3.   To say that labor demand is derived means that labor demand
   a.   is poorly thought of.
   b.   is not related to the wage rate.
   c.   depends upon the demand for output.
   d.   varies from city to city.

4.   When a labor market is in equilibrium,
   a.   there could be a surplus of labor.
   b.   there could be a shortage of labor.
   c.   either a shortage or surplus of labor is possible.
   d.   no shortage nor surplus of labor will occur.

5.   Which is NOT a characteristic of a purely competitive labor market?
        a.   Many buyers and sellers of labor services.
        b.   Firms are wage makers.
        c.   Labor is homogeneous.
        d.   Barriers to entry and exit in the labor market do not exist.

6.   The arrow in Multiple Choice Figure 1 indicates that, the higher is the
        a.   quantity of labor supplied, the higher will be the wage rate.
        b.   quantity of labor supplied, the lower will be the wage rate.
        c.   wage rate, the higher will be the quantity of labor supplied.
        d.   wage rate, the lower will be the quantity of labor supplied.

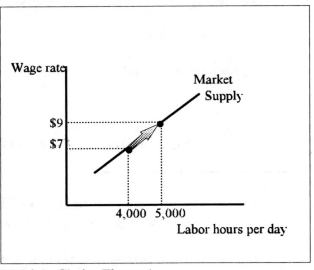

Multiple Choice Figure 1

7.   Joe's Mop-up Crew is the only firm in town that specializes in mopping floors. Joe seeks to hire additional people to mop floors. Joe is likely to face a labor supply curve that
        a.   is nearly horizontal.
        b.   slopes upward steeply.
        c.   is vertical.
        d.   is backward bending.

8.   The marginal revenue product of labor curve
        a.   slopes upward.
        b.   is horizontal.
        c.   slopes downward.
        d.   is vertical.

Refer to the following table to answer the next two questions. Assume the wage rate is constant at $5 per unit of labor, and the price of output is $3 per unit.

Labor	Output
0	0
1	3
2	11
3	15
4	17
5	16

9.   The marginal revenue product of the third unit of labor is
      a. $25.
      b. $20.
      c. $15.
      d. $12.

10.   This firm should hire _____ units of labor in order to maximize profit.
      a.   zero
      b.   two
      c.   three
      d.   four

11.   The marginal revenue product curve would definitely shift to the right if
      a.   average product increased.
      b.   marginal product decreased.
      c.   product price increased.
      d.   product price decreased.

12.   The labor market shown in Multiple Choice Figure 2 is most likely to be
      a.   monopoly.
      b.   monopsony.
      c.   bilateral monopoly.
      d.   pure competition.

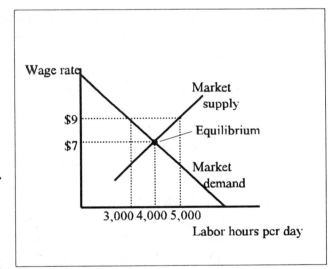

13.   Given the labor market shown in Multiple Choice Figure 2, the output market(s) associated with the output of labor
      a.   must be a monopoly.
      b.   must be a monopsony.
      c.   must be pure competition.
      d.   might be associated with any of the market structures.

Multiple Choice Figure 2

14.   Under a monopsony, the wage rate is given by the point on the
      a.   derived demand curve where it is crossed by the marginal cost of labor curve.
      b.   derived demand curve where it is crossed by the supply curve.
      c.   supply curve below where marginal cost of labor crosses the derived demand curve.
      d.   supply curve where it is equal to marginal cost of labor.

15.   Which of the following is the best example of a monopsony?
a.   The market for astronauts
b.   The United Autoworkers Union
c.   The market for delivery truck drivers
d.   Newspaper coverage of a sensational murder trial

16.   A labor union that maximizes revenue will create which outcome?
a.   Lower wages and lower employment
b.   Higher wages and lower employment
c.   Lower wages and higher employment
d.   Higher wages and higher employment

17.   Of the following, the best example of a bilateral monopoly would be
a.   astronauts at NASA.
b.   Coke and Pepsi.
c.   major league baseball.
d.   the Teamsters Union.

18.   Suppose the firm in Multiple Choice Figure 3 increases its market power in its output market, and that the curves shown in the figure are the firm's marginal revenue product of labor before and after this increase in market power. Curve A is
a.   probably after the increase in the firm's market power.
b.   probably before the increase in the firm's market power.
c.   equally likely to be before or after the increase in the firm's market power.
d.   illogical, because a firm with market power in its output market cannot face a horizontal supply of labor.

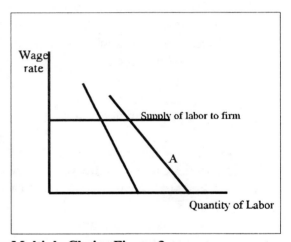

Multiple Choice Figure 3

19.   Lumpy capital means that capital
a.   wears out.
b.   may have a rental price.
c.   is impossible to purchase.
d.   cannot be varied in small amounts.

20. The profit-maximizing rule for capital
    a.   does not exist.
    b.   says to employ capital until its purchase price equals its marginal product.
    c.   says to employ capital until its marginal cost equals its marginal revenue product.
    d.   says to employ capital in the same amount as the profit-maximizing amount of labor.

E&A 21. If it is to be imported into the United States, a product must be labeled with the
    a.   number of jobs the product takes from American workers.
    b.   environmental impact of producing that product.
    c.   name of the importer.
    d.   country where it is made.

22. Regarding labor laws, U.S. multinationals
    a.   make their own laws.
    b.   must abide by U.S. law
    c.   must abide by the laws of countries where they are located.
    d.   must abide by the international law formulated by the United Nations to apply to multinationals.

23. For the most part, those who work for multinational firms
    a.   would prefer to work for companies that are locally based since the multinationals pay less and work their employees harder than local companies.
    b.   prefer to work for multinationals instead of local companies since multinationals pay all workers the same high pay, no matter the country involved.
    c.   receive government assistance for the stresses from working for foreign bosses.
    d.   don't particularly care whether their employer is a multinational firm since such firms must follow local laws and usually follow local customs.

24. Foreigners who work in the U.S. illegally are
    a.   subject to a fine.
    b.   subject to 10 years' imprisonment.
    c.   subject to deportation.
    d.   not subject to any sort of penalty, but are required to quit their jobs within two months of being discovered.

25. U.S. data shows that in the 1990s the country allowed between approximately _____ immigrants a year to enter the country for employment reasons.
    a.   1,000,000 and 2,000,000
    b.   500,000 and 1,000,000
    c.   250,000 and 500,000
    d.   50,000 and 150,000

GRASPING THE GRAPHS
Fill in each box with a concept that applies.

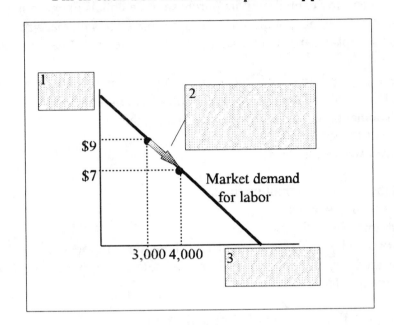

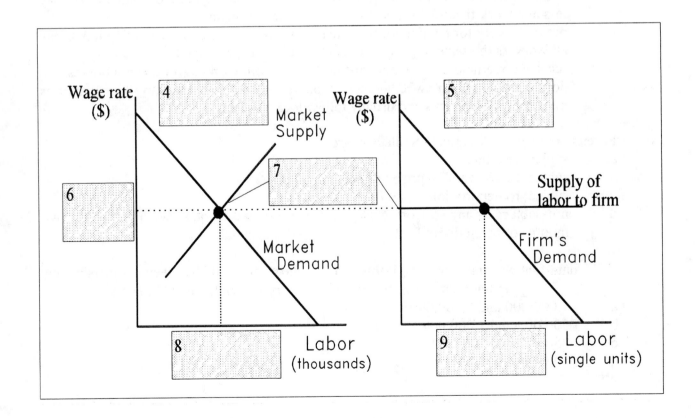

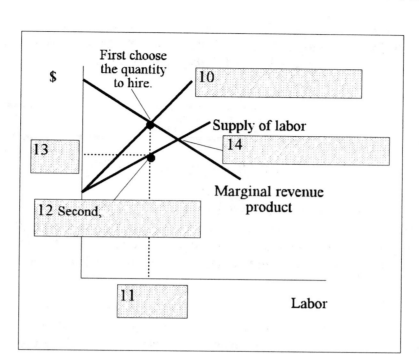

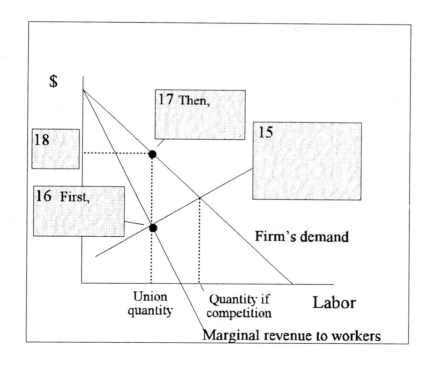

**For additional practice in grasping this chapter's graphs,
visit http://www.prenhall.com/ayers and try *Smart Graph* 31,
along with *Active Graphs* 60 and 61.**

ANSWERS

STUDYCHECKS

1. In the labor market, workers are the sellers and firms are the buyers of labor services. The firm's demand for labor is determined by demand for the output that the labor produces. For this reason, the firm's demand is termed a derived demand. Each worker offers to supply labor so long as the wage rate exceeds that worker's reservation wage.

2. Refer to the following table:

Number of Workers	Output	Marginal Product	Output Price ($)	Total Revenue ($)	Marginal Revenue Product ($)
0	0	undefined	3	0	undefined
1	8	8	3	24	24
2	15	7	3	45	21
3	21	6	3	63	18
4	26	5	3	78	15
5	30	4	3	90	12

a. 3
b. 3
c. $12
d. Yes, marginal revenue product reveals how much labor the firm will hire at each wage rate, and is thus its derived demand for labor.

3. See StudyCheck 3 Figure.

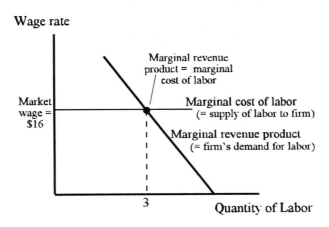

StudyCheck 3 Figure

4. Unlike a competitive firm, the monopsonist faces a marginal cost of labor that exceeds the wage. Thus, the monopsonist will not hire to the point where marginal revenue product equals the wage rate. This is seen in StudyCheck 4 Figure, which shows the monopsonist's choice relative to what the firm's choice would have been if the firm was a price taker in the labor market.

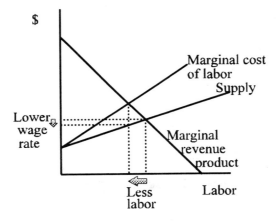

StudyCheck 4 Figure

5. The Internet allows some kinds of work to be done in other countries. For example, software development can be done by foreign workers and be sent to the U.S. over the Internet using e-mail. American workers find themselves in competition with these workers. The Internet also allows merchants in other countries to sell their wares to foreigners. Likewise, American entrepreneurs must compete with these business people.

FILL IN THE BLANKS

1. labor market
2. wage rate
3. market, lower
4. downward
5. derived
6. positive
7. equilibrium
8. surplus, shortage
9. decrease, increase
10. many, homogeneous, barriers
11. wage takers, zero
12. supply
13. marginal revenue product
14. marginal cost, market wage rate
15. marginal revenue product
16. horizontal, downward
17. monopsony, monopoly, bilateral monopoly
18. less
19. upward, increase
20. higher, less, Bilateral monopoly
21. multinational
22. demonstrates that no American citizen is available to fill the job
23. million, 10
24. entrepreneurs
25. Internet

TRUE/FALSE/EXPLAIN

1. True.
2. True.
3. False, marginal revenue product is the change in total revenue divided by the change in input.
4. True.
5. True.
6. False, each firm would be a wage taker.
7. True.
8. False, a firm's demand for labor is given by its marginal revenue product of labor.

9. False, the union that represents all potential workers would be an example of a monopoly.
10. False, although a monopsony would pay workers less than the competitive wage, it would also hire fewer of them.
11. False, the firm maximizes profit by hiring up to the point where the wage rate equals the marginal revenue product.
12. True.
13. True.
14. True.
15. False, pure monopsony occurs when there is one buyer of labor's services.
16. False, with a monopsony labor market, there is only one employer in the market.
17. False, a monopsony pays less than the competitive wage.
18. True.
19. False, the wage rate under bilateral monopoly would depend on the relative bargaining power of the monopsony and monopoly involved.
20. True.
21. False, some U.S. imports from abroad come from American owned factories.
22. True.
23. True.
24. False, employment is only one of the reasons that an immigrant might be allowed into the United States.
25. False, in Japan it is difficult for the foreign-born to get jobs.

MULTIPLE CHOICE

1	c	8	c	15	a	22	c
2	d	9	d	16	b	23	d
3	c	10	d	17	c	24	c
4	d	11	c	18	b	25	d
5	b	12	d	19	d		
6	c	13	d	20	c		
7	a	14	c	21	d		

GRASPING THE GRAPHS
Examples of correct answers

1 Wage rate
2 As the wage rate falls, the quantity of labor demanded rises.
3 Units of labor
4 The competitive labor market

5   The firm
6   Market wage rate
7   The firm is a wage taker.
8   Market equilibrium quantity of labor
9   Quantity of labor chosen by the firm
10   Marginal cost of labor
11   Quantity to hire
12   Pay as little as possible.
13   Wage rate
14   Equilibrium if market were competitive instead of monopsony
15   Marginal cost if union or supply if competition
16   The union determines what quantity to offer.
17   It gets the highest wage it can.
18   Wage rate

**Visit the Ayers/Collinge companion Website at <u>http://www.prenhall.com/ayers</u>
for further activities and exercises for this chapter.**

Chapter 13

EARNINGS
AND INCOME DISTRIBUTION

CHAPTER REVIEW

13.1 Measuring Incomes

- Wages and salaries provide 72 percent of U.S. national income. Businesses provide another 18 percent in the form of corporate profits plus the income from proprietorships. Interest earnings provide another 8 percent, while rents received by landlords provide 2 percent.

- Wages are the incomes that workers earn from their jobs. The size of their incomes depends on two variables: the quantity of labor they supply and the amount they are paid. The quantity of labor supplied is usually measured in hours. The price of labor is the *wage rate*—the amount an individual is paid per hour. When the wage rate is multiplied by hours worked, the result is *earnings*, the income from labor.

- Hours in excess of 40 are called *overtime* hours. Overtime wage rates are 50 percent greater than the *straight-time* rate that a worker receives for the first 40 hours worked. The Department of Labor enforces these rules, which arise from the *Fair Labor Standards Act*, enacted by Congress in 1938.

- Workers who are paid a *salary* receive a fixed amount of income, no matter how many hours they work. Employers expect salaried employees to work a minimum number of hours per week, typically corresponding to the regular operating hours of the business. If such employees work additional hours, they are not paid for those hours. Labor Department rules govern what types of jobs pay salaries versus hourly wages.

- An employer's *total labor costs* are the sum of wages and salaries plus fringe benefits. Some benefits are voluntarily offered by employers; others are required by government. Benefits received by workers include paid vacations, sick leave, and employer contributions to Social Security. *Workers' compensation* coverage, which provides workers who are injured on the job with a stipend while they recuperate from their injuries, paid time off for lunch, and health benefits round out the list of typical benefits. For the typical U.S. employer, benefits account for about 28 percent of labor costs.

13.2 Individual Labor Supply

- *Labor force participation* reflects the decisions of individuals to offer their services in the labor market. To be counted as a member of the labor force, a person must either have paid employment or be actively looking for it. Examples of nonparticipants include full-time students and retirees.

- Individual preferences play a key role in explaining labor force participation, and hence earnings. These preferences are evidenced in the individual's labor supply curve. Below the **reservation wage,** individuals "reserve" their labor—they choose not to work at all. Note that, unlike supply curves for other things, the individual's supply curve of labor services has a *backward-bending* portion.

- As wage rates rise at first, the **substitution effect** of the change in wage rates causes individuals to work more—they substitute away from leisure, because the opportunity cost of leisure becomes higher as wage rates rise. The result is that people offer more hours in response to higher wages, causing the supply curve to slope upward. In place of leisure, workers consume goods and services with their increased earnings.

- As wage rates rise, eventually the **income effect** of the wage change tugs the worker in the opposite direction relative to the substitution effect. Higher wages bring higher incomes, which prompt workers to demand more of all normal goods. *Leisure,* time away from work, is a normal good. To "buy" more leisure, workers pay the opportunity cost of giving up the income from some work hours. The result is that, as wage rates rise, the income effect prompts workers to offer fewer hours of work. The supply curve bends backward when the income effect outweighs the substitution effect. The substitution effect tends to be stronger at lower wage rates, and the income effect stronger at higher wage rates. The result is a supply curve that first slopes upward and then bends backward.

- Individuals' labor supply curves will vary depending on whether they are *primary workers,* the main source of income in households, or *secondary workers,* whose incomes are not as critical to their households' well-being.

- The labor supply curves of primary workers are nearly vertical, meaning that they will choose to work about the same number of hours, no matter the wages they are able to receive. The quantity of labor supplied by a primary worker is typically in the range of 35 to 45 hours per week. In contrast, secondary workers have a much more pronounced upward slope and backward-bend to their supply curves. Secondary workers are more likely to hold part-time jobs than primary workers.

StudyCheck 1

Describe how the income and substitution effects determine the shape of an individual's labor supply curve. Why does it matter if the worker is primary or secondary?

- Labor supply curves may shift. Many persons receive *nonlabor income* from investments, pension funds, government transfer payments, interest on bank deposits, gifts from relatives, and other sources. The amount of nonlabor income received can affect labor market choices. Generally, a greater amount of nonlabor income will reduce the labor a worker supplies.

- The *market labor supply* sums the quantity of labor supplied at various wage rates for all the individuals in a labor market. Market supply curves of labor are upward sloping in the range of income that is usually relevant to employers.

StudyCheck 2

Explain why the market supply of labor will slope upwards, even if some individuals have backward-bending labor supply curves.

- An *industry labor supply* sums the quantity of labor supplied to a particular industry at various wage rates. Because higher wage rates in one industry attract workers from other industries, any particular industry supply curve of labor is nearly always upward sloping. It is also usually quite elastic, meaning that a small increase in the wage rate would result in a large increase in the quantity of labor supplied.

13.3   Sources of Earnings Differentials

- Wage differentials among workers sometimes seem intuitive. We expect a heart surgeon to earn more than a janitor. Many wage differentials are not so easy to understand, however. Individual earnings differ because of a combination factors, which we examine next.

- Numerous occupations exist. Over 700 basic occupations are cataloged on the Internet database *Occupational Information Network*, also known as *O*Net*, which was created by the U.S. Department of Labor. Occupational choice plays a significant role in earnings power. Generally, the highest-paying occupations are those that require the greatest skills, and the lowest paying are the unskilled occupations.

- Different jobs have their own advantages and disadvantages. Most people would rather work at safe jobs in air-conditioned comfort rather than at dangerous jobs outside in the extremes of weather. Higher pay in the latter jobs will be necessary in order to equalize their attractiveness relative to the former jobs. Such increases in pay are termed **compensating wage differentials.**

- Sanitation workers, coal miners, and others have unpleasant or dangerous jobs. To induce workers to take those jobs, employers must pay a compensating differential. Note that even with compensating differentials included, the pay in such jobs may still be relatively low, because skill requirements in many of these jobs are low.

- People choose jobs on the basis of many job characteristics. Pay, the *pecuniary* attribute, is the most important for some. For others, job security, status, the likelihood of advancement, safe working conditions, interest in the work, or the flexibility of employers in matters of dress or hours is most important. Job features unrelated to pay are called the *nonpecuniary* attributes. Positive nonpecuniary features can offset low pay.

- Workers join labor unions to improve their pay and work environments. At the peak of union membership in 1953, 36 percent of U.S. workers belonged to a union. In 2001 that figure stood at 16.3 million members out of the civilian labor force of 142 million, or about 11.5 percent of the labor force.

- The decline in overall union membership masks the concentration of membership in several key industries. Indeed, government employee unionism has reached record levels, with seven million government workers, equal to about 37.5 percent of such workers, belonging to unions.

- Possibly the most important factor behind the low percentage of union workers in the economy is more global competition in industries where unions have historically been strong. Fewer U.S. workers in these industries mean fewer union members. Examples include steel and autos.

- Also contributing to the decline in unionism has been the increasing importance of white-collar jobs, in which the appeal of unions is relatively weak. Nonetheless, a recent nationwide survey of workers showed one-third of those surveyed who were not union members would like to be.

- In order to reverse the long-term decline in membership, unions reach out for new members. Union efforts to "organize" an employer—have the right to represent its workers—culminate in a secret ballot representation election, under the supervision of the federal government's National Labor Relations Board (NLRB).

- When more than half of a firm's employees vote in favor of a union, the NLRB certifies the union as the bargaining agent for the workers. Once certified, a union engages in **collective bargaining,** negotiations with employers aimed at improving working conditions, pay, and benefits. Legally, employers must bargain with a union, but are not obligated to reach agreement. Consequently, some firms resist unionization by staying within the law and bargaining, but then failing to agree with union demands.

- When firms balk at union demands, which side will prevail? **Union *bargaining power* refers to the ability of a union to win an agreement with greater wages and benefits for its members. The primary weapon providing bargaining power to unions is the *strike,* or work stoppage.** The ability to shut down an employer is a powerful weapon, although strikers have the incentive to settle a strike because they are not paid wages while on strike. Generally, a strike will be preceded by negotiations. Thus, a strike indicates the failure of negotiations. However, there are *wildcat strikes,* work stoppages that occur spontaneously because of workers' grievances against their employers. When an employer faces a strike, its most powerful source of bargaining power is the right to hire permanent replacements for striking workers. However, firms often do not exercise that right for fear of violence toward their property or replacement employees.

- Union bargaining power is reduced in the 23 states with some form of a *right-to-work law,* which permits a unionized firm's workers the option of not joining the union. In these states, union and nonunion workers may work side by side on the job. Hence, workers in right-to-work states are less likely to present a united front when labor disputes arise, a situation which decreases union bargaining power. Union membership is the strongest in New York, and the weakest in North Carolina. In general, right-to-work states have a lower percent of union members than do other states.

- Another union weapon is the *boycott,* a campaign to persuade union members and the public to refrain from purchasing the output of a firm with which the union has a disagreement. Boycotts often go hand in hand with strikes. For a boycott to be effective, a union must have the public on its side.

- Given the weapons unions have, it should not be surprising that union wages are high. Median weekly earnings for union members in 2001 were $718, approximately 25 percent higher than the $575 for those not represented by unions.

- **Higher pay means fewer jobs in the union sector, which increases the supply of labor to the nonunion sector and drives down wages there.** Furthermore, the kinds of jobs held by union members differ from the kinds held by other workers. Some of the higher pay in union jobs is likely to be compensating differentials, which would be paid even in the absence of unions. The consensus of research on union wages is that, after taking account of all other factors affecting wages, **unions raise wages for their members. However, estimates of the increase vary too widely to know its magnitude with certainty.**

- Human capital is another important determinant of earnings differentials. Human capital is the knowledge, skills, and other productivity-enhancing attributes embodied within individual workers. Attending college is a prime example of how to increase one's human capital. Sources of human capital include formal schooling, on-the-job training, and classroom skills training.

- It is costly to build a stock of human capital. There are out-of-pocket, explicit costs, as well as the opportunity costs of forgone earnings. For many college students, opportunity costs far exceed the explicit costs. Is a college degree worth the investment? College graduates are less likely to be unemployed than high school graduates, and earn higher incomes over their adult lives. The $786 median weekly salary in 2001 for college graduates exceeded the median of $474 for high school graduates by about 66 percent. The statistics must be interpreted with caution, however, since those going to college may differ in other respects from those who do not. For example, college graduates may be smarter and more motivated than workers who did not go to college, in which case they would earn more than other people even without college.

- Several studies indicate that the returns to the investment in a college diploma probably increased over the last 20 years, which helps explain why an increasing fraction of high school graduates attend college. The increase in relative earnings is due to many factors. One is the decline in the power of unions to raise wages above competitive levels for their mostly high school-educated membership. Other contributing factors include (1) the flow of relatively unskilled immigrants into the United States, many of whom compete for jobs against high school graduates; (2) the increased desire of employers to hire college graduates for jobs that have not historically required advanced education; and (3) the high-tech economy, which places a premium on education.

- The **signaling** hypothesis provides an alternative to the human capital explanation for the greater earnings of college graduates. In this view, education provides information to employers about the characteristics of job applicants. Employers believe that more education signals that one is easily trained and reliable.

- This view holds that most college courses do little to increase a person's productivity. In effect, college does not train people for the job market, but instead screens out the winners from the losers. Many economists believe that there is truth in both the human capital and signaling views.

- *Wage discrimination* occurs when a worker who is as productive as other workers doing the same job is paid less because of race, sex, color, religion, or national origin. This discrimination is illegal in the United States. It is difficult to ascertain what part of wage differences between workers occurs as a result of wage discrimination and what part occurs because of productivity differences.

- Not all wage differences arise because of employer discrimination. The wages of different groups will differ if there are differences in how productive workers are in each group. The market will tend to pay the members of one group more than the members of the other if the first group is more productive. Productivity differences among workers often result from differences in human capital, which may reflect differing amounts and quality of schooling.

- To the extent that a group, blacks for example, experiences systematic discrimination prior to entering the labor market—*pre-market discrimination*—the outcome is less human capital and lower wages. This situation can also harm blacks with higher-than-average human capital to the extent that employers have imperfect information about individual job applicants and resort to *statistical discrimination,* which is to judge applicants by the average characteristics of their racial or ethnic group.

- Evidence indicates that wage discrimination by employers typically accounts for only a part of wage differentials among racial and gender groups. An individual's age, ability, health, education, marital status, occupation, and number of years of work experience affect his or her productivity and hence earnings. A good part of the lower earnings of minorities and women can be attributed to differences in these attributes.

- Wage differentials exist even among individuals who are identical in all measurable attributes that may affect earnings, including race and gender. Such wage differences reflect the effect of difficult-to-measure factors on earnings. Being in the right place at the right time and other forms of luck play a role in wage differences. Other possible factors creating wage differences include disparities in looks, height, social skills, ambition, selection of marriage partner, and other tangible and intangible attributes.

- Wages tend to be related to the cost of living. In localities where the cost of living is high, wages also tend to be high. Wages also tend to be higher in urban areas than in surrounding rural areas, possibly reflecting a lower cost of living in rural areas. Because of differences in the cost of living, the purchasing power of a particular wage can vary enormously.

13.4 Income Inequality

- *Income inequality* refers to differences in earnings.

- Low wages or lack of a job can create poverty. Poverty is associated with deprivation, which motivates government transfer programs to aid the poor. Some of these transfers are "cash," such as the well-known welfare check. About two-thirds of government transfers to the poor provide *in-kind benefits,* meaning that valuable services are provided instead of money. In-kind benefits include health care, food stamps, subsidized housing, and subsidized school lunches. These programs seek to preserve a minimum standard of living for the poor and are commonly referred to as the *social safety net.*

- Most households in poverty are very close to the government-set **poverty line**. This income varies by household size and composition. From 1959 to 1973 the number of persons falling below the poverty line decreased from 22 percent to 11 percent of the population, then stayed within the range of 11 to 15 percent over the following years. The poverty rate in 2000 was 11 percent. Poverty rates vary by family status, age, and race. For example, about 28 percent of families with a female household head and no husband present fell below the poverty line in 2000. With the safety net provided by Social Security, poverty among the elderly has fallen to 10 percent of people over 65, from 35 percent in 1959. Poverty rates are about 3 times higher among blacks than whites. Poverty also varies among the states.

- Earnings differentials exist between groups of people. The average full-time female worker in the United States earns about 74 cents for every dollar earned by the average male. This figure is up from 59 cents in 1978. The closing of the earnings gap is explained by women workers developing specialized job skills, thereby allowing women to move into professional and managerial jobs.

- Although less so now than in earlier decades, women's earnings and rank are negatively affected by *discontinuous labor force participation,* which occurs when a person leaves and later reenters the labor force. Many women leave their jobs after childbirth and do not return to work for several years in order to care for their children. This in-and-out pattern of labor force participation causes women's human capital to depreciate and reduces their years of labor-market experience relative to men.

- Explanations for the remaining earnings gap focus on women's occupational choices. Many occupations are dominated by females. Many of the female-dominated occupations pay less than the male-dominated ones that involve comparable education and responsibility.

- **Occupational segregation,** the concentration of women workers in certain jobs, such as nursing and teaching, is commonly cited as evidence that women are discriminated against in hiring. The reasoning is that women are forced into these jobs because other jobs are not open to them. However, many economists deem this view simplistic. Interruptions in women's careers because of childbearing, child rearing, and the need to change jobs because of a husband's job transfer may motivate women to select occupations in which interruptions in labor force participation will be least harmful to their careers. The skills required in these traditionally female occupations are easily transferred from one employer to another and become obsolete only very slowly.

- There are other possible explanations for occupational segregation. Gender-based differences in interests may be one factor. In addition, there might be discrimination against women by the educational system, such as school guidance that channels women away from subjects that lead to employment in traditionally male jobs. Employer discrimination in hiring women for some higher-paying jobs is another explanation.

- Turning to black-white differences, the data show a significant earnings gap between black and white males, with the median black male earning about 76 percent of the amount earned by the median white male in 2000. While narrowing over time, this gap continues to be a source of concern. In contrast, black women earned 86 percent of the earnings of white women in 1997.

- The wage gap based upon gender is a worldwide phenomena, not confined just to the United States. According to the latest data from the Organization for Economic Co-operation and Development (OECD), women workers in the United Kingdom earn 76 percent of what men earn; in France, 87 percent; Spain, 71 percent; Japan, 61 percent; and in Sweden, 83 percent. Just as in the United States, there are many reasons why women earn less in these countries, including differences in years of education and type of training. Tradition and discrimination also probably play a significant role.

StudyCheck 3

List five reasons why wages differ across people and jobs.

13.5 Other Incomes

- **Economic rent** describes earnings in excess of opportunity costs for a unique input—one that is in fixed supply. Movie stars, top corporate executives, and well-known people in law, academia, and other professions likewise can attribute their high incomes in large part to economic rents. When such people have talents and abilities that are exceptionally scarce and valued in the marketplace, they often find themselves earning much more than they could from their next best alternative. The combination of fixed supply and high demand for the talents of superstars results in sky-high earnings. Yet their opportunity cost, their best earnings opportunity outside their current employment, is usually not nearly so spectacular.

StudyCheck 4

Define a person's economic rent, and illustrate with a graph how its size is determined by demand. Be sure to label the axes.

- Economists use the term interest in the same way as your bank: **Interest is the price paid for the use of money.** In the U.S. in 2001, interest income represented 8 percent of the total income received. The payment of interest is made by borrowers, while lenders receive interest payments. Often, a *financial intermediary*, such as a bank, credit union, or savings and loan attracts deposits from savers and lends these savings to borrowers. Government also pays interest to the owners of government *bonds*, IOUs of the government. Interest is usually expressed in terms of a percentage, the **interest rate**.

- Interest rates have sometimes been a source of controversy, with some countries and religions over the centuries questioning whether charging money for the use of money should be allowed. However, while those with substantial wealth certainly gain by being able to "live on interest," the economy gains as well. The reason is twofold: (1)The payment of interest to lenders promotes savings that are used to pay for investments in physical and human capital that improve standards of living. (2)The requirement that borrowers pay interest makes sure that the money available for investment is used where it will be most productive. Investments should be productive enough to at least be able to cover interest payments.

- Profit motivates entrepreneurs, who perform the following functions:
  - Combining resources—organizing land, labor, and capital into productive uses;
  - Innovation— implementing new production methods and creating new products; and
  - Taking risks—entrepreneurs face the risk of failure.

- These entrepreneurial functions separate the entrepreneur from the hired manager, whose job is to carry out the vision of the entrepreneur. Entrepreneurs face the possibility of losses as well as profits. Losses can result from a variety of causes, including faulty decision making, bad luck, or stiff competition from other firms. For this reason, some people perceive entrepreneurship as risky business.

- Economic profit can also be more than just a reward for the successful practice of entrepreneurial skills. Barriers to entry create monopoly and other markets where economic profits arise due to lack of competition. Barriers to entry include those created by innovation that results in patents. Perhaps the most surprising aspect of profit is that profit accounts for such a small fraction of national income. From profit comes a significant part of the funds used to push the economy along to greater prosperity, as profits held by firms as retained earnings are used to make productive investments.

E✢A **13.6 SCHOOLING AND THE LIFE CYCLE OF EARNINGS**

- Clearly, some students do not stay in school as long as they should. We read of the problem of high-school dropouts, whose economic futures look bleak. We also read of the need for more skilled labor, such as more air conditioner repairers, automobile mechanics, computer technicians and programmers, and the like.

- Considering the model of the life cycle of earnings can help us understand better the decision to pursue additional education. The costs of schooling include both direct costs and opportunity costs.

- Consider first the opportunity costs. The six year old in modern-day America can spend the day in school with minimum opportunity cost, at least in terms of money. Young children in America are not expected to work. Indeed, there are laws against child labor. Even if they or their parents wanted them to work, there are few job opportunities for six-year-old children. Recognize, however, that bans on child labor were not common until the 20th century. In the 18th and 19th America's economic foundation was agriculture, and children had to earn their keep by working in the fields. Education was a luxury that many families could not afford. That is still true today in some less-developed countries. Even when child labor is outlawed, it is often commonplace. The opportunity cost of the lost income from sending children to school is often too great to bear, and so the children work.

- Once an American student becomes a teenager, the opportunity cost rises. Many high-school students stay in school, but work a part-time job to offset the increase in the opportunity cost.

- From kindergarten through 12th grade, the costs of public schooling are absorbed by the taxpayer—the student need not worry about tuition, books, or fees. Once a student enters college, even a public college, the student or the student's parents must pay out of their own pocket. The cost of tuition and fees in a public university varies from state to state, but averages about $5,000 a year. That cost is far higher at most private universities. When a college student decides to live away from home rather than commute to classes at a local community college or university, the direct cost of schooling rises accordingly. The cost of providing their children with a college education is a significant economic burden on working families. Many college students hold part-time jobs in order to ease that burden. Financial aid of various sorts is also available to reduce the burden of college expenses.

- Balanced against the costs of schooling are the benefits. We can classify the benefits into two categories: tangible and intangible. The *tangible benefits* of a college education are the increases in the ability to consume goods and services. Among the tangible benefits that college graduates enjoy are:(1) A higher lifetime income (2) Greater job security (3) Relatively safe, pleasant working conditions that contribute to better health.

- The *intangible benefits* of an action are the benefits unrelated to the acquisition of material goods and services. Two examples of the intangible benefits of a college education are:
  - *Consumption benefits:* College can provide students with the enjoyment that arises from being exposed to new ideas and new ways of thinking.
  - *Social benefits:* College offers students the opportunity to make new friends, find mentors, and even meet their future spouses.

- The *life cycle of earnings* refers to the pattern of an individual's real earnings over time, from entry into the labor force until retirement. A typical life cycle of earnings is illustrated with a curve called an *age/earnings profile*.

- The age/earnings profile of a college graduate rises steeply in the early years of work as the individual acquires the *human capital* associated with increasing experience and responsibility. The rise in earnings reflects the individual's increasing productivity. The age/earnings profile eventually stops rising and even turns down slightly in later years. When the individual retires at age 66, earnings from labor stop.

- The age/earnings profile of a high school graduate starts at age 18 rather than age 21, as in the earnings profile of the college graduate. This earnings profile starts lower than the earnings profile of the college graduate and stays lower. Typically, the gap between the two age/earnings profiles would increase over time because the slope of the earnings profile of the high school graduate will be less than the slope of the earnings profile of the college graduate. This lower slope reflects the reduced opportunities on the job for the high school graduate to acquire human capital.

- The age/earnings profile of a drop out starts at the minimum wage and after rising due to initial on the job training remains flat throughout the individual's lifetime. The flat earnings profile assumes that the dropout is not able to acquire any additional human capital on the job, which would increase productivity and thus put a positive slope on the age/earnings profile. It also assumes that the minimum wage keeps up with inflation. If the minimum wage rises more slowly than inflation, the age/earnings profile would slope downward. Alternatively, if the minimum wage increased more rapidly than inflation, the age/earnings profile would slope upward.

- The study of life cycles of earnings for different types of workers can provide revealing insights into the workings of the labor market. For example, the age/earnings profiles of white workers will have a steeper slope than the age/earnings profiles of minority workers when minority workers are discriminated against on the job. Another example relates to women workers. The discontinuous labor force participation of women will be revealed by a break in the earnings profile. Some kinds of jobs, such as school teaching, allow workers who return to work to resume their earnings at the same level as when they left the labor force. Other jobs, those where human capital depreciates rapidly because of rapid advances in knowledge in the field, punish discontinuous labor force participation by offering lower wages to workers who return after being out of the labor force.

- The higher, steeper earnings profile for college graduates indicates that a college education has value. Despite the high costs of obtaining that college education, labor economists have consistently found that a bachelor's degree is a good investment.

StudyCheck 5

Why does the age/earnings profile of a high school dropout remain flat after some initial on the job training?

FILL IN THE BLANKS

1.   Wages and salaries provide _____ percent of U.S. national income. Businesses provide another _____ percent in the form of corporate profits plus the income from proprietorships. Interest earnings provide another _____ percent, while rents received by landlords provide _____ percent.

2.   Hours in excess of 40 are called _____ hours. The wage rate for these hours is 50 percent greater than the straight-time rate that a worker receives for the first 40 hours worked. Workers who are paid a _____ receive a fixed amount of income, no matter how many hours they work. An employer's _____ _____ _____ are the sum of wages and salaries plus fringe benefits. Some benefits are voluntarily offered by employers; others are required by government. For the typical U.S. employer, benefits account for about _____ percent of labor costs.

3.   _____ _____ _____ reflects the decisions of individuals to offer their services in the labor market. To be counted as a member of the labor force, a person must either have paid employment or be actively looking for it.

4.   Individual preferences play a key role in explaining labor force participation, and hence earnings. These preferences are evidenced in the individual's labor supply curve. Below the _____ _____ , individuals "reserve" their labor—they choose not to work at all. The individual's supply curve of labor services has a _____ _____ portion.

5.   As wage rates rise at first, the _____ effect of the change in wage rates causes individuals to work more—they substitute away from leisure, because the opportunity cost of leisure becomes higher as wage rates rise. The result is that people offer more hours in response to higher wages, causing the supply curve to slope upward.

6.   As wage rates rise, eventually the _____ effect of the wage change tugs the worker in the opposite direction relative to the substitution effect. Higher wages bring higher incomes, which prompt workers to demand more of all normal goods. Leisure, time away from work, is a normal good. To "buy" more leisure, workers pay the opportunity cost of giving up the income from some work hours. The result is that, as wage rates rise, the income effect prompts workers to offer _____ hours of work.

7.   The supply curve bends backward when the _____ effect outweighs the _____ effect. The substitution effect tends to be stronger at lower wage rates, and the income effect stronger at higher wage rates. The result is a supply curve that first slopes _____ and then bends backward.

8.　Individuals' labor supply curves will vary depending on whether they are _____ workers, the main source of income in households, or _____ workers, whose incomes are not as critical to their households' well-being.　The labor supply curves of primary workers are nearly _____ meaning that they will choose to work about the same number of hours, no matter the wages they are able to receive. Labor supply curves may shift. Many persons receive _____ income from investments, pension funds, government transfer payments, interest on bank deposits, gifts from relatives, and other sources. Generally, a greater amount of this type of income will _____ the labor a worker supplies.　The _____ labor supply sums the quantity of labor supplied at various wage rates for all the individuals in a labor market.　This supply curve is _____ sloping in the range of income that is usually relevant to employers.

9.　Higher pay in dangerous or unpleasant jobs will be necessary in order to equalize their attractiveness relative to safe or pleasant work. Such increases in pay are termed _____ _____ _____.

10.　People choose jobs on the basis of many job characteristics. Pay, the _____ attribute, is the most important for some. For others, job security, status, the likelihood of advancement, safe working conditions, interest in the work, or the flexibility of employers in matters of dress or hours is most important. Job features unrelated to pay are called the _____ attributes.

11.　Workers join labor unions to improve their pay and work environments. At the peak of union membership in 1953, _____ percent of U.S. workers belonged to a union.　In 2001 that figure stood at 16.3 million members out of the civilian labor force of 142 million, or about _____ percent of the labor force.

12.　In order to reverse the long-term decline in membership, unions reach out for new members. Union efforts to "organize" an employer—have the right to represent its workers—culminate in a secret ballot representation election, under the supervision of the federal government's _____ _____ _____ _____ (NLRB). When more than _____ of a firm's employees vote in favor of a union, the NLRB certifies the union as the bargaining agent for the workers. Once certified, a union engages in _____ _____, negotiations with employers aimed at improving working conditions, pay, and benefits. Union _____ _____ refers to the ability of a union to win an agreement with greater wages and benefits for its members. The primary weapon providing bargaining power to unions is the _____ or work stoppage. A _____ _____ is a work stoppage that occurs spontaneously because of workers' grievances against their employer. When an employer faces a work stoppage, its most powerful source of bargaining power is the right to hire _____ _____ for striking workers.

13.   Union bargaining power is reduced in the 23 states with some form of a _____ law, which permits a unionized firm's workers the option of not joining the union.

14.   Another union weapon is the _____, a campaign to persuade union members and the public to refrain from purchasing the output of a firm with which the union has a disagreement. Boycotts often go hand in hand with strikes.

15.   The _____ hypothesis provides an alternative to the human capital explanation for the greater earnings of college graduates. In this view, education provides information to employers about the characteristics of job applicants. Employers believe that more education signals that one is easily trained and reliable.

16.   _____ discrimination occurs when a worker who is as productive as other workers doing the same job is paid less because of race, sex, color, religion, or national origin. This discrimination is illegal in the United States. Not all wage differences arise because of employer discrimination. The market will tend to pay the members of one group more than the members of the other if the first group is more _____, perhaps from differences in human capital, which may reflect differing amounts and quality of schooling.

17.   To the extent that a group, blacks for example, experiences systematic discrimination prior to entering the labor market—_____ discrimination—the outcome is less human capital and lower wages. This situation can also harm blacks with higher-than-average human capital to the extent that employers have imperfect information about individual job applicants and resort to _____ discrimination, which is to judge applicants by the average characteristics of their racial or ethnic group.

18.   _____ _____ refers to differences in earnings. Low wages or lack of a job can create poverty. Poverty is associated with deprivation, which motivates government transfer programs to aid the poor. Some of these transfers are cash. About two-thirds of government transfers to the poor provide _____ benefits, meaning that valuable services are provided instead of money. These programs seek to preserve a minimum standard of living for the poor and are commonly referred to as the _____ _____ _____.

19.   Earnings differentials exist between groups of people. The average full-time female worker in the United States earns about _____ cents for every dollar earned by the average male. This figure is up from 59 cents in 1978. Although less so now than in earlier decades, women's earnings and rank are negatively affected by _____ labor force participation, which occurs when a person leaves and later reenters the labor force. _____ _____ is the concentration of women workers in certain jobs, such as nursing and teaching.

20. _____ _____ describes earnings in excess of opportunity costs for a unique input—one that is in fixed supply. _____ is the price paid for the use of money, usually expressed in terms of a percentage, the _____ _____. Profit motivates _____, who perform the following functions: (1) Combining resources—organizing land, labor, and capital into productive uses; (2)Innovation—implementing new production methods and creating new products; and (3) Taking risks.

E&A   21. The costs of schooling include both _____costs and _____costs.

22. Balanced against the costs of schooling are the benefits. The _____ benefits of a college education are the increases in the ability to consume goods and services.

23. The _____ benefits of an action are the benefits unrelated to the acquisition of material goods and services. Two examples of these benefits of a college education are consumption benefits and social benefits.

24. The age/earnings profile of a college graduate rises steeply in the early years of work as the individual acquires the _____ _____associated with increasing experience and responsibility. The rise in earnings reflects the individual's increasing productivity.

25. The age/earnings profile of a high school graduate starts at age 18 rather than age 21, as in the earnings profile of the college graduate. This earnings profile starts lower than the earnings profile of the college graduate and stays lower. Typically, the gap between the two age/earnings profiles would _____ over time because the slope of the earnings profile of the high school graduate will be less than the slope of the earnings profile of the college graduate. This lower slope reflects the reduced opportunities on the job for the high school graduate to acquire human capital. The age/earnings profile of a drop out starts at the minimum wage and after rising due to initial on the job training remains flat throughout the individual's lifetime. The flat earnings profile assumes that the dropout is not able to acquire any additional _____ _____on the job, which would increase productivity and thus put a positive slope on the age/earnings profile. The age/earnings profiles of white workers will have a _____ slope than the age/earnings profiles of minority workers when minority workers are discriminated against on the job.

TRUE/FALSE/EXPLAIN
If false, explain why in the space provided.

1. Profit accounts for about half of national income in the United States.

2. The sum of all wages an employer pays reveals the employer's total labor costs.

3. Paid vacations are an example of a fringe benefit.

4. People will only work for pay when wages exceed their reservation wages.

5. The substitution effect of a wage increase tends to reduce the number of hours a person works.

6. The income effect of a wage increase tends to reduce the number of hours a person works.

7. The income effect of a wage increase dominates the substitution effect for the labor market as a whole.

8. Right-to-work laws outlaw unions in the states with such laws.

9. Compensating wage differentials explain why unpleasant jobs pay more than pleasant jobs requiring comparable skills.

10. Human capital is concerned with education and training.

11.   On the-job-training is an example of human capital acquisition.

12.   The theory of compensating wage differentials says that garbage collectors will be paid more in order to compensate them for the unpleasant aspects of the job.

13.   Occupational segregation is about the concentration of workers in certain occupations.

14.   Women earn about 50 percent of men's earnings.

15.   One of the widest pay gaps is between the earnings of black women and white women.

16.   Economic rent is income in excess of opportunity costs.

17.   Each person with a unique talent is able to earn a large economic rent.

18.   Inequality as measured by the income distribution would be less if in-kind government assistance to the poor were included in income.

19.   Interest is a payment made by a borrower to compensate a lender for the use of money.

20.   The interest rate is the percentage of borrowers relative to the population is a whole.

E&A 21. Statistics show that average yearly earnings are lowest for those with less than a 9th grade education and highest for those with a doctorate degree.

22. Among the tangible benefits of a college education is the opportunity to make new friends.

23. Typically, an age/earnings profile will rise throughout a person's life, even to the point where the person retires.

24. The age/earnings profile for a college graduate may be below that of a dropout while the college graduate is in school, but will be above that of the dropout later.

25. While the cost of tuition and fees at a public university varies from state to state, it is normally about the same as at a private university.

MULTIPLE CHOICE
Circle the letter preceding the one best answer.

1. Over 70 percent of U.S. national income comes from
    a. profits.
    b. wages.
    c. rents.
    d. interest.

2. The difference between salaried workers and workers who are paid wages is that the former
    a. receive fringe benefits and the latter do not.
    b. receive a fixed income, while the income of the latter depends on how many hours are worked.
    c. receive overtime pay, while the latter do not.
    d. are nonunion workers, while the latter are union members.

3.   Monthly labor costs at Gizmo Magic Manufacturing Company, which employs 1000 workers, equal $10,000 in wages, and $2,700 in fringe benefits. Per worker, total labor costs at Gizmo Magic are
a. $2.7 million.
b. $12,700.
c. $12.70.
d. $10.00.

4.   In order for an individual to be counted as part of the U.S. labor force, he or she must
a.   have a job.
b.   simply want a job.
c.   have a job or be looking for a job, no matter his or her age.
d.   be at least 16 years of age and have a job or be looking for a job.

5.   An unemployed worker who is offered less than a reservation wage will
a.   voluntarily choose to remain unemployed.
b.   choose to work, but only part time.
c.   choose to work, but actively look for another job.
d.   choose to work, but do a poor job.

6.   If the income effect of a wage change is stronger than the substitution effect,
a.   demand for labor will shift outward.
b.   demand for labor will shift inward.
c.   labor supply will be vertical.
d.   labor supply will be backward bending.

7.   Of the following, the rightward shift in supply in Multiple Choice Figure 1 is most likely to be caused by
a.   a decrease in a person's wealth.
b.   an increase in a person's wealth.
c.   an increase in competition.
d.   a more effective union.

8.   The downwardly pointing arrow in Multiple Choice Figure 1 represents
a.   a decrease in economic rent.
b.   an increase in economic rent.
c.   a decrease in demand.
d.   a decrease in the person's reservation wage.

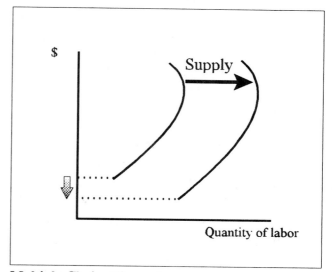

Multiple Choice Figure 1

9.   Which of the following labor supply curves is likely to be the most inelastic?
      a.   The labor supply of a primary worker.
      b.   The labor supply of a secondary worker.
      c.   The market supply of labor.
      d.   The supply of labor to a particular industry.

10.   Which of the following represents a compensating wage differential?
      a.   Wages paid to Jenny, a nurse on the night shift, exceed wages paid for the same kind of work on the day shift.
      b.   Although they are both equally qualified special education teachers, Gayla is paid less than Joe, the son of the school board president.
      c.   As a petroleum engineer, Judy saw her wages jump when the price of oil increased.
      d.   Unlike the rest of us, Michael Jordan has earned millions of dollars each year because of his accomplishments as a basketball star.

11.   Right-to work laws _____ union bargaining power.
      a.   increase
      b.   decrease
      c.   leave unchanged
      d.   sometimes increase and other times decrease

12.   Which is NOT a means by which unions try to attain their goals?
      a.   Strike
      b.   Boycott
      c.   Negotiations
      d.   Lockout

13.   When workers invest in human capital, their earnings would be expected to
      a.   remain the same.
      b.   decrease because there are few jobs for skilled workers.
      c.   decrease because there is not much demand for skilled workers.
      d.   increase.

14.   Statistical discrimination means
      a.   to judge applicants by the average characteristics of their racial or ethnic group.
      b.   that the odds are strongly against a workforce being composed of the exact same racial and ethnic makeup as the community or the workforce.
      c.   that, on average, people discriminate.
      d.   that employers tend to hire people who are good with numbers, even if those skills are not needed on the job.

15. The poverty line
    a. extends from near Richmond, Virginia, to Akron, Ohio, then southwest to Memphis, east to Knoxville, and then north again to Richmond.
    b. is constructed by the government.
    c. is computed after adding the value of in-kind transfers received by the poor.
    d. is another name for the Mason-Dixon line.

16. To qualify for access to subsidized school luches an other in-kind government assistance, individuals whose incomes are low are most likely to have an incentive to
    a. increase their incomes.
    b. decrease their incomes.
    c. maintain their same incomes, but earn it from multiple employers.
    d. maintain their same incomes, and keep their same job.

17. Compared to men in the United States, women in the United States earn
    a. 43 cents for every dollar earned by the average male.
    b. 59 cents for every dollar earned by the average male.
    c. 74 cents for every dollar earned by the average male.
    d. 89 cents for every dollar earned by the average male.

18. In recent years, the number of women holding executive, administrative, or managerial positions has been
    a. declining.
    b. remaining constant.
    c. steadily increasing.
    d. fluctuating, with no apparent trend.

19. If the government passes a law that women's wages be increased by ten percent, the most likely result would be
    a. higher unemployment for women.
    b. lower unemployment for women.
    c. lower wages for women.
    d. that men's wages also rise by ten percent.

20. It has been observed that janitors receive higher wages than secretaries. Which of the following explanations would be consistent with economic analysis?
    a. Social pressures have the effect of directing women toward secretarial careers, thereby increasing the supply relative to the demand.
    b. Being a janitor has more prestige than being a secretary.
    c. Janitors need more money because they are often primary workers, while secretaries usually have husbands to support them.
    d. Janitors perform an essential service, while secretaries do not.

E&A 21.   For a young child, the opportunity cost of schooling is
       a.   equal to the cost of books and tuition.
       b.   equal to the amount of school taxes paid by taxpayers.
       c.   essentially zero.
       d.   a significant determinant of whether those children are put to work in family businesses today.

22.   An intangible benefit to a college graduate would be
       a.   an increased ability to consume goods and services.
       b.   greater job security.
       c.   better working conditions.
       d.   the enjoyment that comes with learning new things.

23.   A person's expected stream of earnings over time is referred to as
       a.   the earnings curve.
       b.   an age/earnings profile.
       c.   the educational attainment function.
       d.   the income quotient (I. Q.).

24.   The age/earning profile that will typically rise the highest is the profile of a
       a.   high-school dropout.
       b.   high-school graduate.
       c.   college graduate with a bachelor's degree.
       d.   person who earns a professional degree.

25.   Health problems will most likely be associated with
       a.   a rising age/earnings profile.
       b.   a flat age/earnings profile.
       c.   a falling age/earnings profile.
       d.   a vertical age/earnings profile.

GRASPING THE GRAPHS
Fill in each box with a concept that applies.

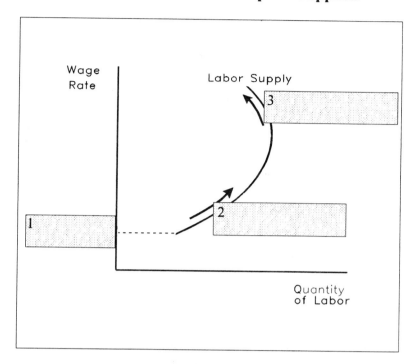

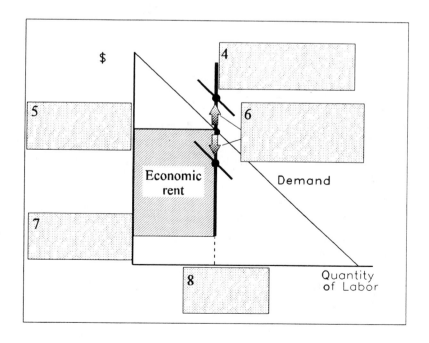

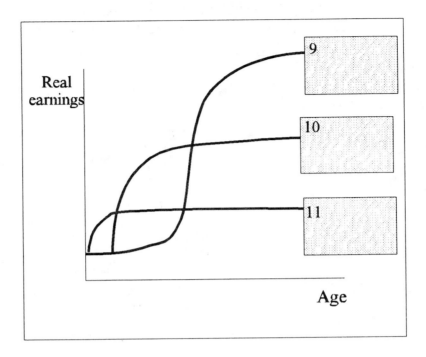

ANSWERS

STUDYCHECKS

1. At first, the worker's labor supply curve slopes upward. The worker works more because higher wages cause leisure to have a higher opportunity cost than before. That is the substitution effect. When income is high, however, the income effect may come to dominate. That effect may cause the labor supply curve to become backward-bending, as workers take more time off to enjoy their wealth. The upward-sloping and backward-bending portions of the individual's supply of labor are likely to be most pronounced for secondary workers, who have more discretion over whether to work. Primary workers have a more nearly vertical supply curve.

2. The reason that the market supply of labor will slope upwards, even if some individuals have backward-bending labor supply curves is that higher wages will attract new entrants into specific labor markets and also into the labor force as a whole.

3. Five of the possible reasons are: 1) compensating wage differentials; 2) unionization; 3) human capital; 4) discrimination; 5) luck.

4.   A payment to a worker in excess of the person's opportunity costs is termed economic rent. See how an increase in demand increases rent in StudyCheck 4 Figure.

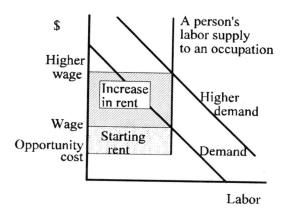

StudyCheck 4 Figure

5.   The high school drop out is assumed to have no opportunities to acquire additional human capital, which would cause the age/earnings profile to slope upward.

FILL IN THE BLANKS

1.   72, 18, 8, 2
2.   overtime, salary, total labor costs, 28
3.   Labor force participation
4.   reservation wage, backward-bending
5.   substitution
6.   income, fewer
7.   income, substitution, upward
8.   primary, secondary, vertical, nonlabor, reduce, market, upward
9.   compensating pay differentials
10.   pecuniary, nonpecuniary
11.   36, 11.5
12.   National Labor Relations Board, half, collective bargaining, bargaining power, strike, wildcat strike, permanent replacements
13.   right-to-work
14.   boycott
15.   signaling
16.   Wage, productive
17.   pre-market, statistical

18. Income inequality, in-kind, social safety net
19. 74, discontinuous, Occupational segregation
20. Economic rent, Interest, interest rate, entrepreneurs
21. direct, opportunity
22. tangible
23. intangible
24. human capital
25. increase, human capital, steeper

TRUE/FALSE/EXPLAIN

1. False, profit accounts for less than 10 percent of income in the United States.
2. False, an employer's total labor costs included fringe benefits as well as wages and salaries.
3. True.
4. True.
5. False, the substitution effect of a wage increase tends to increase the number of hours people work.
6. True.
7. False, both the income effect and the substitution effect of the wage increase apply to an individual's labor supply, not to market labor supply.
8. False, right-to-work laws do not outlaw unions, but rather state that employees cannot be forced to join a union.
9. True.
10. True.
11. True.
12. True.
13. True.
14. False, the typical full-time female worker in the United States earns about 74 cents for every dollar earned by the typical male.
15. False, there is a much wider pay gap between men and women in general than between black women and white women.
16. True.
17. False, the amount of economic rent earned by someone with a unique talent depends entirely on demand.
18. True.
19. True.
20. False, the interest rate is the price of borrowed money, expressed as a percentage.
21. True.
22. False, that benefit would be intangible.
23. False, the profile will flatten out and possibly drop at some point as a person approaches retirement.

24. True.
25. False, the cost of tuition and fees is ordinarily much higher at a private university.

MULTIPLE CHOICE

1.	b	8.	d	15.	b	22.	d
2.	b	9.	a	16.	b	23.	b
3.	c	10.	a	17.	c	24.	d
4.	d	11.	b	18.	c	25.	c
5.	a	12.	d	19.	a		
6.	d	13.	d	20.	a		
7.	a	14.	a	21.	c		

GRASPING THE GRAPHS
Examples of correct answers

1. Reservation wage
2. Substitution effect dominates
3. Income affects dominates
4. Supply of a unique talent
5. Wage rate
6. Changes in demand change the wage rate and change economic rent.
7. Opportunity cost = reservation wage
8. Quantity supplied
9. Earnings profile for college graduate
10. Earnings profile for high school graduate
11. Earnings profile for dropout

**Visit the Ayers/Collinge companion Website at http://www.prenhall.com/ayers
for further activities and exercises for this chapter.**

Part 5

MARKET FAILURE
AND GOVERNMENT ACTION

Chapter 14

PUBLIC GOODS, REGULATION, AND INFORMATION

CHAPTER REVIEW

14.1 Identifying Market Failures

• The invisible hand of the marketplace leads profit-seeking producers to offer consumers an efficient variety of goods and services. Competition ensures that these goods and services are produced at least cost and in efficient quantities.

• Efficiency is the market's great success and the reason that market economies have been able to improve living standards over time. However, there are also instances of **market failure,** in which markets do not bring about economic efficiency.

• There are two sources of market failure, The first is a lack of competition, which you learned about in the monopoly chapter. The second occurs when a good is not purely private.

• **Private goods** are *excludable* and *rival,* meaning that people can be excluded from consuming the good and any one person's consumption diminishes the amount that is available for everyone else. Most goods are private goods.

• At the opposite extreme from private goods lie **public goods,** which are *nonexcludable* and *nonrival,* meaning that people can neither be kept from consuming the good nor does their consumption reduce the amount available for others. The nonrival nature of a public good means that the marginal cost of providing service to additional consumers is zero. The nonexcludable nature of the public good means that, although different people value it differently, we have no choice but to each consume the same amount. National defense provides the best example of a public good.

• *Pure public goods* are completely nonexcludable and nonrival. To some extent, almost all public goods are impure. An *impure public good* is one that is not consumed with complete equality or that some people can be excluded from consuming at all.

- Impurities in public goods often involve **congestion**, which occurs when the addition of one more user reduces the availability of the good for all other users. **Congestion violates the assumption of nonrivalry needed for a pure public good.** Fees can serve to reduce congestion.

- Public goods can extend over a wide or limited area. A city's air quality is an example of a **local public good.** Local public goods provide an economic justification for local and regional governments.

- In between pure public and pure private goods are common property resources and private goods with externalities. Sometimes the ownership of something is common property, meaning that it is shared. Shared ownership occurs most frequently with natural resources, thus leading to the term **common property resource.** A common property resource generates contention over who gets to use it.

- Other times, the production or consumption of private goods leads to costs or benefits to third parties—people or businesses who were not party to the transaction. Such spillover effects onto third parties are termed **externalities.**

- Externalities can be either negative or positive. Pollution is an example of a negative externality. Negative externalities impose **external costs** on others. Conversely, positive externalities confer **external benefits.**

- Private goods are consumed and paid for by the individual. Public goods, on the other hand, are consumed simultaneously by everyone regardless of who pays.

- Unlike a private good, each unit of a public good is simultaneously consumed by everyone. The value of a public good is thus the sum of its values to all consumers. It would be efficient to provide this good only if total benefits exceed total costs.

- In most applications, the quantity of a public good can vary, which means we must compare the increment to costs to the increment to benefits from producing more of the public good. In other words, we must consider not only total benefits and costs, but also marginal benefit and marginal cost.

- **The efficient quantity of a public good is achieved when marginal cost equals marginal benefit.** That quantity maximizes social surplus, which is the difference between total benefit and total cost.

- With public goods, the amount you consume seems unaffected by how much you spend. You can still consume just as much of the public good as everyone else. The result is a **free-rider problem,** in which everyone has the incentive to let others pay the costs of providing the public good.

StudyCheck 1

Explain how the free rider problem dissuades the private marketplace from providing public goods. When is there most likely to be private provision of public goods? Provide an example of a public good that is provided in the free marketplace.

- The laws of supply and demand apply as much to public goods as to private goods. The lower is the price of a public good, the less producers are willing to sell and the more consumers are willing to buy. Unfortunately, because public goods are nonexcludable, they are free to use. While we value public goods collectively, we do not volunteer to pay for them individually. So public goods will not be produced unless government gets involved.

- The solution to the free-rider problem involves taxation. Government compels everyone to contribute, since everyone shares in consuming public goods.

14.2 Policy Options

- In cases of pure public goods, government has little recourse but to produce the goods itself or provide government payment to private companies who in turn would produce the goods. However, as we move along the spectrum of market failure away from pure public goods, it becomes possible for government to use regulations or price incentives to guide the marketplace toward efficiency.

- Government might charge for the use of particular highways through the assessment of *user fees*, known more familiarly as tolls. For such impure public goods, government's policy alternatives are of three general sorts:
    - **Government can price the good.** For example, tolls can be used to discourage driving when roads are congested.
    - **Government can produce the good.** For example, most highways are built by government contractors and subcontractors.
    - **Government can regulate the good.** For example, certain highway lanes are reserved for busses or other high-occupancy vehicles.

- Highways are subject to congestion, which is a special case of externality in which adding another user detracts from the benefits going to other users. In the case of highways, additional drivers slow each other down.

- The marginal cost of highway usage is assumed to be zero until the point at which congestion sets in. That assumption is largely true for passenger cars, as almost all degradation of highways comes from weather and heavy trucks. After the point of congestion, however, adding more vehicles of any sort slows everybody down, which is costly.

- The individual driver is motivated to avoid these congested roads only to the extent that it affects that driver—marginal private cost. However, there are additional costs to society—marginal social cost—because that driver's presence on the highway makes the problems of congestion worse for everybody else. The result is too much congestion as drivers make their decisions without reference to their own impact on the traffic jam. A toll could be used to achieve the efficient amount of congestion by raising the marginal cost perceived by the entering driver.

- Most drivers prefer the inefficient highway congestion to the tolls. The reason is that, although achieving efficiency means that society has more to go around, the drivers themselves would be worse off because the toll would collect a large amount of money from them.

- What if the highway is usually congested—should a new one be built? For the answer to that question and a myriad more, government turns to cost-benefit analysis. Government uses **cost-benefit analysis** to estimate and compare the costs and benefits of alternative courses of action. Cost-benefit analysis is often complex.

- Consider the seemingly simple matter of speed limits. We can save lives by reducing the speed limit on expressways to ten miles per hour. But we value our time as well as our safety and so prefer to go faster. But how much faster? In order to choose the best speed limit requires comparison of *intangibles*, which have no market price. However, researchers can often infer the value we implicitly place on intangibles, including the intangibles of safety and time.

- Consider the value of a *statistical life*, which is the expectation of a life saved or lost as a result of a government action, without knowing exactly whose life it will be. Raising speed limits costs statistical lives. Likewise, adding police officers saves statistical lives. We do not set speed limits at zero, nor do we spend all of our money on cops. So implicitly, we place a value on life in a statistical sort of way. Getting a handle on how much a statistical life is worth to us might involve looking at pay differentials between risky and nonrisky jobs, such as how much more construction workers are paid to work on high-rise buildings where their lives are more at risk.

- Another intangible is that, unlike private firms, the government cannot observe the prices at which its products sell in the marketplace because the market for its products does not exist. What is the value of saving a wetland? No one offers to purchase public goods of this sort.

- Some of the best techniques to reveal benefits of intangibles involve observing other market prices that relate to the good in question. For example, the cost of noise pollution from airplanes can be estimated by observing market prices for homes under takeoff and landing flight paths, and comparing those to market prices of similar homes in less noisy locations. Attaching dollar values provides a common measuring rod by which to measure things that are otherwise seemingly incomparable. Because the economy has scarce resources, such choices must be made.

- **Regulation** occurs whenever government acts to influence the specifications of goods and services or the manner in which they are produced. Speed limits, smoking bans, seat belt requirements, product standards, and workplace safety laws are a few of the many regulations.

- In determining the type and amount of regulations to apply, policymakers should be aware of the regulations' *administrative and compliance costs.* Regulations should only be imposed to the extent that their benefits outweigh their costs, including costs of administration of compliance.

- **The marginal benefit of additional regulation should equal its marginal cost.** While it is often hard to quantify these benefits and costs, there is often a suspicion that regulation has gone overboard.

StudyCheck 2

Explain why, even though regulations are usually enacted for good purposes, people and businesses often get highly incensed over them. Provide an example of a regulation for which this is so.

- The **specificity principle** says to target the problem in as precise and narrow a manner as possible. Using the specificity principle, the best solution to a market failure is often not to abandon markets altogether by resorting to command and control, but rather to correct only the problem within the market that is keeping it from being a success.

- **The specificity principle can be used to resolve urban water crises.** In most cases, the reaction of urban water authorities is to make rules and regulations that govern how water can be used. However, **the specific problem is not the specifics of water usage, but rather the lack of a market-clearing price.**

- The complication is that municipal water distribution is a natural monopoly, and thus a legitimate candidate for regulation. In most major American cities, local government either controls the water supply or regulates the price charged by a protected monopoly franchise.

- Traditionally, as discussed in the chapter on monopoly, regulation takes the form of average-cost pricing, in which the authorities set price so as to allow the firm only a normal profit. Unlike in other cases of regulated monopoly, though, the quantity of water available at any given time is not easily adjustable. Unfortunately, aiming price to achieve a revenue objective does not allow it to also target the objective of allocative efficiency. That would require marginal-cost pricing, which might be quite a bit higher in some regions.

- Alternatively, local governments frequently price discriminate, with some users paying a much higher price than is paid by others. While price discrimination could be efficient, in this case it is usually constrained to maintain only normal profit. For example, authorities might raise the rates to punish large-volume users, and use the extra revenues to lower rates for everybody else. The result still does not clear the market.

- Local government authorities might aim to keep prices low for the poor, to avoid having a so-called water tax. If those authorities were to specify their objective more fundamentally, though, it would be that they do not want their actions to cause additional impoverishment. So really there are two goals: 1) to avoid a water shortage; 2) to avoid hurting the poor. Price can only meet one of them. Since there are two goals, the specificity principle would suggest two separate policies, such as:
  - A single market-clearing price that adjusts as needed to prevent shortages.
  - Financial aid on the basis of income needs.

StudyCheck 3

Distinguish between the following two alternatives for pricing municipal tap water: (a) marginal-cost pricing; (b) average-cost pricing. Explain which is more likely to lead to a water shortage and why. What guidance would the specificity principle offer regarding these prices?

14.3 Imperfect Information

- **Imperfect information** occurs when we do not fully understand the choices available to us, or the consequences of those choices.

- Investors in Enron Corporation learned firsthand about the implications of imperfect information. At the start of 2001, Enron Corporation had a market value that placed it within the top 10 of all U.S. corporations. Yet by the end of that year, Enron was bankrupt. The investors who had bid the price of Enron stock so high had been deceived by complicated and shady accounting practices that they did not understand. The market had made a mistake.

- As a result of the Enron debacle, investors and analysts pored over the accounting statements of other companies very, very carefully. This scrutiny caused investors to reallocate their money away from companies with suspect accounting practices, a process that increased both information flow and the efficiency of the market. But government had a role to play, too. The Securities and Exchange Commission took action to reevaluate the information that public companies were required by law to report to shareholders and when they were required to report it.

- When one person has access to more information than another on a subject of mutual interest, they are said to possess **asymmetric information**. Asymmetric information is responsible for several puzzling facets of modern life. For example, the value of an automobile drops by a couple of thousand dollars as soon as it is first sold. The reason is that prospective buyers of a used car are aware that the seller knows more about the car—the shoppers are aware of what they don't know.

- Asymmetric information may be important to the value of the degree you seek. If you are studying at one of the top ten universities in the country, for example, you are likely to find that your degree will be worth a great deal more in the job market than degrees held by people who have acquired an equal amount of knowledge at lesser-known schools. This is the problem of *credentialism*, in which people's skills and abilities are judged by the reputation of their degrees or other credentials. It often seems inequitable, but it can be efficient.

- Asymmetric information provides at least part of the explanation for another phenomenon—*cronyism*. Cronyism occurs when employers hire friends, relatives, fellow church members, and so forth. Fair or not, cronyism offers a way to circumvent asymmetric information.

- The search for profit motivates firms to implement numerous safety measures, even when no regulation forces them to do so. The rationale is that unsafe working conditions lead to various costs, such as those associated with interruptions in production. A dangerous firm must also offer higher wages and better benefits to attract workers. It would be forced to pay higher insurance premiums to cover Healthcare expenses and liability. If these costs exceed the cost of the safety measures, a profit-maximizing firm will undertake the safety measures.

- It can be shown, in principle, how to choose an efficient amount of safety. The idea is to keep adding safety measures so long as the marginal benefit exceeds the marginal cost. While the search for profit motivates the firm to implement safety measures, not all of the benefits from safety improvements might affect those profits. If they don't then firms will not choose to be safe enough. This situation might occur if workers have insufficient information about the value of safety improvements.

- If firms do not undertake an efficient number of safety measures, there is a role for government regulators. Specifically, government regulators might estimate the efficient amount of safety and force firms to achieve that amount.

- It is impractical for government safety regulations to be tailored to the wants of different groups of workers. The result is that both firms and workers often complain about rigid work rules and safety measures.

StudyCheck 4

Using a graph, show how the market equilibrium quantity of workplace safety might be less than the efficient quantity. Why might this result occur?

- The costs of crime and crime prevention take many forms. People lose life and property. What makes an individual turn to a life of crime? From an economic perspective, a criminal would consider the relative monetary and nonmonetary returns and weigh them against expected costs. **Because there is uncertainty attached to the outcome of criminal activity, the economic model of crime posits that criminals make decisions based on the** *expected marginal benefits* **and** *expected marginal costs* **of criminal activity.** On the cost side, the prospective criminal considers the uncertain expected punishment, where the expected punishment = punishment for the crime × probability of being caught and convicted.

- The uncertainties of catching and convicting criminals mean that, for the punishments to serve as effective deterrents, they often seem harsh relative to the actual crime that the person committed. The challenge facing government is to find new deterrents to crime that raise the cost to criminals of committing crimes, without a commensurate rise in cost to taxpayers.

E&A   **14.4 Healthcare—Can the Ills be Cured?**

- Healthcare accounts for roughly 14 percent of U.S. spending, compared to about 10 percent in Canada and 7 percent in Japan. Over time, healthcare has come to include increasingly sophisticated techniques.

- Because of healthcare's high and often unpredictable expenses, we typically resort to insurance. Sometimes that insurance is privately provided. Sometimes it is provided by government through Medicaid for the poor or Medicare for the elderly.

- For both physicians and patients, health insurance alters incentives. For example, a patient might pay *co-insurance*—a percentage of costs over some deductible amount. For example, a patient might pay 20 percent of yearly Healthcare expenses after paying a $300 deductible out-of-pocket.

- Healthcare is provided by the insurance company in exchange for annual premiums, usually paid for by a person's employer. Because the per-unit price of Healthcare is reduced to the patient, patients seek more of it, just as the law of demand would suggest. However, this lower price to patients does not mean the price paid to the health service providers has fallen. The result is the problem of *moral hazard* in which the insurance has led to the overconsumption of healthcare services. Moral hazard leads patients to consume too much medical care.

- Typically, healthcare providers bill the insurance company for more than contractually agreed-upon rates. This is not usually a problem, as the insurer merely adjusts the charges downward to what is allowable. However, it becomes a problem if for some reason the patient is not covered by insurance. In that case, the patient is surprised with the full charge. If the surprise price was known beforehand, patients would have shopped for lower rates or reduced their quantities demanded. The surprise price is a way for hospitals, physicians, and other healthcare providers to supplement the low rates paid under government and private insurance plans, rates that cover variable costs but not always fixed costs. The problem revolves around the fairness of this practice to the patient and the efficiency of patient choices in the absence of complete information.

- The price of buying insurance is also high for individuals. To understand why, consider the incentives facing insurance companies. These companies are in business to provide a positive return to their investors, not to give away services that cost more than the value of the premiums they receive. Consequently, they try to distinguish between ex ante (before the fact) and ex post (after the fact) conditions. The laws of probability allow insurers to cover conditions ex ante. For example, suppose you have the same chance as everybody else of coming down with some medical condition. By covering many people, most of whom will have no cause to file claims, the insurer can profitably offer you coverage at a fraction of treatment costs. Ex post is another story altogether.

- If you already have a condition, the insurance company could make money only if they charged you at least the full cost of treatment. That would be no insurance at all!

- Even if you do not have any particular medical problems, you still cannot get an individual policy at a price approaching that of a group insurance plan. The reason revolves around asymmetric information. Even if you do not have any particular condition yet, you probably know much better than the insurance company which conditions you would be most susceptible to. Asymmetric information leads to the problem of *adverse selection*—those who seek out insurance coverage are the most likely to need it.

- Because of adverse selection, the expected cost to the insurance company of writing an individual policy is much higher than the expected cost per person under a group policy. The lowest rates go to groups that are likely to be healthier than average, such as pools of employees at large businesses.

- Healthcare expenses can vary dramatically and unpredictably from person to person. This uncertainty motivates us to want insurance. We want others to be covered, too, including the sick and injured who cannot help themselves. This is a motivation for *universal coverage*, equal access to Healthcare for everyone, which requires government action to achieve.

- Universal coverage would overcome the problem of adverse selection—we would all be in the same group. By forcing everyone to participate, universal coverage would also avoid the free-rider problem, which occurs when people figure that some safety-net level of coverage will be available to them whether they contribute insurance premiums or not.

- In 1993, President Clinton submitted to Congress a sweeping 1,342 page proposal that called for all Americans to be provided with national health insurance, giving citizens complete freedom to chose their own doctors. However, doctors would have been forced to charge the same "community standard" price, a form of price controls. That prospect frightened many people, and led to the proposal's defeat.

- Under community standard pricing, doctors with the best reputations would be flooded with potential patients. The patients wind up paying extra, but the payments are in time, not money. Likewise, doctors with good reputations cannot be expected to spend time on tricky cases when they could process the easy ones much faster for more money. The result would be inefficiency. The best doctors would take the easy cases, leaving the tough ones for the less highly skilled.

- Even though price controls under universal coverage do not work well, the issue of costly care demands attention. Unfortunately, the solutions remain elusive.

StudyCheck 5

Explain how health maintenance organizations (HMOs) might reduce moral hazard in some ways, but increase it in others.

FILL IN THE BLANKS

1.   Efficiency is the market's great success and the reason that market economies have been able to improve living standards over time. However, there are also instances of _____ _____, in which markets do not bring about economic efficiency.

2.   Private goods are _____ and _____.

3.   The nonrival nature of a public good means that the marginal cost of providing service to additional consumers is _____. The nonexcludable nature of the public good means that, although different people value it differently, we have no choice but to each consume the same amount. _____ _____provides the best example of a public good.

4.   Pure public goods are completely nonexcludable and nonrival. To some extent, almost all public goods are _____. Such a public good is one that is not consumed with complete equality or that some people can be excluded from consuming at all.

5.   Impurities in public goods often involve _____, which occurs when the addition of one more user reduces the availability of the good for all other users.

6.   Public goods can extend over a wide or limited area. A city's air quality is an example of a _____ public good.

7.   In between pure public and pure private goods are _____ _____ resources and private goods with _____.

8.   Sometimes the production or consumption of private goods leads to costs or benefits to third parties—people or businesses who were not party to the transaction. Such _____ effects onto third parties are termed _____.

9.   Unlike a private good, each unit of a public good is simultaneously consumed by everyone. The value of a public good is thus the _____ of its values to all consumers. It would be efficient to provide this good only if total _____ exceed total costs.

10. The efficient quantity of a public good is achieved when _____cost equals _____ benefit. That quantity maximizes _____ _____, which is the difference between total benefit and total cost. With public goods, the amount you consume seems unaffected by how much you spend. You can still consume just as much of the public good as everyone else. The result is a_____ problem, in which everyone has the incentive to let others pay the costs of providing the public good. The solution to this problem involves _____.

11. The individual driver is motivated to avoid congested roads only to the extent that it affects that driver—marginal _____cost. However, there are additional costs to society—marginal _____ cost—because that driver's presence on the highway makes the problems of congestion worse for everybody else. The result is too _____ congestion as drivers make their decisions without reference to their own impact on the traffic jam. A_____ could be used to achieve the efficient amount of congestion by raising the marginal cost perceived by the entering driver.

12. What if the highway is usually congested—should a new one be built? For the answer to that question and a myriad more, government turns to _____-_____analysis.

13. The value of a _____ _____ is the expectation of a life saved or lost as a result of a government action, without knowing exactly whose life it will be.

14. _____occurs whenever government acts to influence the specifications of goods and services or the manner in which they are produced.

15. The _____ principle says to target a problem in as precise and narrow a manner as possible.

16. _____information occurs when we do not fully understand the choices available to us, or the consequences of those choices. When one person has access to more

information than another on a subject of mutual interest, they are said to possess _____ information.

17.   You are likely to find that your degree from a top university will be worth a great deal more in the job market than degrees held by people who have acquired an equal amount of knowledge at lesser-known schools. This is the problem of _____.

18.   Asymmetric information provides at least part of the explanation for _____, which occurs when employers hire friends, relatives, fellow church members, and so forth.

19.   It can be shown, in principle, how to choose an efficient amount of safety. The idea is to keep adding safety measures so long as the marginal_____ exceeds the marginal

_____.

20.   The costs of crime and crime prevention take many forms. People lose life and property. What makes an individual turn to a life of crime? From an economic perspective, a criminal would consider the relative monetary and nonmonetary returns and weigh them against expected costs. Because there is uncertainty attached to the outcome of criminal activity, the economic model of crime posits that criminals make decisions based on the expected _____ _____ and expected _____ _____ of criminal activity. On the cost side, the prospective criminal considers the uncertain expected punishment, where the expected punishment = punishment for the crime × _____ of being caught and convicted.

E&A   21.   Healthcare accounts for roughly _____ percent of U.S. spending, compared to about 10 percent in Canada and 7 percent in Japan.

22.   Healthcare is provided by the insurance company in exchange for annual premiums, usually paid for by a person's employer. Because the per-unit price of Healthcare is reduced to the patient, patients seek more of it, just as the law of demand would suggest. However, this lower price to patients does not mean the price paid to the health service providers has fallen. The result is the problem of _____ _____ in which the insurance has led to the overconsumption of healthcare services.

23.   The price of buying insurance is also high for individuals. To understand why, consider the incentives facing insurance companies. These companies are in business to provide a positive return to their investors, not to give away services that cost more than the value of the premiums they receive. Consequently, they try to distinguish between _____(before the fact) and _____ (after the fact) conditions.

24.   Even if you do not have any particular medical problems, you still cannot get an individual policy at a price approaching that of a group insurance plan. The reason revolves around asymmetric information. Even if you do not have any particular condition yet, you probably

know much better than the insurance company which conditions you would be most susceptible to. Asymmetric information leads to the problem of _____ _____—those who seek out insurance coverage are the most likely to need it.

25. Healthcare expenses can vary dramatically and unpredictably from person to person. This uncertainty motivates us to want insurance. We want others to be covered, too, including the sick and injured who cannot help themselves. This is a motivation for _____ _____, equal access to Healthcare for everyone, which requires government action to achieve.

TRUE/FALSE/EXPLAIN
If false, explain why in the space provided.

1. A pure public good is non-excludable and non-rival.

2. A public good will probably be produced in a technologically inefficient manner in the free market.

3. The free-rider problem is usually associated with monopolies.

4. The free-rider problem causes common property resources to be overused.

5. The efficient quantity of a public good is that for which marginal social benefit equals marginal social cost.

6. A local public good is something that all localities across the country consume jointly.

7. The value of a public good is computed by adding the quantity that each person desires at each price.

8.   The actual number of cars on a congested highway will be less than the number that would be efficient.

9.   Cost-benefit analysis is a technically precise means to eliminate controversy over whether or not government should undertake a project.

10.   In evaluating public projects, cost-benefit analysis requires that dollar values be placed on intangibles, such as airplane noise and risk of death.

11.   According to the specificity principle, policy should be directed as precisely as possible toward the problem at hand.

12.   The specificity principle suggests that it is efficient for a single government policy to address multiple policy goals.

13.   Imperfect information can lead to market failure.

14.   Problems of imperfect information are reduced in part by actions of the marketplace and in part by actions of the government.

15.   Asymmetric information occurs when one party to a transaction has access to more information than does the other party.

16.   Part of the value of a college degree revolves around asymmetric information.

17.   The problem of credentialism occurs when people hire their buddies.

18.   To achieve efficiency, firms must use every possible means to safeguard the well-being of their workers.

19.   The expected punishment facing a criminal equals the punishment if caught and convicted multiplied by the probability of that happening.

20.   If criminals were rational, they would not be criminals.

E&A 21.   Moral hazard can lead to excessive medical spending when payments under health insurance plans reduce the cost of care to patients or physicians.

22.   The adverse selection problem in health care causes patients to overuse medical services.

23.   The problem of moral hazard forces individuals to join "groups" in order to obtain insurance coverage.

24.   If all physicians are forced to charge the same schedule of fees, health care costs would decline without any loss of competition or efficiency.

25.   In the 1990s, President Clinton proposed legislation that would have established national health insurance in the United States.

MULTIPLE CHOICE
Circle the letter that corresponds to the one best answer.

1. Market failure occurs whenever
    a.   companies go out of business.
    b.   products are no longer produced.
    c.   a market fails to achieve efficiency.
    d.   market prices are unfair.

2. If Multiple Choice Figure 1 represents the spectrum of market failure, point A would represent
    a.   a purely private good.
    b.   a pure public good.
    c.   an externality or common property resource.
    d.   an impure public good or local public good.

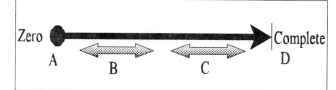

Multiple Choice Figure 1

3. If Multiple Choice Figure 1 represents the spectrum of market failure, region B would include
    a.   purely private goods.
    b.   pure public goods.
    c.   externalities or common property resources.
    d.   impure public goods or local public goods.

4. If Multiple Choice Figure 1 represents the spectrum of market failure, region C would include
    a.   purely private goods.
    b.   pure public goods.
    c.   externalities or common property resources.
    d.   impure public goods or local public goods.

5. If Multiple Choice Figure 1 represents the spectrum of market failure, line segment D would represent
    a.   a purely private good.
    b.   a pure public good.
    c.   an externality or common property resource.
    d.   an impure public good or local public good.

6. Which of the following is the best example of a pure public good?
    a.   A dolphin swimming in the ocean.
    b.   A hamburger served in a fast-food restaurant.
    c.   The books in a public library.
    d.   National defense.

7. Which of the following is most likely to be a common property resource?
    a. Water in a river.
    b. Electricity.
    c. A can of Mountain Dew soft drink.
    d. National defense.

8. Relative to use of a privately owned resource, users of a common property resource have _____ economic incentive to conserve that resource for the future.
    a. more
    b. the same
    c. slightly less
    d. no

9. In the absence of government action, external costs are borne by
    a. producers of the good causing the external cost.
    b. consumers of the good causing the external cost.
    c. other parties who are not directly involved in the production or consumption of the good.
    d. everyone equally.

10. The efficient quantity of a public good occurs at the point where
    a. marginal private cost = marginal private benefit.
    b. marginal social cost = marginal social benefit.
    c. total private cost = total social benefit.
    d. total social cost = total social benefit.

11. Of the choices below, the best example of the free-rider problem is
    a. Sharky pays nothing for the water he pumps from the Snake river to fill his fish farm.
    b. The local bus company allows its employees free bus trips at taxpayer expense.
    c. Gabriel is unwilling to pay anything for local mosquito control, unless the other residents in the area also pay.
    d. The local bus company has no incentive to reduce emissions from its buses, unless it is forced to by government rules or regulations.

12. Public goods are usually provided by government because
    a. the private marketplace would result in the rich getting more than the poor.
    b. the free-rider problem makes the goods difficult to sell.
    c. people don't know how much they need them.
    d. the definition of a public good is any good provided by government!

13.   A radio station's signals are an example of a
     a.   privately produced public good.
     b.   common property resource.
     c.   private good provided by government.
     d.   regulation.

14.   In Multiple Choice Figure 2, area A represents the amount of
     a.   time wasted by drivers stuck in traffic.
     b.   driving time saved the following the assessment of an efficient toll.
     c.   revenue collected by an efficient toll.
     d.   money it would take to implement an efficient toll.

15.   In Multiple Choice Figure 2, arrow B shows how a toll would increase
     a.   marginal private benefit.
     b.   marginal social benefit.
     c.   marginal external benefit.
     d.   marginal private cost.

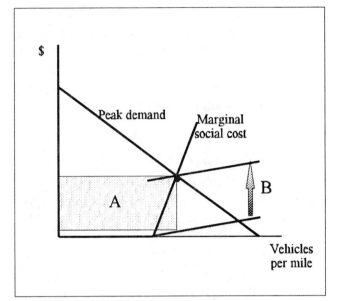

Multiple Choice Figure 2

16.   The optimal size of a governmental project would be that which
     a.   equates marginal social benefits and marginal social costs.
     b.   equates total benefits and total costs.
     c.   maximizes the benefit/cost ratio.
     d.   costs the least.

17.   In cost-benefit analysis, intangibles are usually
     a.   listed separately, since they must be weighed separately from dollar benefits and costs.
     b.   assigned dollar values based on their intrinsic worth, as determined by biological and physical science.
     c.   assigned dollar values which are based upon related values in the private marketplace.
     d.   omitted altogether, thus providing the basis for the most frequent criticism of the cost-benefit technique.

18.   The specificity principle is in keeping with which of the following phrases?
     a.   "It don't amount to a hill of beans."
     b.   "Hit the nail on the head."
     c.   "If at first you don't succeed, try, try again."
     d.   "Rules are made to be broken."

19.   Cities that face water shortages could avoid those shortages in an efficient manner by using
   a.   average-cost pricing, although this would probably cause excess revenue.
   b.   average-cost pricing, although this would probably cause a revenue shortfall.
   c.   marginal-cost pricing, although this would probably cause excess revenue.
   d.   marginal-cost pricing, although this would probably cause a revenue shortfall.

20.   Cronyism and credentialism are symptoms of
   a.   imperfect information.
   b.   externality.
   c.   common property resources.
   d.   congestion.

E&A 21.   Moral hazard occurs when insurance
   a.   causes "job lock" that makes it costly to switch jobs.
   b.   increases the price of risk, thus leading people to become unduly cautious.
   c.   lowers the price of risk, thus causing people to take more risks.
   d.   does not help the needy, because they could not afford to buy insurance policies.

22.   As a result of Great Britain's free national health service, non-urgent conditions are likely to be treated
   a.   more efficiently.
   b.   more quickly.
   c.   more slowly.
   d.   with concern for the patient.

23.   In the United States, payments by private insurers account for about
   a.   1/5 of total medical spending.
   b.   1/3 of total medical spending.
   c.   half of total medical spending.
   d.   3/4 of total medical spending.

24.   Which of the following is intended to solve the problem of adverse selection?
   a.   Requiring that insured people pay a deductible.
   b.   Requiring that insured people pay coinsurance.
   c.   Universal coverage, in which all citizens are guaranteed insurance coverage.
   d.   Health maintenance organizations (HMOs).

25.   Requiring all doctors to charge according to community-standard fee schedules would most likely result in
   a.   a reduction in waiting times to see doctors with the best reputations.
   b.   a competitively efficient provision of medical services, but at higher costs.
   c.   a competitively efficient provision of medical services, but at lower costs.
   d.   inefficiency, as doctors with the best reputations would likely treat the least demanding patients.

GRASPING THE GRAPHS
Fill in each box with a concept that applies.

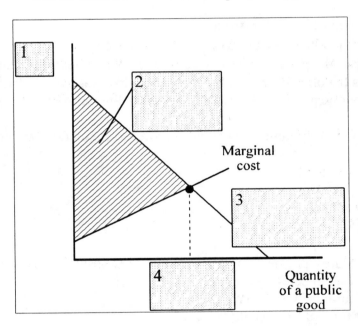

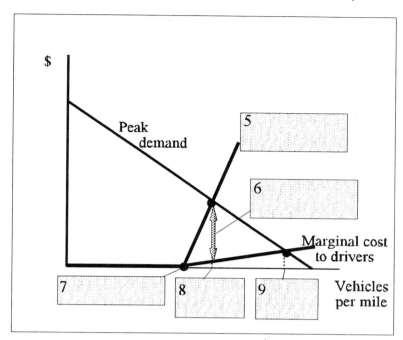

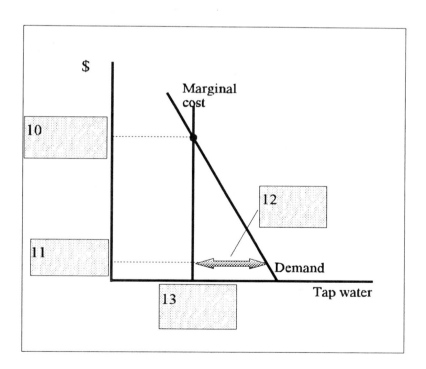

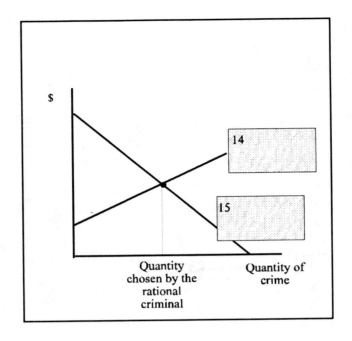

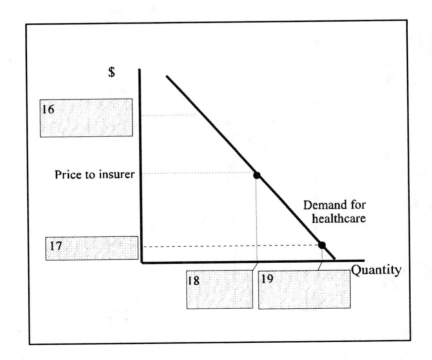

For additional practice in grasping this chapter's graphs,
visit **http://www.prenhall.com/ayers** and try *Smart Graphs* **32 and 33,**
along with *Active Graph* **62.**

ANSWERS

STUDYCHECKS

1. The free-rider problem ordinarily makes it impossible for private firms to sell public goods. Some private provision of public goods does occur in special instances, such as when firms are able to bundle the public good with a private good. For example, radio broadcasts are public goods, but are tied to the private good of advertising.

2. Regulations restrict people's freedom to do as they wish. There are often good economic reasons for regulation, such as the correction of externalities. However, regulations are usually broad-brush and may seem unreasonable and inflexible in numerous special circumstances. For example, the cost of requiring a cross country ski lodge to provide wheelchair access to its restaurant and rest rooms may be far less than the likely benefits, and yet the Americans with Disabilities Act allows no flexibility to recognize this. Other examples could be mentioned.

3. a. Marginal-cost pricing sets the price equal to marginal cost at the point where marginal cost and marginal benefit (demand) intersect. The result is a market-clearing quantity of water and that water is allocated to its most highly valued uses.
    b. Average-cost pricing sets the price so that the water utility earns no excess profit. Unless average cost is equal to marginal cost at their intersection with the demand curve, average-cost pricing will not equal marginal-cost pricing and will not clear the water market.

    During a drought or at other times when water supplies are tight, average-cost pricing leads to a water shortage because it does not increase price, or at least not enough, to reflect the increased scarcity of water. According to the specificity principle, one price cannot both allocate water efficiently and also achieve the goal of zero excess revenue. For this reason, policymakers would need to choose which goal is more important or else add an additional element of policy.

4. See StudyCheck 5 Figure. Marginal social benefit might exceed market demand if workers have imperfect information that causes them to underestimate benefits.

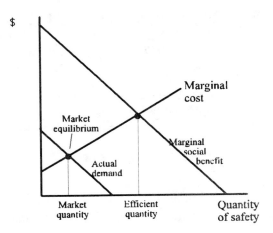

StudyCheck 5 Figure

5.   HMOs reduce the moral hazard of physicians performing too many medical services, because HMOs take away the financial incentive to do so. However, because physicians are rewarded the best for seeing the most patients, the moral hazard can go the other way. Specifically, physicians might skimp on the time and services they provide patients in order to achieve a higher head count.

FILL IN THE BLANKS

1.   market failure
2.   excludable, rival
3.   zero, National defense
4.   impure
5.   congestion
6.   local
7.   common property, externalities
8.   spillover, externalities
9.   sum, benefits
10.   marginal, marginal, social surplus, free-rider, taxation
11.   private, social, much, toll
12.   cost-benefit
13.   statistical life
14.   Regulation
15.   specificity
16.   Imperfect, asymmetric
17.   credentialism
18.   cronyism

19.   benefit, cost
20.   marginal benefits, marginal costs, probability
21.   14
22.   moral hazard
23.   ex ante, ex post
24.   adverse selection
25.   universal coverage

TRUE/FALSE/EXPLAIN

1.   True.
2.   False, it is not the manner of production that is inefficient, but rather the amount of production that causes allocative inefficiency.
3.   False, the free-rider problem is associated with public goods.
4.   False, the free-rider problem causes public goods to be underproduced.
5.   True.
6.   False, all local public good is one that is jointly consumed only within a particular region.
7.   False, the value of a public good is computed by adding each person's willingness to pay, since people consume the public good jointly.
8.   False, the actual number of cars on a congested highway will exceed the number that would be efficient.
9.   False, cost-benefit analysis is contentious and frequently dependent on the assumptions that are used.
10.   True.
11.   True.
12.   False, the specificity principle suggests that achieving multiple policy goals is likely to require multiple policies.
13.   True.
14.   True.
15.   True.
16.   True.
17.   False, it is the problem of cronyism that occurs when people hire their buddies.
18.   False, to achieve efficiency, firms must increase safety to the point that the marginal benefit of additional safety just equals its marginal cost.
19.   True.
20.   False, although there are other reasons to not be criminals, rationality would merely stop the criminal from committing crimes for which the expected marginal cost exceeds the expected marginal benefit.
21.   True.
22.   False, adverse selection makes it difficult for patients to get insurance, which in turn might somewhat reduced the moral hazard problem.

23. True.
24. False, it would be inefficient for all physicians to charge the same fees, since differences in fees are what allocate the most difficult cases to the most capable doctors.
25. True.

MULTIPLE CHOICE

1.	c	8.	d	15.	d	22.	c
2.	a	9.	c	16.	a	23.	b
3.	c	10.	b	17.	c	24.	c
4.	d	11.	c	18.	b	25.	d
5.	b	12.	b	19.	c		
6.	d	13.	a	20.	a		
7.	a	14.	c	21.	c		

GRASPING THE GRAPHS
Examples of correct answers

1. $
2. Social surplus
3. Marginal willingness to pay ("demand")
4. Efficient quantity
5. Marginal social cost
6. Efficient toll
7. Congestion point
8. Efficient quantity
9. Market quantity
10. Marginal-cost price
11. Average-cost price
12. Water shortage
13. Sustainable quantity
14. Expected marginal cost
15. Expected marginal benefit
16. Price to the unexpectedly uninsured
17. Coinsurance
18. Efficient quantity
19. Actual quantity (after moral hazard)

Visit the Ayers/Collinge companion Website at http://www.prenhall.com/ayers for further activities and exercises for this chapter.

Chapter 15

EXTERNALITIES AND COMMON PROPERTY RESOURCES

CHAPTER REVIEW

15.1 Externalities and Common Property Resources

- Externalities can be either negative or positive. Pollution is an example of a negative externality. Negative externalities impose **external costs** on others.

- Conversely, positive externalities confer **external benefits,** such as when a neighbor kills all the mosquitos on her property, which leaves fewer to fly into your own backyard.

- Externalities in the form of external benefits or external costs are all around us, although frequently of minor significance. Externalities occur when the **private costs or benefits** of an action—those borne by the ones taking the action—differ from social costs or benefits.

- **Social costs or benefits** are defined to equal all costs or benefits within the economy, including both private and external costs and benefits, as follows: Social cost = private cost + external cost, and Social benefit = private benefit + external benefit.

- By the same token, consider the costs and benefits associated with each additional unit of output, as follows: Marginal social cost = marginal private cost + marginal external cost, and Marginal social benefit = marginal private benefit + marginal external benefit.

- It is externalities that occur at the margin—**marginal external costs** and **marginal external benefits**—that are of most interest in economics, because these externalities at the margin cause market outcomes to differ from what is efficient. Significant external benefits are not as widespread as significant external costs.

- Because external costs or benefits are not felt by the person or firm causing the externality, the free market price signal fails to generate efficient outputs. In the case of an external benefit, market demand does not capture all social benefits. External benefits might arise from education, perhaps because the educated person makes better choices in the voting booth. While of value to others, there is no payment to the individual. For that reason, **when**

marginal external benefits are present, the free market produces too little—output falls short of that which would be efficient.

- The most obvious external cost is from environmental pollution. Because external costs or benefits are not felt by the person or firm causing the externality, the free market price signal fails to generate efficient outputs. Thus, **when marginal external costs are present, the free market produces too much**—output exceeds that which would be efficient.

StudyCheck 1

Why do common property resources and externalities lead to inefficiencies? In general terms, how can public policy help?

- Marginal external cost rises with output, meaning that the difference between supply and marginal social cost rises with increasing output. This is a typical result, because the usual external cost comes from pollution and results in a degradation in environmental quality. The marginal external costs of pollution are nothing more than the marginal benefits of environmental quality forgone. The presence of external costs does not imply that the externality-generating activity should cease. It is efficient to have some pollution, for example.

- Pollution results from firms using common-property air or water to remove the wastes that are generated by their production of goods and services. Lacking government action, polluters pollute too much. The reason is that there is no market for many environmental services. The outcome when there is no market is a price of zero. There is, however, a market for some environmental services,, such as for landfill services.

- If environmental services provided by common-property water and air were priced, as they would be if sold in a market, firms would economize and pollute less. They would also look for alternate ways to produce their output with less pollution. The upshot is that firms would pollute only when the value of that pollution exceeds its environmental costs. That would be efficient.

- Typically, competition forces firms to be environmentally neglectful unless there are public policy incentives to be otherwise. Were a firm to go to the expense of cutting back its pollution, that firm would be at a disadvantage in competing against other firms in its industry. Only the heaviest polluters would survive. This is why pollution externalities represent a market failure, one calling for government action to change the rules of the game. The Clean Air Act was one such action. This Act, amended in 1970, has caused the emission of major air pollutants to fall dramatically.

- While reliance on public policy is commonplace, it is not the only means to resolve externalities. An alternative would rely upon legal safeguards against damage to the property of others. This school of thought is supported by the **Coase theorem,** named after Nobel Laureate Sir Ronald Coase. The Coase theorem holds that parties to an externality would voluntarily negotiate an efficient outcome, without government involvement. Government need merely define and clearly enforce property rights.

- Few people believe the Coase theorem offers a general solution to externality problems. The problem of *strategic behavior* interferes with the practical application of the Coase theorem. That problem becomes significantly worse when the effects of the externality are widespread.

- In addition, identifying specific culprits and bringing together victims becomes quite difficult when many parties are involved. *Transaction costs,* the expense of coordinating market exchanges, would be high. Thus, the Coase theorem applies only in the absence of transaction costs and strategic behavior. In practice, this means we either resort to public policy to remedy the externality or ignore the problem and let the market fail.

StudyCheck 2

Describe the Coase Theorem and its limitations.

- Common property resources are owned jointly. Common property resources include groundwater, public lands, wild animals, and fish in the oceans, lakes, and rivers. Unless government sets up policies to prevent it, anyone can hunt, fish, pump water, and in other ways capture the common property to make it that person's private property.

- Common property resources lead to too much production in the present with insufficient regard for the future. The problem is that, when many people own the same resource, no one has any personal incentive to conserve it.

- Government can solve common property resource problems by selling the common property to a single owner. Most often, however, complete transfers would be impractical or politically unacceptable. The alternative is for government to act as the owners' agent and apportion use of the common property so that overuse is avoided. This is the rationale behind fishing and hunting permits, regulation of mesh size on fishing nets, mandated water-saving toilets, and various other restrictions and **user fees**—fees for use of a publicly owned resource.

15.2 Policy Tools

- Appeals to our social conscience—called **moral suasion**—are the easiest and most high-profile form of public policy available to fight problems associated with externalities and common property resources. Moral suasion makes it clear to the public that the government is taking action. Unfortunately, moral suasion is rarely adequate to the task and often has undesirable side effects.

- A fundamental drawback to moral suasion is that it has no way of achieving any particular target, efficient or otherwise. Also, moral suasion imposes all costs of cutbacks on the "moral." A third and perhaps most troubling problem is that moral suasion can lead to a self-righteous intrusion on personal privacy.

- **Technology mandates** occur when government instructs producers as to the exact technology to install to remedy some public problem. Low-flow showerheads and low-flush toilets are examples of technology mandates designed to avoid wasting water.

- Sometimes the mandates are indirect, as with scrubbers on powerplants' smokestacks, and other specific pollution control strategies. Here, the Environmental Protection Agency (EPA) specifies emission *standards* that must be met and suggests technologies that will meet these standards.

- Technology mandates are often much more expensive and annoying than other policy options. If external costs can be added directly to the prices of products, the higher prices would induce conservation in ways that regulators might be unable to mandate. Using prices avoids the inefficiencies caused by the broad brush of technology mandates.

- Economic studies on pollution control estimate that market-based alternatives to technology mandates and standards can achieve the same amounts of emission cutbacks at roughly one-third the cost. For example, the EPA's *bubble plan* allows a firm to increase its emissions from some sources if it offsets those increases by decreasing its emissions from other sources within its plant. The EPA's *offsets plan* extends this flexible concept across firms to capture even more cost savings.

StudyCheck 3

Describe and give an example of a technology mandate. Why might technology mandates not be the most efficient way of addressing market failure?

- As an alternative to technology mandates, pollution taxes can reduce pollution without creating the problems associated with technology mandates. Economists often advocate this action, which is referred to as *internalizing* the cost of an externality directly into prices.

- How would such a tax work? If an activity generates damages, the value of those damages would be estimated, and a tax imposed equal to the amount of the marginal external cost at the efficient level of output. In this way, the tax causes perpetrators of the external cost to pay the full marginal social cost of their activities. This means that externalities become part of the decisions of those who cause them, and efficient choices will be made in the marketplace.

- If smoking a pack of cigarettes causes an average of $1 in health damages to others, then a tax of $1 per pack would represent those damages. Such a tax is sometimes referred to as an environmental user fee, since polluters are charged for using the common property environment. A corrective tax on cigarettes shifts the supply curve up by the amount of that tax, since sellers now have to collect that extra payment and pass it along to government. The price would rise and the quantity fall, as the market equilibrium changes.

- Using fees to remedy externalities often encounters difficulties. External damages may depend upon time and place. Measurement of pollution is another hurdle in the way of applying pollution taxes. Of greater concern, however, is political support for taxing pollution and providing effective penalties to ensure compliance. Pollution taxes have proven to have little political support.

- To overcome political barriers to pollution taxes, policymakers sometimes resort to paying for pollution abatement instead. For example, municipal wastewater treatment plants receive significant federal **subsidies,** which are payments from the federal government meant to encourage actions with external benefits or that reduce external costs. Unfortunately, subsidies for reducing pollution have two undesirable side effects, which are: (1) Subsidies drain government revenues. (2) Subsidies reward polluters and, for this reason, can lead to too many polluting firms.

- **Marketable permits** offer the same economic advantages as taxes, but in a way that has much more political appeal. In application to pollution, marketable permits represent property rights to a certain amount of pollutant emissions. Government sets the overall quantity, and then divides up that quantity into a limited number of permits for the various polluters. While these permits could be auctioned, politics causes them more typically to be given away to preexisting polluters without charge.

- Marketable permits are valuable property rights. The term *marketable* means that those rights can be bought and sold. This feature has appeal not only to producers, but also to economists. If pollution rights are traded, buyers would be firms with high costs of pollution abatement. Likewise, sellers would be firms with low costs of cutting back emissions. This means that emission reductions are undertaken by firms able to do so at least cost. Trading in emission rights has mushroomed in recent years, so much so that it has formed an industry of its own.

- Since most pollution comes from production rather than from consumption, it is usually best to apply a tax or permit approach directly to pollution rather than to outputs. Sometimes this is difficult or impossible to do. When pollution control policy is applied to output, however, pollution is reduced only to the extent that output falls. In contrast, when pollution is taxed directly, polluters also have the incentive to reduce the amount of pollution per unit of that output. It is often feasible to tax pollution directly in cases of stationary-source polluters, such as factories. Such taxes require that government be able to monitor the quantity of pollution that is emitted.

- Firms do not pollute for its own sake. Rather, they use the environment to remove waste products, with pollution being the result. For this reason, firms have a demand for the right to emit pollution into the environment. In other words, firms are willing to pay because using the environment to remove wastes is a valuable service to them, just like the services of labor. Firms value this service because consumers value the output that the firms produce. Thus, the benefit of pollution is really the extra value that consumers receive because producers pollute.

- Since environmental services are not priced, there is no one in the free market to charge firms for environmental services, because no one owns the environment. For this reason, in the absence of government action, firms are free to pollute as much as they want. In effect, there is a missing market. If a market were to exist, the market supply curve would correspond to marginal social cost, the market equilibrium would an efficient quantity. The equilibrium price would equal the efficient tax.

- To substitute for an efficient market price, government could charge firms a fee per unit of emissions. This fee is commonly referred to as a pollution tax. **To remedy an externality with a tax, the tax rate must be set equal to marginal external cost at the efficient level of pollution.** Polluters would be forced to buy emission rights at that price in the same manner that they must pay for their other inputs. In this case, it is in effect government selling them the input of environmental services.

- Alternatively, regulators could issue an efficient quantity of marketable permits, which would have the effect of limiting emissions to no more than that amount. The value of the marginal unit of emissions would be the same as the efficient tax, so that competition of emission rights in the marketplace would set a price on those rights just as though there had been an emissions tax.

- While the tax solution brings in revenue to the government for every unit of emissions, a marketable permit system will typically bring little or no revenue to the government. The reason is that emission permits are usually given free of charge to firms in a region, with those firms then free to sell the emission rights as they see fit. The reason for this manner of distribution is mainly political. Since either the tax or permit approach allows regulators to create a market that allocates emission rights efficiently, marketable permits have become the policy instrument of choice.

StudyCheck 4

Explain in words how either taxes or marketable permits can be used to achieve an efficient quantity of pollution.

15.3 Caring for the Global Environment

• Policies to control pollution or preserve common property resources require a government to administer them. Yet, oftentimes, these market failures go beyond the confines of any single country. In these situations, the best solutions often involve international cooperation.

• It sounds like a good idea for countries of the world to somehow get together and protect the common property resources that we all share. Indeed, countries have gotten together to agree upon such matters as *the law of the sea*, including allowing countries to claim up to 200 miles from shorelines as the countries' own territories.

• Agreements are often difficult to reach. For example, President Bush reiterated in 2002 that the United States would not abide by the multilateral *Kyoto accords* on global warming.

• Economists identify pollution as a market failure, because firms and consumers ignore the external costs of their actions. In addition, it is important to recognize that many countries' governments have been responsible for the world's pollution. The environmental legacy of the Soviet Union and its European allies provides a tragic illustration.

E&A **15.4 Borderlands of the Southwest—Whose Pollution? Whose Solution?**

- As in other parts of the country, citizens of the Southwest must abide by U.S. environmental laws. Much of the pollution has its source in Mexico, an industrializing country with a rapidly growing population and less stringent control over pollutants. Exemplifying the problem of border air pollution, the city of El Paso, Texas, is in noncompliance with guidelines set by the U.S. Environmental Protection Agency (EPA). However, the EPA allows this noncompliance to continue without penalty.

- Transborder pollution is a problem of growing magnitude around the world. The problems are worsening for two reasons. On the one hand, economic growth in the less-developed countries does not emphasize pollution control. Of greater concern to those countries are such tangibles as food, clothing, and shelter. On the other hand, the increased wealth of the developed countries has allowed them the luxury to focus beyond immediate necessities toward the quality and long-term sustainability of lifestyles. Environmental quality is important to both of those lifestyle goals.

- Transborder pollution problems come in many forms. Some are global in nature, such as concerns that emissions of chlorofluorocarbons are depleting the earth's ozone layer. The pollution problem of most concern in America's Southwest is more local in nature. Here we have two countries, each of which feels the effects of the other's pollution. What trouble does this cause?

- The problem of localized transborder pollution centers on incentives. There is much more incentive to control pollution that affects your own residents than there is incentive to control pollution absorbed elsewhere.

- It would be very difficult for the United States to apply any particular pollution control strategy to firms in Mexico. Options that work well within a jurisdiction don't work as well across jurisdictions. For example, one option long advocated by economists is for government to impose a tax on emissions of pollutants, such that the *external costs* of pollution are *internalized* into the production process. The idea is to make firms pay for environmental services.

- A *second-best*, less desirable, alternative would be to tax the output of the firm. This approach would not give firms any incentive to reduce the amount of pollution per unit of output, but it would at least drive up the price of that output. Higher prices would mean fewer sales and thus less pollution. Could we apply either of these tax ideas to transborder pollution?

- The answer is the United States probably could not effectively use pollution taxes on Mexican polluters. The United States could not tax pollution emissions effectively, because it lacks the authority to monitor pollution in Mexico and lacks the authority to impose taxes even if it could monitor that pollution.

- Other policy instruments, such as pollution permits or mandated pollution control technologies, would also be infeasible for the same reasons taxes would not work.

- The best solution may be voluntary cooperation between the United States and Mexico based on mutual self-interest. This cooperative spirit is attested to by the 1994 implementation of the North American Free Trade Agreement (NAFTA), which incorporated Mexico into a revised and expanded free trade agreement between the United States and Canada.

- NAFTA broke new ground in international trade by writing environmental safeguards directly into the treaty and side accords. For example, NAFTA signatories are obligated to maintain effective enforcement of their own environmental laws, even when the affected pollutants spill over the border. While NAFTA does not itself solve the problems of border pollution, it does provide a framework for cooperation.

- The United States cannot expect the world to follow its standards, at least not without granting the rest of the world's citizens voting rights in U.S. elections. Moreover, uniform environmental standards would not make sense across all countries. After all, maintaining those standards is expensive, and incomes in some countries are much lower than incomes in the United States.

- One of the best ways for the United States to see greater control of pollution in Mexico is to see greater per capita income in Mexico. The reason is that environmental quality is a normal good, meaning that people want more as their incomes rise.

- it must be noted that the environment is a *common property resource,* meaning that we can all use it, but that no one really owns it. This gives us no incentive as individuals to maintain it in the present or invest in its future. The way that government solves pollution problems is, in effect, to lay its own claim to the common property environment. Government then seeks to represent the interests of present and future users of the environment. Policy is implemented via such tools as carefully designed pollution charges, allocation of pollution permits, or mandated pollution controls.

- Along the border, local governments have an incentive to cooperate in order to address the common pollution problem jointly. That is exactly what El Paso and Juárez have done. Specifically, those governments have formed a single international air quality management district for their region. This district is empowered with the authority to set air quality goals and employ market mechanisms to meet those goals.

- For example, the market mechanism might grant limited emission rights to local polluters, but allow them to buy and sell these rights in the marketplace. In this way, overall pollution would be reduced and the firms that actually undertake pollution reduction would be those who can do so least expensively. The idea is for government to allocate property rights to the quantity of pollution that is permitted, and then let the free market determine which firms actually use those rights. For this approach to work, though, firms must not fear losing future allocations of pollution rights if they do not use those rights in the present. That has been a problem that has bedeviled such programs in the past. Markets function efficiently only when property rights are clear and reliable.

• The *North American Development Bank* is financed by the governments of Mexico and the United States to fund border cleanup projects. Yes, the hands of government and the pockets of taxpayers are likely to be major parts of any final resolution to the transborder pollution problems of the American Southwest.

StudyCheck 5

Describe two possible strategies the United States could use to address Canadian pollution of Lake Ontario, which lies between the United States and Canada. Indicate which is better, and why.

FILL IN THE BLANKS

1. Externalities can be either negative or positive. Pollution is an example of a _____ externality. Such externalities impose external _____ on others.

2. Conversely, _____ externalities confer external _____, such as when a neighbor kills all the mosquitos on her property, which leaves fewer to fly into your own backyard.

3. Externalities occur when the _____ costs or benefits of an action—those borne by the ones taking the action—differ from social costs or benefits.

4. Social costs or benefits are defined to equal _____ costs or benefits within the economy, as follows: Social cost = _____ cost + _____ cost, and Social benefit = _____ benefit + _____ benefit.

5. It is externalities that occur at the margin—_____ external costs and _____ external benefits—that are of most interest in economics, because these externalities at the margin cause market outcomes to differ from what is _____.

6. Because external costs or benefits are not felt by the person or firm causing the externality, the free market price signal fails to generate _____ outputs. For example, in the case of an external benefit, market demand does not capture all _____benefits. For that reason, when marginal external benefits are present, the free market produces too _____.

7. The most obvious external cost is from environmental pollution. Because external costs or benefits are not felt by the person or firm causing the externality, the free market price signal fails to generate efficient outputs. Thus, when marginal external costs are present, the free market produces too _____.

8. Marginal external cost _____ with output, meaning that the difference between supply and marginal social cost rises with increasing output. The marginal external costs of pollution are nothing more than the marginal _____ of environmental quality forgone.

9. Lacking government action, polluters pollute too much. The reason is that there is no market for many environmental services. The outcome when there is no market is a price of _____.

10. If environmental services provided by common-property water and air were priced, as they would be if sold in a market, firms would pollute _____. The upshot is that firms would pollute only when the value of that pollution exceeds its environmental costs. That would be _____.

11. Typically, competition forces firms to be environmentally neglectful unless there are public policy incentives to be otherwise. Were a firm to go to the expense of cutting back its pollution, that firm would be at a disadvantage in competing against other firms in its industry. Only the heaviest polluters would survive. This is why pollution externalities represent a _____ _____, one calling for government action to change the rules of the game.

12. The _____ _____ holds that parties to an externality would voluntarily negotiate an efficient outcome, without government involvement. Government need merely define and clearly enforce property rights.

13. _____ _____ _____ are owned jointly. Examples include groundwater, public lands, wild animals, and fish in the oceans, lakes, and rivers. The problem is that, when many people own the same resource, no one has any personal incentive to _____ it.

14. From U.S. Presidents to Smokey the Bear, we are exhorted to do the right thing. These appeals to our social conscience—called _____ _____—are the easiest and most high-profile form of public policy available to fight problems associated with externalities and common property resources.

15. _____ _____ occur when government instructs producers as to the exact technology to install to remedy some public problem.

16. Economic studies on pollution control estimate that market-based alternatives to technology mandates and standards can achieve the same amounts of emission cutbacks at roughly one-third the cost. For example, the EPA's _____ _____ allows a firm to increase its emissions from some sources if it offsets those increases by decreasing its emissions from other sources within its plant. The EPA's _____ _____ extends this flexible concept across firms to capture even more cost savings.

17. As an alternative to technology mandates, pollution taxes can reduce pollution without creating the problems associated with technology mandates. Economists often advocate this action, which is referred to as _____ the cost of an externality directly into prices. If an activity generates damages, the value of those damages would be estimated, and a tax imposed equal to the amount of the _____ _____ _____ at the efficient level of output.

18.   For example, if smoking a pack of cigarettes causes an average of $1 in health damages to others, then a tax of $1 per pack would represent those damages. Such a tax is sometimes referred to as an _____ _____ _____, since polluters are charged for using the common property environment. A corrective tax on cigarettes shifts the supply curve _____ by the amount of that tax, since sellers now have to collect that extra payment and pass it along to government. The price would _____ and the quantity _____, as the market equilibrium changes.

19.   To overcome political barriers to pollution taxes, policymakers sometimes resort to paying for pollution abatement instead. For example, municipal wastewater treatment plants receive significant federal _____, which are payments from the federal government meant to encourage actions with external benefits or that reduce external costs.

20.   In application to pollution, _____ _____ represent property rights to a certain amount of pollutant emissions.

E↕A   21.   Exemplifying the problem of border air pollution, the city of El Paso, Texas, is in noncompliance with guidelines set by the U.S. Environmental Protection Agency (EPA). However, the EPA allows this noncompliance to continue without penalty. One option long advocated by economists is for government to impose a _____ on emissions of pollutants, such that the external costs of pollution are internalized into the production process. The idea is to make firms pay for environmental services.

22.   A second-best, less desirable, alternative would be to tax the _____ of the firm. This approach would not give firms any incentive to reduce the amount of pollution per unit of output, but it would at least drive up the price of that output. Higher prices would mean fewer sales and thus _____ pollution.

23.   The best solution may be voluntary _____ between the United States and Mexico based on mutual _____. This cooperative spirit is attested to by the 1994 implementation of the _____ _____ _____ _____ _____ (NAFTA), which incorporated Mexico into a revised and expanded free trade agreement between the United States and Canada.

24.   One of the best ways for the United States to see greater control of pollution in Mexico is to see greater per capita income in Mexico. The reason is that environmental quality is a _____ good, meaning that people want more as their incomes rise.

25.   The_____ _____ _____ _____ is financed by the governments of Mexico and the United States to fund border cleanup projects.

TRUE/FALSE/EXPLAIN
If false, explain why in the space provided.

1.   In daily life, most people will not encounter externalities.

2.   If external costs are present, marginal social costs exceed marginal private costs.

3.   The Coase theorem provides a theoretical justification for extensive use of taxes and permits to control pollution.

4.   It is efficient to allow some pollution.

5.   The "tragedy of the commons" is a common property resource problem that could be resolved through regulation.

6.   Government can address common property resource problems with the same set of tools that it uses to address problems from pollution.

7.   If moral suasion persuades a paper mill to voluntarily cut back its pollution, that paper mill will be at a cost disadvantage to its competitors.

8.   Moral suasion is illegal in the United States, since it violates the separation of church and state.

9.   Technology mandates usually achieve objectives of economic efficiency at the least possible social cost.

10. Marketable pollution permits represent property rights that can be bought and sold.

11. Polluters usually prefer taxes over marketable permits as a means of pollution control.

12. The most efficient quantity of pollution would be none at all.

13. If a tax is placed on pollution, all of that tax will be passed along to consumers and the quantity of pollution will remain unchanged.

14. If pollution itself is to be taxed, then the amount of pollution must be monitored.

15. It is efficient to pollute if the marginal social benefit from doing so exceeds the marginal social cost.

16. To correct pollution externalities with a tax or permit system, government regulators must estimate the efficient amount of each type of pollution that is to be controlled.

17. The quantity of pollution in the free market is less than the efficient quantity.

18. Marketable permits ordinarily lead to more pollution than do other forms of pollution control.

19. If an efficient amount of marketable permits is issued, the resale price of those permits will approximate the efficient tax rate.

20. To remedy an externality with a tax, the tax rate must be set equal to marginal external cost at the efficient level of pollution.

E↓A 21. Since environmental quality is an inferior good, we should expect Mexico to make fewer efforts toward controlling pollution as per capita income in Mexico rises.

22. NAFTA and its side agreements recognize the importance of the North American environment and include environmental safeguards.

23. An unrestricted free market will lead to the efficient amount of transborder pollution.

24. In theory, a tax can internalize the external costs of pollution, although putting theory into practice is often quite difficult.

25. Taxing the output of a polluting firm rather than taxing the pollution itself is a second-best policy that gives firms no incentive to reduce pollution per unit of output.

MULTIPLE CHOICE
Circle the letter that corresponds to the one best answer.

1. Social costs equal
    a. private costs minus external costs.
    b. private costs plus external costs.
    c. social benefits minus private costs.
    d. private benefits minus private costs.

2. If Multiple Choice Figure 1 represents a market with an external benefit, the demand curve would be shown by
    a. line E.
    b. line F.
    c. the difference between line F and line E.
    d. the difference between the supply curve and line E.

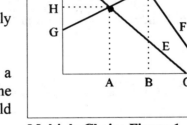

Multiple Choice Figure 1

3. If Multiple Choice Figure 1 represents a market with an external benefit, the schedule of marginal external benefits would be shown by
    a. line E.
    b. line F.
    c. the difference between line F and line E.
    d. the difference between the supply curve and line E.

4. If Multiple Choice Figure 1 represents a market with an external benefit, marginal social benefits would be shown by
    a. line E.
    b. line F.
    c. the difference between line F and line E.
    d. the difference between the supply curve and line E.

5. If Multiple Choice Figure 1 represents a market with an external benefit, the efficient quantity of output would be given by point
    a. A.
    b. B.
    c. C.
    d. D.

6.   If Multiple Choice Figure 1 represents a market with an external benefit, the market price in the absence of any government action would be given by
   a.   G.
   b.   H.
   c.   I.
   d.   J.

7.   When the private costs of an action differ from the social costs,
   a.   common property resources are underconsumed.
   b.   there is a free-rider problem.
   c.   an externality exists.
   d.   the result is an impure public good.

8.   Goods associated with external costs are produced
   a.   in efficient quantities by the market.
   b.   in greater than the efficient quantities by the market.
   c.   in less than the efficient quantities by the market.
   d.   only by government.

9.   When property rights are clearly defined, the Coase theorem states that government action is _____ to achieve an _____ amount of pollution.
   a.   necessary; equitable
   b.   necessary; efficient
   c.   unnecessary; equitable
   d.   unnecessary; efficient

10.   Which of the following is an example of moral suasion?
   a.   The "only YOU can prevent forest fires" campaign.
   b.   Pollution taxes.
   c.   Limits on toilet tank capacities.
   d.   The Coase theorem.

11.   The Environmental Protection Agency has traditionally chosen to use technology mandates for each of the following reasons, EXCEPT
   a.   it is easy to observe whether firms are complying.
   b.   other approaches require that emissions be monitored, which is sometimes difficult.
   c.   technology mandates make it obvious that pollution is being controlled.
   d.   technology mandates are usually the most efficient way to control pollutants that can be monitored.

12. To internalize an external cost refers to
    a. placing tariffs on imports.
    b. banning economic activities that create social costs.
    c. forcing producers to take into account the costs they impose on others.
    d. the costs of government.

13. If a tax is placed on the output of all firms in a polluting industry, pollution would
    a. be reduced because firms would reduce the amount of pollution per unit of output.
    b. be reduced because the market price of the industry's output would rise, thus leading to fewer sales, less production, and thus less pollution.
    c. stay the same, because firms would merely pass along the cost of the tax to consumers.
    d. stay the same, because firms would absorb the extra cost of the tax.

14. Relative to technology mandates, achieving an overall pollution target through marketable permits is
    a. more efficient, because firms with low costs of pollution control would pollute the least and sell their extra permits to other firms with higher costs of pollution control.
    b. more efficient, because marketable permits do not require that emissions be monitored.
    c. less efficient, because marketable permits do not require that emissions be monitored.
    d. less efficient, because government research scientists know best which pollution control technologies are most cost-effective.

15. The efficient quantity of pollution occurs at the point where
    a. total benefit equals total cost.
    b. marginal benefit equals marginal cost.
    c. marginal cost equals zero.
    d. total benefit is maximized.

16. If a pollution tax were to be used to control pollution, the tax per unit of pollution should be set
    a. equal to the marginal external cost at the efficient level of pollution.
    b. equal to the marginal external cost at the initial level of pollution.
    c. high enough to prevent firms from polluting.
    d. at any level, since the firm will just pass it along to consumers and continue to pollute the same amount as before.

17.   Line A in Multiple Choice Figure 2 is most likely to represent the
        a.   marginal external cost curve.
        b.   demand for emission rights.
        c.   supply of marketable emissions permits.
        d.   supply of emission rights implied by an emissions tax.

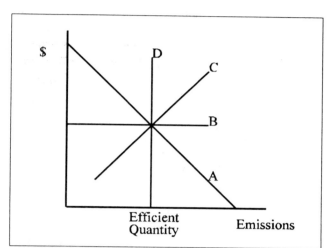

Multiple Choice Figure 2

18.   Line B in Multiple Choice Figure 2 is most likely to represent the
        a.   marginal external cost curve.
        b.   demand for emission rights.
        c.   supply of marketable emissions permits.
        d.   supply of emission rights implied by an emissions tax.

19.   Line C in Multiple Choice Figure 2 is most likely to represent the
        a.   marginal external cost curve.
        b.   demand for emission rights.
        c.   supply of marketable emissions permits.
        d.   supply of emission rights implied by an emissions tax.

20.   Line D in Multiple Choice Figure 2 is most likely to represent the
        a.   marginal external cost curve.
        b.   demand for emission rights.
        c.   supply of marketable emissions permits.
        d.   supply of emission rights implied by an emissions tax.

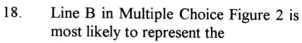

21.   As countries develop, they pollute
        a.   more and more over time.
        b.   less and less over time.
        c.   more at first, and then less later.
        d.   less at first, and then more later.

22.   Of the following, second-best pollution control is most likely to involve
        a.   ignoring pollution.
        b.   bringing the level of pollution down to zero in spite of the jobs this might cost.
        c.   taxing the outputs of polluting firms.
        d.   a tax on pollution itself.

23. Of the following, the best way to reduce pollution that comes from other countries is likely to be to
    a. place a trade embargo against the polluting country.
    b. threatening military action unless the pollution stops.
    c. send pollution back across the border to give them "a taste of their own medicine."
    d. negotiate treaties to control transborder pollution.

24. Relative to per capita income in the United States, per capita income in Mexico is
    a. much smaller.
    b. much larger.
    c. about the same, but Mexico has much more pollution.
    d. about the same, but Mexico has much less pollution.

25. The North American Development Bank that funds cleanup projects along the border between the U.S. and Mexico is financed by
    a. a consortium of major banks, including Citibank and Wells Fargo.
    b. the U.S. government alone.
    c. the Mexican government alone.
    d. both the U.S. and Mexican governments.

GRASPING THE GRAPHS
Fill in each box with a concept that applies.

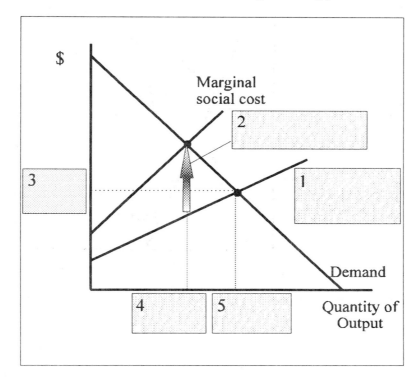

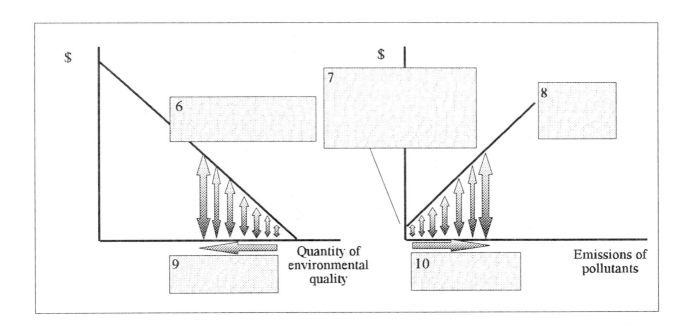

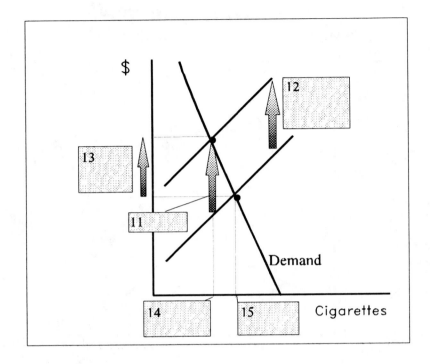

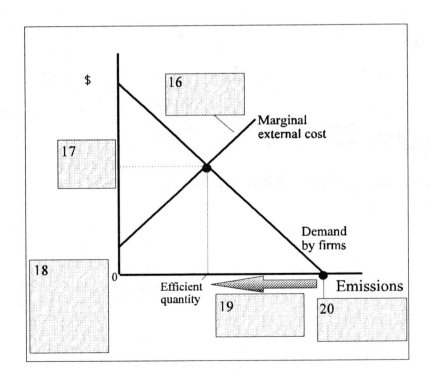

**For additional practice in grasping this chapter's graphs,
visit http://www.prenhall.com/ayers and try *Smart Graph* 34,
along with *Active Graphs* 63 and 64.**

ANSWERS

STUDYCHECKS

1. Because common property resources are owned jointly, they are normally overconsumed (in the absence of government policy) because no one has any personal incentive to conserve them. Externalities also lead to market failures. In the case of external costs, the market produces more than an efficient amount of output. If there are external benefits, the market produces less than an efficient amount of output. The reason is that private decision makers consider only private costs and benefits, and ignore external costs and benefits. Government can solve this problem if it can internalize those externalities into the decision-making process of individuals and firms.

2. The Coase theorem suggests that, if property rights are clearly defined, government action is unnecessary. Rather, those affected by the externality will negotiate with whoever is responsible for causing the externality until an efficient solution is obtained. However, transaction costs and strategic behavior can defeat the efficiency of the Coasian solution.

3. Technology mandates are directives from government pertaining to how something is to be done. For example, directives requiring water-conserving irrigation equipment or smog-reducing catalytic converters are both technology mandates. Because technology mandates are not tailored to individual circumstances, they tend to be an excessively costly way to achieve desired results.

4. The efficient quantity can be obtained by issuing marketable permits that sum to that quantity, or by imposing a tax that raises costs to the point where the market equilibrium occurs at that quantity. The optimal tax equals the marginal external cost at the optimal level of output. Under either the tax or marketable permit approach, the outputs will go to those consumers who value them most and be produced by those producers with the lowest costs. That outcome is efficient.

5. The most practical strategy involves negotiations between the United States and Canada, in which each side recognizes their joint interests in pollution control. (This has been the route actually taken.) Another strategy is for the United States to impose duties on Canadian products in retaliation for Canadian pollution. However, this strategy violates the specificity principle and invites retaliation. Other strategies could be mentioned.

FILL IN THE BLANKS

1. negative, costs
2. positive, benefits
3. private
4. all, private, external, private, external
5. marginal, marginal, efficient
6. efficient, social, little
7. much
8. rises, benefits
9. zero
10. less, efficient
11. market failure
12. Coase theorem
13. Common property resources, conserve
14. moral suasion
15. Technology mandates
16. bubble plan, offsets plan
17. internalizing, marginal external cost
18. environmental user fee, up, rise, fall
19. subsidies
20. marketable permits
21. tax
22. output, less
23. cooperation, self-interest, North American Free Trade Agreement
24. normal
25. North American Development Bank

TRUE/FALSE/EXPLAIN

1. False, although they are often of no greater significance than mere personal appearance, externalities are everyday events for most of us.
2. True.
3. False, the Coase theorem suggests that private negotiations will resolve externalities issues.
4. True.
5. True.
6. True.
7. True.
8. False, moral suasion involves nothing more than exhorting people or firms to "do the right thing," and is often one of the first policies that is tried.

9. False, technology mandates are unlikely to be technologically efficient, except when the activity being regulated cannot be measured are monitored directly.

10. True.

11. False, taxes require polluters to turn over money to the government, while marketable permits have the potential of keeping that money within the industry.

12. False, the efficient quantity of pollution would equate marginal social cost and marginal social benefit.

13. False, if firms tried to pass along the entire tax in the form of higher prices for their products, there would be a surplus of those products as consumers cut back on the quantity demanded. The result is that, while there will be an increase in product prices, there will also be a decrease in output and an attempt by firms to reduce the quantity of pollution associated with each unit of output.

14. True.

15. True.

16. True.

17. False, while efficiency would call for pollution up to the point where marginal social cost equals marginal social benefit, the free market would pollute beyond that point to where the marginal benefit is zero.

18. False, since the cost of a system of marketable permits tends to be less than or equal to the cost of alternative policies, the amount of pollution allowed under marketable permits is likely to be less than or equal to that allowed under alternative policy approaches.

19. True.

20. True.

21. False, environmental quality is a normal good, and so we could expect greater pollution control in Mexico as Mexican incomes rise.

22. True.

23. False, an unrestricted free market leads to excessive pollution.

24. True.

25. True.

MULTIPLE CHOICE

1.	b	8.	b	15.	b	22.	c
2.	a	9.	d	16.	a	23.	d
3.	c	10.	a	17.	b	24.	a
4.	b	11.	d	18.	d	25.	d
5.	b	12.	c	19.	a		
6.	b	13.	b	20.	c		
7.	c	14.	a	21.	c		

GRASPING THE GRAPHS
Examples of correct answers

1. Marginal private cost
2. Marginal external cost
3. Market price
4. Efficient quantity
5. Market quantity
6. Marginal social benefit ("demand" for the public good)
7. The marginal external cost curve starts above zero, since there is some naturally occurring pollution.
8. Marginal external cost
9. Reduced environmental quality . . .
10. . . .caused by an increase in pollution
11. Tax
12. Shift in supply
13. Higher price
14. Quantity after tax
15. Quantity before tax
16. So-called missing supply
17. Efficient tax
18. Without the tax, the price of emissions would be zero.
19. Pollution abatement
20. Free-market quantity

Visit the Ayers/Collinge companion Website at <u>http://www.prenhall.com/ayers</u> for further activities and exercises for this chapter.

Chapter 16

PUBLIC CHOICE

CHAPTER REVIEW

- In addition to market failure, there is **government failure**, which involves inefficiencies within government itself. These inefficiencies are not unexpected, since without them, there would be no reason to have markets at all. The field of **public choice** looks at economic incentives within government.

16.1 Choosing a Political System

- There is no realistic way to get rid of government failure, at least not entirely. But it can help to imagine what a government might be like, which is where we start.

- Economists define a *benevolent dictatorship* as a form of government in which well-meaning and well-informed officials make all of the best choices. Obviously, there is no such thing in practice anywhere in world. A benevolent dictatorship is an abstract form of government that implements the people's wishes without costly political processes and without worrying about providing public servants with incentives.

- Dictatorships do not look so benevolent when found in the real world. Although a dictatorship might at first seem like an efficient form of government because it avoids wasting money on political campaigns and political rivalries, there are other inefficiencies that are far more significant. Dictatorships have little incentive to follow the wishes of the public or to avoid waste in government actions.

- The moral here is that a dictatorship cannot be expected to act in a benevolent manner. This provides justification for a more complicated form of government, one that provides incentives for the government to respond to the wishes of the people.

- Democracy is an answer to the inefficiencies of dictatorship. It provides for a representative government that responds to the wishes of the public. The processes of democracy are costly and messy, however.

- Economic incentives appear in every aspect of government. Voters face economic incentives in determining whether and how to vote. Legislators face economic incentives in determining which policies to enact and which taxes to levy. Public servants also face economic incentives in determining the level and type of service to provide.

- The political process does not provide definitively efficient answers. For example, there is the problem of **cycling,** in which the order of political choices determines the outcome.

- An example shows how cycling can occur. The first representative, Agnes, prefers increasing spending to cutting taxes, but prefers a tax rebate to the poor over an across-the-board tax cut. The second representative, Biff, prefers cutting taxes to new spending, but would rather that the tax cut be directed to the poor rather than across the board. The third representative, Christina, prefers an across-the-board tax cut and strongly opposes sending out rebate checks. Christina views increased defense spending as preferable to sending out rebate checks, but not as desirable as an across-the-board tax cut. The following table summarizes the preferences of Agnes, Biff, and Christina.

Preferences of Subcommittee Members

Option	Ranking by Agnes	Ranking by Biff	Ranking by Christina
Increased defense spending	1	3	2
Tax rebates to the poor	2	1	3
Across-the-board tax cut	3	2	1

The Subcommittee's Recommendation

Choices	Agnes' vote	Biff's vote	Christina's vote	The Subcommittee's Choice
Tax rebates to the poor or Increased defense spending	for defense	for rebates	for defense	increased defense spending
Increased defense spending or Across-the-board tax cut	for defense	for tax cut	for tax cut	across-the-board tax cut
Across-the-board tax cut or Tax rebates to the poor	for rebates	for rebates	for tax cut	tax rebates to the poor

- Note that the recommendation of the subcommittee will depend on the order in which members consider the alternatives. Whoever sets the *agenda* of which alternatives will be considered first winds up in effect choosing the alternatives that they will recommend to Congress. In this manner, cycling illustrates a certain irrationality within the collective choice process.

- Democracy in the United States is characterized by *federalism*, meaning that there are multiple layers of government. This arrangement has an economic basis: it allows those citizens to vote who are most directly affected by the consequences of the choice.

- **Fiscal federalism** examines the design of a federal system of government from an economic standpoint. It suggests that decisions should be make by the level of government most directly affected by those decisions.

- Many issues are national in scope and thus appropriate to consider at the federal level, meaning at the level of government that presides over all of the other governments. Certainly national defense is one such issue. Another is income redistribution. If income redistribution is left to state-owned localities, little of it can occur. The reason is that only the federal government can effectively take from the rich and give to the poor. If such income redistribution is tried by states and cities on their own, the rich wind up moving out and the poor wind up moving in.

- There is sometimes a conflict between the federal governments and states over which government should be the final authority. For example, Oregon legalized medically assisted suicide for terminally ill elderly patients who are capable of making such a choice. The federal government recognizes no such right and promised to prosecute doctors who assist in such suicides.

16.2 Choices by the Voters

- Because we delegate decisions collectively, none of us gets exactly what we want. Moreover, each candidate represents a **bundled good**, meaning that the voter cannot pick and choose which items on a candidate's agenda to support, and which to oppose—one vote buys all. The result is a compromise that is not fully satisfying to anyone. In the case of public goods, such as national defense, the quantity that is chosen by public officials must then be consumed by everyone, no matter their personal preferences. However, the culprit is not the public officials, but the nature of the public good itself—public goods are consumed jointly. Where possible, people prefer to make choices for themselves.

- A second source of concern over government action has to do with the **principal-agent problem**. Over 19 million workers in this country are employed by government as public servants. No matter the job, they are all *agents* of the public (the *principal*). However, because the public is so large, no individual has direct control. This generalized accountability provides a great deal of leeway on the part of the agents to do as they please.

- A funny thing happens on the road to public office. In U.S. presidential campaigns, for example, Democratic and Republican candidates for president often sound much farther apart on the issues in the primaries than they do when it comes time for the general election. For an explanation of this and other aspects of election outcomes, we can turn to the **median voter model**.

- The median voter model says that candidates will seek the decisive swing voter that can tilt the balance from one candidate to the other. This median voter will be quite different in the general election than the median voter in either the Democratic or Republican primaries. The median voter model thus predicts that successful politicians will seek to always follow that median to wherever it moves.

- The median voter model is applicable when voters—those who actually vote—can be lined up along a spectrum from left to right. Maybe the spectrum is political, ranging from the left wing to the right wing. Perhaps the spectrum is budgetary, ranging from a lower budget to a higher budget. In any case, the *median voter* is the one for whom 50 percent of the other voters prefer further to the right on the spectrum and 50 percent prefer further to the left. In an election in which all voters pick between two candidates, the candidate chosen by the median voter will win by garnering just over 50 percent of the vote.

StudyCheck 1

Explain the median voter model and why it predicts that candidates will change their positions between the primary and general elections.

- In most elections below the level of presidential elections, considerably less than half of registered voters bother to vote. Even when registered voters do vote, they often have little idea of what they are voting on. There are many things on the typical ballot, so many in fact that voters do not have time enough to research all of the candidates and propositions seen on the ballot. Even people who want to be involved find themselves with insufficient time to prepare as well as they would like for the voting process. The result is **rational ignorance** on the part of the voters, meaning that they make a rational choice to remain uninformed on many public choices.

- Most voting choices are for people rather than on specific policy actions. A voter will vote for a candidate based on that candidate's reputation and positions on certain issues. The voter relies on the candidate to address other issues in a similar way. So voters delegate authority to politicians, who in turn delegate to the administrative bureaucracy. The amount of detail involved in governing the country is too overwhelming to do otherwise. If voters were asked to vote on every issue directly, the amount of rational ignorance would be much greater than it is under the system of voting for candidates.

- Political parties are in part a response to the rational ignorance of voters. Instead of having to figure it all out for themselves, voters can select political parties they trust and according to their philosophical preferences. In this way, voters rely on the political parties to do much of the detailed research into the issues and into the candidates that are running for office. So-called "voting the party line" can be a reasonable way to address the problem of rational ignorance. If voters pay too little attention, though, political parties and the politicians they produce might too closely aligned themselves with special interests that do pay attention.

StudyCheck 2
Do people get what they individually want out of the public choice process? Explain.

16.3 Candidates and Coalitions

- To achieve the results constituents expect, the holder of a political office will often find it necessary to compromise and bargain with other elected representatives. In addition, voters' rational ignorance means that politicians and bureaucrats can often safely follow their own personal agendas, even when those agendas conflict with what the public would want them to do.

- Most elected officials want to remain in office. Incumbent politicians routinely get reelected, even though *term limitations*—laws that restrict the number of sequential times a politician can hold one public office—are quite popular. Achieving this objective can be accomplished through **logrolling**—vote trading—in order to obtain projects of direct benefit to constituents. Logrolling unfortunately results in massive spending packages that contain numerous local spending projects of questionable merit. These projects (often called *pork*) and other accomplishments are then reported back to constituents through a newsletter. Left out is any focus on cost, however, even though the pork does not come cheaply.

- Remember, to obtain projects for their districts, legislators must vote for all of the other costly items in the legislation, including those of no benefit to their constituents. When voters focus on visible benefits from projects and ignore the less-obvious costs, they are said to suffer from **fiscal illusion**, which tends to bring about excessive spending.

- Even if the costs of logrolling are considered, they are still likely to be of little concern to the electorate. After all, the costs are in terms of other districts' wasteful projects that are included in an appropriations bill. However, if a majority of other legislators are signing onto the bill, you don't want your district left out. In other words, if you are going to be paying for other districts' pork, you want pork of your own. Thus, constituents rarely hold pork-barrel politics against their own legislators, even though they may disapprove of the practice in general. There is good reason to disapprove. *Pork-barrel politics* leads to excessive government spending, as the cost of the myriad of relatively small projects gets lost in the general budget.

- One check on logrolling is the line-item veto powers of many state governors. The **line-item veto** allows a governor to veto parts of appropriations bills, rather than having to accept or reject the bills in their entireties. The result would be much less pork. The governors of 43 states have some form of line-item veto authority. Although Congress voted in 1996 to grant the president line-item veto power, the Supreme Court subsequently ruled this application of line-item veto authority to be unconstitutional.

- Not all vote trading is inefficient. For example, a worthy project might serve only a portion of the country. Consider levees along a river that benefit the residents of only a few states. Without vote trading, the project would not pass through Congress, since a majority of states would perceive no benefits. Such projects could still be undertaken, however, if the affected states join forces and proceed on their own. Payment for the project would then come from the residents of those states instead of from general tax revenues.

- Sometimes government spending can be financed without or tax, or at least without anything labeled as a tax. A favorite in the political recipe book is to use *unfunded mandates*, which means that government requires business to implement government programs, but to do so at their own expense. When government does not have to pay the costs itself, it is much easier to say yes to projects than if those projects must be financed explicitly out of tax revenue. With unfunded mandates, the tax is effectively hidden in the higher costs to firms and higher prices to their customers.

- The United States prides itself on its majority rule. Yet legislation is often influenced by small, well-organized minorities, aligned according to special interests. *Special-interest groups* are characterized by a tightly focused agenda and **lobbyists**—agents who promote that agenda within the political system.

- The agendas of the special interests often conflict with the interests of most voters. Special interests are frequently able to get their way, however, by paying close attention to the details of legislators' votes. Legislators who vote against special interests know they lose their votes and campaign contributions. However, legislators who favor the special interests and vote against the wishes of the majority often face no adverse consequences. The reason is that general interest is often more diffuse, with few voters keying their votes around specific issues. In short, **when the benefits of an action are spread broadly and the costs are concentrated, special interests are frequently successful at preventing the action from occurring.**

- Lobbying by special-interest groups is efficient when it provides information that prevents legislative errors. When legislation targets the actions of a particular industry, for example, that industry's lobbyists are in the best position to provide relevant information on the industry's business practices.

- Unfortunately, special interest lobbying is frequently inefficient, because it involves wasteful rent seeking. **Rent seeking** occurs when lobbyists or others expend resources in an effort to come out a winner in the political process. Since economic efficiency looks at the size of the economic pie, not how it is sliced, the time and money lobbyists spend trying to get the pie sliced to their liking is inefficient.

- **Block grants** represent sums of money designated to go toward a range of state-administered programs. For example, Congress designates a single block grant to finance many of the welfare programs administered in a state. By leaving the details up to the states, block grants mean that Congress need merely decide on the number of dollars to include in the grant, something that voters will monitor relatively closely. Lobbyists must then compete with each other, state by state, over the allocation of that money.

StudyCheck 3

Explain how opportunities for inefficiency arise at each stage of the public choice process. Given these inefficiencies, why have that process at all?

StudyCheck 4

Describe and give an example of rent-seeking behavior in reference to public policy. Explain why rent seeking is usually wasteful.

16.4 The Government Bureaucracy

- Employees of the many agencies of government are commonly referred to as government *bureaucrats*. The employees of government agencies have personal agendas that sometimes conflict with the intent of voters and their elected representatives. Most significantly, for both public-spirited and self-serving reasons, bureaucrats almost always desire budgets for their agencies that exceed what the average citizen and elected official would prefer.

- Who enters government at all? For the most part, it's people who think government is relatively more important than most citizens realize. Thus, employees of government in general and agencies in particular truly believe that their missions are more deserving than the political process acknowledges. For these public-spirited motives, they seek to expand the size of their agencies beyond what is efficient. There are also self-serving reasons why government employees want larger budgets for their agencies.

- Consider the marginal net benefit of increasing an agency's budget, where *marginal net benefit* equals marginal social benefit minus marginal social cost. At first, if the agency directs its spending toward its most essential missions, the value of agency spending far exceeds its budgetary cost. As the budget size is increased, however, the agency must fund programs of increasingly less merit. When the value of extra spending is less than the cost of that spending, the agency has spent too much. To achieve economic efficiency, the agency budget should equal the amount for which marginal net benefit is zero.

- It is one thing for bureaucrats to want an inefficiently large budget—to expand their turf. Getting that budget is another matter. Unfortunately, the struggle over the size of agency budgets is rather one-sided, because the agency is best positioned to know what its spending options are. If an agency is aware of ways to save money, for example, it has little incentive to reveal them. Such *asymmetric information*, in which one party to a transaction knows more than the other, put legislators at a disadvantage in overseeing agencies.

- There are various strategies government agencies use to obtain the budgets they want. For example, agency spending is commonly guided by "use it or lose it." Agencies want to avoid getting caught with extra cash at the end of the fiscal year when the budget expires.

- The strategy of selecting widely supported projects for potential cuts has been used so often, it's acquired its own name—the **Washington Monument strategy.** Using this strategy, the agency bluffs by offering a bare-bones budget that cuts its most popular functions. For instance, the National Park Service might propose to save money by restricting access to the Washington Monument to between 9 A.M. and 5 P.M. on weekdays, with no access at all on weekends. Evenings and weekends are cut because they are the times of peak tourist demand.

16.5 Addressing Government Failures

- Is there anything citizens can do to counter all the incentives within government to spend too much? The options are limited. For example, limiting the number of years legislators can serve might keep representatives more in touch with the voters. However, such term limits deprive government of experienced legislators, and also run the danger of focusing legislators' attentions on personal profit opportunities once they leave office.

- There is no easy way to provide the proper incentives for efficiency within government. That should come as little surprise. After all, if government were efficient, there would be little reason to adopt competitive free markets. We resort to government when markets fail. We must merely keep in mind that market failure does not imply government success.

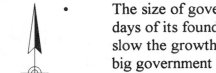

16.6 Growing the Government

- The size of government and its proper role has been debated in the United States from the days of its founding. President Ronald Reagan, for example, was well known for trying to slow the growth of government. In 1996, even President Clinton proclaimed, "The era of big government is over."

- On the flip side, Treasury Secretary Alexander Hamilton, pictured on the $10 bill, favored change that would strengthen the power of the federal government. He offered strong arguments favoring the creation of a Bank of the United States, an early version of what we now refer to as a central bank. More recently, in leading the fight against terrorism, President George W. Bush pushed through significant increases in government spending and powers. Government spending as a fraction of GDP is today more than three times its value in 1929. Transfer payments as a fraction of government spending rose to historic highs in the 1990s.

- What led the country down the path to bigger government? The U.S. Constitution says that government is obligated to "promote the general welfare." The welfare of the country covers a lot. Earliest efforts by government to promote a growing economy focused on filling the transportation needs of a young nation. From building roads and canals at first, and then later railroads, government provided the resources needed to build a transportation system that would tie the states together and promote commerce. But government was always limited in what it could do because it had no way to raise the money to fund the cost of a "big government," even if there had been agreement that government ought to be bigger.

- Following the expansion of government power and influence that necessarily accompanied the Civil War and the Reconstruction era, the federal government continued to take on more responsibilities. To regulate commerce, the Interstate Commerce Commission was created in 1887. The first antitrust law, the Sherman Act, designed to halt the growth of monopoly power was enacted in 1890. Then came two major events that were to allow an unprecedented expansion in the size of the federal government.

- The federal income tax was enacted into law in 1913. This act and the other new laws, agencies, and obligations of government were controversial because they expanded government power and influence. Yet by1929, the eve of the Great Depression, government's share of aggregate spending was still only a small fraction of its current share.

- President Franklin D. Roosevelt promised the nation a New Deal to overcome the misery of the Great Depression. The Supreme Court soon declared unconstitutional a number of these policies, thus acting as a brake on the expansion of government. Not even the popular FDR could bring the American people along in support of his plan to "pack" the Court with new justices who would support all his proposals.

- After World War II ended in 1945, an explosion of American prosperity enriched consumers as never before. U.S. prosperity ultimately spread to the war-shattered countries of Western Europe and Japan, as the U.S. served as the engine of growth and these countries got pulled along for the ride. While the government had not been particularly successful in ending the depression in the 1930s, the government proved in the 1940s that it could successfully wage war. Americans were united in their support of their government's war effort and it was natural that these good feelings toward government would continue following the war.

- The expansion of government reached it pinnacle with President Lyndon Johnson's Great Society, which added about 500 social programs between 1965 and 1968. Some programs, such as Medicare, have become familiar standbys. Others, such as Model Cities, have long since been forgotten. These programs aimed to meet nearly all of the social issues of the time, and more. They included programs to solve the problems of hunger, homelessness, discrimination, and excess immigration. Great Society programs provided higher minimum wages, vocational training, agricultural subsidies, fair labeling, pensions, clean highways, and on and on.

- The big-government expansion of the 1960s seemed too much to many citizens by the end of the 1970s. In 1980, Americans elected Ronald Reagan as their 36th President. Reagan promised to "get the government off the backs of the American people." As President, Mr. Reagan spoke of the need for less government regulation, saying, "Millions of individuals making their own decisions in the marketplace will always allocate resources better than any centralized government planning process." Reagan sold to the American people his view that government should be smaller partly with his quick wit. A sample: "Government's view of the economy could be summed up in a few short phrases: If it moves, tax it. If it keeps moving, regulate it. And if it stops moving, subsidize it." More pointedly, Reagan stated "There is a threat posed to human freedom by the enormous power of the modern state. History teaches the dangers of government that overreaches—political control taking precedence over free economic growth— secret police, mindless bureaucracy, all combining to stifle individual excellence and personal freedom."

- Reagan did oversee a buildup in military spending, but one that was directed at convincing the Soviet Union that it could not afford to maintain its adversarial stance. With the demise of the Soviet Union, the U.S. in the 1990s was able to reap a so-called peace dividend of lower defense spending needs. Military spending was cut dramatically during the administrations of the first George Bush and of Bill Clinton in the 1990s.

- In light of terrorist threats and a perception that cuts in the 1990s were too deep, the military spending trend has turned once more to the upside under President George W. Bush, as has spending on farm subsidies and other programs. Time will tell the extent to which GW oversees another federal government expansion.

StudyCheck 5

What can explain the nearly continual growth in transfer payments relative to other elements of government spending over the last many decades?

FILL IN THE BLANKS

1. In addition to market failure, however, there is also _____ _____, which involves inefficiencies within government itself. The field of_____ _____ looks at economic incentives within government.

2. Economists define a _____ _____ as a form of government in which well-meaning and well-informed officials make all of the best choices. Obviously, there is no such thing in practice anywhere in world.

3. The political process does not provide definitively efficient answers. For example, there is the problem of _____, in which the order of political choices determines the outcome. The recommendation of the subcommittee will depend on the order in which members consider the alternatives. Whoever sets the _____ of which alternatives will be considered first winds up in effect choosing the alternatives that they will recommend to Congress.

4. Democracy in the United States is characterized by _____, meaning that there are multiple layers of government. This arrangement has an economic basis: it allows those citizens to vote who are most directly affected by the consequences of the choice.

5. _____ _____ examines the design of a federal system of government from an economic standpoint. It suggests that decisions should be make by the level of government most directly affected by those decisions.

6. Many issues are national in scope and thus appropriate to consider at the federal level, meaning at the level of government that presides over all of the other governments. Certainly _____ _____ is one such issue. Another is _____ _____ _____.

7. Because we delegate decisions collectively, none of us gets exactly what we want. Moreover, each candidate represents a _____ good, meaning that the voter cannot pick and choose which items on a candidate's agenda to support, and which to oppose—one vote buys all. The result is a compromise that is not fully satisfying to anyone.

8. A source of concern over government action has to do with the _____ problem. Over 19 million workers in this country are employed by government as public servants. No matter the job, they are all _____ of the public (the _____).

9. The _____ _____ model says that candidates will seek the decisive swing voter that can tilt the balance from one candidate to the other. The median voter is the one for whom _____ percent of the other voters prefer further to the right on the spectrum and _____ percent prefer further to the left. In an election in which all voters pick between two candidates, the candidate chosen by the median voter will win by garnering just over _____ percent of the vote.

10.   In most elections below the level of presidential elections, considerably less than half of registered voters bother to vote. Even when registered voters do vote, they often have little idea of what they are voting on. There are many things on the typical ballot, so many in fact that voters do not have time enough to research all of the candidates and propositions seen on the ballot. Even people who want to be involved find themselves with insufficient time to prepare as well as they would like for the voting process. The result is _____ _____ on the part of the voters, meaning that they make a rational choice to remain uninformed on many public choices.

11.   Most elected officials want to remain in office. Incumbent politicians routinely get reelected, even though _____ _____—laws that restrict the number of sequential times a politician can hold one public office—are quite popular.

12.   Achieving this objective can be accomplished through _____—vote trading—in order to obtain projects of direct benefit to constituents.

13.   When voters focus on visible benefits from projects and ignore the less-obvious costs, they are said to suffer from _____ _____, which tends to bring about excessive spending.

14.   _____ politics leads to excessive government spending, as the cost of the myriad of relatively small projects gets lost in the general budget.

15.   One check on logrolling is the _____ _____ powers of many state governors. The power allows a governor to veto parts of appropriations bills, rather than having to accept or reject the bills in their entireties.

16.   Sometimes government spending can be financed without a tax, or at least without anything labeled as a tax. A favorite in the political recipe book is to use _____ _____, which means that government requires business to implement government programs, but to do so at their own expense.

17.   The United States prides itself on its majority rule. Yet legislation is often influenced by small, well-organized minorities, aligned according to special interests. Special-interest groups are characterized by a tightly focused agenda and _____—agents who promote that agenda within the political system.

18.   Unfortunately, special interest lobbying is frequently inefficient, because it involves wasteful _____ _____, which occurs when lobbyists or others expend resources in an effort to come out a winner in the political process.

19.   _____ _____ represent sums of money designated to go toward a range of state-administered programs.

20. Consider the marginal net benefit of increasing an agency's budget, where marginal net benefit equals marginal social benefit minus marginal social cost. To achieve economic efficiency, the agency budget should equal the amount for which marginal net benefit is _____.

E&A 21. The size of government and its proper role has been debated in the United States from the days of its founding. In 1996, President _____ proclaimed, "The era of big government is over."

22. On the flip side, Treasury Secretary _____ _____, pictured on the $10 bill, favored change that would strengthen the power of the federal government. He offered strong arguments favoring the creation of a Bank of the United States, an early version of what we now refer to as a central bank. More recently, in leading the fight against terrorism, President George W. Bush pushed through significant increases in government spending and powers. Government spending as a fraction of GDP is today more than three _____ times its value in 1929.

23. The U.S. Constitution says that government is obligated to "promote the _____ _____."

24. The federal _____ _____ was enacted into law in 1906 and the Federal Reserve was created in 1913. All these new laws, agencies, and obligations of government were controversial because they expanded government power and influence. Yet by 1929, the eve of the Great Depression, government's share of aggregate spending was still only a small fraction of its current share.

25. President Franklin D. Roosevelt promised the nation a _____ _____ to overcome the misery of the Great Depression. The expansion of government reached it pinnacle with President Lyndon Johnson's _____ _____, which added about 500 social programs between 1965 and 1968. Some programs, such as Medicare, have become familiar standbys. Others, such as Model Cities, have long since been forgotten. These programs aimed to meet nearly all of the social issues of the time, and more.

TRUE/FALSE/EXPLAIN
If false, explain why in the space provided.

1. Economic incentives appear in every aspect of government.

2. Federalism occurs when there are multiple layers of government.

3.   If there is cycling, then whoever sets the agenda will control the outcome.

4.   In democracy, the outcome is sometimes inefficient, but is never random.

5.   It is irrational for voters to select candidates without first examining in detail all of the information available about those candidates.

6.   The median voter model can be used to explain why political candidates often sound so much alike.

7.   According to the median voter model, a candidate will have the best chance of winning an election if he or she takes positions exactly in the middle, irrespective of where potential voters line up on the issues.

8.   When voters suffer from fiscal illusion, they tend to focus too much on the costs and not enough on the benefits of federal programs.

9.   Voters usually choose candidates who promise to stay out of pork-barrel politics.

10.   The line-item veto is meant to reduce logrolling.

11.   Although Congress had voted to grant the president line-item veto authority, the Supreme Court subsequently ruled it unconstitutional.

12. In recent years, Congress has become increasingly involved in specifying the details of welfare programs administered by the states.

13. When states use tax incentives to compete over the location of a new automobile manufacturing plant, they are engaging in rent-seeking.

14. When lobbyists fight over who will benefit from government programs, they are engaging in rent seeking.

15. Whenever an agency's budget exceeds that which would be efficient, society would be better off if the agency did not exist.

16. The professionals who staff government agencies provide an important safeguard against politicians' tendency to spend too much.

17. Employees of government agencies usually have both selfish and idealistic reasons to favor a higher budget for their agencies.

18. If a government agency adopts the Washington Monument strategy, the agency will be totally honest in revealing all potential cost-saving measures.

19. An example of the Washington Monument strategy is when a government employee becomes a high-profile "whistle blower" by telling the news media about waste in his or her agency.

20. Unfunded mandates offer a means for government to accomplish its goals without the spending showing up in the public budget.

E&A   21.   President Clinton once proclaimed, "The era of big government is over."

22.   President George W. Bush has pushed through significant reductions in government spending and powers.

23.   U.S. history has shown that the balance of power has shifted back and forth between those favoring a bigger government and those who disagreed.

24.   Following the carnage of World War II, Americans were disgusted with government and successful at reducing its size.

25.   In the 1990s, the U.S. federal government saw revenues increase as a result of increases in stock dividends.

MULTIPLE CHOICE
Circle the letter that corresponds to the one best answer.

1.   Inefficiencies within government are lumped together in the term
   a.   rational ignorance.
   b.   government failure.
   c.   benevolent dictatorship.
   d.   cycling.

2.   The field of study that examines incentives within government is called
   a.   democracy.
   b.   rent seeking.
   c.   externality.
   d.   public choice.

3.   To the extent that the political process is characterized by cycling, it will not provide
a.   a social safety net.
b.   national defense.
c.   definitive choices.
d.   integrity.

4.   The principle of fiscal federalism suggest that a mass transit project intended to benefit the residents of Philadelphia be voted on
a.   and paid for by Philadelphia residents.
b.   by the federal government and paid for by all U.S. taxpayers.
c.   by Philadelphia residents, but paid for by the federal government.
d.   by the federal government, but paid for by Philadelphia residents.

5.   The principle of fiscal federalism suggests that income redistribution should
a.   not occur.
b.   be done at the local level.
c.   be done at the state level.
d.   be done at the national level.

6.   One advantage of following the principle of fiscal federalism is that it
a.   allows policies to be tried out on of small-scale before they are used on a large-scale.
b.   avoids the inefficiencies of competition.
c.   is more likely to generate a benevolent dictator.
d.   provides more good government jobs.

7.   Because a voter cannot pick and choose which items on candidate's agenda to support, the candidate is referred to as
a.   pork.
b.   dimpled chad.
c.   a bundle good.
d.   the principle agent.

8.   An assumption of the median voter model is that political candidates
a.   engage in pork-barrel politics.
b.   can be lined up along a spectrum.
c.   are rarely of more than average intelligence.
d.   participate for public-spirited reasons rather than their own personal self-interests.

9.   Of the following, the median voter model is most likely to explain
a.   why presidential elections are often very close.
b.   why voters have fiscal illusion.
c.   the persistence of logrolling.
d.   rent-seeking behavior on the part of lobbyists.

10. The line-item veto is intended to address the problem of
    a. rent seeking.
    b. pork-barrel politics.
    c. rational ignorance.
    d. cycling.

11. A person is most likely to be rationally ignorant because of limited
    a. income.
    b. intelligence.
    c. freedom.
    d. time.

12. As applied to government, the essence of the principle-agent problem is that _____ are principals, _____ are agents, and _____ follow their own agendas.
    a. citizens; public servants; citizens
    b. citizens; public servants; public servants
    c. public servants; citizens; citizens
    d. public servants; citizens; public servants

13. Logrolling is likely to result in
    a. an efficient amount of government spending.
    b. an excessive amount of government spending.
    c. too little government spending.
    d. personal injury to those who are too careless to get out of the way.

14. When lobbyists or others expend resources in an effort to come out a winner in the political process, _____ is said to occur.
    a. rent seeking
    b. the Washington Monument strategy
    c. a capital gain
    d. value added

15. When the benefits of an action are spread broadly and the costs are concentrated, it is likely that special-interest groups will
    a. not form.
    b. be effective at preventing the action from happening.
    c. be ineffective at preventing the action from happening.
    d. convert to general-interest groups.

16. In favoring larger budgets for their agencies, government employees are usually motivated by
   a. fear of whistle-blower laws.
   b. self-interest and a belief in the value of their agencies' goals.
   c. self-interest, despite believing that too much is already spent on their agencies.
   d. the public interest, despite knowing that their personal self-interests are better served by the lower taxes that would be made possible by smaller budgets for their agencies.

17. Which of the following is the best example of the Washington Monument strategy?
   a. A school district says it must eliminate school crossing guards if its budget is cut.
   b. General Jones orders that all of the roads on her base be converted from asphalt to concrete, because there is extra money in the budget.
   c. The Secretary of Education organizes a large rally in support of a higher budget for his agency.
   d. Representative Curry votes for Representative Favor's project in return for Favor's support of Curry's project.

18. An efficient agency budget is one for which marginal net benefit is
   a. positive.
   b. negative.
   c. zero.
   d. maximized.

19. When an agency uses up its budget at the end of the fiscal year in order to achieve a larger budget in the following year, it is counting on there being
   a. unfunded mandates.
   b. logrolling.
   c. pork-barrel politics.
   d. asymmetric information.

20. When government fails to provide businesses with the money they need to carry out a required public policy, government is said to have
   a. a budget surplus.
   b. difficulty in carrying out fiscal policy.
   c. issued an unfunded mandate.
   d. made a transfer payment.

E&A 21. An example of a transfer payment would be government spending
   a. to deliver the mail.
   b. to defend the country.
   c. to help the poor.
   d. on investments.

22. As a percentage of federal spending, transfer payments are
    a. as high or higher than they have ever been before.
    b. as low or lower than they have ever been before.
    c. higher than in 1929, but much lower than in the 1970s.
    d. lower than in the 1940s and 1980s, but higher than at any time since then.

23. Of the following, which event was most responsible for a dramatic expansion in the size of the federal government?
    a. Creation of the Bank of the United States
    b. Creation of the Interstate Commerce Commission in 1887
    c. The Sherman Act of 1890
    d. Enactment of the federal income tax in 1906

24. The expansion of government reached its pinnacle with the Great Society programs of President
    a. William Henry Harrison.
    b. Grover Cleveland.
    c. Lyndon B. Johnson.
    d. Bill Clinton.

25. The fraction of U.S. GDP devoted to national defense
    a. was much lower in the 1990s than in the 1980s, but has increased in the last few years.
    b. was much higher in the 1990s than in the 1980s, but has decreased in the last few years.
    c. has increased steadily since 1988.
    d. is a military secret and not revealed to the American public.

GRASPING THE GRAPHS
Fill in each box with a concept that applies.

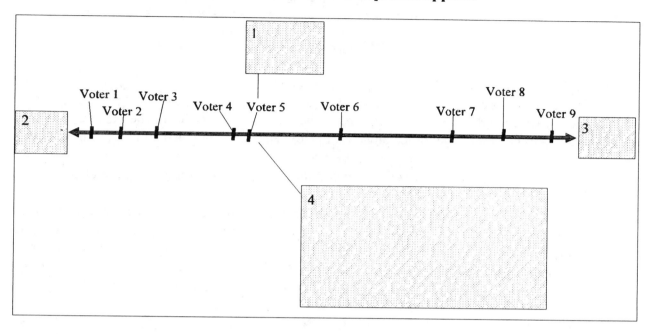

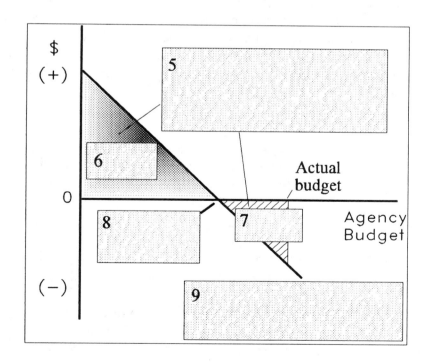

ANSWERS

STUDYCHECKS

1. The median voter model requires that voters can be lined up from left to right on an issue. The median voter is the one for whom 50 percent of other voters are to the left and 50 percent to the right. The candidate best satisfying the preferences of the median voter will win in a contest with any other single candidate. However, the median in the primaries will differ from the median in the general election. Thus, candidates who win the primaries are well served to adjust their positions toward the new median voter in the general election.

2. Public choice processes respond to voters collectively and imprecisely. In the case of public goods, even an efficient quantity rarely satisfies individual voters, because residents each consume the same collectively determined quantity rather than the quantity that they would most prefer as individuals. Similarly, political candidates are bundled goods, meaning that voters must accept all of the positions and attributes of the people they vote into office.

3. Opportunities for inefficiency arise at each stage of the public choice process. Because of rational ignorance, voters often do not know what they vote upon. Legislators rationally engage in logrolling that leads to inefficiently high spending. For reasons of self-interest and their perceptions of the public interest, bureaucrats seek to inflate their budgets and, because of asymmetric information, often have the opportunities to do so. Even the beneficiaries of legislation waste time and money in socially unproductive rent seeking. Still, government action may be needed to address inequities and market failures. The challenge is to weigh government failures against market failures and arrive at the optimal mix of public and private action.

4. Rent-seeking behavior is the attempt to be the beneficiary of a public policy or other action. The costs of competing to be the winner squanders the value of the winnings. One example is when the EPA gives away pollution rights. In that case, individual polluters are likely to engage in rent seeking by spending heavily on lobbying efforts to influence the permit distribution formula in their individual directions. Other examples could be presented.

5. Transfer payments have grown as a percentage of government spending as the country has come to rely more and more on the social safety net, such as Social Security. Many safety-net programs got their start in President Roosevelt's New Deal. Redistributional programs got a big boost in the 1960s with the Great Society agenda of President Lyndon Johnson. The Social Security component has continued to grow as the population profile continues to age in response to improve medical care and the retirement of baby boomers.

FILL IN THE BLANKS

1.   government failure, public choice
2.   benevolent dictatorship
3.   cycling, agenda
4.   federalism
5.   Fiscal federalism
6.   national defense, income redistribution
7.   bundled
8.   principal-agent, agents, principals
9.   median voter, 50, 50, 50
10.   rational ignorance
11.   term limitations
12.   logrolling
13.   fiscal illusion
14.   Pork-barrel
15.   line-item veto
16.   unfunded mandates
17.   lobbyists
18.   rent seeking
19.   Block grants
20.   zero
21.   Clinton
22.   Alexander Hamilton, three
23.   general welfare
24.   income tax
25.   New Deal, Great Society

TRUE/FALSE/EXPLAIN

1.   True.
2.   True.
3.   True.
4.   False, when there is cycling, the outcome can be random.
5.   False, because voters have limited time, it is rational for them to remain ignorant of much of the information that is available.
6.   True.
7.   False, the median voter model says that a candidate is most likely to when by taking the positions of the median voter, irrespective of whether those positions are exactly in the middle of the political spectrum.

8.   False, fiscal illusion causes voters to focus too much on the benefits of federal programs, with not enough attention to the costs.

9.   False, although voters may disapprove of pork-barrel politics in general, it is in their interests to vote for candidates who will participate in that process.

10.   True.

11.   True.

12.   False, Congress has turned toward block grants as a way of letting states make decisions as to the details of welfare programs.

13.   True.

14.   True.

15.   False, while society would be better off if the agency had an efficient budget, it may nevertheless be the case that the gains from the agency's spending up to the efficient amount offset the losses from spending beyond that amount.

16.   False, the staff of a government agency can be expected to favor a larger budget for that agency, irrespective of whether that budget would be efficient.

17.   True

18.   False, the Washington Monument strategy can only be effective if there is asymmetric information..

19.   False, the Washington Monument strategy relies on a misrepresentation of potential budgetary alternatives.

20.   True.

21.   True.

22.   False, President G. W. Bush has pushed for significant increases in government spending and powers.

23.   True.

24.   False, following World War II, Americans were very proud of the U.S. government and the size of government increased.

25.   False, there was a so-called peace dividend in the 1990s that allowed for reduced military spending after the demise of the Soviet Union.

MULTIPLE CHOICE

1.	b	8.	b	15.	b	22.	a
2.	d	9.	a	16.	b	23.	d
3.	c	10.	b	17.	a	24.	c
4.	a	11.	d	18.	c	25.	a
5.	d	12.	b	19.	d		
6.	a	13.	b	20.	c		
7.	c	14.	a	21.	c		

GRASPING THE GRAPHS
Examples of correct answers

1. The median voter
2. The left
3. The right
4. By adopting the positions of the median voter, a candidate maximizes the odds of winning a two-candidate election.
5. If the gains from agencies spending exceed the losses from excessive spending, the agency is worth having.
6. Gains
7. Losses
8. Efficient budget
9. Marginal net benefit equals marginal social benefit minus marginal social cost.

Visit the Ayers/Collinge companion Website at http://www.prenhall.com/ayers for further activities and exercises for this chapter.

Part 6

THE GLOBAL ECONOMY

Chapter 17

INTO THE
INTERNATIONAL MARKETPLACE

CHAPTER REVIEW

- International trade involves all of the elements of the economy within a country's borders—its *domestic* economy. In addition, international trade must also take into account foreign currencies and conflicting interests among countries.

17.1 Measuring International Transactions

- Countries trade with one another in order to increase their standards of living. Each country records the details of trade in its **balance of payments accounts**. The balance of payments accounts of the United States measure the economic interactions of the U.S. with other countries.

- The balance of payments accounts contain subaccounts that categorize the major types of international economic interactions. The two primary subaccounts are the current account and the capital account.

- A country **exports** goods and services when it sells them to another country. A country **imports** goods and services when it purchases them from another country. **The current account** measures the value of exports and imports for a specific period of time.

- The balance on the current account is the dollar value of exports minus the dollar value of imports.

- The current account divides up trade into categories of merchandise and services. The **balance of trade** refers to the merchandise portion only, meaning that it is the value of exported merchandise—tangible goods—minus the value of imported merchandise. The balance of trade is currently in deficit—the **trade deficit**—which means that the value of imported merchandise exceeds the value of exported merchandise.

- When it comes to services—intangible items—the United States exports more than it imports. The result is that the services component of the current account is in *surplus*. Because the trade deficit exceeds the services surplus, the current account overall is in deficit, which means that the value of all imports exceeds the value of all exports.

- The current account looks at flows of investment into and out of the country. Investments counted in the current account are primarily of two types: *direct investments and financial investments.*

- The balance on the U.S. capital account is the dollar value of capital inflows minus the dollar value of capital outflows. *Capital inflows* represent dollars that foreigners spend on investments in the United States. *Capital outflows* represent dollars that United States citizens and firms spend on investments abroad. Thus, when looking at the direction of dollar movements, capital inflows are similar to exports, and capital outflows are similar to imports.

- The following figure summarizes the balance of payments accounts.

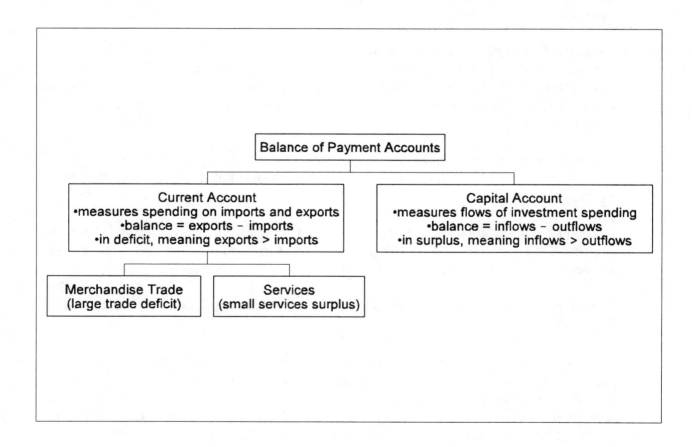

StudyCheck 1

The United States has a substantial current account deficit. Does this deficit imply anything about the capital and financial accounts? Explain.

17.2 The Impact of International Commerce

- The reason a country opens its doors to international trade, like the purpose of market trade within countries, is to get more value from the country's resources. However, while the economic pie grows because of trade, some of the slices get smaller.

- Opportunities in specific industries and types of occupations can change markedly because of international trade.

- The United States has an abundance of both physical and human capital relative to most, but not all, other countries. This means that the United States is likely to specialize in goods that are capital intensive. In other words, for the United States to gain from international trade, it exports goods that use a high proportion of capital in their production.

- Japan is in some respects more capital intensive than the United States, which explains why Japan exports so many electronic goods to this country. Over all, though, international trade causes the United States to specialize somewhat in capital-intensive goods. Exports thus increase the demand for different kinds of capital in the United States and increase the prices paid for capital.

- By increasing the return to human capital in the United States, international trade opens up attractive employment opportunities for those who have acquired skills and abilities. The return to a college education, a significant source of human capital, is higher than it would be without international trade. Conversely, job opportunities for low-skilled labor in the U.S. are harmed by international trade, as imports of labor-intensive goods lead to lower wages and fewer job openings in those industries.

- **International investment can substitute for trade.** Immigration can also substitute for trade by affecting trade patterns and the distribution of income within a country. Both capital investment and labor can move among countries, although there are usually some barriers to this migration.

- The barriers to capital movements arise from diverse sources. Investors often lack information about the risks involved in setting up shop in another country. Many of these risks are referred to as *political risks* because they involve instabilities associated with government.

- These kinds of political risks are in addition to general business risks associated with investing, and help slow down the flow of capital from one country to another. A further barrier to capital movements occurs when a government refuses to allow foreign investors into their country, or when government limits the amount of foreign investment.

- If a country has abundant capital relative to labor, it tends to have lower prices than other countries on capital-intensive goods. That country then tends to export goods that are produced with a relatively high proportion of capital and import goods that employ more labor. Likewise, labor-abundant countries tend to export goods that require a lot of labor to produce and import goods that require a lot of capital. Immigration provides countries that have relatively less labor an opportunity to increase their amount of labor.

StudyCheck 2

What would be the effect on international trade if all countries were to have identical ratios of capital to labor?

17.3 Exchange Rates

- Each country usually has its own currency. Different monies can be exchanged for each other in *currency markets,* also known as **foreign exchange markets**.

- The amount of one country's currency that trades for a unit of another country's currency is called an **exchange rate**.

- Although global in nature, the basic operation of the currency market is easily understood using supply and demand analysis. Those on the demand side for yen include U.S. buyers of imported goods and services from Japan. They also include U.S. investors interested in such things as Japanese property, stocks, and bonds. Those supplying yen have the same sort of interests, except now the roles are reversed. They may be wanting U.S. goods or services, or U.S. investments. The exchange of currencies thus represents the exchange of goods, services, and investments—both buyers and sellers have a use for each other's currencies.

- As usual with supply and demand analysis, the horizontal axis represents the quantity of a good, and the vertical axis represents its price. Quantity here is the total amount of one currency, and price is its value per unit in terms of the other currency. That price is the exchange rate. In our example, we look at the quantity of yen and see its price in terms of dollars per yen. The market equilibrium exchange rate is associated with the intersection of demand and supply.

- At the market equilibrium exchange rate, the total quantity of yen offered for sale is just equal to the total quantity of yen purchased. Moreover, the total number of dollars being spent to obtain yen is just equal to the total number of dollars being received by those selling yen.

StudyCheck 3
How does international trade affect employment? Does it matter if there is a trade deficit?
Explain, making reference to the role of the foreign exchange markets.

- Exchange rates can greatly affect the prices we see at our local stores. For example, imported products will seem cheaper if the dollar *strengthens*, meaning that it appreciates against many currencies. A stronger dollar buys more of other currencies, although just how much purchasing power is needed to make the dollar strong or how little to make it weak is a normative issue—a matter of subjective opinion. U.S. consumers and U.S. tourists abroad both like a strong dollar.

- Moreover, not only does a stronger dollar mean that the price of imports is lower to U.S. consumers, it also means that U.S. firms must keep their own prices lower to the extent that their products and imports are good substitutes among consumers.

- Although U.S. consumers benefit from a stronger dollar, U.S. producers of products that compete with imports and foreign tourists in the U.S. prefer to see the dollar weaken. A weak dollar means that U.S. goods and services seem cheap to foreigners, and foreign goods and services seem expensive to U.S. citizens.

- Some have argued that exchange rates will adjust until there is **purchasing power parity**, meaning that prices would be the same around the world for easily tradeable items. In reality, there are often too many costly details of trade for purchasing power parity to be a good guide. The most significant of these details are transportation and storage costs.

- Exchange rates do not remain constant. Currency **appreciation** occurs when a currency gets stronger. **Depreciation** occurs when the currency becomes weaker.

- The depreciation of the dollar against the yen from the early 1980s through the mid-1990s can be traced to an increase in U.S. demand for yen, which drove the dollar price of those yen higher. A dominant force behind the strong yen during this period was the demand by American importers for yen to buy the Japanese electronics and automobiles that they sold to U.S. consumers.

StudyCheck 4

Using a graph, show the effects on the exchange rate between the dollar and French franc of a major telecommunications advance in France that leads France to become a significant exporter to the United States of telecommunication services. Be sure to label both axes of your graph. (Hint: Place the quantity of French francs exchanged on the horizontal axis.)

StudyCheck 5

Suppose the U.S. government borrows more money, which in turn has the effect of increasing interest rates and the desirability of investing in the United States. On a supply and demand diagram for Japanese yen priced in terms of U.S. dollars, show the effect of this action on the exchange rate between the yen and the dollar. Label XR0 as the initial exchange rate, and XR1 as the new exchange rate. (Hint: Place the quantity of yen on the horizontal axis.)

- Governments sometimes try to influence the market exchange rates. The huge volume of global currency transactions overwhelms the efforts of any individual country. Countries have been slightly more effective when they work in synchrony. The most important of these joint efforts is conducted through a group of eight countries, called *the G8*, whose members include the United States, Britain, France, Germany, Japan, Italy, Canada and Russia. **The value of currencies exchanged worldwide in a single week exceeds the value of an entire year's worth of U.S. output.**

- In the period after World War II, governments from around the world adhered to the *Bretton Woods agreement*. The Bretton Woods agreement was a treaty signed in 1944 at Bretton Woods, New Hampshire, by most of the world's major trading countries. This agreement *pegged* the dollar to gold ($35/ounce) and all other currencies to the dollar, thereby implying *fixed exchange rates*. Governments agreed to take whatever actions would be necessary to maintain these rates. The system of fixed exchange rates was modified in stages and ultimately abandoned as unworkable. Since 1972 the system has been one of **floating exchange rates**, meaning that exchange rates have been allowed to adjust to whatever level the market dictates. However, **because governments still take actions intended to affect market exchange rates, the system is referred to as a *managed float* or *dirty float*.**

- Government inability to control exchange rates was highlighted by the precipitous depreciation of Asia's currencies as their values tumbled during the Asian currency crisis of 1998. By late July, 1998, for example, the Indonesian rupiah had dropped to 14,000 per dollar from 2,600 per dollar one year earlier. This plunge of the rupiah occurred in spite of efforts by the Indonesian government to prevent it. This abrupt depreciation of the rupiah dramatically increased the purchasing power of dollars in Indonesia and decreased the purchasing power of rupiah in the United States.

- Companies that import or export products do so in response to market prices, prices that depend centrally upon exchange rates. **Relatively higher prices at home than abroad lead to imports, while relatively lower prices at home than abroad cause exports.** The result of the prices in the free market is that countries export goods in which they have comparative advantages and import goods in which they do not.

- Recall from chapter 2 that comparative advantage occurs whenever the country can produce a good at a lower opportunity cost than could other countries. Looking at England in the following table, we see its comparative advantage is in the production of oil because the opportunity cost of oil is lower in England than in Japan. This means that Japan will export to England some of the computer chips it produces, while importing some of its oil from England.

Relative Prices within Countries in the Absence of Trade

Country	Price of a Computer Chip	Price of a Barrel of Oil	Opportunity Cost of a Barrel of Oil	Opportunity Cost of a Computer Chip
Japan	¥2,000	¥5,000	2.5 computer chips (¥5000/¥2000)	2/5 of a barrel of oil (¥2000/¥5000)
England	£3	£5	1.67 computer chips (£5/£3)	3/5 of a barrel of oil (£3/£5)

- Were the two countries to trade, the terms at which the countries could exchange oil for computer chips would settle somewhere between the two countries opportunity costs of oil for computer chips. For example, they might be 2 computer chips per barrel of oil. Equivalently, then, a computer chip would trade for ½ a barrel of oil. Currency exchange rates would adjust to make it so.

- The equilibrium exchange rate causes each country to export the good for which it has a comparative advantage and import the other good. In this way, both countries are better off by specializing and trading, meaning that their consumption possibilities would grow beyond their production possibilities. By trading, Japan obtains a barrel of oil in trade for 2 computer chips , which is less than the 2.5 computer chips a barrel of oil would cost in Japan. Trade allows England to obtain computer chips at the cost of ½ a barrel of oil rather than the cost of 3/5 of a barrel of oil that would prevail without trade.

E&A 17.4 Immigration and the Melting-Pot World

- Today immigrants account for about 8 percent of the U.S. population. The Immigration Act of 1965 opened the door to a new wave of mass immigration into the United States, totaling about 800,000 persons per year.

- Opposition to immigration arises from the following root causes:
    - Ethnic tensions arising prior to the assimilation of the newcomers into the existing culture;
    - A backlash stemming from concerns that immigration has high economic costs, such as in terms of subsidized education and social programs;
    - Concerns that immigration exposes the country to terrorist acts by those with interests hostile to America.

- The U.S. Census Bureau estimates that by the year 2050, the immigration rates established by the 1965 act will result in a U.S. population of up to 500 million people, which is about twice the population counted in the 1990 census.

- Immigration affects the economy in a variety of ways. Most controversially, immigration can change relative wages. Immigration of low-skilled workers can increase competition for low-skilled jobs and drive wages there down. Conversely, immigration of skilled workers can drive down wages that are available to other skilled workers. So immigration has the potential to either widen or reduce the wage gap between the skilled and unskilled.

- Immigrants also buy products and influence the buying habits of consumers in their new home country. Foreign products have often become popular after being introduced by immigrants.

- Another way that immigration can affect trade patterns is through the skills that immigrants bring to their new country. Also, opportunities for success in a country encourages particularly inventive and entrepreneurial immigrants. The entrepreneurship and development of technology arising from the efforts of these immigrants expands the country's production possibilities and in the process changes its patterns of trade.

- Whether or not a country allows easy immigration has a lot to do with the ownership of resources and the distribution of income within that country. For example, immigration can decrease the incomes and job opportunities for workers who find themselves in competition with the immigrants. Also, if immigrants can claim property rights or subsidies from longer-term citizens, the well-being of those citizens could easily fall, even as the country's output goes up. Thus, whether a country wants to allow easy immigration depends on its objective. If the country seeks to maximize the well-being of its longer-term citizens, it has to consider immigration's effects on those citizens' incomes and tax burdens, and might choose a relatively tight immigration policy.

- As a middle ground, many countries make special provisions for guest workers. *Guest workers* are temporary immigrants, granted limited rights to work and live in a country.

StudyCheck 6

Describe the manner in which the immigration of unskilled labor can substitute for the import of labor-intensive goods. What is a significant difference between the two alternatives?

FILL IN THE BLANKS

1. International trade involves all of the elements of the economy within a country's borders—its _____ economy. Each country records the details of trade in its_____ ___ _____ accounts.

2. The balance of payments accounts contain subaccounts that categorize the major types of international economic interactions. The two primary subaccounts are the _____ account and the _____ account.

3. A country _____ goods and services when it sells them to another country. A country _____ goods and services when it purchases them from another country. The _____ account measures the value of exports and imports for a specific period of time.

4. The balance on the current account is the dollar value of _____ minus the dollar value of _____. The current account divides up trade into categories of merchandise and services.

5. The _____ _____ _____ refers to the merchandise portion only, meaning that it is the value of exported merchandise—tangible goods—minus the value of imported merchandise. The _____ _____ is means that the value of imported merchandise exceeds the value of exported merchandise.

6. When it comes to services—intangible items—the United States exports more than it imports. The result is that the services component of the current account is in _____. Because the trade deficit exceeds the services surplus, the current account overall is in _____, which means that the value of imports exceeds the value of exports.

7. The current account looks at flows of investment into and out of the country. Investments counted in the current account are primarily of two types: _____ investments and _____ investments.

8. The balance on the U.S. capital account is the dollar value of capital inflows minus the dollar value of capital outflows. Capital _____ represent dollars that foreigners spend on investments in the United States. Capital _____ represent dollars that United States citizens and firms spend on investments abroad.

9.   The United States has an abundance of both physical and human capital relative to most, but not all, other countries. This means that the United States is likely to specialize in goods that are _____ intensive.

10.   The barriers to capital movements arise from diverse sources. Investors often lack information about the risks involved in setting up shop in another country. Many of these risks are referred to as _____ risks because they involve instabilities associated with government.

11.   If a country has abundant capital relative to labor, it tends to have lower prices than other countries on _____-intensive goods. That country then tends to export goods that are produced with a relatively high proportion of _____ and import goods that employ more _____.

12.   Each country usually has its own currency. Different monies can be exchanged for each other in currency markets, also known as _____ _____ markets. The amount of one country's currency that trades for a unit of another country's currency is called an _____ _____.

13.   At the market equilibrium exchange rate, the total quantity of yen offered for sale is _____ to the total quantity of yen purchased. Moreover, the total number of dollars being spent to obtain yen is _____ to the total number of dollars being received by those selling yen.

14.   Exchange rates can greatly affect the prices we see at our local stores. For example, imported products will seem cheaper if the dollar _____, meaning that it appreciates against many currencies. U.S. producers of products that compete with imports and foreign tourists in the U.S. prefer to see the dollar _____.

15.   Some have argued that exchange rates will adjust until there is _____ _____ _____, meaning that prices would be the same around the world for easily tradeable items.

16.   Exchange rates do not remain constant. Currency _____ occurs when a currency gets stronger. _____ occurs when the currency becomes weaker.

17.   Governments sometimes try to influence the market exchange rates. The most important of these joint efforts is conducted through a group of eight countries, called the _____, whose members include the United States, Britain, France, Germany, Japan, Italy, Canada and Russia. The value of currencies exchanged worldwide in a single week exceeds the value of an entire _____worth of U.S. output.

18.   In the period after World War II, governments from around the world adhered to the _____ _____ agreement, which pegged the dollar to gold ($35/ounce) and

all other currencies to the dollar, thereby implying _____ exchange rates. Since 1972 the system has been one of _____ exchange rates, meaning that exchange rates have been allowed to adjust to whatever level the market dictates. However, because governments still take actions intended to affect market exchange rates, the system is referred to as a _____ float or a _____ _____.

19. Relatively higher prices at home than abroad lead to _____, while relatively lower prices at home than abroad cause _____. The result of the prices in the free market is that countries export goods in which they have comparative advantages and import goods in which they do not. In the following table, _____ has a comparative advantage in computer chip production and _____ has a comparative advantage in oil production..

Relative Prices within Countries in the Absence of Trade

Country	Price of a Computer Chip	Price of a Barrel of Oil	Opportunity Cost of a Barrel of Oil	Opportunity Cost of a Computer Chip
Japan	¥2,000	¥5,000	2.5 computer chips (¥5000/¥2000)	2/5 of a barrel of oil (¥2000/¥5000)
England	£3	£5	1.67 computer chips (£5/£3)	3/5 of a barrel of oil (£3/£5)

20. The equilibrium exchange rate causes each country to _____ the good for which it has a comparative advantage and _____ the other good. In this way, both countries are better off by specializing and trading, meaning that their consumption possibilities would grow beyond their _____ _____.

E↓A 21. Today immigrants account for about ____ percent of the U.S. population. The _____ Act of 1965 opened the door to a new wave of mass immigration into the United States, totaling about 800,000 persons per year. The U.S. Census Bureau estimates that by the year 2050, the immigration rates established by the 1965 act will result in a U.S. population of up to 500 million people, which is about _____ the population counted in the 1990 census.

22. Immigration affects the economy in a variety of ways. Most controversially, immigration can change relative wages. Immigration of low-skilled workers can increase competition for low-skilled jobs and drive wages there _____. Conversely, immigration of skilled workers can drive _____ wages that are available to other skilled workers. So immigration has the potential to either widen or reduce the _____ gap between the skilled and unskilled.

23. Another way that immigration can affect trade patterns is through the skills that immigrants bring to their new country. Also, opportunities for success in a country encourages

particularly inventive and entrepreneurial immigrants. The entrepreneurship and development of technology arising from the efforts of these immigrants expands the country's _____ _____ and in the process changes its patterns of trade.

24. Whether or not a country allows easy immigration has a lot to do with the ownership of resources and the distribution of income within that country. For example, immigration can decrease the _____ and job opportunities for workers who find themselves in competition with the immigrants.

25. _____ workers are temporary immigrants, granted limited rights to work and live in a country.

TRUE/FALSE/EXPLAIN
If false, explain why in the space provided.

1. The current account and the capital account are the two main subaccounts of the balance of payments

2. Imported goods are entered into the balance of payments accounts as capital inflows.

3. When Japanese investors buy U.S. golf courses, their purchases show up in the capital account of the U.S. balance of payments accounts.

4. The persistent U.S. trade deficit in recent years must mean that the number of U.S. dollars that have left the country and have not returned has risen dramatically.

5. The services account has shown a surplus in recent years.

6. The larger is the U.S. trade deficit, the larger is the U.S. unemployment rate

7.   The smaller and less diverse is a country, the more important is international trade.

8.   Imports lead to job losses in specific industries, but there is no reason to believe that imports cause job losses in the aggregate.

9.   International trade increases the return to human capital in the U.S.

10.   An appreciation in the dollar means that consumers pay less for imports.

11.   U.S. producers prefer a stronger dollar.

12.   When a currency strengthens, it appreciates.

13.   In foreign exchange markets, a managed float refers to an issuance of government bonds payable in the currency of another country.

14.   U.S. manufacturers seeking to attract consumers away from rival foreign imports will have more success if the dollar strengthens against other currencies.

15.   Exchange rates among the world's currencies are currently set in accordance with the Bretton Woods Agreement.

16.   Relatively higher prices at home than abroad cause a country to import a good.

17. International trade forces banks around the world to pay their depositors the same interest rates, no matter the currency in which interest is paid.

18. If the inauguration of international trade causes the price of widgets in a country to rise from 1 peso apiece to 2 pesos apiece, the most likely reason is that the country is exporting widgets.

19. If the start of international trade causes the price of widgets in a country to rise from 1 peso apiece to 2 pesos apiece, the country can be presumed to have a comparative advantage in the production of widgets.

20. Some countries have comparative advantages in all of the goods they consume.

E&A 21. The Immigration Act of 1965 reduced the number of immigrants to the U.S.

22. If immigrants bring new skills and technology to a country, they can expand that country's production possibilities.

23. The wage gap between skilled and unskilled labor can be increased or decreased by immigration.

24. No matter what a country's goals are, a tight immigration policy that limits the number of immigrants can never be justified.

25. The Bracero program is an example of allowing guest workers to enter the country.

MULTIPLE CHOICE
Circle the letter preceding the one best answer.

1. Which of the following is not included in the balance of payments accounts?
   a. Imports and exports of goods.
   b. Imports and exports of services.
   c. Immigration.
   d. Gifts and foreign aid.

2. If the services account is in surplus, this means that
   a. the value of imports and exports of services are equal.
   b. the value of imports of services is less than the value of the exports of services.
   c. the value of imports of services is more than the value of the exports of services.
   d. consumers gain more than producers lose.

3. A capital outflow in the U.S. balance of payments accounts occurs when
   a. Americans purchase imported goods.
   b. Americans purchase imported services.
   c. Americans invest in other countries.
   d. citizens of other countries invest in the U.S.

4. If capital outflows exceed capital inflows, the balance on the capital account will be
   a. positive.
   b. negative.
   c. either positive or negative depending upon the balance of trade.
   d. zero.

5. U.S. exports tend to be
   a. labor intensive.
   b. capital intensive.
   c. a combination of capital and labor intensive in equal proportions.
   d. not intensive in either capital or labor.

6. Regarding capital and labor,
   a. they cannot move from one country to another.
   b. they can move freely from one country to another.
   c. they can move from one country to another, with some barriers to their movement.
   d. labor can move, but capital cannot.

7. The takeover of American property by the Cuban government in the early 1960s is an example of
   a. currency appreciation.
   b. currency depreciation.
   c. purchasing power parity.
   d. political risk.

8. If a country has abundant capital relative to labor, it is likely to
   a. import goods that are capital-intensive and export goods that are labor-intensive.
   b. export goods that are capital-intensive and import goods that are labor-intensive.
   c. export more goods than it imports.
   d. import more goods than it exports.

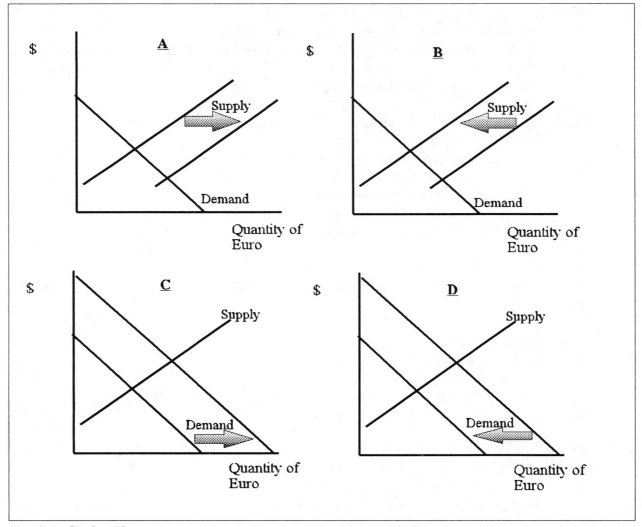

Multiple Choice Figure 1

9.   In Multiple Choice Figure 1, appreciation of the dollar would occur following the supply and demand shifts shown in graphs
   a.   A and B.
   b.   A and C.
   c.   A and D.
   d.   B and C.

10.   In Multiple Choice Figure 1, appreciation of the euro would occur following the supply and demand shifts shown in graphs
   a.   A and B.
   b.   A and C.
   c.   A and D.
   d.   B and C.

11.   In Multiple Choice Figure 1, depreciation of the dollar would occur following the supply and demand shifts shown in graphs
   a.   A and B.
   b.   A and C.
   c.   A and D.
   d.   B and C.

12.   In Multiple Choice Figure 1, depreciation of the euro would occur following the supply and demand shifts shown in graphs
   a.   A and B.
   b.   A and C.
   c.   A and D.
   d.   B and C.

13.   Suppose that, ceteris paribus, European investors decide that investment in the United States is safer than it used to be. Which of the graphs in Multiple Choice Figure 1 is the most likely result of this decision?
   a.   A
   b.   B
   c.   C
   d.   D

14.   Suppose that, ceteris paribus, American investors decide that investment in Europe is safer than it used to be. Which of the graphs in Multiple Choice Figure 1 is the most likely result of this decision?
   a.   A
   b.   B
   c.   C
   d.   D

15.   Suppose that, in response to a "buy American" advertising campaign, U.S. consumers become less inclined to buy goods made in Europe. Which of the graphs in Multiple Choice Figure 1 is the most likely result of this decision?
   a.   A
   b.   B
   c.   C
   d.   D

16.   Suppose that Europeans decide that travel to the United States is less pleasant than it used to be. Which of the graphs in Multiple Choice Figure 1 is the most likely result of this change?
   a.   A
   b.   B
   c.   C
   d.   D

17.   Suppose the initial exchange rate between U.S. dollars and the Japanese yen is one dollar per 100 yen. If the Japanese demand for U.S. output increases, the dollar would _____ and exchange for ____ than 100 yen.
   a.   appreciate; more
   b.   appreciate; less
   c.   depreciate; more
   d.   depreciate; less

18.   The Asian currency crisis of 1998 provided an example of
   a.   government control of exchange rates.
   b.   the crisis that can occur when a country's currency appreciates.
   c.   the crisis that can occur when a country's currency depreciates.
   d.   the crisis that can occur when a country decides to stop all international trade with other countries.

19.   Under a managed float, government
   a.   sets an exchange rate directly, thereby eliminating the currency market.
   b.   backs its currency with gold, thus limiting the fluctuations that occur in the price of its currency.
   c.   does not intervene in free currency markets, with the result that exchange rates often fluctuate dramatically because of speculators and international capital movements.
   d.   intervenes in the foreign exchange market by buying and selling currencies.

20. Suppose that fish and fowl are the only two tradeable goods. In the absence of trade, suppose that fish sold for 5,000 yen in Japan and for 5 pounds in England. Likewise, in the absence of trade, fowl sold for 3,000 yen in Japan and 2 pounds in England. We can conclude
   a.   nothing about the comparative advantages of the countries.
   b.   that England has a comparative advantage in the production of fowl and Japan has a comparative advantage in the production of fish
   c.   that England has a comparative advantage in the production of fish and Japan has a comparative advantage in the production of fowl.
   d.   that England has a comparative advantage in the production of both goods.

E&A 21. Immigrants make up about _____ percent of the U.S. population.
   a.   2
   b.   8
   c.   22
   d.   33

22. If immigration into the U.S. continues at its current pace it will take about ____ years for the U.S. population to be double what it was in 1990.
   a.   15
   b.   25
   c.   50
   d.   100

23. Allowing low-skill workers to immigrate into the U.S. would be expected to
   a.   lead to no change in the wage gap between the skilled and unskilled.
   b.   widen the wage gap between the skilled and unskilled.
   c.   diminish the wage gap between the skilled and unskilled.
   d.   change the wage gap between the skilled and unskilled in unpredictable ways.

24. Providing subsidies to immigrants
   a.   always makes the current residents of a country better off since the immigrants will add to the country's production.
   b.   will have no effect on the well being of current residents since the government will be paying the subsidies in question.
   c.   could make current residents worse off, even if the country's production rises due to immigration.
   d.   could increase the tax burden on current residents, but the new skills and entrepreneurial spirit of immigrants guarantee that the higher taxes will be more than offset.

25. Guest workers are
    a.   permanent immigrants.
    b.   temporary immigrants.
    c.   working illegally.
    d.   students in a country other than the country where they have citizenship.

GRASPING THE GRAPHS
Fill in the boxes with a concept that applies.

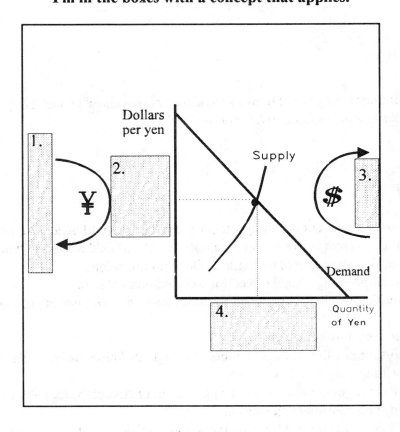

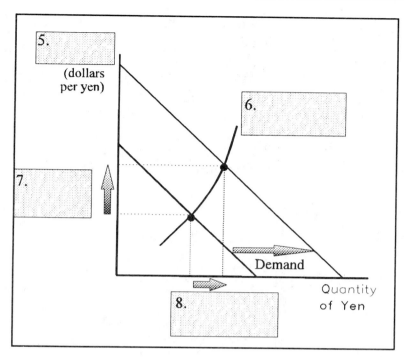

**For additional practice in grasping this chapter's graphs, visit
http://www.prenhall.com/ayers and try *Active Graphs* 65, 66, and 67.**

ANSWERS

STUDYCHECKS

1. Yes, to compensate for the current account deficit, there must be a surplus in the capital and financial accounts. The result is a net inflow of foreign investment spending. Overall, by definition, the balance of payments must be zero.

2. If migration resulted in all countries having identical ratios of capital to labor, world trade would shrink considerably. This is because countries with abundant capital tend to export goods that are capital-intensive, while countries with abundant labor tend to export labor-intensive goods.

3. International trade changes the distribution of jobs in a country. However, there is no reason to expect any effect on employment in total, even if the country runs a substantial trade deficit. The reason for this result can be found in the foreign exchange markets. A currency

is primarily of value in the country that issues it. Thus, when currencies enter the foreign exchange market, they ordinarily bounce back to their respective countries in the form of payments for exports, investments, or in other ways. Since a country's central bank can also replace any currency that does stay abroad, foreign trade and investment is unlikely to affect aggregate spending and employment in the home country. However, foreign trade and investment do lead to more of some jobs and fewer of others.

4.   See StudyCheck 4 Figure. The dollar depreciates and the franc appreciates as U.S. telecommunication customers increase their demands for French products.

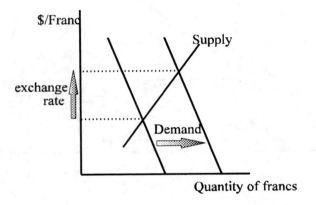

StudyCheck 4 Figure

5.   See StudyCheck 5 Figure. The dollar appreciates and the yen depreciates as Japanese investors supply more yen in exchange for dollars to invest.

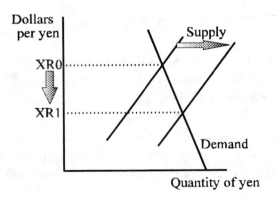

StudyCheck 5 Figure

6. Immigration of unskilled labor lowers wage rates and thus promotes the development of labor-intensive industries within the country. This means the country need not import as many of those goods: it has substituted domestic production for imports. However, not only do the immigrants increase domestic production of labor-intensive goods, they also increase population. More people means more to share in the consumption of both private-sector and public-sector goods and services. Because the immigrants in question earn income through the sale of unskilled labor services, their incomes are low. Thus, on average, they contribute less tax revenue and consume more services than the average citizen.

FILL IN THE BLANKS

1. domestic, balance of payments
2. current, capital
3. exports, imports, current account
4. exports, imports
5. balance of trade, trade deficit
6. surplus, deficit
7. direct, financial
8. inflows, outflows
9. capital
10. political
11. capital, capital, labor
12. foreign exchange, exchange rate
13. equal, equal
14. strengthens, weaken
15. purchasing power parity
16. appreciation, Depreciation
17. G8, year's
18. Bretton Woods, fixed, floating, managed, dirty
19. imports, exports, Japan, England
20. export, import, production possibilities
21. 8, Immigration, twice
22. down, down, wage
23. production possibilities
24. incomes
25. Guest

TRUE/FALSE/EXPLAIN

1. True.
2. False, imports represented negative entry in the current account.
3. True.
4. False, countervailing flows of dollars show up elsewhere in the current account, in the capital account, and in the statistical discrepancy.
5. True.
6. False, the record trade deficits of the 1980s and 1990s were associated with very low U.S. unemployment.
7. True.
8. True.
9. True.
10. True.
11. False, producers prefer a weaker dollar because it makes their exports cheaper and their competitors' imports more expensive.
12. True.
13. False, a managed float occurs when governments attempt to influence market exchange rates.
14. False, a stronger dollar makes imports less expensive and consumers more likely to buy them.
15. False, supply and demand in the marketplace determine exchange rates.
16. True.
17. False, banks in countries with high inflation or high risk will have to pay more to attract deposits.
18. True.
19. True.
20. False, since comparative advantage is defined terms of opportunity costs, it is not possible for country to have comparative advantages and all the goods that it consumes.
21. False, the Immigration Act of 1965 increased U.S. immigration.
22. True.
23. True.
24. False, a tight immigration policy can be justified if current residents are made worse off by immigration.
25. True.

MULTIPLE CHOICE

1.	c	8.	b	15.	d	22.	c
2.	c	9.	c	16.	b	23.	b
3.	c	10.	d	17.	a	24.	c
4.	b	11.	d	18.	c	25.	b
5.	b	12.	c	19.	d		
6.	c	13.	a	20.	b		
7.	d	14.	c	21.	b		

GRASPING THE GRAPHS
Examples of correct answers

1. Japan
2. Equilibrium exchange rate
3. USA
4. Equilibrium quantity of yen
5. Exchange rate
6. Supply of yen
7. Dollar depreciates, yen appreciates
8. Larger quantity of yen exchanged

**Visit the Ayers/Collinge companion Website at http://www.prenhall.com/ayers
for further activities and exercises for this chapter.**

Chapter 18

POLICY TOWARD TRADE

CHAPTER REVIEW

18.1 Assessing Gains from Trade

- International trade occurs in response to differences between the price of a good in the country's own market—its domestic market—and the price that the good sells for in the rest of the world—the *world price*. When a country opens its doors to international trade, the price in the domestic market will come to equal that in the world market. If that means that the domestic price rises to meet the higher world price, then the country exports the good. If the world price causes the domestic price to drop, then the country imports the good.

- Before free trade, the country's prices would have been based solely on its own domestic supply and demand curves. However, goods and services that are widely traded among countries have a *world price*, which is the price that the good trades for in the global marketplace.

- The world price of a good is determined by supply and demand for the good from all trading countries. **Free trade implies that a country's producers must accept world market prices, which would entail a higher price for some goods and a lower price for others.**

- **Imports allow domestic consumers to pay a lower price for goods.** They benefit from a lower price per unit for goods that they buy. **They also gain by consuming more of the good**, supplementing the lower quantity supplied by domestic producers with imports from other countries. The gains to consumers are measured by the increase in consumer surplus, defined as the difference between demand and price.

- The price drop from imports causes producers to lose, however. In general, producer surplus is defined as the difference between price and supply. After the lower price that results from international trade, producer surplus drops.

- **The gains to consumers from imports more than offset the losses to producers, which reveals that the country as a whole is better off allowing imports.**

StudyCheck 1

Graph a situation in which the world price leads to imports. Label the domestic quantity demanded, domestic quantity supplied, and the amount imported. Indicate the amount that consumers gain or lose. Also indicate the amount that producers gain or lose.

- Suppose the world price is above the domestic price. In this case, the price difference causes the domestic quantity supplied to be greater than the domestic quantity demanded. This difference between quantity supplied and the quantity demanded results in an excess quantity of the product. This excess quantity is exported.

- **In the case of exports, producers win and consumers lose.** Producers win because they sell more at a higher price. Their gain is measured by the increase in producer surplus. Consumers lose because they must pay the higher world price, and thus consume less. Their consumer surplus drops. Because producer surplus increases by more than consumer surplus shrinks, producers gain more than consumers lose. So, on balance, **the country as a whole gains by allowing exports.** In short, both imports and exports lead to more gains than losses.

StudyCheck 2

Graph a situation in which the world price leads to exports. Label the domestic quantity demanded, domestic quantity supplied, and the amount exported. Indicate the amount that consumers gain or lose. Also indicate the amount that producers gain or lose.

18.2 Trade Agreements

- Countries must choose how wide to open their doors to international trade. An **open economy** is a country that erects no barriers to international trade and investment. In contrast, a *closed economy* shuts itself off from foreign investment and trade.

- Countries design their trade policies with an eye toward their own self interests. Since governments are by nature political, trade strategies usually contain a mix of political and economic objectives. However, most countries recognize that their interests are usually best served by freeing up trade with other countries. In a misguided fight against the high unemployment of the Great Depression of the 1930s, the U.S. and other countries engaged in a *trade war*, a situation in which countries punish each other and themselves through retaliatory trade restrictions.

- Most countries have signed the **General Agreement on Tariffs and Trade (GATT)** that aims to avoid trade wars and promote free trade. The GATT was initially signed in 1947 by the 23 major trading countries of the world at that time. Over the intervening years, the agreement has been updated and membership has grown to 110 countries.

- Since 1995, the GATT has been administered by the **World Trade Organization,** an arm of the GATT created to settle trade disputes among GATT members and monitor compliance with provisions of the GATT.

- The initial impetus for the GATT agreement was the prohibitively high **tariffs**—taxes on imports— imposed by the United States and some other countries in the decade prior to World War II. Most significantly, the **Smoot-Hawley Act** was passed by the U.S. Congress in 1930 as a means to fight the unemployment of the Great Depression. The Act raised import tariffs to an average rate of 52 percent on more than 20,000 products, a level that was so prohibitively high that imports nearly ceased. Such *beggar-thy-neighbor* protectionist policies didn't work for the U.S. or anybody else.

- The GATT required significant tariff reductions. It has been strengthened over the years through rounds of trade negotiations that have achieved further reductions in tariffs. The negotiations have also placed restrictions on **quotas,** which limit the quantity of imports of products a country allows, and on other **nontariff barriers,** which is a catch-all category for the variety of other actions a country can take to restrict trade. Most recently, the *Uruguay round* of negotiations took eight years of often contentious bargaining before being ratified by the United States and other countries in late 1994. It established the World Trade Organization and dealt with various thorny issues, such as tariffs, agricultural subsidies, services, and intellectual property.

- In addition to joining the GATT, most countries have also gone the route of forming regional **trading blocs,** agreements that lower trade barriers among member countries. For example, the European Economic Community is considered a trading bloc, because it has lower trade barriers among its member countries than to the rest of the world. By signing the **North American Free Trade Agreement,** commonly known as **NAFTA,** the United States, Canada, and Mexico also formed a trading bloc. The *Mercosur* is primarily a South American trading bloc.

- To the extent that regional trading blocs reduce tariffs and other trade restrictions, the trading blocs promote trade among their members. This trade can come from two sources. First is the **trade creation effect,** which involves an increase in world trade. The trade creation effect is efficient, since it allows countries to specialize according to comparative advantage.

- The second is the **trade diversion effect,** which represents trade that would have occurred with countries outside the trading bloc, but that is diverted to countries within a trading bloc in response to lower tariff rates. Trade diversion is inefficient, since it causes trade to respond to price signals from government—relative tariff rates—rather than to comparative advantage.

- Economists generally support regional trading blocs as a step toward free trade. However, even supporters of regional agreements have reservations about trade-diversion effects.

18.3 Trade Policy Options

- Counter to the spirit of the GATT and regional trading blocs, all major countries have some restrictions on trade. Policies that accomplish this goal are termed *protectionist,* even though these policies usually harm rather than protect the economy as a whole.

- Protectionist policies come in two basic forms: tariffs and nontariff barriers. Nontariff barriers can be either quotas—quantity restrictions on imports—or any of a variety of other actions that make importing more difficult.

- A tariff is a tax on an imported product. Demand for an imported product tells the quantities of the product consumers would purchase from foreign sources at each possible price. This demand is sometimes called *residual demand,* since it represents demand that is left over after consumers have bought from domestic suppliers. **Tariffs increase the cost of selling imported products.**

- By raising barriers to the entry of foreign products, **tariffs can be viewed as a form of price support for domestic producers.** The higher price of imports causes the demand curve to shift to the right for domestic products that are close substitutes.

- Tariffs are said to be *transparent,* meaning that their effects on prices are clear for all to see. The United States has an extensive array of tariffs, most of which are currently below 6 percent and falling. Most other major trading countries also have similar tariffs. With some exceptions, tariff rates are kept low by the GATT.

- Import quotas are an alternative to import tariffs and can accomplish the same goals as a tariff. Unlike an import tariff, an import quota restricts the quantity of imports directly and thus cuts off supply from abroad at the quota quantity.

StudyCheck 3
Graph the effects of an import quota, indicating the quantity that is allowed to be imported, and the amount by which the domestic price would rise in response to the quota.

- As an alternative to tariffs and import quotas, the United States and some other countries have chosen to negotiate **voluntary export restraints,** in which individual exporting countries agree to limit the quantities they export. The alternative would be for the United States or other importing countries to impose import quotas.

- Exporting countries can charge higher prices per unit under a voluntary export restraint than they could if they face import quotas. Exporting countries charge more because they are not competing against each other—they each have their preassigned export restraints and are not allowed to fill those of other exporting countries.

- Quotas and voluntary export restraints are examples of nontariff barriers to trade, which include all ways other than tariffs that countries make importing difficult. Most nontariff barriers do not restrict imports explicitly; their effects are even less transparent than quotas. For example, paperwork and red tape delays can inhibit trade.

18.4 The Free Trade Debate
- If the arguments for and against free trade were to be counted, free trade would come up very short. However, the number of objections is not important. It is their validity that matters.

The objections to free trade commonly have limited applicability or are based on questionable logic.

- If imports or exports seriously threaten national defense, it makes sense to restrict them. However, translating national defense interests into policy requires judgments and debate. The judgments are often difficult and the source of debate.

StudyCheck 4

Why is it difficult to determine when international trade should be restricted for reasons of national defense? Provide an example where the choice is unclear.

- The United States sometimes uses *trade sanctions*, which restrict trade with countries such as Cuba and Iraq that have policies it opposes. Note that Cuba's Fidel Castro and Iraq's Saddam Hussein have had remarkable staying power, even as the trade sanctions contributed to the poverty of their economies. Despite their lack of effectiveness, trade sanctions are often popular with the public.

- Some U.S. industries cannot produce products as cheaply as products from abroad, perhaps because foreign producers face weak standards of behavior. For example, they might not need to do as much to protect the environment and the health and safety of their workers. Should the United States attempt to estimate the extra costs of complying with U.S. standards and then add that cost to imports by imposing an appropriate set of tariffs? Some critics of current trade policy suggest that this approach is the only way to achieve a *level playing field*.

- **Dumping** is defined as the selling of a good for less than its cost of production. Countries dump for many reasons. For example, the company might have overestimated demand for its product and finds itself stuck with too much—a clearance sale, so to speak. Alternatively, a company may be selling output at a price that covers wages, materials, and other operating expenses of production, but does not cover the cost of its capital and other costs that it must pay whether it produces or not. However, dumping is illegal across countries according to the GATT.

• The United States presumes dumping whenever a foreign company charges less in the United States than it does at home, irrespective of its costs. The GATT and U.S. law permit anti-dumping tariffs when dumping harms a domestic industry.

• Consumers gain from the low prices that result from dumping. The only strong economic argument in favor of restricting dumping occurs in the special case of strategic dumping. **Strategic dumping** is dumping that aims to drive the competition out of business so that the firms doing the dumping can monopolize output and drive prices up in the future. However, the prospects for successful strategic dumping are highly questionable in most industries.

• Developing countries often try to nurture new industries they hope will one day become a source of export earnings. These **infant industries** are thought to need protection in the rough world marketplace. The infant industry argument claims that government must first identify promising industries and then erect import barriers to protect them. When the infants grow strong enough to fend for themselves, government should remove the barriers.

• The infant industry argument is unconvincing if markets function efficiently. In the free marketplace, *venture capitalists* and other private investors will often support firms through many years of losses. They will do so if they expect that the firms will eventually become profitable and reward their patience. Unfortunately, there is much less assurance that government will pick industries that are likely to survive on their own. Governments often use political considerations to select so-called infant industries. By requiring government subsidies to stay afloat, and by charging prices above prices in the rest of the world, such industries have proven to be expensive for governments and consumers alike.

E&A 18.5 Energy Security—A Question of Oil Imports

• There are many possibilities for developing *alternative fuels*, so-called because they provide an alternative to the traditional fossil fuels of coal, natural gas and crude oil. These alternative fuels have one thing in common—they all cost more than the oil and other fossil fuels that they would replace. For that reason, without government assistance, the marketplace has not financed the development and production of such alternative fuels as ethanol, wind power, and solar power.

• The price of oil in the world market has fluctuated from under $20 per barrel to over $30 per barrel in the last few years. However, the cost of importing that oil into the United States might be significantly higher. There are costs that the importers do not currently pay that perhaps the country as a whole does pay. These are the costs having to do with energy freedom.

- The U.S. economy consumes tremendous amounts of petroleum, about 777 million gallons per day as of January, 2002. The U.S. imports 55 - 60 percent of the oil it uses, with imports exceeding 50 percent of the total for the first time in 1994. Because the oil market is global, a disruption in oil exports from the Middle East would bring Europeans and other countries into competition for oil that would otherwise go to the United States. By the same token, the U.S. presence in world oil market increases petroleum prices and the wealth of oil exporters. This situation means that:
    - The U.S. is vulnerable to political instability in the Middle East and in other oil-exporting countries.
    - The U.S. is a source of income to Middle Eastern countries with interests hostile to those of the United States.

- These *external costs* of oil imports are not reflected in the price paid by importers. To "internalize" them, the United States could levy an *oil import fee*, an common name for an import tariff when applied to oil.

- An oil import fee would raise the price of imported oil and encourage the development of alternative fuels. U.S. producers would produce more, and consumers consume less.

- If the U.S. raises the price of imported oil, U.S. producers will substitute domestic oil, which increases the price of domestic oil relative to oil available on the world market. The higher price would attract resources from elsewhere in the economy to increase production from existing U.S. oilfields, as well as to increase the search for new supplies. Likewise, some existing industries that consume large amounts of oil would shrink or leave the country. For example, a higher oil price in the U.S. relative to other countries would probably cause petrochemical production to be moved abroad.

- Since oil is a nonrenewable resource, opponents of oil import fees argue that such a fee would "drain America first." Down the road, as U.S. wells are pumped dry more quickly, the U.S. might be forced to rely even more heavily on foreign supplies. In that view, oil import fees might help in the present, but would make matters worse over time. The economy would grow faster and stronger with cheaper energy and be better positioned to weather energy disruptions if they ever do materialize.

- Also, higher oil prices could prompt the substitution of coal and nuclear power, both of which can harm the environment. Oil production itself can cause significant environmental damage. For example, the General Accounting Office estimated in July, 2002, that oil companies pumping oil from the Alaska's North Slope oil fields will face about $6 billion worth of environmental cleanup costs when their wells run dry. Since the opening of the Trans-Alaska pipeline in 1977, oil companies have pumped more than 13 billion barrels of oil and provided about 20 percent of the oil produced in the United States. The prospect of an additional environmental damages to the Alaska National Wildlife Refuge caused to the U.S. Congress to reject President Bush's proposal to allow oil exploration in that area.

- The subject of oil import fees is obviously contentious, with the topic discussed off and on for decades. While the U.S. does not have an oil import fee, it does have another policy that gives it a measure of protection from the uncertainties of oil politics. Specifically, the U.S. maintains a *Strategic Petroleum Reserve* in the form of a huge quantity of oil that the U.S. government has been stashing away each year. That reserve was tapped when, in the face of oil prices that had doubled to more than $30 per barrel in 2000, President Clinton ordered a limited sale from that reserve. Whether for this reason or other reasons, the price did drop back after that action.

StudyCheck 5

Explain the effects of an oil import fee on domestic production and consumption, as well as the amount imported. Why might the fee increase the use of alternative fuels? How might these alternative fuels be more environmentally damaging than the oil they replace?

FILL IN THE BLANKS

1. International trade occurs in response to differences between the price of a good in the country's own market—its _____ market—and the price that the good sells for in the rest of the world—the world price. When a country opens its doors to international trade, the price in the domestic market will come to _____ that in the world market. If that means that the domestic price rises to meet the higher world price, then the country _____ the good. If the world price causes the domestic price to drop, then the country _____ the good.

2. Imports allow domestic consumers to pay a _____ price for goods. The gains to consumers are measured by the increase in _____ _____, defined as the difference between demand and price. The price _____ from imports causes producers to lose, however. In general, producer surplus is defined as the difference between price and supply. After the lower price that results from international trade, however, producer surplus _____. The gains to consumers from imports more than offset the losses to producers, which reveals that the country as a whole is better off allowing imports.

3. Suppose the world price is above the domestic price. In this case, the price difference causes the domestic quantity supplied to be _____ than the domestic quantity demanded. This difference between quantity supplied and the quantity demanded results in an _____ quantity of the product, which is then _____.

4. In the case of exports, producers win and consumers lose. Producers win because they sell more at a higher price. Their gain is measured by the _____ in producer surplus. Consumers lose because they must pay the higher world price, and thus consume less. Their consumer surplus drops _____. Because producer surplus increases by more than consumer surplus shrinks, producers gain more than consumers lose. So, on balance, the country as a whole gains by allowing exports. In short, both imports and exports lead to more gains than losses.

5. Countries must choose how wide to open their doors to international trade. An _____ economy is a country that erects no barriers to international trade and investment. In contrast, a _____ economy shuts itself off from foreign investment and trade.

6. Most countries have signed the _____ _____ _____ _____ (GATT) that aims to avoid trade wars and promote free trade. Since 1995, the GATT has been administered by the _____ _____ _____, an arm of the GATT created to settle trade disputes among GATT members and monitor compliance with provisions of the GATT.

7.   The initial impetus for the GATT agreement was the prohibitively high tariffs—taxes on imports— imposed by the United States and some other countries in the decade prior to World War II.   Most significantly, the _____-_____ Act was passed by the U.S. Congress in 1930 as a means to fight the unemployment of the Great Depression. The Act raised import tariffs to an average rate of 52 percent on more than 20,000 products. Such _____-thy-neighbor protectionist policies didn't work for the U.S. or anybody else.

8.   The GATT required significant tariff _____.   Most recently, the _____round of negotiations took eight years of often contentious bargaining before being ratified by the United States and other countries in late 1994.

9.   In addition to joining the GATT, most countries have also gone the route of forming _____ _____ _____, agreements that lower trade barriers among member countries.   Examples include the European Economic Community and the North American Free Trade Agreement.

10.   To the extent that regional trading blocs reduce tariffs and other trade restrictions, the trading blocs promote trade among their members. This trade can come from two sources. First is the _____ _____effect, which involves an increase in world trade. This effect is efficient, since it allows countries to specialize according to comparative advantage.

11.   The second is the _____ _____effect, which represents trade that would have occurred with countries outside the trading bloc, but that is diverted to countries within a trading bloc in response to lower tariff rates. This effect is inefficient, since it causes trade to respond to price signals from government—relative tariff rates—rather than to comparative advantage.

12.   Protectionist policies come in two basic forms: _____ and _____barriers. Nontariff barriers can be either quotas—quantity restrictions on imports—or any of a variety of other actions that make importing more difficult.

13.   A _____is a tax on an imported product. Demand for an imported product tells the quantities of the product consumers would purchase from foreign sources at each possible price. This demand is sometimes called _____demand, since it represents demand that is left over after consumers have bought from domestic suppliers.

14.   Tariffs are said to be _____, meaning that their effects on prices are clear for all to see. The United States has an extensive array of tariffs, most of which are currently below ____ percent and falling.

15.   Import_____are an alternative to import tariffs and can accomplish the same goals as a tariff by restricting the quantity of imports directly.

16. As an alternative to tariffs and import quotas, the United States and some other countries have chosen to negotiate _____ _____ _____, in which individual exporting countries agree to limit the quantities they export.

17. Exporting countries can charge _____ prices per unit under a voluntary export restraint than they could if they face import quotas. Exporting countries charge more because they are not competing against each other—they each have their preassigned export restraints and are not allowed to fill those of other exporting countries.

18. Quotas and voluntary export restraints are examples of _____ _____to trade, which include all ways other than tariffs that countries make importing difficult.

19. _____ is defined as the selling of a good for less than its cost of production. _____ _____aims to drive the competition out of business so that the firms doing the dumping can monopolize output and drive prices up in the future.

20. Developing countries often try to nurture new industries they hope will one day become a source of export earnings. These _____industries are thought to need protection in the rough world marketplace.

E&A 21. There are many possibilities for developing alternative fuels, so-called because they provide an alternative to the traditional fossil fuels of coal, natural gas and crude oil. These alternative fuels have one thing in common—they all cost _____ than the oil and other fossil fuels that they would replace. For that reason, without _____ assistance, the marketplace has not financed the development and production of such alternative fuels as ethanol, wind power, and solar power.

22. The price of oil in the world market has fluctuated from under _____per barrel to over _____ per barrel in the last few years.

23. The U.S. economy consumes tremendous amounts of petroleum, about 777 million gallons per day as of January, 2002. The U.S. imports_____ to _____percent of the oil it uses, with imports exceeding 50 percent of the total for the first time in 1994.

24. The _____ costs of oil imports are not reflected in the price paid by importers. To "internalize" them, the United States could levy an _____ _____fee, an common name for an import tariff when applied to oil. Such a fee would raise_____ the price of imported oil and encourage the development of alternative fuels. U.S. producers would produce _____, and consumers consume _____. If the U.S. raises the price of imported oil, U.S. producers will substitute domestic oil, which _____ the price of domestic oil relative to oil available on the world market.

25.   While the U.S. does not have an oil import fee, it does have another policy that gives it a measure of protection from the uncertainties of oil politics. Specifically, the U.S. maintains a _____ _____ _____ in the form of a huge quantity of oil that the U.S. government has been stashing away each year.

TRUE/FALSE/EXPLAIN
If false, explain why in the space provided.

1.   Free trade refers to when a country uses quotas rather than tariffs as a way to restrict imports.

2.   When a country imposes an import tariff or other trade restriction, the gains to the country's producers will normally exceed the loss to the country's consumers.

3.   When a tariff is imposed on imports of gizmos, both the country's gizmo producers and the government treasury will benefit.

4.   Imposing a tariff on the import of a good will raise its price in the domestic market, unless the good is also produced and sold domestically.

5.   Tariffs bring in government revenues, but have no effect on the quantity of goods imported.

6.   A quota can be set to have the same effect as a tariff in terms of the quantity of a product allowed into the country and the prices paid by consumers.

7.   A sugar import quota benefits producers of corn-based sweeteners.

8.   The United States restricts the import of sugar through a set of country-by-country quotas.

9.   Other countries would prefer that the United States negotiate import quotas rather than voluntary export restraints.

10.   Both voluntary export restraints and import quotas drive up prices to U.S. consumers.

11.   When other countries voluntarily limit their exports to the United States, the United States pays less per unit for those exports.

12.   Economists usually call for greater restrictions on imports than politicians will agree to.

13.   The General Agreement on Tariffs and Trade (GATT) is a pact among countries who seek to protect their domestic industries against foreign competition through the maintenance of high tariff barriers.

14.   The United States belongs to a regional trading bloc, entitled the NAFTA.

15.   In the absence of government protection, private investors are likely to support infant industries that promise to mature into profitable companies in the future.

16.   It is often difficult to determine in practice the extent to which imports or exports truly threaten national defense.

17. The only time it makes economic sense for government to restrict imports is in the case of infant industries.

18. At least temporarily, dumping by foreign companies results in lower prices for U.S. consumers.

19. Strategic dumping refers to when a country's producers use unprofitably low prices as a way to drive producers in other countries out of business, after which prices would be set much higher.

20. Prospects for successful strategic dumping are common in most industries.

E↔A 21. Alternative fuels have typically cost more than the coal, natural gas, or crude oil that they are intended to replace.

22. One reason for government to subsidize alternative fuels is to promote energy security.

23. Oil imported into the United States comes almost exclusively from countries of the Middle East.

24. External costs of oil imports could be internalized by an oil import fee.

25. Opponents of an oil import fee argue that such a fee would "drain America first."

MULTIPLE CHOICE
Circle the letter preceding the one best answer.

1. In Multiple Choice Figure 1, the point labeled G represents the
    a. domestic quantity produced when international trade is allowed.
    b. domestic quantity consumed when international trade is allowed.
    c. domestic quantity both produced and consumed when international trade is not allowed.
    d. quantity of imports when international trade is allowed.

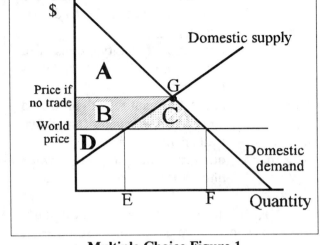

Multiple Choice Figure 1

2. In Multiple Choice Figure 1, the amount of social surplus in the absence of international trade is given by the areas
    a. A + B + C.
    b. A + B + C + D.
    c. A + B + D.
    d. A + B + D − C.

3. In Multiple Choice Figure 1, point E represents the quantity _____ and point F represents the quantity _____ when international trade is allowed.
    a. produced domestically; consumed domestically
    b. consumed domestically; produced domestically
    c. imported; exported
    d. consumed domestically; exported

4. In Multiple Choice Figure 1, the distance between point E and point F represents the quantity that is
    a. imported.
    b. exported.
    c. produced domestically.
    d. consumed domestically.

5. In Multiple Choice Figure 2, the point labeled G represents the
    a. domestic quantity produced when international trade is allowed.
    b. domestic quantity consumed when international trade is allowed.
    c. domestic quantity both produced and consumed when international trade is not allowed.
    d. quantity of imports when international trade is allowed.

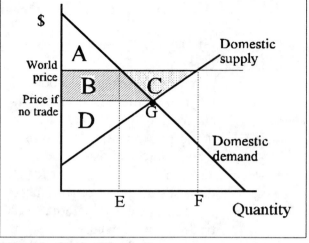

Multiple Choice Figure 2

6. In Multiple Choice Figure 2, the amount of social surplus in the presence of international trade is given by the areas
    a. A + B + C.
    b. A + B + C + D.
    c. A + B + D.
    d. A + B + D – C.

7. In Multiple Choice Figure 2, point E represents the quantity _____ and point F represents the quantity _____ when international trade is allowed .
    a. produced domestically; consumed domestically
    b. consumed domestically; produced domestically
    c. imported; exported
    d. consumed domestically; exported

8. In Multiple Choice Figure 2, the distance between point E and point F represents the quantity that is
    a. imported.
    b. exported.
    c. produced domestically.
    d. consumed domestically.

9. If the United States imposes a tariff on the import of tin, which of the following groups will lose?
    a. U.S. tin producers.
    b. The U.S. Treasury.
    c. U.S. producers of substitutes for tin.
    d. The U.S. economy as a whole.

10. As a general rule, a country gains the most when it
    a. restricts neither imports nor exports.
    b. prohibits all foreign trade.
    c. restricts imports but not exports.
    d. restricts exports but not imports.

11. One reason for the enactment of tariffs into law is that they
    a. result in net job creation in the countries that enact them.
    b. reflect the overwhelming belief among economists that free trade is harmful.
    c. act as a price support for domestic producers.
    d. encourage consumers to purchase imported goods.

12. Which of the following has the effect of increasing the price that foreigners receive for exporting their products to the United States?
    a. A voluntary export restraint.
    b. An import quota.
    c. A tariff.
    d. Nontariff barriers.

13. If the United States gives other countries a choice between voluntary export restraints or the U.S. imposition of import quotas, the other countries are likely to choose
    a. import quotas, because this allows them to compete with other countries to fill those quotas.
    b. import quotas, because this allows them to charge higher prices.
    c. voluntary export restraints, because that would allow them to charge higher prices.
    d. voluntary export restraints, because they are voluntary.

14. The U.S. requirement that Mexican bricks imported into the United States be stamped "Made in Mexico" is an example of a
    a. tariff.
    b. quota.
    c. subsidy.
    d. nontariff barrier.

15. The General Agreement on Tariffs and Trade is administered by the
    a. president of the United States.
    b. U.S. Department of Commerce.
    c. United Nations.
    d. World Trade Organization.

16. Which of the following forms a trading bloc?
    a.   The United States.
    b.   The United Nations.
    c.   The World Trade Organization.
    d.   The North American Free Trade Agreement.

17. A favorable effect of a trading bloc is
    a.   trade diversion.
    b.   trade creation.
    c.   devaluation of the currency.
    d.   the regional effect.

18. Regarding the numerous arguments against free trade,
    a.   a number of them are so convincing that it is clear that the United States should restrict trade.
    b.   free trade is widely recognized as inefficient, so that additional arguments against free trade are unnecessary.
    c.   most of them apply to a country's exports, but not to its imports.
    d.   they are mostly based on questionable assumptions or have limited applicability.

19. If the United States were to impose a fee on the import of shoes, it would be likely to do all of the following EXCEPT
    a.   violate GATT.
    b.   benefit U.S. shoe producers.
    c.   provide government revenues.
    d.   provide benefits to the United States greater than costs to the United States.

20. In his 1999 State of the Union Address, President Clinton warned the Japanese against dumping steel in the U.S. market. If the Japanese had been doing this, then
    a.   U.S. producers of steel lost more than U.S. consumers of steel gained while the dumping occurred.
    b.   the Japanese priced their steel sold in the United States below the price for which it was sold in Japan, and possibly below cost.
    c.   the United States need for steelmaking capacity during wartime clearly required that retaliatory action be taken until this dumping stopped.
    d.   the quality of products made with dumped Japanese steel cannot be relied upon.

E&A 21. Which of the following would be an advantage to the United States of imposing a fee on imported oil?
   a.   U.S. consumers would paying lower prices for gasoline.
   b.   U.S. fuel-using industries would see their costs go down relative to similar industries in other countries.
   c.   the U.S. environment would be better protected.
   d.   the United States would have less reason to try to influence political events in oil-producing countries.

22. An oil import fee would cause U.S. oil production to _____ and U.S. oil consumption to _____.
   a.   increase; increase
   b.   increase; decrease
   c.   decrease; increase
   d.   decrease; decrease

23. If the United States raises the price of imported oil,
   a.   there would be no effect on the amount of oil pumped from existing fields.
   b.   less effort would be put into finding new U.S. oilfields or other sources of energy supply.
   c.   some existing industries that consume large amounts of oil would shrink or leave the country.
   d.   demand would decrease for coal and nuclear power.

24. Since the opening of the Trans Alaskan pipeline, oil from Alaska has accounted for about ___ percent of total oil production in the United States.
   a.   10
   b.   20
   c.   50
   d.   75

25. The strategic petroleum reserve is a
   a.   huge quantity of oil the U.S. government has been stashing away in order to offset potential disruptions in the supply of oil from other countries.
   b.   military force that can be deployed at short notice in order to protect the world's oilfields.
   c.   military force that is composed of Army reservists who are called to active-duty in order to protect America's oilfields in a time of crisis.
   d.   very large oilfield that is found under the Alaskan National Wildlife Refuge, and which the U.S. government has set aside for use only in time of national emergency.

GRASPING THE GRAPHS
Fill in each box with a concept that applies.

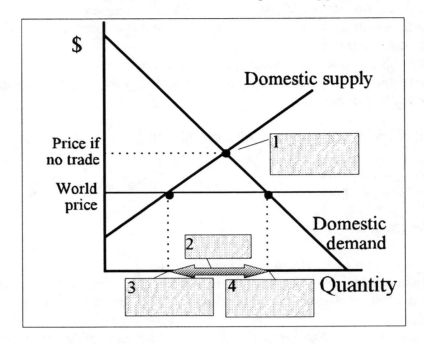

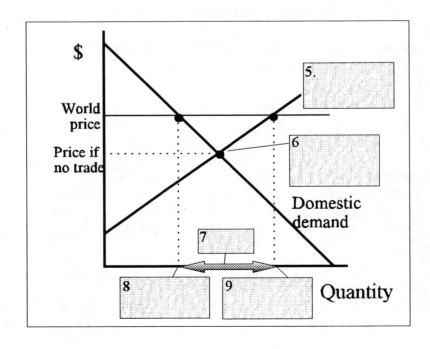

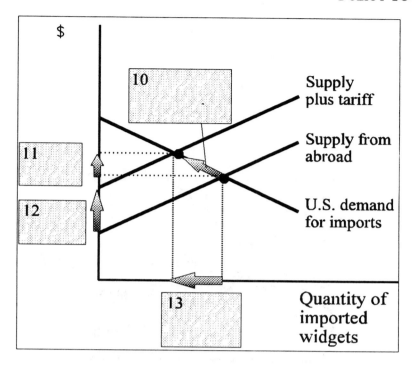

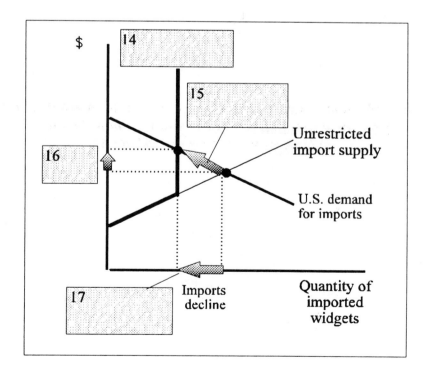

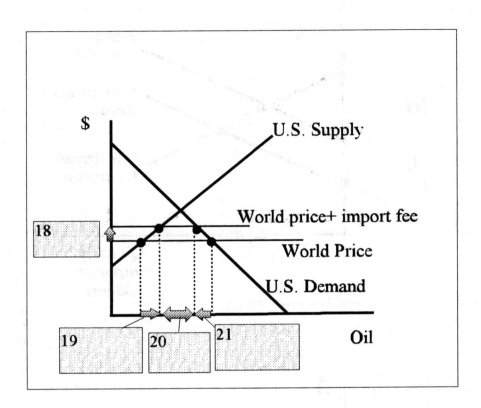

**For additional practice in grasping this chapter's graphs, visit
http://www.prenhall.com/ayers and try *Smart Graph* 35,
along with *Active Graphs* 68 and 69.**

ANSWERS

STUDYCHECKS

1. See StudyCheck 1 Figure. Consumer surplus rises from area A to areas A + B + C, while producer surplus drops from areas B + D down to area D. Since the gains to consumers exceed the loss to producers, the country on balance is better off.

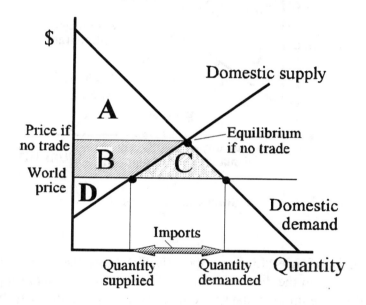

StudyCheck 1 Figure

2.   See StudyCheck 2 Figure. The country's consumers see their consumer surplus drop from areas A + B to only area A. However, producer surplus rises from area D to area B + C + D, meaning that on balance, the country is better off.

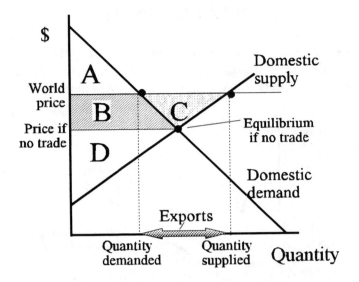

StudyCheck 2 Figure

3.   See StudyCheck 3 Figure. Like an import tariff, a quota also reduces the quantity of imports and increases price in the domestic market. The quota truncates supply from abroad at the maximum allowable import quantity, thus causing import supply to become vertical at that point.

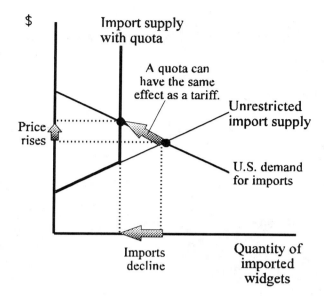

StudyCheck 3 Figure

4.   Exports or imports that can be used militarily also have valuable civilian uses. In addition, the United States may be incapable of preventing world trade in these items. U.S. export or import restrictions may merely serve to transfer production from the United States to other countries. For example, if the United States prohibits the export of high-powered computers, new computer research and production efforts will tend to migrate to other countries. This occurrence would be unfortunate for the United States because it would both harm that industry and cause the United States to forgo some of the important external benefits to the rest of the U.S. economy from high-tech industries.

5.   By raising the price of imported oil, an oil import fee would reduce oil imports and increase the U.S. price of oil to match the price of the imports. The higher price might prompt additional domestic oil production or discoveries. It might also trigger the development of alternative fuels, such as coal or nuclear power, both of which present significant environmental hazards.

FILL IN THE BLANKS

1.   domestic, equal, exports, imports
2.   lower, consumer surplus, decrease, decreases
3.   greater, excess, exported

4.   increase, decreases
5.   open, closed
6.   General Agreement on Tariffs and Trade, World Trade Organization
7.   Smoot-Hawley, beggar
8.   reductions, Uruguay
9.   regional trading blocs
10. trade creation
11. trade diversion
12. tariffs, nontariff
13. tariff, residual
14. transparent, six
15. quotas
16. voluntary export restraints
17. higher
18. nontariff barriers
19. Dumping, Strategic dumping
20. infant
21. more, government
22. $20, $30
23. 55, 60
24. external, oil import, raise, more, less, increases
25. Strategic Petroleum Reserve

TRUE/FALSE/EXPLAIN

1.   False, free trade refers to when a country does not restrict imports or exports at all.
2.   False, import restrictions lead to losses to consumers that are greater than the gains to producers.
3.   True.
4.   False, a tariff will increase the price of a good in the domestic market whether or not the good is produced and sold domestically.
5.   False, although tariffs do bring in government revenues, they also decrease the quantity of goods imported.
6.   True.
7.   True.
8.   True.
9.   False, voluntary export restraints allow other countries to sell to the United States at higher prices.
10. True.
11. False, the United States winds up paying more per unit to import the exports of those countries.

12. False, economists usually come down the side of free trade, even though there are often strong political pressures to restrict it.
13. False, the GATT is a pact among countries that promotes freer trade.
14. True.
15. True.
16. True.
17. False, it is not clear that infant industries make for a good argument for protectionist trade policy, while it is clear that some other arguments are at times valid, such as the national defense argument.
18. True.
19. True.
20. False, it is very difficult to drive all of your competitors out of business and prevent them from coming back in once you raise prices.
21. True.
22. True.
23. False, the Middle East provides about a quarter of the oil imported into the United States.
24. True.
25. True.

MULTIPLE CHOICE

1.	c	8.	b	15.	d	22.	b
2.	c	9.	d	16.	d	23.	c
3.	a	10.	a	17.	b	24.	b
4.	a	11.	c	18.	d	25.	a
5.	c	12.	a	19.	d		
6.	b	13.	c	20.	b		
7.	b	14.	d	21.	d		

GRASPING THE GRAPHS
Examples of correct answers

1. Equilibrium before international trade
2. Imports
3. Domestic quantity produced
4. Domestic quantity consumed
5. Domestic supply
6. Equilibrium before international trade

7.   Exports
8.   Domestic quantity consumed
9.   Domestic quantity produced
10.   Change in equilibrium
11.   Higher price
12.   Tariff
13.   Lower quantity
14.   Supply with quota
15.   Change in equilibrium
16.   Higher price
17.   Quantity of imports
18.   Higher price
19.   Increased domestic production
20.   Reduced domestic consumption
21.   Imports after fee

**Visit the Ayers/Collinge companion Website at http://www.prenhall.com/ayers
for further activities and exercises for this chapter.**